# Algorithms and Data Structures

# Algorithms
# and Data Structures

## Design, Correctness, Analysis

Second edition

Jeffrey H Kingston

**Addison-Wesley**

Harlow, England • Reading, Massachusetts • Menlo Park, California
New York • Don Mills, Ontario • Amsterdam • Bonn • Sydney • Singapore
Tokyo • Madrid • San Juan • Milan • Mexico City • Seoul • Taipei

Addison Wesley Longman Limited
Edinburgh Gate
Harlow
Essex CM20 2JE
England

and Associated Companies throughout the World.

The right of Jeffrey Kingston to be identified as author of this Work has been asserted by him in accordance with the Copyright, Designs and Patents Act 1988.

The programs in this book have been included for their instructional value. They have been tested with care but are not guaranteed for any particular purpose. The publisher does not offer any warranties or representations nor does it accept any liabilities with respect to the programs.

Many of the designations used by manufacturers and sellers to distinguish their products are claimed as trademarks. Addison Wesley Longman Limited has made every attempt to supply trademark information about manufacturers and their products mentioned in this book. Eiffel is a trademark of Nonprofit International Consortium for Eiffel (NICE)

Cover designed by Designers & Partners, Oxford, UK
and printed by The Riverside Press, Reading, UK
Typesetting and illustrations by the author
Printed and bound in Great Britain
by Biddles Ltd, Guildford and King's Lynn.

First printed 1997. Reprinted 1997

ISBN 0-201-40374-9

**British Library Cataloguing-in-Publication Data**
A catalogue record for this book is available from the British Library

# Contents

# Contents

# Contents

# Preface

This book is intended as a text for a one-semester second or third year course on algorithms and data structures. It aims to present the central topics of the subject under a coherent organization, with emphasis more on depth of treatment than on broad survey.

My motive in choosing depth over breadth was a desire to involve the student by making all the material fully accessible. For example, an average complexity analysis is the best way to justify the use of Quicksort, but since this is not easy to perform, some preparation in analysis techniques is needed. Similarly, the correctness of Dijkstra's algorithm is not clear, and it requires a proof using loop invariants. Thus are we led naturally to depth of treatment.

I have retained the traditional organization by application area for most of the book (Chapters 5–12). This brings together the alternative solutions to the various problems, and makes manifest to the student the general scope of the subject, in a way that a text structured around design or analysis techniques cannot do. Chapters 1–4 are devoted to techniques: correctness, analysis, the use of abstract data types, and algorithm design.

Finding the right level of treatment for correctness is difficult. Proofs of correctness are essential for the graph algorithms of Chapter 12, and the presentation of even quite simple algorithms can be improved by giving their loop invariants; but a formal treatment including predicate transformers would easily fill an entire book. I have compromised, using informal arguments to establish formal invariants, and including an introductory chapter that could be assigned as reading.

By counting the number of times that a characteristic operation is performed, the analyses give quite precise results, without excessive detail. Amortized complexity, an unusual feature of this book, is the key to some exciting new data structures – notably Fibonacci heaps, which lead to an optimal implementation of Dijkstra's algorithm.

Abstract data types have helped greatly in organizing the subject matter, both by classifying and specifying data structures, and by removing them from the algorithms. They permeate the book, and there are whole chapters devoted to the implementation of three important ones: the symbol table, the priority queue, and the disjoint sets structure.

For algorithm design, the usual list of strategies is presented, and the reader is invited to consider applying each to the problem at hand. Backtracking and branch-and-bound have been omitted, since they are most often applied to NP-hard and artificial intelligence problems that lie outside the scope of this book.

As I wrote this book, I perceived a need for a more systematic classification of iterative algorithms than is usually given. To this end, I have identified two distinctive kinds of loop invariant, the first occurring in such trivial algorithms as summing an array and insertion sort, and the second in more subtle algorithms, including the greedy algorithms. This classification is presented in Section 4.2.

This book is entirely self-contained in its treatment of correctness, analysis of algorithms (except basic probability theory), data abstraction, and algorithm design. Some knowledge of the kind usually imparted in a second programming course is assumed: familiarity with a Pascal-like programming language, linked structures, and recursion.

Specific attributions are given throughout the text. More generally, I am indebted to a number of previous authors, especially to Aho et al. (1983) for my choice of subject areas, as well as many of the individual topics; to Tarjan (1983), whose monograph provided a model for my organization, and some of its most interesting material; to Knuth (1973a) for general inspiration, and to Knuth (1973b) for most of the analyses in Chapters 6–9.

Several people generously gave their time during the development of the book at Sydney University. Greg Ryan carefully read the manuscript; Stephen Russell and John Gough assisted with Modula-2; and Bryden Allen, Greg Butler, Norman Foo, and Alan Fekete gave reviews and advice. My thanks also to my thesis supervisor, Allan Bromley, for his encouragement over the years.

This book has grown from courses taught while visiting the University of Iowa in 1984–7, and in a general way owes much to my colleagues there, especially Donald Alton, Keith Brinck, and Douglas Jones, and to the congenial environment I found at Iowa. Accordingly, I dedicate the book with gratitude to my many American friends.

## Preface to the second edition

In revising this book for the second edition, I have been pleased to be able to incorporate the suggestions of several readers and reviewers. Early material on lists, stacks, queues, and trees has been expanded, and many exercises used in courses based on this book at the University of Sydney have been added. There are also new sections on the Indexed List ADT, network flow, and bipartite matching.

The major change, however, has been the replacement of Modula-2 by Eiffel as the programming notation. The result has been code that expresses the book's ideas more clearly than was possible in Modula-2. Readers unfamiliar with Eiffel but familiar with Pascal, Modula-2, Ada, or C should have no difficulty reading Eiffel; the few points that are not self-evident are explained in a short appendix. Once again all the code except a few fragments in exercises has been compiled and carefully tested. It is available, free, from *ftp://ftp.cs.usyd.edu.au/jeff/kedsal.*

This edition was typeset by me using the Lout document formatting system. My thanks go to the Basser Department of Computer Science at the University of Sydney, and to the Department of Computer Science at the University of Nottingham, for the use of their facilities; to my colleague Antonios Symvonis; and to David Barnett, Victoria Henderson, Karen Mosman, Simon Plumtree, Dylan Reisenberger, and Andrew Ware from Addison Wesley Longman.

Jeffrey H Kingston
*jeff@cs.usyd.edu.au*

# Chapter 1

# Algorithm Correctness

Most algorithms are straightforward and obviously correct. For example, the algorithm for summing the elements of a set of numbers, by adding each in turn into a *sum* variable, is of this kind. If all algorithms were like this, there would be no need to study algorithm correctness.

Here is an algorithm, simple to state, whose correctness is not nearly so obvious. We are given a map showing cities and the distances between them:

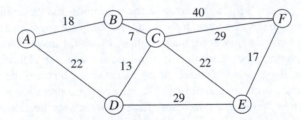

The problem is to connect all the cities together with fiber-optic cable, using links whose total distance is as small as possible. For the map just given, the answer is

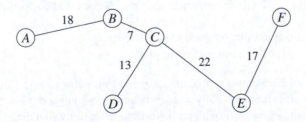

One algorithm for this problem (Kruskal's algorithm from Section 12.2) takes each link in turn, from the shortest to the longest, and adds it to the growing result whenever doing so would not introduce a cycle. This is plausible, and it works

for the instance above, but is it obviously correct in every instance? Not at all. To understand Kruskal's algorithm and others like it, intuition is not enough: something more formal is needed.

The study of algorithm correctness, as this book goes about it, is known as *axiomatic semantics*, and it is principally owing to Floyd (1967) and Hoare (1969). It is possible, using the methods of axiomatic semantics, to prove that an algorithm is correct as rigorously as one can prove a theorem in logic. This will not be attempted here, because it is an entire subject in itself; see, for example, Dijkstra (1976) and Gries (1981). Instead, a less rigorous approach will be used which is compatible with the fully rigorous one, but which is more appropriate to our aim of understanding why algorithms are correct.

## 1.1 Problems and specifications

A *problem* is a general question to be answered, usually possessing one or more *parameters*. A problem is specified by describing the form the parameters are to take, and the question that is being asked about them. For example, the *minimum-finding problem* is '*S* is a set of numbers. What is a minimum element of *S*?' It has one parameter, the set of numbers *S*.

An *instance* of a problem is an assignment of values to the parameters. For example, '*S* = {5, 2, 6, 9}' is an instance of the minimum-finding problem.

An *algorithm* is a step-by-step procedure for taking any instance of a problem and producing a correct answer for that instance. If several answers are equally correct, as often happens, the algorithm may produce any one. An algorithm is *correct* if it is guaranteed to produce a correct answer to every instance of the problem.

Specifying a problem can be difficult, because great precision is needed. For example, the empty set has no minimum element, so the specification above for the minimum-finding problem is flawed. A good way to state a specification precisely is to give two boolean expressions, or *conditions*: the first, the *precondition*, states what may be assumed true initially; the second, the *postcondition*, states what is to be true about the result. The minimum-finding problem could be specified like this:

> *Pre*:     *S* is a finite, non-empty set of integers
> *Post*:    *m* is a minimum element of *S*

By writing (there exists $x \in S$ such that $m = x$) **and** (for all $x \in S, m \le x$), it is possible to express more formally what it means for $m$ to be a minimum element of *S*. Whether this degree of formalism is worthwhile or not will depend on the use to which the specification is put.

By assuming that all instances are non-empty, we are saying that we don't care what an algorithm for this problem does if it is given the empty set. It is the user's responsibility to supply only instances in accord with the precondition.

## 1.2 Recursive algorithms

Newcomers to recursion are often confused by the apparent circularity of recursive definitions: to solve a problem, first solve the problem. As a first, simple example, consider this well-known recursive algorithm for calculating $n!$, the product of the first $n$ natural numbers:

> *factorial*(*n*: *INTEGER*): *INTEGER* **is**
>    **do**
>        **if** $n = 0$ **then**
>           *Result* := 1
>        **else**
>           *Result* := *n* ∗ *factorial*(*n*–1)
>        **end**
>    **end**

A naive approach to understanding this algorithm, based on tracing its behavior, is possible but becomes very confusing as the recursive calls build up.

A much clearer view is obtainable when the ideas of problems, instances, and formal specification using preconditions and postconditions are used. The problem of calculating $n!$ has specification

> -- *Pre*: $n$ is an integer such that $n \geq 0$
> $x := factorial(n)$
> -- *Post*: $x = n!$

The convention used here is to include the conditions as comments in a program fragment at the points where they should be true.

Instead of trying to understand the algorithm by tracing it, the approach recommended here is to prove that the program satisfies its specification, and to use the proof as a guide to understanding the algorithm.

It must be shown that for all $n \geq 0$, *factorial*(*n*) returns $n!$. This statement is clearly suited to a proof by induction on $n$. First it must be shown that *factorial*(0) returns 0!, and second, that if *factorial*(*j*) returns $j!$ for all $j$ such that $0 \leq j \leq n - 1$, then *factorial*(*n*) returns $n!$.

The key point is that during the proof we will be *assuming* that *factorial*(*n*–1) returns $(n - 1)!$, as proof by induction permits us to do. That is, to understand this algorithm there is no need to trace the call to *factorial*(*n*–1), and in fact to do so only leads to confusion. Instead, the recursive call is assumed correct by induction, and the formal specification defines its effect without any need to trace it.

Here is the formal proof:

**Theorem 1.1:** For all integers $n \geq 0$, *factorial*(*n*) returns $n!$.
**Proof:** by induction on $n$.
**Basis step:** $n = 0$. Then the test $n = 0$ succeeds, and the algorithm returns 1. This is correct, since $0! = 1$.

**Inductive step:** The inductive hypothesis is that *factorial*(*j*) returns *j*! for all *j* in the range $0 \leq j \leq n - 1$. It must be shown that *factorial*(*n*) returns *n*!. Since $n > 0$, the algorithm returns $n * factorial(n-1)$. By the inductive hypothesis, *factorial*(*n*–1) returns $(n - 1)!$, and so *factorial*(*n*) returns $n \times (n - 1)!$, which equals *n*!.  □

Notice that the proof is only possible because the recursive call is given a smaller instance than the original, so that the inductive hypothesis may be applied to it. Also, the theorem says nothing about the behavior of *factorial*(*n*) for $n < 0$, and in fact the algorithm never halts for these *n*.

For a second example, consider the *binary search* algorithm, whose goal is to determine whether *x* is present in the sorted array *entries.item*(*a..b*):

> -- *Pre*: $a \leq b + 1$ **and** *entries.item*(*a..b*) is a sorted array
> *found* := *binary_search*(*a*, *b*, *x*);
> -- *Post*: *found* = $x \in$ *entries.item*(*a..b*) **and** *entries* is unchanged

The code is

```
binary_search(a, b: INTEGER; x: KEY_TYPE): BOOLEAN is
    local
        mid: INTEGER;
    do
        if a > b then
            Result := false
        else
            mid := (a + b) // 2;
            if x = entries.item(mid) then
                Result := true
            elseif x < entries.item(mid) then
                Result := binary_search(a, mid−1, x)
            else
                Result := binary_search(mid+1, b, x)
            end
        end
    end
```

where // denotes integer division. Binary search first compares *x* with the middle entry of the array, *entries.item*(*mid*). If $x <$ *entries.item*(*mid*), *x* must lie in the left half of the array if it is present at all; if $x >$ *entries.item*(*mid*), it must lie in the right half. The proof is by induction on the size of the array *entries.item*(*a..b*):

**Theorem 1.2:** For all $n \geq 0$, where $n = b - a + 1$ equals the number of elements in the array *entries.item*(*a..b*), *binary_search*(*a*, *b*, *x*) correctly returns the value of the condition $x \in$ *entries.item*(*a..b*).
**Proof:** by induction on *n*.
**Basis step:** $n = 0$. The array is empty, so $a = b + 1$, the test $a > b$ succeeds, and the algorithm returns **false**. This is correct: *x* cannot be present in an empty array.

**Inductive step:** $n > 0$. The inductive hypothesis is that, for all $j$ lying in the range $0 \le j \le n - 1$, where $j = b' - a' + 1$, $binary\_search(a', b', x)$ correctly returns the condition $x \in entries.item(a'..b')$. From the calculation $mid := (a + b) \,//\, 2$ it follows that $a \le mid \le b$. If $x = entries.item(mid)$, clearly $x \in entries.item(a..b)$ and the algorithm correctly returns the value **true**. If $x < entries.item(mid)$, then since $entries$ is sorted it follows that $x \in entries.item(a..b)$ if and only if $x \in entries.item(a..mid - 1)$. By the inductive hypothesis, this second condition is returned by $binary\_search(a, mid-1, x)$. The inductive hypothesis does apply, since $0 \le (mid - 1) - a + 1 \le n - 1$. The case $x > entries.item(mid)$ is similar, and so the algorithm is correct for all instances of size $n$. □

## 1.3 Iterative algorithms

Iterative algorithms (those containing a loop) are much easier to trace than recursive algorithms, but they are not always easier to understand. For example, the mysterious algorithm given at the beginning of this chapter, for building communication networks, has a simple iterative form.

It turns out that proofs of correctness of iterative algorithms can supply the ideas needed to understand such algorithms. In particular, a condition called the *loop invariant*, which lies at the heart of every such proof, is the key to understanding even the most mysterious iterative algorithms.

A *loop invariant* $I$ of an algorithm containing an **until** loop is a condition which is true at the beginning of each iteration of the loop, at the moment just before the **until** condition is tested.

Two questions are raised by this. First, how do we go about finding loop invariants? And second, how do we use them to prove that algorithms are correct? It seems best to tackle both questions simultaneously, by way of examples. Our first, very simple, example finds the sum of the elements of the array $entries.item(a..b)$:

> -- *Pre*: $a \le b + 1$
> **from** $i := a$; $sum := 0$ **until** $i = b + 1$ **loop**
>     $sum := sum + entries.item(i)$;
>     $i := i + 1$
> **end**
> -- *Post*: $sum = \sum_{j=a}^{b} entries.item(j)$

As usual, the precondition and postcondition have been included as comments at the points where they should be true. By definition, $entries.item(a..a-1)$ denotes an empty array whose sum is 0, and this algorithm calculates this empty sum correctly.

Now, what is the loop invariant of this algorithm? We are looking for a condition which is true at the beginning of each iteration of the loop. Some trivial examples are **true** and $i \ge a$; but, to be useful, a loop invariant must express everything that the algorithm has achieved up to the point where it occurs.

It is often helpful to imagine the state of affairs when about half the iterations are complete: what is true then? At that point, the *sum* variable contains the sum of all the items examined so far. More precisely,

$$sum = \sum_{j=a}^{i-1} entries.item(j)$$

This condition is the loop invariant of the summing algorithm; the reader may easily verify intuitively that this condition holds at the beginning of each iteration.

Even without proof, the loop invariant is very useful to know. For example, it makes an excellent comment (at least, it does for loops less trivial than this summing example). To know the loop invariant is to understand the algorithm.

For the record, and as a model for the more difficult proofs that appear later in this book, here is a proof that the condition really is a loop invariant:

**Theorem 1.3 (Loop invariant of summing algorithm):** At the beginning of the $k$th iteration of the summing algorithm above, $sum = \sum_{j=a}^{i-1} entries.item(j)$.

**Proof:** by induction on $k$.

**Basis step:** $k = 1$. At the beginning of the first iteration, the initialization statements ensure that $sum = 0$ and $i = a$. Since $0 = \sum_{j=a}^{a-1} entries.item(j)$, the condition holds.

**Inductive step:** The inductive hypothesis is that $sum = \sum_{j=a}^{i-1} entries.item(j)$ at the beginning of the $k$th iteration. Since the aim here is to prove that this condition holds after one more iteration, it may also be assumed at this point that the loop is not about to terminate, or in other words, that $i \neq b + 1$. Let $sum'$ and $i'$ be the values of $sum$ and $i$ at the beginning of the $(k + 1)$st iteration. It is required to show that $sum' = \sum_{j=a}^{i'-1} entries.item(j)$. Since $sum' = sum + entries.item(i)$, and $i' = i + 1$,

$$sum' = sum + entries.item(i)$$

$$= \sum_{j=a}^{i-1} entries.item(j) + entries.item(i)$$

$$= \sum_{j=a}^{i} entries.item(j)$$

$$= \sum_{j=a}^{i'-1} entries.item(j)$$

and so the condition holds at the beginning of the $(k + 1)$st iteration. □

Establishing the loop invariant is invariably the hard part of the proof, but there are two easier steps remaining. First, it must be shown that the postcondition holds at the end. Consider the last iteration of the loop in the summing algorithm. At the end of it, the loop invariant holds, as has been shown. Then the test $i = b + 1$ is made, succeeds, and execution passes to the point after the loop. Clearly, at that moment the condition

$$sum = \sum_{j=a}^{i-1} entries.item(j) \text{ and } i = b + 1$$

holds. But this condition implies

$$sum = \sum_{j=a}^{b} entries.item(j)$$

which is the desired postcondition; so the postcondition holds when the algorithm terminates. Notice that this conclusion could not have been reached so simply if $i > b$ (the condition that is usually written in practice) had been used as the condition at the top of the loop. In general, just after the completion of the execution of the loop '**from** ... **until** $B$ ...', with loop invariant $I$, the condition $I$ **and** $B$ holds, and it is necessary to prove that this implies *Post*.

The final step is to show that there is no risk of an infinite loop. This is usually obvious, so may be done briefly. The method of proof is to identify some integer quantity that is strictly increasing (or decreasing) from one iteration to the next, and to show that when this becomes sufficiently large (or small) the loop must terminate. For the summing algorithm, $i$ is strictly increasing, and when it reaches $b + 1$, the loop must terminate. This argument depends on $i$ being no greater than $b + 1$ initially; in other words, the condition $a \leq b + 1$ must be true initially in order for termination to be guaranteed.

To summarize, then, the steps required to prove that the iterative algorithm

```
-- Pre
from ... until B loop
    ...
end
-- Post
```

is correct are as follows:

1.  Guess a condition $I$.

2.  Prove by induction that $I$ is a loop invariant.

3.  Prove that $I$ **and** $B \Rightarrow Post$.

4.  Prove that the loop is guaranteed to terminate.

With practice, a clear intuitive understanding of the correctness of an algorithm will lead immediately to the loop invariant. Remember that the loop invariant must mention all the variables whose values change within the loop, but that it expresses an unchanging relationship among those variables. It must also contain complete information about what the algorithm has achieved up to the point in the program text where it occurs.

For example, the loop invariant

$$sum = \sum_{j=a}^{i-1} entries.item(j)$$

makes good intuitive sense. It simply expresses the fact that, at the beginning of each iteration, *sum* contains the sum of all the values examined so far.

Some guidance on the general form of the loop invariant may be obtained from *Post*, since *I* must satisfy *I* **and** *B* $\Rightarrow$ *Post*, where *B* and *Post* are known. In fact, it is good policy to take *Post* and generalize it in some way to obtain *I*. For example, in the summing algorithm above, *I* is just *Post* with *b* replaced by *i* − 1. This simple relationship ensures that the condition *I* **and** *B* $\Rightarrow$ *Post* is readily proved.

At the other extreme, check that the initialization statements establish *I*. If they do, and *I* **and** *B* $\Rightarrow$ *Post*, it is probably worthwhile to proceed with the main part of the induction.

## Correctness of selection sorting

Selection sorting is a simple sorting method which works by repeatedly finding the smallest item among those that remain unsorted, and adding it to the end of a growing sorted sequence. It makes an interesting example because there is a natural choice of loop invariant which turns out to be too weak, as will be seen.

Assuming that the items to be sorted are stored in an array *entries.item(a..b)*, the sorting problem may be specified like this:

-- *Pre*: $a \leq b + 1$
-- *Post*: *entries.item(a..b)* contains some permutation of its initial values
            **and** *entries.item(a)* $\leq$ *entries.item(a + 1)* $\leq$ ... $\leq$ *entries.item(b)*

The precondition permits the array to be empty, when $a = b + 1$. The first part of the postcondition prevents an algorithm from changing (as distinct from moving) the items in the array; without it, a 'sorting' algorithm could replace every item by zero and declare the array to be sorted.

In the following algorithm, it is assumed that *min_index(entries, i, j)* returns the index of a smallest item in *entries.item(i..j)*, and that *swap(entries, i, j)* exchanges items *i* and *j*. Here then is the selection sorting algorithm:

```
from i := a until i = b+1 loop
    j := min_index(entries, i, b);
    if j /= i then swap(entries, i, j) end;
    i := i + 1
end
```

On the first iteration of the loop, *min_index(entries, a, b)* finds an overall smallest item, and then *swap(entries, a, j)* swaps it into *entries.item(a)*. On the second iteration of the loop, *min_index(entries, a+1, b)* finds a smallest remaining item, and *swap(entries, a+1, j)* swaps it into *entries.item(a+1)*. This process continues until the array is sorted.

It should be clear that the first part of the postcondition, '*entries.item(a..b)* contains some permutation of its initial values,' may be incorporated into the loop invariant without change. It is trivially true at the beginning of the algorithm, and since the only changes to *entries* are those made by *swap(entries,i, j)*, which permutes items but does not change them, it remains true throughout the entire execution of the algorithm.

It is clear informally that the purpose of one iteration is to get the correct item into *entries.item(i)*; so at the beginning of this iteration,

$$entries.item(a) \leq \ldots \leq entries.item(i - 1)$$

and since this condition plus the termination condition $i = b + 1$ implies the remainder of the postcondition, it is a natural candidate for the remainder of the loop invariant. However, although this condition is true, it is inadequate: something is missing.

A simple way to see the problem is to consider the special case $i = a + 1$, that is, to consider the state of affairs at the beginning of the second iteration. The condition is

$$entries.item(a) \leq \ldots \leq entries.item(a)$$

which is vacuously true. But at this moment the loop invariant should be expressing everything that the algorithm has achieved, which in this case is to have swapped a smallest item into *entries.item(a)*. We need to strengthen the loop invariant, which altogether comes to

> *entries.item(a..b)* contains some permutation of its initial values
> **and** *entries.item(a)* $\leq \ldots \leq$ *entries.item(i − 1)* $\leq$ *entries.item(i..b)*

The last inequality means that the items of *entries.item(i..b)* are no smaller than the items of *entries.item(a..i − 1)*.

The actual proof of correctness is now quite straightforward. The loop invariant clearly holds initially, since *entries.item(a..i − 1)* is empty, and when $i = b + 1$ it trivially implies the postcondition. The combined action of *min_index(entries, i, b)* and *swap(entries, i, j)* clearly produces

$$entries.item(a) \leq \ldots \leq entries.item(i) \leq entries.item(i + 1..b)$$

and the final $i := i + 1$ returns us to the loop invariant.

### Correctness of binary search

This section concludes with a study of the correctness of the following non-recursive binary search algorithm:

```
binary_search(a, b: INTEGER; x: KEY_TYPE): BOOLEAN is
    local
        i, j, mid: INTEGER;
        found: BOOLEAN;
    do
        found := false;
        from i := a;  j := b until i = j + 1 or found loop
            mid := (i + j) // 2;
            if x = entries.item(mid) then
                found := true
            elseif x < entries.item(mid) then
                j := mid − 1
            else
                i := mid + 1
            end
        end;
        Result := found
    end
```

From the discussion of the recursive binary search algorithm in Section 1.2, it is fairly evident that the loop invariant should state that $x \in entries.item(a..b)$ if and only if $x \in entries.item(i..j)$. This takes care of the variables $i$ and $j$.

The harder question is how to bring *found* and *mid* into the loop invariant, especially since *mid* is undefined at the beginning of the first iteration. Perhaps the best way to handle these two is to imagine another version of the algorithm in which we actually return the index of $x$ if it is found. For this version it would be necessary to add *found* $\Rightarrow (a \leq mid \leq b$ **and** $x = entries.item(mid))$ to the postcondition, and this immediately suggests that it be included in the loop invariant:

$(x \in entries.item(a..b)$ if and only if $x \in entries.item(i..j))$ **and**
$(found \Rightarrow (a \leq mid \leq b$ **and** $x = entries.item(mid)))$

The initialization *found* := **false**; $i := a; j := b$; clearly establishes this invariant.

At termination, the loop invariant holds and so does $i = j + 1$ **or** *found*. If *found* is true, the loop invariant shows that $a \leq mid \leq b$ **and** $x = entries.item(mid)$, so it must be that $x \in entries.item(a..b)$; on the other hand, if *found* is false, then $i = j + 1$ and so $x \notin entries.item(i..j)$ and therefore $x \notin entries.item(a..b)$. Thus the postcondition holds.

The rest of the proof is left as an exercise; it is quite similar to the argument used to prove that the recursive binary search algorithm was correct.

## 1.4 Exercises

1.1    Consider the following recursive algorithm:

```
g(n: INTEGER): INTEGER;
    do
        if n <= 1 then
            Result := n
        else
            Result := 5*g(n-1) - 6*g(n-2)
        end
    end
```

Prove by induction on $n$ that $g(n)$ returns $3^n - 2^n$ for all $n \geq 0$.

1.2    Prove that the specification

        -- *Pre*: $a \leq b + 1$
        -- *Post*: *entries.item*$(a) \leq$ *entries.item*$(a + 1) \leq \ldots \leq$ *entries.item*$(b)$

is satisfied by the routine

```
selection_sort(a, b: INTEGER) is
    local
        i: INTEGER;
    do
        if a = b + 1 then
            -- do nothing
        else
            i := min_index(entries, a, b);
            if i /= a then swap(entries, i, a) end;
            selection_sort(a + 1, b)
        end
    end;
```

You may assume that *min_index*(*entries*, $i, j$) will return the index of a minimum element of the non-empty subarray *entries.item*$(i..j)$, and that *swap*(*entries*, $i, a$) swaps the two indicated elements.

1.3    It is not within the scope of this book to explain how program correctness may be reduced to a formal logical system. Here though is a glimpse. Consider an assignment statement:

        -- *Pre*: ?
        $x := E$
        -- *Post*: $f(x)$

where $x$ is any variable, $E$ is any expression, and $f(x)$ is any condition. Show that $f(E)$ must be true to guarantee the truth of the given postcondition.

1.4     Use the method of the previous question to show formally that the precondition **true** is sufficient to make the given postcondition true:

$$i := a;$$
$$sum := 0$$
$$\text{-- } Post: sum = \sum_{j=a}^{i-1} entries.item(j)$$

Then use the method to show formally that the postcondition shown below will be true where it occurs if that same condition is true at the beginning:

$$sum := sum + entries.item(i);$$
$$i := i + 1$$
$$\text{-- } Post: sum = \sum_{j=a}^{i-1} entries.item(j)$$

These two results taken together prove formally that the given condition is a loop invariant of the summing algorithm from Section 1.3.

1.5     Prove that the following linear search algorithm is correct with respect to the given precondition and postcondition:

```
-- Pre: a ≤ b and x ∈ entries.item(a..b)
from i := a until x = entries.item(i) loop
   i := i + 1
end
-- Post: a ≤ i ≤ b and x ∉ entries.item(a..i − 1)
     and  x = entries.item(i)
```

1.6     This algorithm for evaluating the polynomial $a_0 + a_1 x + \cdots + a_{k-1} x^{k-1}$ at the point $x = x_0$ is named after William G. Horner:

```
horner(a: ARRAY[INTEGER]; x0: INTEGER): INTEGER is
   local
      i: INTEGER;
   do
      Result := 0;
      from i := k − 1 until i < 0 loop
         Result := a.item(i) + Result * x0;
         i := i − 1
      end
   end
```

Find the loop invariant of this algorithm and prove it correct.

1.7     In addition to finding whether $x \in entries.item(a..b)$, the following iterative version of binary search finds the index of the place where $x$ lies, or, if $x$ is not present, the index of the place just to the left of $x$'s place in the ordering:

```
binary_search(a, b: INTEGER; x: KEY_TYPE): INTEGER is
    local
        i, j, mid: INTEGER;
        found: BOOLEAN;
    do
        found := false;
        from i := a; j := b until i = j + 1 or found loop
            mid := (i + j) // 2;
            if x = entries.item(mid) then
                found := true
            elseif x < entries.item(mid) then
                j := mid − 1
            else
                i := mid + 1
            end
        end;
        if found then Result := mid else Result := j end
    end
```

where // is integer division. Prove that this satisfies the specification

    -- Pre:
    $a \leq b + 1$ and $entries.item(a) \leq \ldots \leq entries.item(b)$
    -- Post:
    (found $\Rightarrow a \leq Result \leq b$ and $entries.item(Result) = x$) and
    (**not** found $\Rightarrow a − 1 \leq Result \leq b$ and
        (for all $k$ such that $a \leq k \leq Result, entries.item(k) < x$) and
        (for all $k$ such that $Result + 1 \leq k \leq b, x < entries.item(k)$)))

Your first task is to determine what must be true just after the loop terminates, in order for the final **if** statement to establish the postcondition.

1.8   *The bill-splitting problem* (J. McCormack). A group of $p$ people living in a shared household receive a bill for $c$ cents. They want to split the bill $p$ ways as fairly as possible, given that fractions of one cent are not allowed. The following algorithm is proposed:

```
from m := c; n := p until n < 0 loop
    r := m // n;
    output.put_int(r);
    output.next_line;
    m := m − r;
    n := n − 1
end
```

where // is integer division. Does it always work?

1.9   *Tail recursion elimination.* Recursion is a powerful tool for expressing algorithms, and it is used extensively throughout this book. However, when a recursive algorithm is heavily used in a production system, it may be worthwhile to tune it by eliminating some or all of the recursive calls. In general, recursion elimination requires the replacement of the runtime stack with an explicit stack appearing in the algorithm; but, in the case where there is only one recursive call, and it is the last statement in the body of the routine, the recursion can be replaced with a loop. This case is known as *tail recursion*. In general, the tail-recursive routine

> *tail_rec*(*x*: *instance_type*): *result_type* **is**
>   **local**
>     *y*: *instance_type*;
>   **do**
>     **if** *b*(*x*) **then**
>       *Result* := *c*(*x*)
>     **else**
>       *y* := *d*(*x*);
>       *Result* := *tail_rec*(*y*)
>     **end**
>   **end**

has identical effect to the non-recursive routine

> *non_rec*(*x*: *instance_type*): *result_type* **is**
>   **do**
>     **from until** *b*(*x*) **loop**
>       *x* := *d*(*x*)
>     **end**;
>     *Result* := *c*(*x*)
>   **end**

where *b*(*x*), *c*(*x*), and *d*(*x*) are any functions of type *BOOLEAN*, *result_type*, and *instance_type* respectively. Prove this assertion by showing that the two routines execute identical statements in identical order.

1.10　Eliminate tail recursion from the *selection_sort* routine of Exercise 1.2.

1.11　Although the recursive binary search given in Section 1.2 is not in the form of a tail-recursive routine, since it has two recursive calls within its body, it can be made tail-recursive by careful rewriting. Do this and compare the non-recursive version obtained by eliminating tail recursion with the version given in Section 1.3.

# Chapter 2

# Analysis of Algorithms

The speed of computation has increased so much over the past 40 years that it might seem that efficiency in algorithms is no longer important. But, paradoxically, efficiency matters more today than ever before. The obvious reason why this is so is that our ambition has grown with our computing power. Virtually all applications of computing – the simulation of continuous systems, high-resolution graphics, and the interpretation of physical data, for example – are demanding more speed.

The more subtle, and more important reason is as follows. The time that many algorithms take to execute is a non-linear function of the size of their input, and this can greatly reduce their ability to benefit from increases in speed. For example, consider an algorithm that sorts $n$ numbers into increasing order in $n^2$ steps. Suppose that over the course of a few years, computing speed increases by a factor of 100. In the time that it used to take to execute the $n^2$ steps, it is now possible to execute $100n^2 = (10n)^2$ steps. Thus, only 10 times as many numbers can be sorted as before. One of the potential two orders of magnitude improvement has been lost to an inefficient algorithm.

Another example is the multiplication of integers. It takes longer to perform one 64-bit multiplication than it does to perform two 32-bit multiplications, as far as anyone knows.

The faster computers run, the more are efficient algorithms needed to take advantage of their power. The branch of computer science that studies efficiency is known as *analysis of algorithms.*

## 2.1 Characteristic operations and time complexity

Consider the following algorithm, which finds the index of a minimum element of the non-empty array *entries.item(a..b)*:

```
min_index(a, b: INTEGER): INTEGER is
    local
        i: INTEGER
    do
        Result := a;
        from i := a + 1 until i > b loop
            if entries.item(i) < entries.item(Result) then
                Result := i
            end;
            i := i + 1
        end
    end
```

How long does $min\_index(1, n)$ take to execute? The answer to this question depends on the particular implementation (that is, computer and compiler) used to execute the algorithm, and on the size of the array, $n$. Since our interest is in the algorithm itself, and not in any particular implementation of it, these two factors must be separated. In general, this will be done as follows. Choose some *characteristic operation* that the algorithm performs repeatedly. Define the *time complexity* $T(n)$ of an algorithm to be the number of characteristic operations it performs when given an input of size $n$.

For example, if the operation $Result := a$ is chosen as the characteristic operation for $min\_index(1, n)$, it turns out that $T(n) = 1$, since this operation is performed exactly once. Or, if the comparison $entries.item(i) < entries.item(Result)$ is taken as the characteristic operation, $T(n)$ is the number of times the body of the loop is executed. It is not hard to see that this is $T(n) = n - 1$, since $entries.item(Result)$ is compared once with each of the $n - 1$ numbers $entries.item(2..n)$. Finally, if $Result := i$ is chosen as the characteristic operation, $T(n)$ could be anything from 0 to $n - 1$, depending on the values in the array: if the first entry is the smallest, $T(n) = 0$; if the first entry is the largest and then every entry after the first is smaller than the preceding one, $T(n) = n - 1$. This dependence on values will be considered further in the next example.

One way to choose among these answers is to refer to some particular implementation. Suppose it takes $p$ microseconds to execute the body of the loop once, and $q$ microseconds to execute the initialization and return parts. Then the execution time is $p(n - 1) + q$, which is $pT(n) + q$ if the second complexity function is chosen. A characteristic operation and its corresponding complexity function $T(n)$ are called *realistic* if the execution time with respect to some implementation is bounded by a linear function of $T(n)$. By choosing a realistic characteristic operation, the inherent complexity $T(n)$ is neatly separated from the implementation-dependent details $p$ and $q$. The choice of a realistic characteristic operation is almost always so obvious that it rarely needs justification; in principle the analysis could be done for every possible operation and the largest answer taken.

Now consider the following algorithm for determining whether $x$ is an element of $entries.item(a..b)$:

```
linear_search(a, b: INTEGER; x: KEY_TYPE): BOOLEAN is
    local
        i: INTEGER;
        found: BOOLEAN
    do
        found := false;
        from i := a until i > b or found loop
            found := (x = entries.item(i));
            i := i + 1
        end;
        Result := found
    end
```

The time complexity of $linear\_search(1, n, x)$ depends on the value of $x$ and on the contents of the array. This leads to two questions:

Over all instances of size $n$, what is the maximum time the algorithm takes to execute? This is its *worst-case time complexity*, denoted $W(n)$.

Over all instances of size $n$, what is the average time the algorithm takes to execute? This is its *average time complexity*, denoted $A(n)$.

More formally, suppose algorithm $P$ accepts $k$ different instances of size $n$. Let $T_i(n)$ be the time complexity of $P$ when given the $i$th instance, for $1 \le i \le k$, and let $p_i$ be the probability that this instance occurs. Then

$$W(n) = \max_{1 \le i \le k} T_i(n)$$

$$A(n) = \sum_{i=1}^{k} p_i T_i(n)$$

Incidentally, it follows that $A(n) \le W(n)$, with equality, assuming all the probabilities are non-zero, if and only if $T_1(n) = T_2(n) = \ldots = T_k(n)$ (Exercises 2.1 and 2.2).

Average complexity analysis is complicated by the need to find suitable values for the probabilities $p_i$. In one sense, any values would do, but if the result is to be useful the values must reflect the conditions under which the algorithm will be used – a hazy and subjective requirement. For some problems, no consensus on suitable probabilities has been reached (for example, graph problems).

Here now is the calculation of $W(n)$ and $A(n)$ for $linear\_search(1, n, x)$, choosing $x = entries.item(i)$ as the characteristic operation. Two reasonable assumptions are (a) the probability that $x$ will be found somewhere in the array is a constant, $p$; and (b) if $x$ is present, it is equally likely to be found at any position in the array.

Although $linear\_search(1, n, x)$ has an infinite number of instances, they fall into just $k = n + 1$ classes. If $x = entries.item(i)$, the algorithm will determine this and stop after comparing $x$ with $entries.item(1)$, $entries.item(2)$, $\ldots$, $entries.item(i)$; that is, after performing $i$ characteristic operations. Since the probability $p$ of $x$ being present is spread equally among the $n$ cases $x = entries.item(1)$, $x = entries.item(2)$, $\ldots, x = entries.item(n)$, each must have probability $p/n$. If $x$ is not present, then $x$ is compared with all $n$ elements of the array before stopping. This is all summarized in the following table:

| $i$ | Instance | | $p_i$ | $T_i(n)$ |
|-----|----------|---|-------|----------|
| 1 | $x = entries.item(1)$ | | $p/n$ | 1 |
| 2 | $x = entries.item(2)$ | | $p/n$ | 2 |
| | | $\ldots$ | | |
| $i$ | $x = entries.item(i)$ | | $p/n$ | $i$ |
| | | $\ldots$ | | |
| $n$ | $x = entries.item(n)$ | | $p/n$ | $n$ |
| $n+1$ | $x \notin entries.item(1..n)$ | | $1-p$ | $n$ |

From this table, it is clear that $linear\_search(1, n, x)$ has worst-case time complexity $W(n) = n$ comparisons. This occurs when $x = entries.item(n)$, and also when $x$ is not present. The average complexity is

$$A(n) = \sum_{i=1}^{n+1} p_i T_i(n)$$

$$= \sum_{i=1}^{n} p_i T_i(n) + p_{n+1} T_{n+1}(n)$$

$$= \sum_{i=1}^{n} \frac{p}{n} i + (1-p)n$$

$$= \frac{p(n+1)}{2} + (1-p)n$$

For example, if $p = 1$ the algorithm scans halfway along the array on average.

## 2.2 Recursive algorithms

In Section 1.2 it was shown how the correctness of a recursive algorithm is proved by induction on $n$, the size of its input. That approach allowed the recursive calls to be assumed correct; no investigation of them was needed.

A similar strategy often applies to the analysis of a recursive algorithm. By definition, for all $n$, $T(n)$ is the time complexity of the algorithm when given an input of size $n$. By definition, then, a recursive call of size $n/2$, say, has time complexity $T(n/2)$; no further investigation of it is needed. Just as the algorithm is defined in terms of itself, this approach will lead to an expression for $T(n)$ in terms of itself: a *recurrence equation* for $T(n)$, which must then be solved.

For example, consider the *Towers of Hanoi* problem, defined as follows. There are three pegs, labelled *a*, *b*, and *c*.  On peg *a* there is a stack of *n* disks, each with a hole in the middle to accommodate the peg:

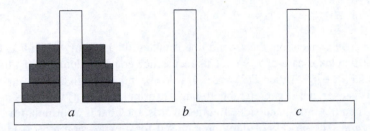

As the diagram shows, the disks increase in size going down.  The problem is to transfer the stack of disks to peg *c*, one disk at a time, in such a way as to ensure that no disk is ever placed on top of a smaller disk.  Here is a well-known algorithm for the Towers of Hanoi problem:

> *hanoi(n: INTEGER; from_peg, to_peg, spare_peg: CHARACTER)* **is**
> **do**
>   **if** *n > 0* **then**
>     *hanoi(n−1, from_peg, spare_peg, to_peg)*;
>     *output.put_string("Move the top disk from peg ")*;
>     *output.put_character(from_peg)*;
>     *output.put_string(" to peg ")*;
>     *output.put_character(to_peg)*;
>     *output.next_line*;
>     *hanoi(n−1, spare_peg, to_peg, from_peg)*
>   **end**
> **end**

Incidentally, it is the policy of this book to make the base of recursive algorithms as low as possible.  In the case of *hanoi*, it makes sense to move zero disks from one peg to another.  This policy invariably leads to simpler algorithms.

Let $T(n)$ be the time complexity of *hanoi(n, x, y, z)*, when the characteristic operation is the printing of one line.  Clearly, $T(0) = 0$, because the test $n > 0$ fails and nothing is printed.  For larger *n*, the following statements are executed and costs incurred:

| | |
|---|---|
| *hanoi(n−1, from_peg, spare_peg, to_peg)*; | $T(n-1)$ |
| *output.put_string( ... )*; | 1 |
| *hanoi(n−1, spare_peg, to_peg, from_peg)*; | $T(n-1)$ |

As discussed above, the time complexity of *hanoi(n−1, x, y, z)* is $T(n-1)$ by definition, and no further investigation of it is needed. (Many beginners to recursion stumble at this point; they persist in attempting to enter and investigate the recursive calls, when the whole point of recursion is that all needed information about the recursive calls may be *assumed*, by induction.) Summing these contributions gives the *recurrence equation*

$$T(0) = 0$$
$$T(n) = 2T(n-1) + 1$$

for $T(n)$. By convention, the second line is taken to apply only when $n \geq 1$, since the first line takes care of $n = 0$. This recurrence equation defines $T(n)$ for all $n$: $T(1) = 2T(0) + 1 = 1$, then $T(2) = 2T(1) + 1 = 3$, and so on. In one sense, then, the analysis is over, but it is preferable to have a formula for $T(n)$ that does not have $T(n-1)$ on the right-hand side. In other words, the goal is a formula for $T(n)$ in *closed form*. The process of deriving a closed form expression for $T(n)$ is called *solving* the recurrence equation.

Of the variety of techniques for solving recurrence equations, only the simplest technique, *repeated substitution*, is used in this book. Since the formula $T(n) = 2T(n-1) + 1$ holds for all $n \geq 1$, it is valid to substitute $n-1$ for $n$ in it to obtain $T(n-1) = 2T(n-2) + 1$ for all $n \geq 2$. Similarly, $T(n-2) = 2T(n-3) + 1$. Therefore

$$T(n) = 2T(n-1) + 1$$

$$= 2[2T(n-2) + 1] + 1$$

$$= 2[2[2T(n-3) + 1] + 1] + 1$$

$$= 2^3 T(n-3) + 2^2 + 2^1 + 2^0$$

(provided $n \geq 3$), expanding the brackets in a way that elucidates the emerging pattern. If this substitution is repeated $i$ times, clearly the result is

$$T(n) = 2^i T(n-i) + 2^{i-1} + 2^{i-2} + \cdots + 2^0$$

($n \geq i$). Induction on $i$ could be used to prove this, but that is rarely necessary. By choosing $i$ as large as possible, the base of the recurrence equation may be used to eliminate $T$ from the right-hand side: if $i = n$, then $T(n-i) = T(0) = 0$. Hence

$$T(n) = 2^n 0 + 2^{n-1} + 2^{n-2} + \cdots + 2^0$$

$$= \sum_{i=0}^{n-1} 2^i$$

$$= 2^n - 1$$

applying the standard formula for the sum of a geometric progression. This completes the analysis of *hanoi*.

There are cases where the information needed for an analysis is in the data, not the code. Consider this algorithm from Section 6.2 for the inorder traversal of a binary tree:

```
inorder_traversal(x: like entry_type) is
    do
        if not nil_entry(x) then
            inorder_traversal(x.left_child);
            visit(x);
            inorder_traversal(x.right_child)
        end
    end;
```

where *visit(x)* stands for some operation to be performed at each node in the tree, such as printing its contents.

Choose *visit(x)* as the characteristic operation. It is performed once for each node in the tree being traversed, so $T(n) = n$, where $n$ is the number of nodes. For want of a better term, this will be called the *global structure* approach to analysis. The global structure over which the algorithm travels is identified, and the number of characteristic operations performed is related to the size of this structure.

## Analysis of binary search

This section ends with an example which shows how to deal with the practical difficulties and complications that often hinder analyses. The binary search algorithm, which was proved correct in Section 1.2, determines whether $x$ is present in the sorted array *entries.item(a..b)*:

```
binary_search(a, b: INTEGER; x: KEY_TYPE): BOOLEAN is
    local
        mid: INTEGER;
    do
        if a > b then
            Result := false
        else
            mid := (a + b) // 2;
            if x = entries.item(mid) then
                Result := true
            elseif x < entries.item(mid) then
                Result := binary_search(a, mid−1, x)
            else
                Result := binary_search(mid+1, b, x)
            end
        end
    end
```

The array size is halved after each comparison between $x$ and *entries.item(mid)*, roughly, and an array of length $n$ can be halved only about $\log_2 n$ times before reaching a trivial length, so the worst-case complexity of *binary_search*(1, *n*, *x*) is about $\log_2 n$.

A more precise analysis can be made using recurrence equations. Let $T(n)$ be the time complexity of *binary_search*(1, *n*, *x*), where the characteristic operation is one comparison between *x* and *entries.item(mid)* (with a three-way outcome).

If $n > 0$, the algorithm begins by setting *mid* to $\lfloor (n + 1)/2 \rfloor$[1] and examination of the program text reveals that

$$T(0) = 0$$
$$T(n) = 1 \qquad\qquad\qquad\qquad \text{if } x = entries.item(mid)$$
$$= 1 + T(\lfloor (n + 1)/2 \rfloor - 1) \quad \text{if } x < entries.item(mid)$$
$$= 1 + T(n - \lfloor (n + 1)/2 \rfloor) \quad \text{if } x > entries.item(mid)$$

Although it is sometimes possible to solve messy recurrence equations like this one, in general it is better to make some simplifying assumptions. The first step in simplifying this recurrence is the elimination of the floor function, which can be done by restricting *n* to values of the form $n = 2^k - 1$, where *k* is a non-negative integer. This choice ensures that the array always breaks symmetrically into two equal pieces plus middle element:

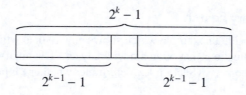

Algebraically this is $\lfloor (n + 1)/2 \rfloor = \lfloor (2^k - 1 + 1)/2 \rfloor = 2^{k-1}$ for $k \geq 1$, giving

$$T(0) = 0$$
$$T(2^k - 1) = 1 \qquad\qquad\qquad\quad \text{if } x = entries.item(mid)$$
$$= 1 + T(2^{k-1} - 1) \quad \text{if } x < entries.item(mid)$$
$$= 1 + T(2^{k-1} - 1) \quad \text{if } x > entries.item(mid)$$

A further simplification can be made by considering only the worst case, which by inspection occurs (for example) when the test $x = entries.item(mid)$ always fails:

$$W(0) = 0$$
$$W(2^k - 1) = 1 + W(2^{k-1} - 1)$$

---

[1]The notation $\lfloor x \rfloor$, 'floor of *x*,' denotes the greatest integer less than or equal to *x*; the result of an integer division of one number by another is always truncated in this way. Similarly, $\lceil x \rceil$, 'ceiling of *x*,' is the smallest integer greater than or equal to *x*.

This may now be solved by repeated substitution:

$$W(2^k - 1) = 1 + W(2^{k-1} - 1)$$

$$= 1 + [1 + W(2^{k-2} - 1)]$$

$$= 1 + [1 + [1 + W(2^{k-3} - 1)]]$$

$$= \dots$$

$$= i + W(2^{k-i} - 1)$$

$(i \leq k)$, and letting $i = k$ gives

$$W(2^k - 1) = k + W(0)$$

$$= k$$

But now $2^k - 1 = n$, and $k = \log_2(n + 1)$, so finally

$$W(n) = \log_2(n + 1)$$

(for $n = 2^k - 1$), which concludes this analysis of binary search.

Although it might seem that the restriction to values of $n$ of the form $2^k - 1$ weakens the result, in practice this does not matter very much: $W(n)$ is a monotone increasing function of $n$, and hence the formula given is a good approximation even when $n$ is not of the form $2^k - 1$ (Exercise 2.15). In Exercise 6.10 it is shown that $W(n) = \lceil \log_2(n + 1) \rceil$ for arbitrary $n$.

## 2.3 Iterative algorithms

Just as recursive algorithms lead naturally to recurrence equations, so iterative algorithms lead naturally to formulas involving summations.

The simplest iterative algorithms to analyze are those containing only loops that iterate over a fixed range of integers. The technique is based on the observation that in the code fragment

```
from i := a until i > b loop
    S;
    i := i + 1
end
```

the statement $S$ is executed $b - a + 1$ times, provided that $a \leq b + 1$. In particular, if $a = b + 1$, $S$ is executed zero times. (This also applies when counting downwards from $b$ to $a$.)

For example, the *min_index* algorithm analyzed earlier in this chapter has this form. The loop executed by *min_index*$(1, n)$ is

```
from i := 2 until i > n loop
    if entries.item(i) < entries.item(Result) then
        Result := i
    end;
    i := i + 1
end
```

By the observation about loops, the **if** statement and hence its comparison is made $n - 2 + 1 = n - 1$ times.

When analyzing an algorithm containing nested loops that iterate over a fixed range of integers in this way, it is generally best to begin with the innermost loop. For example, consider the following algorithm for adding two matrices $a.item(1..n, 1..m)$ and $b.item(1..n, 1..m)$ together:

```
from i := 1 until i > n loop
    from j := 1 until j > m loop
        c.put(a.item(i, j) + b.item(i, j), i, j);
        j := j + 1
    end;
    i := i + 1
end
```

A good choice for the characteristic operation here is $a.item(i, j) + b.item(i, j)$, since it is characteristic of the algorithm and lies inside the inner loop. Having made this choice, the complexity of

```
from j := 1 until j > m loop
    c.put(a.item(i, j) + b.item(i, j), i, j);
    j := j + 1
end;
```

is clearly $m$ additions, by the observation about loops. This reduces the problem to analyzing the outer loop, which now has the form

```
from i := 1 until i > n loop
    perform m additions;
    i := i + 1
end
```

During each of the $n$ iterations of the outer loop, $m$ additions are performed, giving a total of $T(n, m) = nm$ additions overall. The time complexity of the algorithm is a function of two parameters in this example, $n$ and $m$.

In some algorithms, the cost of the inner loop depends on the value of the index variable of the outer loop. Consider this algorithm for sorting the elements of the array *entries.item(a..b)* into non-decreasing order:

```
bubble_sort(a, b: INTEGER) is
    local
        i, j: INTEGER;
    do
        from i := b until i < a loop
            from j := a + 1 until j > i loop
                if entries.item(j−1) > entries.item(j) then
                    swap(entries, j−1, j)
                end;
                j := j + 1
            end;
            i := i − 1
        end
    end
```

It works by 'bubbling' the largest entry up to *entries.item(b)*, the second largest to *entries.item(b−1)*, and so on. The outer loop's invariant is '*entries.item(a..b)* contains a permutation of its original contents, and *entries. item(i+1..b)* contains the $b − i$ largest entries, in sorted order.'

Take the comparison *entries. item(j−1) > entries.item(j)* as the characteristic operation, and consider the analysis of *bubble_sort*$(1, n)$. As before, the first step is to take the inner loop in isolation:

```
from j := 2 until j > i loop
    if entries.item(j−1) > entries.item(j) then
        swap(entries, j−1, j)
    end;
    j := j + 1
end
```

where $a+1$ has been replaced by 2. Applying the observation about loops over fixed ranges shows that the operation *entries.item(j−1) > entries.item(j)* is performed $i − 1$ times, and so the problem reduces to analyzing the outer loop

```
from i := n until i < 1 loop
    perform i−1 comparisons;
    i := i − 1
end
```

where $b$ has been replaced by $n$ and $a$ by 1. The first iteration, when $i = n$, has a cost of $n − 1$ comparisons; the second iteration, when $i = n − 1$, has a cost of $n − 2$ comparisons. Continuing in this way, the total cost is $(n − 1) + (n − 2) + \cdots + 0$ comparisons, so

$$T(n) = \sum_{i=1}^{n}(i − 1) = \frac{n(n − 1)}{2}$$

Compared with the algorithms of Chapter 9, *bubble_sort* is highly inefficient.

Incidentally, it is the policy of this book to produce algorithms that work correctly on the smallest possible input. It makes sense to sort an empty array (that is, an array of length zero); accordingly, this version of *bubble_sort* is well defined when $a = b + 1$, and the analysis is correct too.

As with recursive algorithms, sometimes the information needed for the analysis is in the data, not the code. In such cases the global structure method introduced in the previous section is needed: identify the global structure, and relate $T(n)$ to its size.

Perhaps the simplest example is the traversal of a linked list, using this code taken from Section 5.1:

```
from x := l.first until l.nil_entry(x) loop
    visit(x.value);
    x := l.next(x)
end
```

Using any reasonable linked list implementation, the cost of both *l.first* and *l.next(x)* will be $O(1)$, and so *visit(x.value)* is a realistic characteristic operation. It is clearly performed once for each entry of the list, so the time complexity of traversing a list containing $n$ items is just $n$.

### Tree traversal

For a more complex example of the global structure method just introduced, consider the non-recursive implementation of the inorder traversal of a binary tree, as presented in Figure 6.2 (the recursive version was analyzed in Section 2.2). The idea is to proceed from the first node of the traversal to its successor, to the next successor, and so on:

```
from x := t.inorder_first until t.nil_entry(x) loop
    visit(x);
    x := t.inorder_next(x)
end
```

Parent references are needed in addition to the usual left child and right child links. As explained in detail in Section 6.2, if $x$ has a right child, its successor in the inorder traversal is

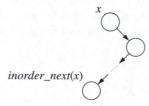

If $x$ has no right child, its successor is

*inorder_next(x)*

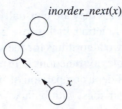

If, following the recursive analysis, *visit(x)* is chosen as the characteristic operation, it follows immediately that $T(n) = n$, the number of nodes in the tree. But it is not clear that this choice is realistic, because *visit(x)* does not lie inside the inner loops of the code just given.

Another characteristic operation, which *is* realistic, is the *edge-traverse*. An edge-traverse is the movement of the algorithm's attention across one link, which could be by any one of the operations $y := t.left\_child(x)$, $y := t.right\_child(x)$, or $y := t.parent(x)$. Examination of examples such as

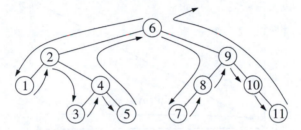

shows that every link is traversed exactly twice: once on the way down, and once on the way back. The final traverse out of the root may be ignored. If $n \geq 1$, there are $n - 1$ edges in an $n$-node binary tree (Exercise 6.1), so $T(n) = 2(n - 1)$. Note that the algorithm treats $n = 0$ as a special case, and accordingly the analysis must do so too: $T(0) = 0$.

## 2.4 Evaluating efficiency, and the *O*-notation

A number of algorithms have been analyzed here, but so far no opinion has been expressed about their efficiency. Consider the Towers of Hanoi algorithm, for example, whose worst-case time complexity was shown in Section 2.2 to be $T(n) = 2^n - 1$ lines of output. Is this an efficient algorithm?

Clearly, the Towers of Hanoi algorithm is not efficient. When given the small instance $n = 10$, the algorithm produces 1023 lines of output; when given the instance $n = 20$, it produces 1 048 575 lines.

Even if its time complexity were $T(n) = 2^n - 100$, or $T(n) = 2^n/100$, the Towers of Hanoi algorithm would still be inefficient. A general assessment of an algorithm's efficiency does not depend very strongly on constant factors in the time complexity function, unless they are unusually large or small. What is important is the general form of the function, in this case $2^n$.

Similarly, when two algorithms for the same problem are compared, the general form of their complexity functions is usually sufficient to determine which is best. For example, consider a comparison of linear search, of worst-case time complexity $W(n) = n$ comparisons, with binary search, of worst-case time complexity $W(n) = \log_2(n + 1)$ comparisons.

It could be argued that this comparison is unfair, since more work is done in binary search per comparison than is done in linear search. This objection can be answered by first adding implementation-dependent constants so as to express the complexities in microseconds. The result might be $W(n) = n + 3$ microseconds for linear search, and $W(n) = 5\log_2(n + 1) + 16$ microseconds for binary search, say. Here is a graph of these two functions:

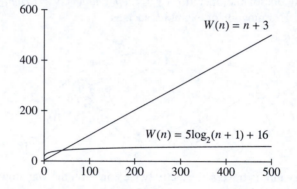

It shows that for $n$ less than about 40, linear search is superior to binary search; for larger $n$, binary search becomes dramatically more efficient: when $n = 500$, for example, binary search is about eight times faster than linear search given these constant factors.

The crossover point is rather sensitive to the values of the constant factors, but the superiority of binary search for large $n$ is not, since it is a well-known fact that for any positive constants $a, b, c,$ and $d$, the quotient

$$\frac{a\log_2(n + 1) + b}{cn + d}$$

approaches 0 as $n$ increases. That is, even without knowing the values of the constant factors, it can be concluded that binary search will be superior for sufficiently large $n$; and unless some exceptionally large constant factors are present, binary search would be preferred for this reason.

## The *O*-notation

A convenient way to express the general form of a function is provided by the *O-notation*. For example, one may say that the time complexity of binary search is $O(\log n)$, pronounced 'big oh of log$n$,' meaning that it has the general form of log$n$. The term *asymptotic time complexity* is also used for the general form of a time complexity function.

The technical definition of the *O*-notation is less important than the idea, explained above, that the asymptotic time complexity determines our evaluation of the efficiency of an algorithm. For the record, however, here is the definition:

**Definition 2.1:** The notation $O(f(n))$, appearing in a formula, stands for a quantity $x_n$ which may not be explicitly known but which is known to satisfy $|x_n| \le M|f(n)|$ for all $n \ge n_0$, where $M$ and $n_0$ are fixed constants.

Let us take the simplest example, $O(1)$. According to the definition, this stands for a quantity $x_n$ which satisfies $|x_n| \le M$ for all $n \ge n_0$. In other words, $O(1)$ is a quantity which is no larger than some fixed constant, whose precise value is not stated. It succinctly describes the time complexity of any algorithm containing no loops and no procedure calls; such an algorithm takes at most some constant amount of time to execute.

Here is another example:

$$\lceil \log_2(n+1) \rceil = O(\log_2 n)$$

This follows from the definition above by letting $x_n = \lceil \log_2(n+1) \rceil$, $f(n) = \log_2 n$, $M = 2$, and $n_0 = 2$, for then it is indeed true that $|x_n| \le M|f(n)|$ for all $n \ge n_0$. It is very convenient to be able to describe binary search as 'an $O(\log_2 n)$ algorithm,' presenting just the essential fact of its asymptotic time complexity.

It turns out that the base of a logarithm is irrelevant inside $O$. In other words, if $x_n = O(\log_a n)$, then $x_n = O(\log_b n)$ for any bases $a$ and $b$ greater than 1. The proof of this is not difficult; it uses the formula $\log_b n = \log_a n / \log_a b$, which shows that the two logarithms only differ by the constant factor $\log_a b$. For this reason, the base of a logarithm is usually omitted inside $O$.

Various useful, if obvious, theorems may be proved about the $O$-notation. For example, if $x_n = O(f(n))$ and $y_n = O(g(n))$, then $x_n y_n = O(f(n)g(n))$. The proofs of these theorems have been left as an exercise (Exercise 2.17); they all follow easily from the formal definition.

Since the definition of the $O$-notation is based on the condition $|x_n| \le M|f(n)|$, it is allowable for $f(n)$ to be a much faster-growing function than $x_n$. For example,

$$\lceil \log_2(n+1) \rceil = O(n^2)$$

is a true statement, although not a very useful one.

This looseness in the definition of the $O$-notation does have one virtue, however. Suppose that analysis reveals that for some algorithm,

$$T(n) = \sum_{i=1}^{n} \lfloor n/i \rfloor$$

The analyst might then proceed to estimate $T(n)$ as follows. Since $\lfloor n/i \rfloor \leq n$,

$$T(n) \leq \sum_{i=1}^{n} n = n^2$$

and this may be correctly reported as $T(n) = O(n^2)$. In fact, it is also true that $T(n) = O(n\log n)$, but more advanced algebra is needed to prove this, and it is not always possible to find the lowest general form in this way. In such cases, an upper bound like the $O(n^2)$ one just given is the next best thing, and the $O$-notation is ideal for reporting it, without making any claim that the result is the best possible.

### The $\Omega$ and $\Theta$ notations

The $\Omega$-notation is defined very similarly to the $O$-notation:

**Definition 2.2:** The notation $\Omega(f(n))$, pronounced 'big omega of $f(n)$,' appearing in a formula, stands for a quantity $x_n$ which may not be explicitly known but which is known to satisfy $|x_n| \geq M|f(n)|$ for all $n \geq n_0$, where $M$ and $n_0$ are fixed constants.

The only change here is the replacement of '$|x_n| \leq M|f(n)|$' by '$|x_n| \geq M|f(n)|$,' and so it follows that $g(n) = \Omega(f(n))$ if and only if $f(n) = O(g(n))$.

The $\Omega$-notation is used in work on lower bounds, to state that every algorithm for some problem must require at least a certain amount of time to execute. For example, we might state that every algorithm for searching an unsorted sequence to determine whether some item $x$ is present must take $\Omega(n)$ time.

It is perhaps worth pointing out that the statement $W(n) = \Omega(f(n))$ does not mean that every instance of some problem takes at least on the order of $f(n)$ time to solve; rather, it means that for all $n$ there exists an instance which takes this long. For example, the complexity of linear search is $\Omega(n)$, since when $x$ is not found the entire list must be searched; but there are instances of arbitrarily large size which require only $O(1)$ time: those where $x$ is present at the front of the list.

Finally, $g(n) = \Theta(f(n))$, 'big theta of $f(n)$,' means that $g(n) = O(f(n))$ and $g(n) = \Omega(f(n))$. It is perhaps surprising that the $\Theta$-notation is not used more widely, in such statements as 'binary search is $\Theta(\log n)$ in the worst case,' but the $O$-notation is much older and more widely used than the other two notations, and is used customarily despite its relative lack of precision.

Problems for which $O(n\log n)$ algorithms exist are said to be *feasible*, meaning that large instances can be solved. Problems for which all algorithms are $\Omega(a^n)$, where $a$ is any constant strictly greater than 1, are *infeasible*, because even on the fastest computing equipment available today or in the foreseeable future, it will be possible to solve only small instances. The feasibility of problems with intermediate complexities, such as $O(n^2)$ and $O(n^3)$, will depend on the size of the instance to be solved. This is illustrated in the following table, which shows the largest instance solvable in a given time, for various complexity functions.

| Complexity (microseconds) | Largest instance solvable in one second | Largest instance solvable in one day | Largest instance solvable in one year |
|---|---|---|---|
| $W(n) = n$ | $n = 1\,000\,000$ | $n = 86\,400\,000\,000$ | $n = 31\,536\,000\,000\,000$ |
| $W(n) = n\log_2 n$ | $n = 62\,746$ | $n = 2\,755\,147\,514$ | $n \approx 798\,160\,978\,500$ |
| $W(n) = n^2$ | $n = 1\,000$ | $n = 293\,938$ | $n = 5\,615\,692$ |
| $W(n) = n^3$ | $n = 100$ | $n = 4\,421$ | $n = 31\,593$ |
| $W(n) = 2^n$ | $n = 19$ | $n = 36$ | $n = 44$ |

## 2.5 Exercises

2.1    Using the formal definitions of $W(n)$ and $A(n)$ given in Section 2.1, prove that $A(n) \leq W(n)$.

2.2    Assuming that all the $p_i$ are non-zero, show that $A(n) = W(n)$ if and only if $T_1(n) = \ldots = T_k(n)$.

2.3    Consider the following algorithm for the linear search of a sorted array *entries.item(a..b)*. The algorithm employs a *sentinel*: it adds $x$ to the end of *entries* before commencing, so as to simplify the search.

```
sorted_search(a, b: INTEGER; x: KEY_TYPE): BOOLEAN is
   local
        i: INTEGER
   do
        entries.put(x, b+1);
        from i := a until entries.item(i) >= x loop
             i := i + 1
        end;
        Result := (i <= b) and (x = entries.item(i))
   end
```

(a)    Choose a characteristic operation. Construct a table of cases for the analysis, similar to the table given in Section 2.1. What is the worst-case complexity of *sorted_search*$(1, n, x)$?

(b)    Making reasonable assumptions about the probabilities of the cases, determine the average complexity of *sorted_search*$(1, n, x)$.

2.4　Consider the following algorithm for finding the index of a minimum element of *entries.item(a..b)*:

```
min_index(a, b: INTEGER): INTEGER is
    do
        if a = b then
            Result := a
        else
            Result := min_index(a + 1, b);
            if entries.item(a) < entries.item(Result) then
                Result := a
            end
        end
    end
```

(a)　Show that, if $T(n)$ is the number of comparisons of the form *entries.item(a) < entries.item(Result)* made by *min_index(1, n)*, then

$$T(1) = 0$$
$$T(n) = 1 + T(n - 1)$$

(b)　Solve this recurrence by repeated substitution. How does the performance of this version of *min_index* compare with the one given in Section 2.1?

(c)　What is the average number of times that the operation *Result := a* will be performed, counting recursive calls? (Hint: it will be performed only when *entries.item(a)* is a minimum element of *entries.item(a..b)*. What is a reasonable probability to assign to this event?)

2.5　The following version of binary search is often preferred because it has a two-way rather than a three-way branch, and so is more amenable to efficient compilation. It assumes that the array to be searched is non-empty.

```
binary_search(a, b: INTEGER; x: KEY_TYPE): BOOLEAN is
    local
        mid: INTEGER;
    do
        if a = b then
            Result := (x = entries.item(a))
        else
            mid := (a + b) // 2;
            if x <= entries.item(mid) then
                Result := binary_search(a, mid, x)
            else
                Result := binary_search(mid+1, b, x)
            end
        end
    end
```

Analyze this algorithm, taking as your measure of complexity the number of comparisons between $x$ and elements of *entries*.

2.6 The *Fibonacci numbers* are defined by the recurrence equation

$$F(0) = 0$$
$$F(1) = 1$$
$$F(n) = F(n-1) + F(n-2)$$

The first few numbers are $0, 1, 1, 2, 3, 5, 8, 13, 21, 34, 55, \ldots$. Unfortunately, the recurrence equation cannot be solved by repeated substitution; a more advanced technique, the use of generating functions, is required. Prove by induction on $n$ that

$$\phi^{n-2} \leq F(n) \leq \phi^{n-1}$$

for all $n \geq 2$, where $\phi = (1 + \sqrt{5})/2 \simeq 1.6180339$. You should begin by showing that $\phi^2 = \phi + 1$, and use this identity to prove the result.

2.7 Consider the following algorithm for calculating $F(n)$, as defined in the previous question:

```
fib(n: INTEGER): INTEGER is
    do
        if n <= 1 then
            Result := n
        else
            Result := fib(n–1) + fib(n–2)
        end
    end
```

Choosing *Result* $:= n$ as characteristic operation, show that $T(n) = F(n+1)$, and use the previous question to conclude that $T(n) = \Theta(\phi^n)$. (A more obviously realistic characteristic operation is $n <= 1$, and analyzing it is an interesting but more difficult exercise.)

2.8 *Euclid's algorithm.* The following algorithm, for finding the greatest common divisor of two positive integers, is similar to one given by Euclid:

```
gcd(n, m: INTEGER): INTEGER is
    do
        if m = 0 then
            Result := n
        else
            Result := gcd(m, n \\ m)
        end
    end
```

where $n \setminus\setminus m$ is the remainder after division of $n$ by $m$. The correctness of Euclid's algorithm follows from a theorem in number theory, and it will not be explored here.

(a) Show that the number of $\setminus\setminus$ operations performed by this algorithm is given by the recurrence equation

$$T(n, 0) = 0$$
$$T(n, m) = 1 + T(m, n \setminus\setminus m)$$

(b) Solve this recurrence equation for the special case of the Fibonacci numbers defined in the previous question; that is, letting $n = F(k + 1)$ and $m = F(k)$.

(c) Show that, for all integers $n$ and $m$ such that $n \geq m > 0$,

$$n + m \geq \frac{3}{2}(m + n \setminus\setminus m)$$

(Hint: let $n = am + b$ where $a \geq 1$ and $0 \leq b < m$, and then consider the fraction $(n + m)/(m + n \setminus\setminus m)$).

(d) Use (c) to prove by induction on $m$ that $T(n, m) \leq \log_{3/2}(n + m)$ provided $n \geq m > 0$.

2.9 Solve the following recurrence equations; $c$ is a constant, and where necessary you may assume that $n = 2^k$.

(a) $T(0) = 1$
$T(n) = cT(n - 1)$

(b) $T(0) = 1$
$T(n) = nT(n - 1)$

(c) $T(1) = 1$
$T(n) = 1 + T(\lfloor n/2 \rfloor)$

(d) $T(1) = 1$
$T(n) = 1 + 2T(\lfloor n/2 \rfloor)$

(e) $T(1) = 0$
$T(n) = c\lceil \log_2 n \rceil + T(\lceil n/2 \rceil)$

(f) $T(1) = 0$
$T(n) = \lceil n\log_2 n \rceil + T(\lceil n/2 \rceil)$

2.10    Show that the solution of the two-dimensional recurrence equation

$$T(n, 0) = 1$$
$$T(0, m) = 1$$
$$T(n, m) = T(n - 1, m) + T(n, m - 1)$$

is the binomial coefficient

$$T(n, m) = \binom{n + m}{n}$$

2.11    Consider the following algorithm for multiplying two *n* by *n* matrices *a* and *b*, placing the result in *Result*:

```
matrix_multiply(a, b: MATRIX): MATRIX is
    local
        i, j, k, total: INTEGER;
    do
        from i := 1 until i > n loop
            from j := 1 until j > n loop
                total := 0;
                from k := 1 until k > n loop
                    total := total + a.item(i, k)*b.item(k, j);
                    k := k + 1
                end;
                Result.put(total, i, j);
                j := j + 1
            end;
            i := i + 1
        end
    end
```

If the characteristic operation is one multiplication of matrix elements, what is the time complexity of this algorithm as a function of *n*?

2.12    Consider the following algorithm for sorting the array *entries.item(a..b)* into non-decreasing order:

```
straight_selection_sort(a, b: INTEGER) is
    local
        i, m: INTEGER;
    do
        from i := a until i >= b loop
            m := min_index(i, b);
            if i /= m then swap(entries, i, m) end;
            i := i + 1
        end
    end
```

where *swap(entries, i, m)* swaps *entries.item(i)* with *entries.item(m)*. Taking as your measure of complexity one comparison between elements of *entries*, as occurs within *min_index* (Exercise 2.4), what is the complexity of this algorithm?

2.13 Consider the following algorithm for finding both the index of a minimum element and the index of a maximum element of the array *e.item(a..b)*. Routine *is_odd* returns **true** when its parameter is an odd number.

```
min_max(a, b: INTEGER) is
   local
      i: INTEGER
   do
      if is_odd(b–a+1) then
         min := a;
         max := a;
         i := a+1
      elseif e.item(a) < e.item(a+1) then
         min := a;
         max := a+1;
         i := a+2
      else
         min := a+1;
         max := a;
         i := a+2
      end;
      from until i > b loop
         if e.item(i) < e.item(i+1) then
            if e.item(i) < e.item(min) then min := i end;
            if e.item(i+1) > e.item(max) then max := i+1 end
         else
            if e.item(i+1) < e.item(min) then min := i+1 end;
            if e.item(i) > e.item(max) then max := i end
         end;
         i := i + 2
      end
   end
```

(a) Explain how this algorithm works, clearly indicating the differences between the odd and even cases. Then give a formal loop invariant.

(b) Analyze *min_max*(1, *n*) for arbitrary $n \geq 1$, using one comparison between elements of *e* as the characteristic operation, and show that its time complexity is

$$T(n) = \left\lceil \frac{3n}{2} \right\rceil - 2$$

Recall that $\lceil x \rceil$ ('ceiling of *x*') means the smallest integer greater than or equal to *x*. (Hint: consider the cases *n* even and *n* odd separately.)

2.14 The following algorithm solves a standard problem encountered by text editors. It searches for the first occurrence of the string (that is, array of characters) *pattern.item*(1..*m*) within the string *text.item*(1..*n*), returning the index where *pattern* begins if found, or else zero. The value *limit* = *n*–*m*+1 is the rightmost place in *text* where *pattern* could possibly begin.

```
string_search(text, pattern: ARRAY[CHARACTER]; n, m: INTEGER):
        BOOLEAN is
    local
        found: BOOLEAN;
        start, i, j, limit: INTEGER;
    do
        found := false;
        limit := n − m + 1;
        from start := 1 until found or start > limit loop
            from
                i := start; j := 1
            until
                j = m+1 or else text.item(i) /= pattern.item(j)
            loop
                i := i + 1;
                j := j + 1
            end;
            found := (j = m + 1);
            start := start + 1
        end;
        if found then
            Result := start − 1
        else
            Result := 0
        end
    end
```

How many times is the comparison *text.item*(*i*) /= *pattern.item*(*j*), which is a realistic characteristic operation, performed in the worst case?

2.15 Prove, by induction on *n*, that the function $W(n)$ defined by

$$W(0) = 0$$
$$W(n) = 1 + W(\lfloor (n + 1)/2 \rfloor - 1)$$

is monotone non-decreasing, or in other words that $W(n) \le W(n + 1)$ for all *n*. You may assume that $\lfloor x \rfloor$ is a monotone non-decreasing function of *x*.

2.16 Suppose you have one hour of computer time each evening to run a certain program. You find that the hour is exactly long enough for your program to process an input of size *n* = 1 000 000. Then your employer buys a computer which runs one hundred times faster than the old one. How large an input will your program handle in one hour now, if its complexity $T(n)$ is, for some constants $k_i$:

(a) $k_1 n$

(b) $k_2 n \log_{10} n$

(c) $k_3 n^2$

(d) $k_4 n^3$

(e) $k_5 10^n$

2.17 Assuming that $x_n = O(f(n))$ and $y_n = O(g(n))$, use the formal definition of the $O$-notation to prove that

(a) $cx_n = O(f(n))$ for any constant $c$

(b) $x_n y_n = O(f(n)g(n))$

(c) $x_n + y_n = O(f(n) + g(n)) = O(\max(f(n), g(n)))$

In the last part, $f(n)$ and $g(n)$ must be non-negative.

2.18 Use the results of the previous question to prove that

$$a_0 + a_1 n + a_2 n^2 + \cdots + a_k n^k = O(n^k)$$

2.19 Does $2^n = \Theta(3^n)$?

# Chapter 3

# Data Abstraction

Data abstraction is one of the two foundations of object-oriented programming (the other being inheritance). In this book, where the programs are not very large, data abstraction is, in essence, a technique for separating data structures from algorithms, so that they may be studied independently of each other.

It is quite remarkable how many parts of the subject are touched, and greatly clarified, by data abstraction. One important technique presented in this chapter (amortized analysis) is scarcely even conceivable without it.

## 3.1 Abstract data types

Modern programming languages provide a variety of features for structuring data: arrays, records or classes, and references or pointers being the principal ones. Before choosing any such concrete representation, however, it is better to take a more abstract view of the data. The right starting point is the concept of a *mathematical entity*, not tied to any particular representation. Here are some standard examples:

A *set*, as in mathematics, is a collection of zero or more entries. An entry may not appear more than once. A set of $n$ entries is denoted $\{a_1, a_2, \ldots, a_n\}$, but the position of an entry has no significance.

A *multiset* is a set, except that repeated elements are allowed.

A *sequence* is an ordered collection of zero or more entries, and is denoted $\langle a_1, a_2, \ldots, a_n \rangle$. The position of an entry in a sequence is significant; for example, one may speak of the fifth entry, or the successor of a given entry.

A *graph* $G = \langle V, E \rangle$ is a set $V$ of *vertices* (nodes) and a set $E$ of *edges* (arcs, links), that is, two-element subsets of $V$. This definition excludes self-loops (edges from a vertex to itself) and parallel edges (two edges connecting the same two vertices). For example,

$V = \{a, b, c, d\}$
$E = \{\{a, c\}, \{c, d\}, \{a, d\}\}$

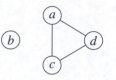

This list of mathematical entities could be extended to include, for example, directed graphs, complex numbers, and matrices.

When one of these entities is used in an algorithm, certain operations are performed on it. For example, the algorithm might do insertions and membership tests on a set, or it might multiply two matrices. An *abstract data type (ADT)* is a mathematical entity together with some operations that may be performed on it.

For example, the mathematical entity *integer*, with the operations addition, subtraction, negation, multiplication, division, and the comparisons, is an ADT which lies at the heart of computing machinery, and it provides a good illustration of the advantages to be gained from recognizing and specifying ADTs. First, users of *integer* never need consider the implementation of the operations: they know what the operations do, and can use them effectively without ever knowing what electronic circuitry is being employed. Second, the implementor of *integer* (in this case a hardware designer) is free to experiment with different implementations, such as carry-lookahead adders, fast multiplication circuits, and so on. All that matters is that the right result be returned. By providing a clean interface between use and implementation, the ADT separates the two and clarifies the task of both.

Our formal notation for an ADT declaration is the short form of an Eiffel class declaration. For example, Figure 3.1 defines the Simple Set ADT. Its mathematical entity is a set of entries, whose representation is not accessible to users of the ADT. Each entry has a *value*, of type *VALUE_TYPE*, defined when the ADT is used. The *new_entry* operation creates a new entry with the specified value.

When an object of type *SIMPLESET* is created, the set is initially empty. The *empty* operation reports whether the set is currently empty; *insert(x)* adds entry $x$ to the set; and *delete_any* deletes and returns an arbitrary element of the set. Notice that this ADT can be used without knowing whether it is implemented using an array, linked list, or whatever.

There are many other examples of ADTs, ranging from *BOOLEAN* with operations **and, or** and **not**, all the way up to databases. Chapters 5, 7, 8, and 10 are concerned with some other standard ADTs.

## An example of the use of ADTs

The remainder of this section is an extended example which demonstrates why ADTs are useful. Given an array of $n$ numbers $a.item(1..n)$, the problem is to determine the $k$ largest elements, where $k \leq n$. For example, if the array $a$ contains $\{5, 3, 1, 9, 6\}$, and $k = 3$, then the result is to be $\{5, 9, 6\}$.

---

**class interface** *SIMPLESET_ADT[VALUE_TYPE]*

   *entry_type*: *SIMPLESET_ADT_ENTRY[VALUE_TYPE]*;

   *make*
         -- Initialize to a new, empty simpleset

   *empty*: *BOOLEAN*
         -- **true** if this simpleset is empty, else **false**

   *new_entry(value*: *VALUE_TYPE*): **like** *entry_type*
         -- A new entry containing *value*

   *insert(x*: **like** *entry_type*)
         -- Insert *x* into this simpleset

   *delete_any*: **like** *entry_type*
         -- Delete and return an arbitrary element of this simpleset

**end** -- *SIMPLESET_ADT*

---

**Figure 3.1** Specification of the Simple Set ADT.

The following algorithm will not be justified in any detail, since that is not the purpose of this example, but it does find the *k* largest elements of *a.item*(1..*n*). The algorithm scans the array from left to right, remembering the *k* largest numbers that it has seen during the scan so far. These numbers are kept in decreasing order in an array *m.item*(1..*k*):

```
from i := 1 until i > k loop
    from j := i − 1 until j <= 0 or else a.item(i) <= m.item(j) loop
        m.put(m.item(j), j+1);
        j := j − 1
    end;
    m.put(a.item(i), j+1);
    i := i + 1
end;

from i := k+1 until i > n loop
    if a.item(i) > m.item(k) then
        from j := k − 1 until j <= 0 or else a.item(i) <= m.item(j) loop
            m.put(m.item(j), j+1);
            j := j − 1
        end;
        m.put(a.item(i), j+1)
    end;
    i := i + 1
end
```

It is difficult to follow the logic of this algorithm, because its structure is obscured by low-level details.

Let us now apply data abstraction to this algorithm. Abstractly, $m$ is a multiset of numbers. What are the operations? It must be possible to initialize $m$ to empty, and to insert a new number into $m$. In the second loop, it is necessary to find the value of a minimum element of $m$, and subsequently to delete it. Assuming the existence of an ADT with these operations, the algorithm becomes

```
!!m.make;
from i := 1 until i > k loop
    m.insert(m.new_entry(a.item(i), Void));
    i := i + 1
end;

from i := k + 1 until i > n loop
    if a.item(i) > m.find_min.key then
        x := m.delete_min;
        m.insert(m.new_entry(a.item(i), Void))
    end;
    i := i + 1
end
```

For a reason that will become clear in a moment, $m$ has been made into a set of entries, each with a *key* equal to *a.item(i)* for some $i$, and a *value* which in this example is always *Void*. The operation *x.key* returns the key of entry $x$.

There are two major reasons for preferring this version to the other. First, it makes clear the structure of the algorithm by hiding away irrelevant details. Second, the purpose of $m$ is now much clearer: it is an ADT that provides the operations *insert(x)*, *find_min*, and *delete_min*. It is now possible to ask whether the particular implementation of $m$ given in the first version is the best, or whether some other data structure would be preferable.

In this case, the operations are standard ones from the Priority Queue ADT of Chapter 8 (hence the *Void* parameters). An efficient implementation of $m$ may thus be taken from a library; the result is not only a clearer algorithm, but also a more efficient one.

## 3.2 Correctness of ADT implementations

An ADT may be specified by giving a precondition and postcondition for each of its operations. These conditions must refer only to the abstract mathematical entity (set, sequence, or whatever) on which the ADT is based; in this way they are made independent of any implementation. For example, the Simple Set ADT of Section 3.1, which is based on the set, may be specified abstractly as in Figure 3.2.

Some explanation of the notation used in Figure 3.2 is required. The precondition of a routine is the conjunction of the labeled boolean expressions following

---

**class interface** *SIMPLESET_ADT[VALUE_TYPE]*

   *entry_type*: *SIMPLESET_ADT_ENTRY[VALUE_TYPE]*;

   *make*
         -- Initialize to a new, empty simpleset
     **ensure**
       *abstract_empty*: *abstract.empty*

   *empty*: *BOOLEAN*
         -- **true** if this simpleset is empty, else **false**
     **ensure**
       *abstract_unchanged*: *abstract* |*equals*| **old** *abstract*
       *result_correct*: *Result* = *abstract.empty*

   *new_entry*(*value*: *VALUE_TYPE*): **like** *entry_type*
         -- A new entry containing *value*
     **ensure**
       *abstract_unchanged*: *abstract* |*equals*| **old** *abstract*
       *result_correct*: *Result.abstract* |*containsvalue*| *value*

   *insert*(*x*: **like** *entry_type*)
         -- Insert *x* into this simpleset
     **require**
       *x_not_member*: *abstract* |*notcontains*| *x.abstract*
     **ensure**
       *x_is_member*: *abstract* |*contains*| *x.abstract*
       *x_unchanged*: *x.abstract* |*equals*| **old** *x.abstract*
       *rest_unchanged*: (*abstract* − *x.abstract*) |*equals*| **old** *abstract*

   *delete_any*: **like** *entry_type*
         -- Delete and return an arbitrary element of this simpleset
     **require**
       *not_empty*: **not** |*isempty*| *abstract*
     **ensure**
       *result_correct*: (**old** *abstract*) |*contains*| *Result.abstract*
       *rest_unchanged*: *abstract* |*equals*| (**old** *abstract* − *Result.abstract*)

**end** -- *SIMPLESET_ADT*

---

**Figure 3.2** Formal specification of the Simple Set ADT. See the accompanying text for an explanation of the notation.

the **require** keyword; or if the **require** keyword is absent, the precondition is **true**. The postcondition of a routine is the conjunction of the labeled boolean expressions following the **ensure** keyword. The Eiffel notation **old** *expression*, which is permitted only in postconditions, returns the value that the expression had when the routine was called.

To these standard Eiffel features the author has added the convention that each ADT (such as Simple Set) should contain a function *abstract* which returns the abstract value of the ADT; in this example, a set of entries. Each entry also has an *abstract* function. (These functions are omitted from the figures in this book.) For example, the postcondition of *insert*,

> **ensure**
>   *x_is_member*: *abstract* |*contains*| *x.abstract*
>   *x_unchanged*: *x.abstract* |*equals*| **old** *x.abstract*
>   *rest_unchanged*: (*abstract* − *x.abstract*) |*equals*| **old** *abstract*

has three clauses: first, the abstract set after the operation must contain *x*; next, *x* itself must not have been modified by the operation; and finally, the remainder of the final abstract set when *x* is taken away must be equal to the original value of the set. How |*equals*| and the other operations are implemented does not strictly matter; but, for the record, the author has defined and implemented an ADT of sets which contains these operations.

It is tedious to say that parameters like *x* are not changed by the operation, but it is necessary, since some operations do indeed change their parameters. For example, *append(other)* from the List ADT appends list *other* to the current list, without copying it first, and this means that *other* cannot be used subsequently. The postcondition of *append(other)* therefore does not say anything about the value of *other* after the operation: the value is undefined.

Although the above has the advantage of being executable and hence precisely defined, it will often be more convenient to use a purely algebraic notation. Let *s* stand for the value of the set before some operation, and *s′* for its value afterwards. Then the postcondition given above may be rewritten loosely as

$$s' = s \cup \{x\}$$

Either way, the significant point is that the specification gives no hint of how the ADT is implemented.

The basic problem in the correctness of ADTs is to take some ADT with its accompanying abstract specification, and a concrete implementation of the ADT, and to prove that the implementation satisfies the specification. For example, consider the problem of proving that the implementation given in Figure 3.3 is correct. The following systematic way to go about this is taken from Liskov and Guttag (1986).

The first step is to find a condition, called the *representation invariant* or (in object-oriented languages) the *class invariant*, denoted $I(s)$, which is true if and only if *s* is a valid concrete value of the class. For the array implementation of the Simple Set ADT, this condition is

$$I(s) = s.free \geq 0 \text{ \textbf{and} for all } i \text{ such that } 0 \leq i < s.free,$$
$$s.entries.item(i) \text{ is well defined and unique}$$

```
class SIMPLESET_ARRAY[VALUE_TYPE]

feature { NONE }

    free: INTEGER;
    entries: ARRAY[like entry_type];
    array_size: INTEGER;

feature

    entry_type: SIMPLESET_ARRAY_ENTRY[VALUE_TYPE];

    initial_array_size: INTEGER is 100;

    make is
        do
            array_size := initial_array_size;
            !!entries.make(0, array_size − 1);
            free := 0
        end;

    empty: BOOLEAN is
        do
            Result := (free = 0)
        end;

    new_entry(v: VALUE_TYPE): like entry_type is
        do
            !!Result.make(v)
        end;

    insert(x: like entry_type) is
        do
            entries.put(x, free);
            free := free + 1;
            if free = array_size then
                array_size := array_size ∗ 2;
                entries.resize(0, array_size − 1);
            end;
        end;

    delete_any: like entry_type is
        do
            Result := entries.item(free − 1);
            free := free − 1;
        end;

end -- SIMPLESET_ARRAY
```

**Figure 3.3** Implementation of the Simple Set ADT using an array of entries.

It is customary to omit things that the compiler checks, such as that *s.free* is an integer; they are implicitly assumed. This example is quite simple, merely ruling out garbage values and duplicate entries; in other cases, $I(s)$ could state that the entries appear in some order (sorted, for example), or define a complex data structure. The condition is *invariant* in the sense of being true throughout the lifetime of *s*.

The second step is to define, for all concrete values *s* satisfying $I(s)$, what the corresponding abstract value is. This is done, as foreshadowed above, by giving an *abstraction function* $A(s)$, which maps the concrete value *s* to its corresponding abstract value. There can be only one such abstract value, otherwise the implementation would be ambiguous (see Exercise 3.3 for more on this). The abstraction function for the array implementation of the Simple Set ADT is

$$A(s) = \{s.entries.item(i) \mid 0 \le i < s.free\}$$

That is, the abstract value of *s* is the set containing *s.entries.item*(0..*s.free*−1). This is the same function as the one denoted *abstract* above.

$I(s)$ and $A(s)$ are an integral part of any ADT implementation; in fact, they are defined (at least implicitly, in the mind of the implementor) before any code is written. So it is reasonable to assume that every ADT implementation comes equipped with its representation invariant and abstraction function.

The third step in proving an ADT implementation correct is to make its specification concrete in the following way. First, replace all references to *s*, *s'*, and so on by $A(s)$, $A(s')$ and so on; this just makes explicit that the values are abstract ones. Next, add $I(s)$ to the precondition of every operation except those that begin by creating a new *s*; and add $I(s')$ to the postcondition of every operation except those that are understood to render *s* unusable subsequently. This will be justified in a moment; the result is a *concrete specification*. For example, this is the concrete postcondition of *insert(x)*:

$$I(s') \text{ and } A(s') = A(s) \cup \{x\}$$

The fourth and final step is to prove the correctness of each operation with respect to its concrete specification. For the *insert(x)* operation, such a proof might run (in outline) as follows. By the precondition $I(s)$, it follows that *s* is well defined, say with abstract value $A(s) = \{x_1, \dots, x_n\}$. The statements of *insert(x)* clearly add *x* to the end of *s*, producing a new value *s'* which satisfies $I(s')$ and has abstract value

$$A(s') = \{x_1, \dots, x_n, x\} = A(s) \cup \{x\}$$

So the postcondition of *insert(x)* holds afterwards.

To justify the addition of $I(s)$ to the preconditions, the following inductive argument is used. Assume that $I(s)$ holds for all values *s* in existence before the *m*th call begins. If the operation is used correctly, its abstract precondition also holds. Hence its concrete precondition holds. The operation has been proved correct, so its concrete postcondition holds afterwards. This postcondition includes $I(s')$. An ADT may be accessed only by its own operations, so no values change between the end of the $m$th call and the beginning of the $(m + 1)$st. Therefore $I(s)$ holds for all $s$ just before the $(m + 1)$st operation.

There are two ways in which this argument may fail: if an $s$ is declared but not initialized to a value satisfying the invariant $I(s)$; and if a call is made to an operation at a time when its abstract precondition does not hold. It is good practice to protect ADT implementations by checking preconditions and invariants, if this can be done efficiently.

## 3.3 Analysis of ADT implementations

Abstract data types were originally developed to protect data structures from invalid operations, so it is natural that they should be valuable aids to correctness. But, perhaps surprisingly, they are equally valuable in time complexity analysis.

Consider an implementation of some ADT with operations $P_1, P_2, \ldots, P_v$. Each operation's implementation is an algorithm, and so may be analyzed in the usual way; the result is a sequence of functions $W_1(n), W_2(n), \ldots, W_v(n)$ which together constitute the *worst-case time complexity of the ADT implementation*. The parameter $n$ is always taken to be the size of the ADT (usually defined to be the number of entries it contains) at the moment the operation is called.

The difficulty of assigning meaningful probabilities to the instances, already noted in Section 2.1, becomes acute here. With one exception, the analysis of the chained hash table in Section 7.7, average complexity analyses of ADT implementations will not be attempted in this book.

For example, consider the Priority Queue ADT of Chapter 8. A priority queue is a set of entries, each containing a key and a value; the size of the ADT is the size of this set. The *make* operation creates a new priority queue whose set of entries is empty; *insert* adds an entry; *find_min* returns an entry with minimum key; and *delete_min* deletes and returns an entry with minimum key.

A simple linked list may be used to implement this ADT, with the entries either sorted into increasing order by key, or left unsorted. Insertion into an unsorted list is trivial, but finding a minimum entry requires a search; the opposite is true for the sorted list. So the worst-case complexities of these two implementations are:

|  | Unsorted linked list | Sorted linked list |
|---|---|---|
| *make* | $O(1)$ | $O(1)$ |
| *empty* | $O(1)$ | $O(1)$ |
| *insert* | $O(1)$ | $O(n)$ |
| *find_min* | $O(n)$ | $O(1)$ |
| *delete_min* | $O(n)$ | $O(1)$ |

When analyzing an algorithm which makes use of an ADT, it is necessary to calculate the total cost of all the calls to the ADT implementation. The usual way to do this is as follows.

Suppose the algorithm makes a total of $m = m_1 + m_2 + \cdots + m_v$ calls to the ADT: $m_1$ to the $P_1$ operation, $m_2$ to $P_2$, and so on, arbitrarily intermixed. Number these calls from 1 to $m$ in the order they occur, and let $t_i$ be the actual complexity of the $i$th call, for $1 \leq i \leq m$. The size of the ADT will vary over the course of the sequence of calls. Let $n_{i-1}$ be the size of the ADT just before the $i$th call, and let

$$n = \max_{1 \leq i \leq m} n_{i-1}$$

Then, if the $i$th call is a $P_j$ operation, $t_i \leq W_j(n_{i-1})$, and the total cost is

$$\sum_{i=1}^{m} t_i \leq \sum_{i=1}^{m} W_j(n_{i-1})$$

$$\leq \sum_{i=1}^{m} W_j(n)$$

$$= m_1 W_1(n) + \cdots + m_v W_v(n)$$

assuming that the $W_j(n)$ are monotone non-decreasing. Note that $n$ here represents the maximum ADT size over the whole sequence of calls, whereas when $W_j(n)$ is given for operation $P_j$ it refers to the ADT size at the moment $P_j$ is called.

It often happens that a different characteristic operation must be chosen for analyzing each operation, so that $W_1(n)$ may count comparisons, $W_2(n)$ may count additions, and so on. In such cases the functions should be multiplied by implementation-dependent constants before being added together, or equivalently the result may be reported as $O(m_1 W_1(n) + \cdots + m_v W_v(n))$.

For example, here is an algorithm (already introduced in Section 3.1) for finding the $k$ largest elements of an array $a.item(1..n)$:

```
!!m.make;
from i := 1 until i > k loop
    m.insert(m.new_entry(a.item(i), Void));
    i := i + 1
end;

from i := k + 1 until i > n loop
    if a.item(i) > m.find_min.key then
        x := m.delete_min;
        m.insert(m.new_entry(a.item(i), Void))
    end;
    i := i + 1
end
```

Its analysis is not difficult. In the worst case, the test $a.item(i) > m.find\_min.key$ always succeeds, and the algorithm makes one call to *make*, $n$ calls to *insert*, $n - k$ calls to *find_min*, and $n - k$ calls to *delete_min*. The maximum ADT size is $k$.

Therefore, if the unsorted linked list is used to implement the priority queue, the total cost of all the calls will be

$$O(1 \times 1 + n \times 1 + (n - k) \times k + (n - k) \times k) = O(nk)$$

If the sorted linked list is used, the total complexity will be

$$O(1 \times 1 + n \times k + (n - k) \times 1 + (n - k) \times 1) = O(nk)$$

so that there is nothing to choose between these two implementations. On the average, however, the test $a.item(i) > m.find\_min.key$ will fail most of the time, so that there will be many more *find_min* calls than insertions and deletions, assuming $k$ is small. Since the sorted linked list provides $O(1)$ complexity for *find_min*, it would be preferred for use with this algorithm.

This example teaches two important lessons. First, only the worst-case complexity of an ADT implementation is needed in order to analyze an algorithm which uses it; the details of the implementation are irrelevant. Second, it is easy to try out a variety of implementations to see which is best for a given algorithm. Indeed, it is even possible to take the extra step of designing the ADT implementation with certain complexity goals in mind (for example, an $O(1)$ *find_min*). This design strategy has been called *balancing* by Aho et al. (1974).

## 3.4 Amortized analysis

The method just given for analyzing algorithms employing ADTs is the standard one, and it usually works well. However, there are cases where the result it produces is wildly pessimistic. The unraveling of this phenomenon will lead to an alternative method called *amortized analysis*, and beyond it to a principle of data structure design with a wealth of applications.

Perhaps the simplest example of an ADT implementation whose worst-case analysis is unsatisfactory is the Parser Stack, a variant of Stack needed by some parsing algorithms, in which the *pop* operation is changed to *pop(k)*, which pops $k$ entries at once. The implementation is a linked list of entries, as in Section 5.1.

Consider now the worst-case analysis of this ADT implementation. The complexity of *push(x)* is clearly $O(1)$, but *pop(k)* requires $k$ reference operations, and so, since $k$ could be as large as the size of the stack, its worst-case complexity is $O(n)$. The total complexity of a sequence of $m_1$ calls to *push(x)* and $m_2$ calls to *pop(k)* will be $O(m_1 + m_2 n)$.

That is the standard argument; now consider the following ad-hoc one. It is impossible to pop more entries off the stack than were pushed onto it, so the total cost of pops cannot exceed the total cost of pushes. Therefore the total cost of any sequence of $m_1$ calls to the $push(x)$ operation and $m_2$ calls to the $pop(k)$ operation must be $O(m_1)$ in the worst case.

The standard analysis was not wrong; it delivered an upper bound on the total complexity which was much larger than it needed to be. This happened because the analysis failed to notice that a sequence of worst-case $pop(k)$ operations is impossible: after one worst-case $pop(k)$ operation, the stack is empty and a second worst-case $pop(k)$ operation cannot occur.

In order to tighten up the analysis, it turns out to be necessary to measure the susceptibility of the state of an ADT implementation to expensive operations. (The state of an ADT implementation is its concrete value at some moment in time – its size, shape, the values it contains, and so on.) This is done by associating with each possible state $S$ a real number $\Phi(S)$, called the *potential of S*, chosen so that the more susceptible a state is, the higher its potential. For example, it would be reasonable to let the potential of a parser stack be the number of entries it contains, because a large stack is susceptible to expensive pops, and a small one is not.

Consider now a sequence of $m$ calls to an ADT. Let $t_i$ be the actual complexity of the $i$th call, as usual. Define the *amortized complexity $a_i$* of the $i$th call by

$$a_i = t_i + \Phi(S_i) - \Phi(S_{i-1})$$

where $S_{i-1}$ is the state of the ADT just before the $i$th call begins, and $S_i$ is the state of the ADT just after it has finished. Now,

$$\sum_{i=1}^{m} t_i = \sum_{i=1}^{m} [a_i - \Phi(S_i) + \Phi(S_{i-1})]$$

$$= \sum_{i=1}^{m} a_i - \Phi(S_m) + \Phi(S_0)$$

$$\leq \sum_{i=1}^{m} a_i$$

assuming that $\Phi(S)$ has been chosen so that $\Phi(S_m) \geq \Phi(S_0)$, which is usually the case since $S_0$ is the initial state and so is likely to have minimal susceptibility to expensive operations. The total amortized complexity is an upper bound on the total actual complexity, and the potentials cancel out.

Suppose, then, that there is an ADT with operations $P_1, P_2, \dots, P_v$, and a sequence of $m = m_1 + m_2 + \cdots + m_v$ calls to the ADT: $m_1$ to $P_1$, $m_2$ to $P_2$, and so on, arbitrarily intermixed. Let $W_{\Phi j}(n)$ be the maximum, over all instances of $P_j$ of size $n$, of the amortized complexity of the instance. (Contrast this with $W_j(n)$, which is the maximum over the same instances of the actual complexity.) Now, if the $i$th operation in the sequence is $P_j$, then $a_i \leq W_{\Phi j}(n_{i-1})$, where $n_{i-1}$ is the ADT size just before the $i$th call begins, and so

$$\sum_{i=1}^{m} t_i \leq \sum_{i=1}^{m} a_i$$

$$\leq \sum_{i=1}^{m} W_{\Phi j}(n_{i-1})$$

$$\leq \sum_{i=1}^{m} W_{\Phi j}(n)$$

$$= m_1 W_{\Phi 1}(n) + \cdots + m_v W_{\Phi v}(n)$$

assuming that the $W_{\Phi j}(n)$ are monotone. So amortized bounds are just as good for bounding the total cost of a sequence of operations as worst-case bounds are; and they may be smaller if $\Phi(S)$ is chosen carefully. The sequence of functions

$$W_{\Phi 1}(n), W_{\Phi 2}(n), \ldots, W_{\Phi v}(n)$$

is called the *amortized complexity* of the ADT implementation.

Choosing a potential function $\Phi(S)$ is a matter of experience and trial and error. For the parser stack example defined above, the size of the stack turns out to be a good choice for $\Phi(S)$. If every operation sequence begins with an empty stack, the condition $\Phi(S_m) \geq \Phi(S_0)$ always holds. Here is a sample operation sequence:

| $i$ | Operation | $S$ | $\Phi(S)$ | $t_i$ | $a_i$ |
|---|---|---|---|---|---|
|  | make | $\langle\rangle$ | 0 |  |  |
| 1 | push(a) | $\langle a \rangle$ | 1 | 1 | 2 |
| 2 | push(e) | $\langle a, e \rangle$ | 2 | 1 | 2 |
| 3 | push(f) | $\langle a, e, f \rangle$ | 3 | 1 | 2 |
| 4 | pop(2) | $\langle a \rangle$ | 1 | 2 | 0 |

In general, for a push $t_i = 1$, $\Phi(S_i) - \Phi(S_{i-1}) = 1$ (the stack size increases by 1), so that $a_i = 2$. For $pop(k)$, $t_i = k$, $\Phi(S_i) - \Phi(S_{i-1}) = -k$ (the stack size decreases by $k$), so $a_i = 0$. The conclusion is that the total complexity of any sequence of $m_1$ pushes and $m_2$ pops is $O(m_1 \times 2 + m_2 \times 0) = O(m_1)$.

As this example shows, an amortized analysis spreads the cost of an occasional expensive operation among nearby calls, like accounting methods which spread the cost of a single large purchase over several years. This is the origin of the term 'amortization.' Amortized analysis is due to Tarjan (1985), although similar ideas may be found in earlier papers. He mentions that its formulation using potential functions is by D. Sleator.

A useful trick for simplifying amortized analyses is to break the operations into small stages and analyze each stage. Consider the $i$th operation. It has actual complexity $t_i$, amortized complexity $a_i$, and it takes the ADT from state $S_{i-1}$ to state $S_i$. Now suppose the ADT passes through some intermediate states during the operation;

call them $S_1', S_2', \ldots, S_{k-1}'$, and let $S_{i-1} = S_0'$ and $S_i = S_k'$. Let $t_j'$ be the actual cost incurred in moving from $S_{j-1}'$ to $S_j'$, for $1 \leq j \leq k$; clearly, the actual complexity of the whole operation is the sum of these numbers:

$$t_i = \sum_{j=1}^{k} t_j'$$

The amortized complexity of each stage may be defined in the usual way, with the formula $a_j' = t_j' + \Phi(S_j') - \Phi(S_{j-1}')$, and this leads to

$$\sum_{j=1}^{k} a_j' = \sum_{j=1}^{k} [t_j' + \Phi(S_j') - \Phi(S_{j-1}')]$$

$$= \sum_{j=1}^{k} t_j' + \Phi(S_k') - \Phi(S_0')$$

$$= t_i + \Phi(S_i) - \Phi(S_{i-1})$$

$$= a_i$$

The amortized complexity of the whole operation is the sum of the amortized complexities of its stages. For example, this approach could have been used to break *pop(k)* into *k* pops of a single element, each of amortized complexity 0.

### The amortized complexity of tree traversal

An interesting example of amortized analysis is provided by the problem of the traversal of a binary tree in inorder, using an ADT whose operations are

> *inorder_first*: **like** *entry_type*
> *inorder_next(x*: **like** *entry_type*): **like** *entry_type*

(Section 6.2). As discussed in Section 2.3, a suitable characteristic operation to choose when analyzing these operations is the edge-traverse, which has the form $x := t.left\_child(x)$, $x := t.right\_child(x)$, or $x := t.parent(x)$. Although a single *inorder_first* or *inorder_next(x)* operation could require up to $n - 1$ edge-traverses, it is shown in Section 2.3 that the full sequence of one *inorder_first* followed by $n$ *inorder_next(x)* operations, required to traverse the tree, takes a total of only $2(n - 1)$ edge-traverses, which is much less than the $O(n^2)$ result of a worst-case analysis. This is just the kind of situation that amortized analysis is suited to, so a potential function should exist which leads to $O(1)$ amortized complexity per operation.

The state of the ADT at any moment is clearly equal to the binary tree being traversed, plus a distinguished node $x$: the place that the traversal has reached. Only $x$ changes over the course of one call to *inorder_first* or *inorder_next(x)*:

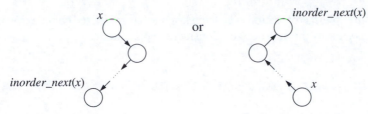

The potential function must cancel completely the cost of traversing down to the left or up to the left, since otherwise the resulting amortized bounds could not be $O(1)$. Define the *rank* of node $x$, $r(x)$, by letting the rank of the root be 0 and

$$r(left\_child(x)) = r(x) - 1$$
$$r(right\_child(x)) = r(x) + 1$$

at each node recursively. Here is a tree showing the ranks:

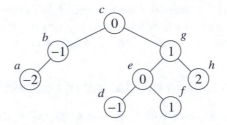

Define $\Phi(S)$ to be the rank of the distinguished node, or 0 initially and finally.

Now an edge-traverse of the form $x := t.left\_child(x)$ has actual complexity 1, but since $r(left\_child(x)) = r(x) - 1$, there is a compensating decrease of 1 in potential, leaving an amortized complexity of 0. Similarly, an edge-traverse from a right child to its parent also has amortized complexity 0.

Here now is a trace of the traversal of the tree above, with a calculation of the amortized complexity of each operation:

| $i$ | Operation | $S$ | $\Phi(S)$ | $t_i$ | $a_i$ |
|---|---|---|---|---|---|
| | | $x = Void$ | 0 | | |
| 1 | $x := t.inorder\_first$ | $x = a$ | $-2$ | 2 | 0 |
| 2 | $x := t.inorder\_next(x)$ | $x = b$ | $-1$ | 1 | 2 |
| 3 | $x := t.inorder\_next(x)$ | $x = c$ | 0 | 1 | 2 |
| 4 | $x := t.inorder\_next(x)$ | $x = d$ | $-1$ | 3 | 2 |
| 5 | $x := t.inorder\_next(x)$ | $x = e$ | 0 | 1 | 2 |
| 6 | $x := t.inorder\_next(x)$ | $x = f$ | 1 | 1 | 2 |
| 7 | $x := t.inorder\_next(x)$ | $x = g$ | 1 | 2 | 2 |
| 8 | $x := t.inorder\_next(x)$ | $x = h$ | 2 | 1 | 2 |
| 9 | $x := t.inorder\_next(x)$ | $x = Void$ | 0 | 2 | 0 |

Every *inorder_next(x)* operation except the last one has amortized complexity 2, and it is easy to see why this must be so. Consider the operation

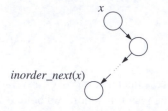

*inorder_next(x)*

The edge-traverse $x := t.right\_child(x)$ has actual complexity 1, and causes a potential increase of 1, for an amortized complexity of 2. The leftward-moving edge-traverses all have amortized complexity 0, as discussed above. Since the sum of the amortized complexities of the edge-traverses equals the amortized complexity of the operation, the amortized complexity of this type of *inorder_next(x)* operation is 2.

It is easy to check that the upward-moving kind of *inorder_next(x)* also has amortized complexity 2 (except the last one, which has amortized complexity 0); and the amortized complexity of *inorder_first* is always 0. It follows that the total complexity of the traversal is exactly $2(n - 1)$ edge-traverses.

## 3.5 Practical issues in the design of container ADTs

This book is largely concerned with *container ADTs*: ADTs that represent a set or sequence of elements, or *entries*. The Simple Set ADT of Section 3.2 is an example of a container ADT.

After correctness, the main objectives to keep in mind when designing ADTs are efficiency in time and space, and ease of use. These are particularly important for container ADTs, since they are among the most frequently used of all ADTs, and in real applications they may hold thousands of entries. With these objectives in mind, then, this section explores two practical issues that arise in the design of container ADTs in general: headers, and references to entries.

### Headers

Most implementations of container ADTs allocate one object for each entry; the objects are linked by references. If that is all the implementation contains, then the container must be accessed from outside by a reference to one of its objects:

access from outside

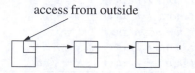

The other possibility is to interpose an additional object, not representing any entry, between the outside and the entries:

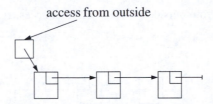

access from outside

Such objects are called *headers*.

It turns out that a header with the same type as the entries can simplify the coding of some ADT implementations by eliminating the special case of an empty structure. A second argument for headers is that sometimes the implementation needs to store information not related to any one entry, such as the number of entries currently in the container. A header provides a natural place to do this.

There is a third, rather subtle, argument for headers. Suppose that a container without a header is being shared by two or more separate parts of a program. For example, one part might be inserting entries, another part might be deleting them:

access from outside           another access from outside

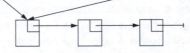

When the second part of the program deletes the first entry, it can easily move its own reference to the container as a whole across to the second entry:

access from outside           another access from outside

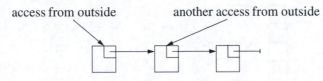

But now there is an inconsistency: the reference from the first part of the program should have moved as well, but it did not and could not because it is not reachable from the second part of the program. This problem is easily avoided with a header:

access from outside           another access from outside

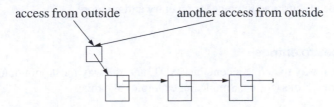

When the first entry is deleted by the second part of the program, the reference to it lying within the header is moved:

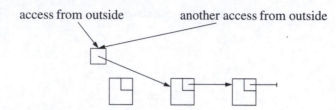

and all references from outside the container remain valid.

The argument against headers is that they waste space and time when there are many small containers. For example, the Mergesort sorting algorithm (Section 9.3) begins by placing each of the $n$ items to be sorted into a container of its own. Clearly, $n$ entry objects are needed to hold the $n$ items, but headers would add a further $n$ header objects, almost doubling the space and memory allocation time.

There seem to be compelling reasons both for and against headers. But it is not reasonable to supply two versions of every container ADT implementation, one with and one without a header.

The simplification of coding achievable by headers that have the same type as the entries is not very great, and is not significant when means exist for effective code re-use. Once this argument is put aside, the container as a whole may be represented by a separate object which serves as a header, and in cases where there are many small unshared containers, these header objects may be declared in Eiffel as **expanded**, avoiding separate memory records for them:

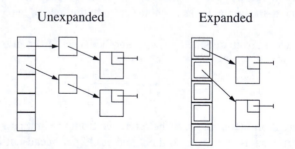

Space efficiency still demands however that the header object contain as little as possible, ideally just one reference to an entry and no more.

### References to entries

The simplest way to define a container ADT, and the way most commonly seen in class libraries, looks (for the Simple Set example) like this:

**class interface** *SIMPLESET[T]*

> *make*
> > -- Initialize to a new, empty simpleset
>
> *empty*: *BOOLEAN*
> > -- **true** if this simpleset is empty, else **false**
>
> *insert(x: T)*
> > -- Insert *x* into this simpleset
>
> *delete_any*: *T*
> > -- Delete and return an arbitrary element of this simpleset

**end** -- *SIMPLESET*

For example, if *s* is a *SIMPLESET[INTEGER]*, then operations such as *s.insert*(128) and *i := s.delete_any* may be performed. This simple plan is not used in this book, because it breaks down when more demanding operations are introduced.

The first problem arises when a *delete* operation is added. Under the simple plan, this can only take the form *delete(x: T)*. But an instance of this operation, *s.delete*(128) say, must search through the container to find an entry containing 128. Of course, searching is a perfectly respectable thing to do, and it is the basis of the Symbol Table ADT of Chapter 7. The point here is that searching has a significant cost: to do it efficiently requires extra memory, and even then it is not possible to achieve $O(1)$ worst-case time complexity. Those who need searching can use a symbol table and pay this inevitable cost; but, as we will see, it is possible to delete without any searching, in $O(1)$ worst-case time, if the simple plan is abandoned.

This avoidance of searching turns out to be crucial to the efficient implementation of Dijkstra's algorithm for shortest paths in graphs. The $O(n\log n + m)$ result obtained in Section 12.1 is not achievable under the simple plan.

The second problem is *traversal*, the examination of each entry in turn. The simple plan accomplishes traversal by means of a *hidden cursor*: a reference to an entry hidden within *s*:

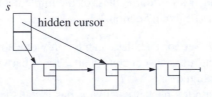

In this diagram, the cursor happens to refer to the second entry. There is a *first* operation, which sets the cursor to the first entry; a *next* operation, which moves it one step to the right; a *finished* operation, which returns **true** when the cursor has moved off the end; and a *current* operation, which returns the value stored in the entry currently pointed to by the cursor.

Unfortunately, many algorithms require two or more simultaneous traversals: checking whether a sequence is a palindrome (the same when reversed), checking whether any two elements are equal, and so on. These are impossible if there is only one cursor, and having two or more hidden cursors leads to clumsy operations and makes headers large, wasting space when there are many small containers.

The third problem arises when entries are moved from one container to another by deletion from the first followed by insertion into the second. If a linked structure is used under the simple plan, every deletion frees one object and every insertion creates one. This memory allocation overhead is severe and cannot be removed by compiler optimizations; for example, it more than doubles the running time of the Mergesort algorithm (Section 9.3). This problem is less awkward than the other two, because it can be avoided (at some cost to elegance) by including explicit *move* operations in all container ADTs.

A better solution is to provide the user of the container with a type whose concrete value is a reference to an entry. This solves all of these problems at once: the parameter of *delete* can be changed to be of this type; instead of one hidden cursor there can be as many cursors (of this type) as the user chooses to declare; and insertion no longer involves a memory allocation step. This is the plan adopted uniformly throughout this book; every container ADT contains an attribute called *entry_type* whose type is a reference to an entry, and the Eiffel notation **like** *entry_type* stands for this type.

Permitting references into the interior of containers naturally raises concerns about breaking the security of the container ADT. But such concerns are quite unfounded: no operations on entry types are provided, and so the only code that can actually follow such a reference is secure code lying within the implementation of the container ADT.

## 3.6 Exercises

3.1    Give an algebraic specification of the Simple Set ADT from Figure 3.2.

3.2    Complete the proof of correctness of the implementation of the Simple Set ADT that was begun in Section 3.2.

3.3    According to Section 3.2, there can be only one abstract value of an ADT corresponding to each concrete value, for otherwise the implementation would be ambiguous.

The author's pocket calculator has a statistics ADT, whose abstract value is a set of numbers. There are buttons to insert or delete a number, and to report the set's size, mean, and standard deviation. The instructions say that the calculator stores just three things: the number of elements, their sum, and the sum of their squares. This means that the abstract values $\{4, 8, 9\}$ and $\{5, 6, 10\}$ have identical concrete values. How can this be?

3.4    Use data abstraction to tidy up the following disgraceful program, which
reads some numbers from input and writes them out again in sorted order:

```
sort is
    local
        n, i, j, min: INTEGER;
        a: ARRAY[INTEGER];
    do
        a.make(max_size);
        from n := 0 until io.endfile loop
            n := n + 1;
            io.read_integer;
            a.put(io.last_integer, n)
        end;

        from i := 1 until i > n loop
            min := i;
            from j := i+1 until j > n loop
                if a.item(j) < a.item(min) then
                    min := j
                end;
                j := j + 1
            end;
            io.put_integer(a.item(min));
            a.put(a.item(i), min);
            i := i + 1
        end;
    end
```

3.5    A group of k people decide to go on a camping trip. Each has a knapsack, and
they wish to divide the n items to be carried into k bundles whose weight is as
equal as possible. Since this is an NP-hard problem, they adopt the following
approximate method: *repeatedly choose the heaviest remaining unpacked
item and pack it into the knapsack which is currently the lightest.* Use data
abstraction to produce an elegant implementation of this method.

3.6    The following code fragment finds the k smallest elements of an array of n
numbers a.item(1..n), using a method quite different to the one used in Section
3.1 to find the k largest:

```
q.make;
from i := 1 until i > n loop
    q.insert(q.new_entry(a.item(i), Void));
    i := i + 1
end;
from i := 1 until i > k loop
    io.put_integer(q.delete_min.key)
    i := i + 1;
end
```

(a)    Perform an abstract worst-case analysis of this algorithm, and thus determine its worst-case time complexity when the priority queue is implemented by (1) a sorted list, (2) an unsorted list, and (3) a heap. Use the method given in Section 3.3; the worst-case time complexity of the heap may be found in the summary at the end of Chapter 8.

(b)    Assuming that $n$ is very large, which of these three implementations is preferable for this algorithm when $k$ is small (say, $k = 3$); which is preferable when $k$ is large (say, $k = n/3$)?

3.7    Consider the following algorithm for adding 1 to a binary number, represented as an array of $n$ bits, assuming that there is no overflow:

```
increment is
  local
    i: INTEGER;
  do
    from i := n until a.item(i) = 0 loop
      a.put(0, i);
      i := i - 1
    end;
    a.put(1, i)
  end
```

This algorithm is clearly $O(n)$ in the worst case. Show that its amortized complexity is $O(1)$.

3.8    One way of finding the convex hull of a set of $n$ points in the plane (see Section 4.3 for a definition of the problem) begins by sorting the points by their $x$ coordinates. As will be seen in Chapter 9, this step can be implemented so as to have $O(n\log n)$ complexity in the worst case. Next, add the points one by one, from left to right, to a growing convex hull:

Verify that a careful implementation of this step can be made to run in $O(k)$ time, where $k$ is the number of edges deleted (that is, the dashed edges in the diagram above). Then find a potential function which makes the amortized complexity of adding one point $O(1)$; this leads to a convex hull algorithm of $O(n\log n)$ complexity in the worst case.

# Chapter 4

# Algorithm Design

Algorithm design is a creative activity, and there is no simple recipe for success. Indeed, there are many important problems for which no efficient algorithms are known. Nevertheless, by classifying algorithms according to similarities in their structure, it is possible to identify certain strategies which often lead to correct, efficient algorithms. These strategies are the subject of this chapter.

## 4.1 The design process

The first step in design is to produce a clear specification of the problem. Petty details, such as the format of the input data, should be ignored, and attention focused on what seems to be the essential part of the problem. When the problem is expressed in this abstract form, it will often resemble a standard one, and no innovation will be needed. Thus, the first rule of algorithm design is to be familiar with the repertoire of standard problems.

For example, consider the following problem. An architect produces a house plan like the one below. The question is, what is the most economical way to install the plumbing?

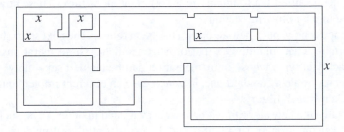

The places where water is needed, and the place where it enters the house, are marked with an *x*; pipes may be installed only in the walls. Although this particular instance is very easy to solve, much larger and more complex instances confront the designers of hospitals and other large buildings.

Is this a standard problem? To begin with, all the information relevant to the problem may be summarized in the form of a graph whose edges are walls, and whose vertices are the places where walls intersect with other walls or with the places where water is needed:

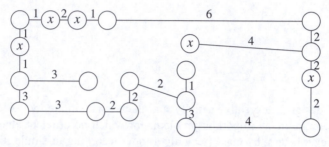

The numbers indicate the lengths of walls.

Having abstracted the problem in this way, it may be expressed as follows: given a graph *G* whose edges have costs, find a way to connect a specified subset of the vertices of *G* together, using only edges from *G*, so as to minimize the total cost of the edges used. In this form, the problem is recognizable as a standard one: finding a Steiner tree of a graph.

This is a particularly instructive example, because the Steiner tree problem is known to be NP-hard, which informally means that it is one of a large class of problems which are known to be equally difficult, but for which no efficient algorithms are known. Someone unaware of this could waste a lot of time in a frustrating search for an efficient algorithm, without knowing that many experienced computer scientists have tried and failed. Garey and Johnson (1979) has the whole story, which is beyond the scope of this book.

Even when the problem seems to be new, all is not lost, because there are strategies for designing algorithms, and experience has shown that application of these strategies often leads quickly to an efficient algorithm. These strategies are described in the following sections.

Suppose now that a new algorithm has been found. The next step is to examine it to determine what operations are performed on its data. These operations constitute an abstract data type, whose implementation can be tackled separately. Often the ADT will resemble a standard one, in which case an efficient implementation of it can be taken from a library.

Finally, the new algorithm is analyzed, evaluated in other ways (such as for its memory consumption, or simplicity), and the process of algorithm design repeated if necessary.

## 4.2  **Incremental algorithms**

When an instance of a problem is first encountered, it is like an unknown country. Somehow it must be explored, and the sought-for answer found.

A natural way to do this is to examine some small piece of the instance, record whatever about it is needed for the solution, then move on to the next piece and repeat until the whole instance has been examined. This *incremental strategy* leads to algorithms with the following structure:

> *incremental(instance*: *INSTANCE_TYPE*): *RESULT_TYPE* **is**
>    **do**
>       **from** *Result* := *some initial value* **until** *instance* = *empty* **loop**
>          *x* := *an element of instance*;
>          *Delete x*;
>          *Update Result to reflect the discovery of x*
>       **end**
>    **end**

The unknown country, *instance*, gradually shrinks until it becomes empty.

Having decided to try this approach, the algorithm designer must next consider the choice of *x* at each stage. There seem to be two broad strategies for choosing *x*, leading to two distinctive kinds of incremental algorithm.

The first kind of incremental algorithm does not invest any time in choosing *x* carefully; it simply selects the most accessible of the remaining elements of *instance*. The advantage of this is that the selection is very simple and efficient; the disadvantage is that the algorithm is blind to the problem instance as a whole, knowing nothing but the values of *x* it has selected. Accordingly, the algorithm is characterized by a loop invariant of the form

> '*Result* is a complete solution to the subproblem represented by the part
> of *instance* that has been deleted'

in which no mention is made of the instance as a whole.

The correctness of an incremental algorithm of this first kind is always obvious. As a very simple example, consider the following algorithm for summing the elements of array *s.item(a..b)*:

> *sum* := 0;
> **from** *i* := *a* **until** *i* > *b* **loop**
>    *sum* := *sum* + *s.item(i)*;
>    *i* := *i* + 1
> **end**

The loop invariant, '*sum* holds the sum of all the elements examined so far,' confirms that this is indeed an incremental algorithm of the first kind. In this book, whenever the correctness of an incremental algorithm is passed over without comment, it may be inferred that it is of this kind.

The problem of sorting a set of numbers into increasing order is a good one for trying all kinds of design strategies on. A sorting algorithm which is an incremental algorithm of the first kind should have loop invariant

> '*Result* is a sorted sequence containing the elements of *instance* that have been deleted'

For example, if the instance is {5, 1, 12, 9, 6, 13}, then after deleting 5, 1, and 12, it must be the case that *Result* = $\langle 1, 5, 12 \rangle$. Then, after deleting 9, *Result* must be $\langle 1, 5, 9, 12 \rangle$. It is clear from this that the updating step requires that $x$ be inserted into its appropriate place in the result sequence, which is quite easy to do.

The next step in the design process is to examine the operations on *instance* and *Result*, to determine what abstract data type these define and so what data structures are appropriate for their representation. This is done in Section 9.1, where the algorithm just designed appears under the name of *insertion sort*.

## Incremental algorithms of the second kind

The danger faced by algorithms that do not look ahead is that a value of $x$ could appear which completely upsets what has been done so far. That is, it may not be possible to update *Result* in any simple way to take account of the discovery of $x$.

For example, imagine a group of people packing their knapsacks for a camping trip. They have a number of items to carry, of varying weights, and they want to equalize the weights of the knapsacks, as far as possible. Suppose that about half the load has been stowed, and the knapsacks are of roughly equal weight. There is no simple way to add one item, keeping the loads balanced: if the new item is heavy, a great deal of repacking is inevitable.

Most people would choose to begin the packing with the heaviest items, in the hope that the lighter ones could be fitted around them without any need for repacking. That is, they would invest more effort in choosing $x$ carefully at each stage, so avoiding any need to modify what they have already done.

There are a number of algorithms which employ this strategy, so in this book they are given a name: *incremental algorithms of the second kind*. They are characterized by a loop invariant of the form

> '*Result* is a part of the solution to the instance as a whole; it will need to be added to, but not modified'

in which the final solution plays a prominent part. This kind of incremental algorithm is invariably more subtle than the other, and indeed this book contains several whose correctness is far from obvious.

The sorting problem again provides a good illustration of this strategy. The output of a sorting algorithm is a sequence like $\langle 1, 5, 6, 9, 12, 13 \rangle$, which suggests that *Result*, if it is to conform to the given loop invariant, should take successively the values $\langle\rangle$, $\langle 1\rangle$, $\langle 1, 5\rangle$, $\langle 1, 5, 6\rangle$, and so on, all of which can be added to without modification to obtain the overall solution. Clearly, the smallest remaining element of *instance* is being chosen at each stage, and added to the end of the result sequence. This algorithm is *selection sort*, and it is studied further in Section 9.2.

## 4.3 Divide-and-conquer

*Divide-and-conquer* is a design strategy which is well known for breaking down efficiency barriers. When the method applies, it often leads to a large improvement in time complexity, from $O(n^2)$ to $O(n\log n)$, for example.

   One notable algorithm employing this strategy is the *fast Fourier transform*, which is used in the physical sciences for transforming a function of time into a function of frequency, both functions being defined by their values at a large number of points. A nuclear magnetic resonance spectrometer, for example, regularly produces $2^{16}$ or more numbers which must be transformed in this way. Without the fast $O(n\log n)$ method made possible by divide-and-conquer, this whole technique would be infeasible. For a full description, see for example Aho et al. (1974).

   The divide-and-conquer strategy is as follows. Divide the problem instance into two or more smaller instances of the same problem, solve the smaller instances recursively, and assemble the solutions to form a solution of the original instance. The recursion stops when an instance is reached which is too small to divide: the solution to this instance can be produced directly, and it forms the basis for a proof of correctness by induction on the size of the instance (see Section 1.2).

   When dividing the instance, it may be best to use whatever division comes most easily to hand; or alternatively it may be worth investing time in making the division carefully so that the assembly is simplified. This design issue is graphically illustrated by the following example.

### Finding the convex hull

Consider finding the *convex hull* of a set of points in the plane, that is, a sequence of points from the set which defines a convex figure enclosing all of them:

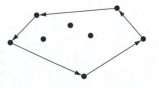

(A convex figure is a closed figure with no indentations, that is, in which no interior angle exceeds 180 degrees.) If the points are not given in any particular order, the simplest way to apply divide-and-conquer is to partition them into two subsets of approximately equal size. For example, beginning with

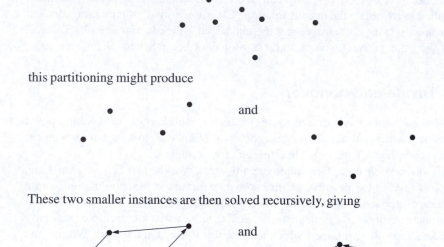

this partitioning might produce

and

These two smaller instances are then solved recursively, giving

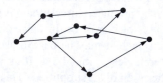

and

Finally, the two hulls resulting from the recursive calls are assembled into one:

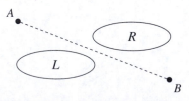

Unfortunately, this seems too complicated to be worth pursuing.

In general, it will not always be possible to reassemble the smaller solutions; but before abandoning divide-and-conquer a more careful partitioning method can be tried. For this problem, observe that the point $A$ with maximum $y$ coordinate must be in the convex hull, as must the point $B$ with minimum $y$ coordinate. This suggests the following partitioning:

A simple algorithm which finds the maximum and minimum of a set of numbers can be used to determine $A$ and $B$ in linear time, and it takes constant time to decide which side of line $AB$ a point lies on. Thus, the partitioning is $O(n)$. Solving subproblems $L$ and $R$ recursively gives

and this is fairly easy to merge into an overall solution. It is necessary to connect $A$ to one of the vertices of the convex hull of $L$. Just which vertex is appropriate is not quite clear, but it turns out that there is a simple geometrical test which can be applied to each vertex to determine if it is the right one. Similarly, $A$ must be connected to $R$, and $B$ to $L$ and $R$, giving the desired hull:

The analysis of this algorithm is similar to Quicksort's (Section 9.4); it turns out to be $O(n\log n)$ on the average, degenerating to $O(n^2)$ if $L$ or $R$ is empty at each stage. For other algorithms for this problem, see Sedgewick (1988).

### Strassen's algorithm

The matrix multiplication algorithm due to Strassen (1969) is perhaps the most dramatic example of the ability of divide-and-conquer to break efficiency barriers.

The usual way to multiply two $n \times n$ matrices $a$ and $b$, yielding result matrix $c$, is the following:

```
from i := 1 until i > n loop
    from j := 1 until j > n loop
        total := 0;
        from k := 1 until k > n loop
            total := total + a.item(i, k)*b.item(k, j);
            k := k + 1
        end;
        c.put(total, i, j);
        j := j + 1
    end;
    i := i + 1
end
```

This algorithm requires $n^3$ scalar multiplications (that is, multiplications of single numbers) and $n^3$ scalar additions. It very simply reflects the definition of matrix multiplication, and it is natural to expect that it cannot be improved upon.

Now apply divide-and-conquer to the problem. It is a fact that, if the three matrices are divided into quarters like this:

$$\begin{pmatrix} a_{11} & a_{12} \\ a_{21} & a_{22} \end{pmatrix} \begin{pmatrix} b_{11} & b_{12} \\ b_{21} & b_{22} \end{pmatrix} = \begin{pmatrix} c_{11} & c_{12} \\ c_{21} & c_{22} \end{pmatrix}$$

then the $c_{ij}$ can be found by the usual matrix multiplication algorithm, substituting matrix operations for scalar ones. That is,

$$c_{11} = a_{11}b_{11} + a_{12}b_{21}$$
$$c_{12} = a_{11}b_{12} + a_{12}b_{22}$$
$$c_{21} = a_{21}b_{11} + a_{22}b_{21}$$
$$c_{22} = a_{21}b_{12} + a_{22}b_{22}$$

This leads to a divide-and-conquer algorithm, which performs an $n \times n$ matrix multiplication by partitioning the matrices into quarters and performing eight $(n/2) \times (n/2)$ matrix multiplications and four $(n/2) \times (n/2)$ matrix additions. The recurrence for the number of scalar multiplications is

$$T(1) = 1$$
$$T(n) = 8T(n/2)$$

which leads to $T(n) = n^3$ when $n$ is a power of 2, as is easily shown.

Strassen's insight was to find an alternative method for calculating the $c_{ij}$, requiring seven $(n/2) \times (n/2)$ matrix multiplications and eighteen $(n/2) \times (n/2)$ matrix additions and subtractions:

$$m_1 = (a_{12} - a_{22})(b_{21} + b_{22})$$
$$m_2 = (a_{11} + a_{22})(b_{11} + b_{22})$$
$$m_3 = (a_{11} - a_{21})(b_{11} + b_{12})$$
$$m_4 = (a_{11} + a_{12})b_{22}$$
$$m_5 = a_{11}(b_{12} - b_{22})$$
$$m_6 = a_{22}(b_{21} - b_{11})$$
$$m_7 = (a_{21} + a_{22})b_{11}$$

$$c_{11} = m_1 + m_2 - m_4 + m_6$$
$$c_{12} = m_4 + m_5$$
$$c_{21} = m_6 + m_7$$
$$c_{22} = m_2 - m_3 + m_5 - m_7$$

It is easy to verify that these formulae for the $c_{ij}$ agree with the ones given above.

If this method is used recursively to perform the seven $(n/2) \times (n/2)$ matrix multiplications, the number of scalar multiplications performed is given by

$$T(1) = 1$$
$$T(n) = 7T(n/2)$$

Solving this for the case $n = 2^k$ is easy:

$$T(2^k) = 7T(2^{k-1})$$

$$= 7^2 T(2^{k-2})$$

$$= \ldots$$

$$= 7^i T(2^{k-i})$$

$$= \ldots$$

$$= 7^k T(1)$$

$$= 7^k$$

That is, $T(n) = 7^{\log_2 n}$. Applying the identity $a^{\log_b c} = c^{\log_b a}$, which may be proved by taking logarithms to base $b$, gives

$$T(n) = n^{\log_2 7} \simeq n^{2.81}$$

The number of scalar additions performed turns out to be also $O(n^{\log_2 7})$, and thus Strassen's algorithm is asymptotically more efficient than the standard algorithm.

In practice, the overhead of managing the many small matrices does not pay off until $n$ reaches the hundreds. Nevertheless, Strassen's algorithm clearly demonstrates the power of divide-and-conquer.

## 4.4 Dynamic programming

Consider the problem of finding the $n$th Fibonacci number, as defined by the recurrence equation

$$F(0) = 0$$
$$F(1) = 1$$
$$F(n) = F(n-1) + F(n-2)$$

One solution is to convert the recurrence into a divide-and-conquer algorithm:

```
fib(n: INTEGER): INTEGER is
    do
        if n <= 1 then
            Result := n
        else
            Result := fib(n–1) + fib(n–2)
        end
    end
```

This is simple, elegant and obviously correct. Unfortunately, it has exponential time complexity (Exercise 2.7). Drawing a tree diagram of all the recursive calls the algorithm makes shows clearly what is slowing it down:

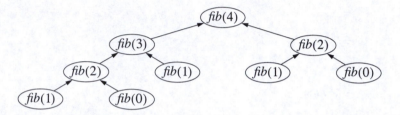

The algorithm solves small instances many times over, and this effect becomes worse as $n$ increases. Arrows are drawn pointing upwards rather than downwards for a reason that will become clear shortly.

Whenever a divide-and-conquer algorithm solves small instances repeatedly in this way, *dynamic programming* may be used to eliminate the redundant work. The solutions are stored in a table, and an instance is solved from scratch only when it is encountered for the first time. Thereafter, whenever that solution is needed, it is simply retrieved from the table. For the Fibonacci problem, this yields

```
fib(n: INTEGER): INTEGER is
    do
        if table.item(n) = empty then
            if n <= 1 then
                table.put(n, n)
            else
                table.put(fib(n–1) + fib(n–2), n)
            end
        end;
        Result := table.item(n)
    end
```

where $table.item(0..n)$ are initialized to the value *empty*, for example $-1$.

Even the test for *empty* can be eliminated by solving the instances in an order that guarantees that when a given instance's turn arrives, all the instances whose solution it needs have already been solved. To find this order, let the instances be vertices in a directed graph, and join $x$ to $y$ by an arrow if the solution to instance $x$ is used when solving $y$. For the Fibonacci numbers problem, this gives

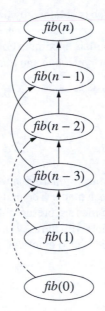

The correct ordering is then a *topological ordering* of the vertices (Section 11.4); in this case, *fib*(0), *fib*(1), *fib*(2), ... , *fib*(n) or *fib*(1), *fib*(0), *fib*(2), ... , *fib*(n).

It often happens that the ordering can be determined in advance and embedded into the algorithm. This can be done for the Fibonacci numbers problem:

```
fib(n: INTEGER): INTEGER is
    local
        i: INTEGER;
    do
        table.put(0, 0);
        table.put(1, 1);
        from i := 2 until i > n loop
            table.put(table.item(i–1) + table.item(i–2), i);
            i := i + 1
        end;
        Result := table.item(n)
    end
```

This algorithm has $O(n)$ complexity. The elimination of recursion is a further practical benefit: dynamic programming is a useful code optimization technique even when it does not reduce the asymptotic time complexity (Exercise 9.5).

## The longest common subsequence

The following problem is typical of the way dynamic programming arises. Let $x$ and $y$ be two sequences of characters, for example $x = abdebcbb$ and $y = adacbcb$.

A *subsequence* of such a sequence is obtained by deleting any number of elements from any positions. A *longest common subsequence* of $x$ and $y$, written $\text{lcs}(x, y)$, is a subsequence of both whose length is maximal. For example, *adcbb* and *adbcb* are longest common subsequences of *abdebcbb* and *adacbcb*:

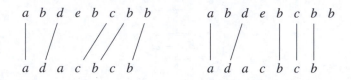

This problem finds application in comparing new and old versions of files to determine where changes have been made. The parts that do not belong to a longest common subsequence of the two files are presumably the changes.

It is always a good idea to start with the easy cases. If either sequence is empty, the longest common subsequence is also empty. Denoting the empty sequence by the symbol $\varepsilon$,

$$\text{lcs}(x, \varepsilon) = \varepsilon$$
$$\text{lcs}(\varepsilon, y) = \varepsilon$$

for any sequences $x$ and $y$.

Next, assuming now that both sequences are non-empty, it is possible to compare their first elements. If they are equal, clearly that first element may be included in the longest common subsequence, so

$$\text{lcs}(ax, ay) = a\text{lcs}(x, y)$$

This notation means that a longest common subsequence of two sequences both beginning with $a$ is $a$ followed by a longest common subsequence of the two remainders.

This leaves just one hard case: two sequences $ax$ and $by$ whose first elements differ. If $\text{lcs}(ax, by)$ does not begin with $a$, it must be equal to $\text{lcs}(x, by)$; otherwise, it does not begin with $b$, so it must equal $\text{lcs}(ax, y)$. Therefore

$$\text{lcs}(ax, by) = \text{lcs}(x, by) \quad or \quad \text{lcs}(ax, y)$$

whichever is the longer; both must be evaluated and their lengths compared.

This is a correct recursive method of evaluating $\text{lcs}(x, y)$, but it is not efficient. In the worst case, the two sequences have no common elements, and the last case always applies. Let the length of $x$ be $n$, and of $y$ be $m$. Then the worst-case complexity of evaluating $\text{lcs}(x, y)$ by this method is

$$W(n, m) = W(n, m - 1) + W(n - 1, m)$$

$$\geq 2W(n - 1, m - 1)$$

which shows that the complexity is exponential in the smaller of $n$ and $m$. In fact, $W(n, m)$ is closely related to the binomial coefficient (Exercise 2.10).

When evaluating lcs($x, y$), eventually lcs($x', y'$) may be called for any suffixes $x$ ' of $x$ and $y'$ of $y$. (A *suffix* of a sequence is a subsequence consisting of any number of rightmost elements; for example, the suffixes of *bac* are ε, $c$, $ac$, and *bac*. Similarly, a *prefix* of a sequence consists of any number of leftmost elements.) Applying dynamic programming, a two-dimensional table is needed. If $x$ has length $n$, and $y$ has length $m$, then the table indexes must run from 0 to $n$ in one dimension and 0 to $m$ in the other.

The following algorithm finds only the length of lcs($x, y$). For convenience in indexing $x$ and $y$, it begins at the right and works leftwards. Thus, *table.item($i, j$)* holds the length of a longest common subsequence of *x.item*($1..i$) and *y.item*($1..j$):

```
lcs(i, j: INTEGER): INTEGER is
    do
        if table.item(i, j) = empty then
            if i = 0 or j = 0 then
                table.put(0, i, j)
            elseif x.item(i) = y.item(j) then
                table.put(1 + lcs(i−1, j−1), i, j)
            else
                table.put(max(lcs(i−1, j), lcs(i, j−1)), i, j)
            end
        end;
        Result := table.item(i, j)
    end
```

To achieve the next optimization – embedding a topological ordering of the subinstances into the algorithm, so eliminating the recursion – the directed graph showing the calls must be constructed. Since lcs($i, j$) depends on lcs($i−1, j−1$), lcs($i−1, j$), and lcs($i, j−1$), this graph is

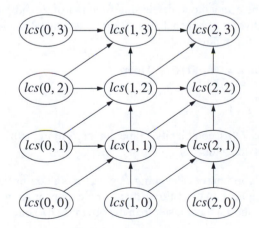

and so on. It is quite easy to find a suitable topological ordering, beginning with the two boundaries:

```
lcs(n, m: INTEGER): INTEGER) is
    local
        i, j: INTEGER
    do
        from i := 0 until i > n loop table.put(0, i, 0) end;
        from j := 1 until j > m loop table.put(0, 0, j) end;
        from i := 1 until i > n loop
            from j := 1 until j > m loop
                if x.item(i) = y.item(j) then
                    table.put(1 + table.item(i–1, j–1), i, j)
                else
                    table.put(max(table.item(i–1, j), table.item(i, j–1)), i, j)
                end
                j := j + 1
            end;
            i := i + 1
        end;
        Result := table.item(n, m)
    end
```

The time complexity of this dynamic programming algorithm is clearly $O(nm)$. The problem of using the values in the table to reconstruct an actual longest common subsequence is left as an exercise.

There is an interesting alternative algorithm for this problem, due to Hunt and Szymanski (1977). For instances typically encountered in the file comparison application mentioned earlier, their algorithm is significantly faster.

## 4.5 Exercises

4.1 Let $f(x)$ be a monotone decreasing function of $x$, and let $n$ be the largest non-negative integer such that $f(n) \geq 0$. Assuming that such an $n$ exists, one algorithm for finding it is

```
from i := 0 until f(i) < 0 loop
    i := i + 1
end;
n := i – 1
```

but it has $O(n)$ complexity. Find an algorithm with better asymptotic complexity than this.

4.2 Find an algorithm for calculating $x^n$, where $n$ is a non-negative integer, using only multiplication operations (that is, no exponentiation). Your algorithm should be substantially faster than the obvious $O(n)$ one.

4.3     The following matrix recurrence equation may be used to define the Fibonacci numbers:

$$\begin{pmatrix} F(1) \\ F(0) \end{pmatrix} = \begin{pmatrix} 1 \\ 0 \end{pmatrix}$$

$$\begin{pmatrix} F(n+1) \\ F(n) \end{pmatrix} = \begin{pmatrix} 1 & 1 \\ 1 & 0 \end{pmatrix} \begin{pmatrix} F(n) \\ F(n-1) \end{pmatrix}$$

Verify this statement, solve the recurrence, and use your result, together with
the solution to the previous question, to find an algorithm for calculating $F(n)$
which is substantially faster than the $O(n)$ dynamic programming algorithm
given in Section 4.4.

4.4     Find an incremental algorithm for the convex hull problem of Section 4.3.

4.5     Suppose we are given a convex polygon, like this one:

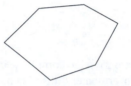

Find an algorithm for determining which two vertices are farthest apart,
given a sequence of the coordinates of the vertices in counterclockwise
order. The obvious algorithm is to calculate the distance between each pair
of vertices, which is $O(n^2)$ if there are $n$ vertices. Try for a substantially
faster algorithm.

4.6     A *celebrity* is someone that everyone knows, but who knows noone. Find
an efficient algorithm for determining whether or not a group of $n$ people
contains a celebrity, based on asking questions of the form 'Excuse me $x$,
do you know $y$?' (Hint: what can you conclude if the answer is yes? if the
answer is no?)

4.7     A computer has a single printer. At a certain instant, $n$ people each send a file
to the printer, then wait beside it for their output. The printer must *schedule*
the files (that is, decide on an order to print them) so as to minimize the total
waiting time of the $n$ people. The size of each file is known, and from this
the printer can determine $t(x)$, the time it will take to print file $x$. Prove that
printing the files in order of increasing $t(x)$ yields an optimal schedule. (Hint:
this is an incremental algorithm of the second kind.)

4.8 A *local minimum* of an array *s.item(a..b)* is an element *s.item(k)* satisfying both *s.item(k)* ≤ *s.item(k − 1)* and *s.item(k)* ≤ *s.item(k + 1)*. It is assumed that *a* ≤ *b*, *s.item(a)* ≤ *s.item(a − 1)*, and *s.item(b)* ≤ *s.item(b + 1)*; from these conditions it follows that a local minimum must exist. Design an algorithm for finding a local minimum of the array *s.item(a..b)* which is substantially faster than the obvious $O(n)$ one, in the worst case.

4.9 One idea for simplifying the algorithm given in Section 4.3 for finding the convex hull of a set of points is as follows. After partitioning into

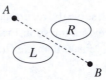

include *A* and *B* in the two subproblems, or in other words, solve

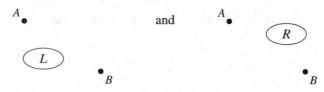

and

whose solutions are trivial to combine, since *BA* is in the first hull and *AB* is in the second. Unfortunately, this idea has a fatal flaw. What is it?

4.10 Design an algorithm for printing out all the subsets of a given finite set. For example, the subsets of {*a*, *b*, *c*} are

| | |
|---|---|
| {} | {*a*} |
| {*c*} | {*a*, *c*} |
| {*b*} | {*a*, *b*} |
| {*b*, *c*} | {*a*, *b*, *c*} |

4.11 When a divide-and-conquer algorithm divides a problem of size *n* into *a* subproblems, each of size *n/b*, its complexity is typically given by the recurrence equation

$$T(1) = d$$
$$T(n) = aT(n/b) + f(n)$$

where $f(n)$ is the cost of dividing a subproblem of size *n*, and subsequently recombining the solutions, and *d* is a constant. Let $n = b^k$ and show that

$$T(b^k) = da^k + \sum_{i=1}^{k} a^{k-i} f(b^i)$$

4.12  The recurrence equation given in the previous question often occurs with $f(n) = cn^r$ for some positive constants $c$ and $r$. Show that in this case the solution of the recurrence equation is

$$T(n) = O(n^r) \qquad \text{if } a < b^r$$
$$= O(n^r \log n) \qquad \text{if } a = b^r$$
$$= O(n^{\log_b a}) \qquad \text{if } a > b^r$$

for $n = b^k$. Thus, divide-and-conquer algorithms become asymptotically less efficient as $a$ increases relative to $b^r$.

4.13  Karatsuba and Ofman (1962). It is usually assumed that the multiplication of two integers can be performed in constant time, but if the numbers are very large this is unrealistic, as the following hand calculation of 1101 times 1010 shows:

$$
\begin{array}{r}
1101 \\
\underline{1010} \\
0000 \\
1101 \\
0000 \\
\underline{1101} \\
10000010
\end{array}
$$

So consider the problem of multiplying two $n$-bit numbers together, and let the characteristic operation be the multiplication of two 1-bit numbers (addition is of course much cheaper, so its cost is ignored).

(a)  Show that the complexity of the hand method is $T(n) = n^2$.

(b)  Now consider the following divide-and-conquer approach. Let $u$ and $v$ be the two $n$-bit binary integers, and assume that $n$ is even. Let $u_1$ be the $n/2$ most significant bits of $u$, and let $u_0$ be the remaining bits, so that $u = 2^{n/2} u_1 + u_0$. Similarly, let $v = 2^{n/2} v_1 + v_0$. The identity

$$uv = (2^n + 2^{n/2}) u_1 v_1 + 2^{n/2} (u_1 - u_0)(v_0 - v_1) + (2^{n/2} + 1) u_0 v_0$$

which may be easily verified by multiplying out the right-hand side, shows that the $n$-bit multiplication $uv$ may be accomplished with the three $n/2$-bit multiplications $u_1 v_1$, $(u_1 - u_0)(v_0 - v_1)$, and $u_0 v_0$, plus some inexpensive additions and shifts. Derive and solve a recurrence equation for the time complexity of this method, assuming $n$ is a power of 2, and show that it is asymptotically more efficient than the traditional method.

4.14 You are given an $n \times m$ matrix $s.item(a..b, c..d)$ in which it is known that $s.item(i, j) \le s.item(i, j + 1)$ and $s.item(i, j) \le s.item(i + 1, j)$ for all $i$ and $j$. That is, the entries are sorted along the rows and columns. Design an efficient algorithm for determining whether a given value $x$ is present in $s$.

4.15 *The subset sum problem.* The following is a simple example of the problems that arise from any attempt to make efficient use of a limited storage space, such as a computer's memory. A set of items $A = \{a_1, a_2, \ldots, a_n\}$ is given. Each item $a_i$ has a *size*, $s(a_i)$, which is a positive integer. The problem is to find a subset of $A$ whose total size (that is, the sum of the sizes of its elements) is as large as possible, but not larger than a given integer $C$, the capacity of the storage space.

This problem may be solved by generating the $2^n$ subsets of $A$, eliminating all those whose total size exceeds $C$, and returning a remaining subset of maximum size. Unfortunately, this has exponential complexity. Find an algorithm which is substantially faster if $C$ is not too large, and determine the complexity of your algorithm. (Hint: $a_1$ is either in or out. Divide the problem into these two cases, and solve the resulting smaller instances. Then apply dynamic programming.)

4.16 *Bin packing.* $K$ bins are given, each of capacity $C$, and a set of items $A = \{a_1, a_2, \ldots, a_n\}$, each with an associated size. The problem is to place all $n$ items into the $K$ bins without exceeding the capacity of any bin, or else to report failure if this is impossible. Using the general approach suggested in the preceding question, design an efficient algorithm for this problem and determine its complexity.

# Chapter 5

# Lists, Stacks, and Queues

The subject of this chapter is a family of ADTs whose principal members, the List, Stack, and Queue, are among the most widely used of all ADTs. The feature that these ADTs share is their mathematical entity: all are based on the sequence, differing only in the operations they provide.

## 5.1 Lists

As defined in Section 3.1, a sequence is a collection of entries whose order matters. To distinguish them from sets, sequences are enclosed in angle brackets:

$$\langle a_1, a_2, \dots , a_n \rangle$$

Since order matters, it makes sense to speak of the first entry, the $i$th entry, the successor of any entry except the last, and so on.

It is easy to think of many useful operations on sequences: insertion, deletion, traversal (examining the entries in order), appending two sequences to form one. The List ADT (Figure 5.1) embraces all of these operations.

A list is empty when first created, and grows by having entries inserted one by one. It turns out that users need four kinds of insertion operation: insertion of an entry at the front of the sequence, at the back, just before an existing entry, and just after. There is just one *delete* operation, however; it deletes a specified entry.

Traversal of a list $l$ is performed by the following code:

```
from x := l.first until l.nil_entry(x) loop
    visit(x.value);
    x := l.next(x)
end
```

---

**class interface** *LIST_ADT[VALUE_TYPE]*

    *entry_type*: *LIST_ADT_ENTRY[VALUE_TYPE]*;

    *empty*: *BOOLEAN*
        -- **true** if this list is empty, else **false**

    *nil_entry*(*x*: **like** *entry_type*): *BOOLEAN*
        -- **true** if *x* is a nil entry, else **false**

    *new_entry*(*value*: *VALUE_TYPE*): **like** *entry_type*
        -- A new entry containing *value*

    *insert_first*(*x*: **like** *entry_type*)
        -- Insert *x* at the front of this list

    *insert_last*(*x*: **like** *entry_type*)
        -- Insert *x* at the back of this list

    *insert_before*(*y*, *x*: **like** *entry_type*)
        -- Insert *x* just before *y* in this list

    *insert_after*(*y*, *x*: **like** *entry_type*)
        -- Insert *x* just after *y* in this list

    *append*(*other*: **like** *Current*)
        -- Append entries of *other* to this list, destroying *other*

    *split*(*x*: **like** *entry_type*): **like** *Current*
        -- Split this list at *x*, creating and returning a new list
        -- If *nil_entry*(*x*), the result list is empty and this list is unchanged
        -- If *x* = *first*, the result list is the whole list and this list is empty

    *delete*(*x*: **like** *entry_type*)
        -- Delete *x* from this list

    *first*: **like** *entry_type*
        -- First entry of this list

    *last*: **like** *entry_type*
        -- Last entry of this list

    *next*(*x*: **like** *entry_type*): **like** *entry_type*
        -- Entry after *x* in this list

    *prev*(*x*: **like** *entry_type*): **like** *entry_type*
        -- Entry before *x* in this list

**end** -- *LIST_ADT*

---

**Figure 5.1** Specification of the List ADT.

The *first* operation returns the first entry of the list, and *next(x)* returns the entry after *x*. The list may be traversed backwards by using *last* and *prev(x)* instead of *first* and *next(x)*. All these operations return a special value *x* such that *l.nil_entry(x)* is true when the requested entry does not exist, and this makes the traversal code very simple, and correct even when the list is empty. The value stored within entry *x* is *x. value*.

The *append(other)* operation attaches an entire list at the back of the current list. The *split(x)* operation is the inverse of this, splitting off the entries from *x* to the end and making a separate list out of them. If *x* is the first entry, this leaves an empty list behind; if *l.nil_entry(x)* is true, the new list is empty.

One operation has been deliberately omitted, because it turns out to be difficult to implement efficiently: *indexing*, or finding the *i*th entry of a list. Lists with an indexing operation are called *indexed lists*, and they are the subject of Section 7.8.

## Formal specification of the List ADT

The informal description of the List ADT just given is perhaps sufficient for most purposes. Still, a formal specification of List makes a good example and throws up some interesting issues.

As mentioned at the beginning of this chapter, the abstract value of a List is a sequence of entries $\langle a_1, a_2, \dots, a_n \rangle$. As usual, we will write *l* for this abstract value before some operation, and *l'* for the abstract value afterwards.

Let us begin with the formal specification of the *empty* operation:

-- *Pre*: **true**
*res* := *l.empty*
-- *Post*: $l' = l$ **and** $res = (l = \langle \rangle)$

The precondition states that *empty* may be called at any time; the postcondition states that *l* is unchanged by the operation, and that the result is true if and only if the list is empty.

Here is another specification, of *l.insert_first(x)*:

-- *Pre*: $l = \langle a_1, a_2, \dots, a_n \rangle$ **and** $x \notin l$
*l.insert_first(x)*
-- *Post*: $l' = \langle x, a_1, a_2, \dots, a_n \rangle$ **and** $x' = x$

The condition $l = \langle a_1, a_2, \dots, a_n \rangle$ does not constrain the value of *l* in any way; it just introduces some notation that is used when expressing the postcondition. So the precondition requires only that *x* not be an element of *l* already. In fact, *x* should not lie in *any* list initially, but expressing this stronger condition formally is quite awkward. Of course, another entry with the same value as *x.value* is permitted. Afterwards, the postcondition specifies that *x* has been added at the front, and that *x* remains unchanged.

The specification of *l.delete(x)* is quite similar:

-- *Pre*: $l = \langle a_1, \ldots, x, \ldots, a_n \rangle$
*l.delete(x)*
-- *Post*: $l' = \langle a_1, \ldots, a_n \rangle$ **and** $x' = x$

It states that *x* must lie in *l* initially, and that *l'* is *l* with *x* removed. Notice that deletion is not destruction: a final *x'* exists and may be used by subsequent operations.

Perhaps the most interesting specification is that for *append*:

-- *Pre*: $l = \langle a_1, \ldots, a_n \rangle$ **and** *other* $= \langle b_1, \ldots, b_m \rangle$ **and** $l \neq$ *other*
*l.append(other)*
-- *Post*: $l' = \langle a_1, \ldots, a_n, b_1, \ldots, b_m \rangle$

As before, the conditions $l = \langle a_1, \ldots, a_n \rangle$ and *other* $= \langle b_1, \ldots, b_m \rangle$ do not constrain the values of *l* and *other*, so the precondition states only that a list may not be appended to itself. The postcondition defines the effect of appending two lists.

It is significant that no mention is made of *other'*, the final value of *other*, in the postcondition of *append*. This means that *other'* is undefined, and the variable *other* must not be used after this operation. Implementations are therefore free to destroy the value held in *other* during the append, and the implementation presented below uses this freedom to make *append* very simple and efficient.

### Implementation of the List ADT

Although it is natural to think first of arrays when implementing any ADT whose mathematical entity is the sequence, it turns out that insertion and deletion cannot be implemented efficiently with an array. Insertion requires that every entry to the right of the insertion point be shifted right one place to create a gap, and conversely deletion requires them all to shift left one place to close up the gap created by the deletion. In the worst case, when the insertion or deletion point is at the left end of the array, the time complexity is $O(n)$ if there are *n* entries. This is unacceptable.

The usual and best implementation employs a *doubly linked list* of entries: each entry *x* contains references *x.prev_entry* and *x.next_entry* to its predecessor and successor in the sequence. The list as a whole is represented by a header containing just a reference to the first entry. For example, the list $l = \langle x_1, x_2, \ldots, x_n \rangle$ is represented like this:

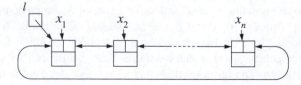

The double-ended arrows are the usual way to show double links, since to show the two references as two separate arrows makes the diagrams too cluttered. Notice that the first and last entries are linked together to form a circle. This clever arrangement permits $O(1)$ access to the back of the list, and turns out to simplify the code as well. An empty list is represented by a header containing a void reference; the special value $x$ that causes $l.nil\_entry(x)$ to return true is also a void reference.

It is not hard to work out how to implement the various operations, by drawing before-and-after diagrams. For example, consider inserting a new entry $x$ after a given entry $y$:

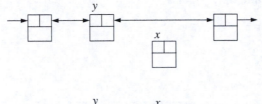

becomes

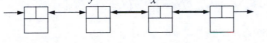

The only references that change are the four shown in bold, and so the cost is a highly efficient $O(1)$, very much better than the array implementation. Owing to the circular linking, $y$ may be the first, last, or even the only entry, without creating a special case.

Perhaps even more remarkably, two lists may be appended just as quickly:

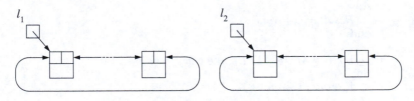

becomes

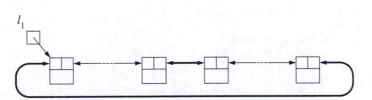

Again, only the four bold references change, and the cost is $O(1)$. In fact, every operation of the List ADT is easily implemented so as to have $O(1)$ worst-case time complexity. A complete implementation appears in Figure 5.2.

```
class LIST_DLL[VALUE_TYPE]

inherit

  LIST_ADT[VALUE_TYPE] redefine entry_type, out end;

feature { LIST_DLL }

  put_first(x: like entry_type) is
    do
      first := x
    end;

feature

  entry_type: LIST_DLL_ENTRY[VALUE_TYPE];

  first: like entry_type;

  empty: BOOLEAN is
    do
      Result := (first = Void)
    end;

  nil_entry(x: like entry_type): BOOLEAN is
    do
      Result := (x = Void)
    end;

  new_entry(v: VALUE_TYPE): like entry_type is
    do
      !!Result.make(v)
    end;

  insert_first(x: like entry_type) is
    do
      if first = Void then
        x.put_next_entry(x);
        x.put_prev_entry(x);
      else
        x.put_prev_entry(first.prev_entry);
        x.prev_entry.put_next_entry(x);
        x.put_next_entry(first);
        x.next_entry.put_prev_entry(x);
      end;
      first := x;
    end;
```

```
insert_last(x: like entry_type) is
    do
        if first = Void then
            x.put_next_entry(x);
            x.put_prev_entry(x);
            first := x
        else
            x.put_prev_entry(first.prev_entry);
            x.prev_entry.put_next_entry(x);
            x.put_next_entry(first);
            x.next_entry.put_prev_entry(x);
        end
    end;

insert_before(y, x: like entry_type) is
    do
        x.put_prev_entry(y.prev_entry);
        x.prev_entry.put_next_entry(x);
        x.put_next_entry(y);
        y.put_prev_entry(x);
        if first = y then first := x end;
    end;

insert_after(y, x: like entry_type) is
    do
        x.put_next_entry(y.next_entry);
        x.next_entry.put_prev_entry(x);
        x.put_prev_entry(y);
        y.put_next_entry(x);
    end;

append(other: like Current) is
    local
        last1, last2: like entry_type;
    do
        if first = Void then
            first := other.first
        elseif other.first = Void then
            -- do nothing
        else
            last1 := first.prev_entry;
            last2 := other.first.prev_entry;
            first.put_prev_entry(last2);
            other.first.put_prev_entry(last1);
            last1.put_next_entry(other.first);
            last2.put_next_entry(first);
        end
    end;
```

```
    split(x: like entry_type): like Current is
        local last1, last2: like entry_type;
        do
            if x = Void then -- do nothing
            elseif x = first then first := Void;
            else
                last1 := x.prev_entry;
                last2 := first.prev_entry;
                first.put_prev_entry(last1);
                x.put_prev_entry(last2);
                last1.put_next_entry(first);
                last2.put_next_entry(x);
            end
            !!Result;
            Result.put_first(x);
        end;

    delete(x: like entry_type) is
        do
            if x = first then
                if first.next_entry = first then first := Void
                else first := first.next_entry
                end
            end;
            x.prev_entry.put_next_entry(x.next_entry);
            x.next_entry.put_prev_entry(x.prev_entry);
        end;

    last: like entry_type is
        do
            if first = Void then Result := Void
            else Result := first.prev_entry end
        end;

    next(x: like entry_type): like entry_type is
        do
            if x.next_entry = first then Result := Void
            else Result := x.next_entry end
        end;

    prev(x: like entry_type): like entry_type is
        do
            if x = first then Result := Void
            else Result := x.prev_entry end
        end;

end -- LIST_DLL
```

**Figure 5.2** Implementation of the List ADT using a doubly linked list.

## 5.2 Stacks

A *stack* is a pile of things on top of each other, such as a pile of dinner plates:

The only plate that can be accessed or removed conveniently is the top one, and the only place where a plate can be added conveniently is on top.

Traditionally, adding to the top of a stack is called *pushing*, and removing from the top is called *popping*. These two operations characterize the Stack ADT (Figure 5.3). Formally, *push* inserts an entry at the back of the sequence, like *insert_last* for lists; *top* returns the last entry, like *last* for lists; and *pop* deletes the last entry, like *delete*(*last*) for lists.

This raises the question, why bother with stacks at all, if their work can be done by lists? Partly because a doubly linked list is not necessary to implement a stack, of which more later; but mainly because there are deep applications of stacks, and to pretend that they are lists would be to obscure their essential nature. The following examples give a good idea of the range of application of stacks.

When a routine begins to execute, some memory is set aside to hold its local variables and a few other things. This memory is called an *activation record*; it is needed while the routine is active, and is reclaimed when the routine returns.

---

**class interface** *STACK_ADT*[*VALUE_TYPE*]

    *entry_type*: *STACK_ADT_ENTRY*[*VALUE_TYPE*];

    *empty*: *BOOLEAN*
          -- **true** if this stack is empty, else **false**

    *new_entry*(*value*: *VALUE_TYPE*): **like** *entry_type*
          -- A new entry containing *value*

    *push*(*x*: **like** *entry_type*)
          -- Insert *x* on top of this stack

    *top*: **like** *entry_type*
          -- Top entry of this stack

    *pop*: **like** *entry_type*
          -- Delete and return the top entry of this stack

**end** -- *STACK_ADT*

---

**Figure 5.3** Specification of the Stack ADT.

For example, suppose there are three routines, *a*, *b*, and *c*:

|  *a* **is** | *b* **is** | *c* **is** |
|:---:|:---:|:---:|
| **do** | **do** | **do** |
| ... | ... | ... |
| *b*; | *c*; | **end**; |
| *b*; | ... | |
| ... | **end**; | |
| **end**; | | |

where the ellipses stand for code that does not contain any routine calls. When *a* begins, its activation record must be created:

*a*

When *a* calls *b* for the first time, the computer first stores in *a*'s activation record the memory address of the point where execution of *a* should resume after *b* returns. Then an activation record is created for *b*, and *b* begins to execute:

*a*        *b*

While *b* is running there may be no use for *a*'s activation record, but it must be kept because it will be needed after *b* returns and *a* resumes.

When *b* calls *c*, an activation record for *c* is created:

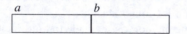

*a*        *b*        *c*

Now when *c* returns, its activation record is no longer required, so it is deleted:

*a*        *b*

and *b* resumes from the point just after the call to *c*.

It should be clear now that the activation records form a stack: when a routine begins, its activation record is pushed onto the stack, and when it ends, its activation record must be on top, and is popped. In abstract terms the trace so far has been

| Operation | Abstract value |
|---|---|
| | $\langle\rangle$ |
| something calls *a* | $\langle a \rangle$ |
| *a* calls *b* | $\langle a, b \rangle$ |
| *b* calls *c* | $\langle a, b, c \rangle$ |
| *c* returns | $\langle a, b \rangle$ |

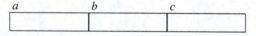

and it continues like this:

| | |
|---|---|
| $b$ returns | $\langle a \rangle$ |
| $a$ calls $b$ (2nd time) | $\langle a, b \rangle$ |
| $b$ calls $c$ | $\langle a, b, c \rangle$ |
| $c$ returns | $\langle a, b \rangle$ |
| $b$ returns | $\langle a \rangle$ |
| $a$ returns | $\langle \rangle$ |

What happens after $a$ returns does not concern us.

Stacks also arise when checking the syntax of input files. A simple example of this is the problem of determining whether a sequence of left and right parenthesis characters is *properly balanced*; that is, whether each left parenthesis has its matching right parenthesis, and conversely. For example, $(()())$ is properly balanced, but $())(()$ is not, even though the number of left and right parentheses is equal.

It turns out that there is a deep connection between this problem and the program tracing problem above. Suppose the symbol $($_r$ means 'routine $r$ begins' and $)_r$ means 'routine $r$ returns.' Then the trace of the program given above can be written as

$$(_a \; (_b \; (_c \; )_c \; )_b \; (_b \; (_c \; )_c \; )_b \; )_a$$

It is no accident that this sequence is properly balanced, because every routine begin has its corresponding return, and all calls that begin while a routine is active must end before it does.

A sequence of labeled parenthesis characters like the above can therefore be checked for proper balance in a single left-to-right scan by pretending that $($_r$ begins a routine $r$, and $)_r$ ends one. Each left parenthesis is pushed onto a stack; each right parenthesis causes one *pop* operation:

$$(_a \; (_b \; (_c \; )_c \; )_b \; (_b \; (_c \; )_c \; )_b \; )_a$$

| | |
|---|---|
| ↑ | $\langle \rangle$ |
| ↑ | $\langle (_a \rangle$ |
| ↑ | $\langle (_a, (_b \rangle$ |
| ↑ | $\langle (_a, (_b, (_c \rangle$ |
| ↑ | $\langle (_a, (_b \rangle$ |
| ↑ | $\langle (_a \rangle$ |
| ↑ | $\langle (_a, (_b \rangle$ |
| ↑ | $\langle (_a, (_b, (_c \rangle$ |

and so on. If some right parenthesis attempts to pop an empty stack, or if the popped item's label does not match, or if the stack is not empty at the end, then the sequence is not properly balanced.

The program trace may also be represented by an ordered tree (Section 6.1):

Because of this correspondence, stacks also arise naturally in tree traversal, in the form of recursive routine calls (Section 6.2).

## Implementation of the Stack ADT

Since the Stack ADT operations are essentially a subset of the List operations, a doubly linked list may of course be used to implement Stack as well as List. However, there are even simpler implementations than this.

A linked implementation needs just one reference in each entry:

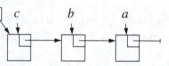

The back of the sequence is at the front of the singly linked list. A push produces

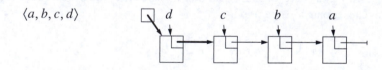

Only the bold references have changed. Popping is even simpler; it just moves the reference in the header one step to the right. These operations are both $O(1)$.

The other implementation in common use is an array of entries:

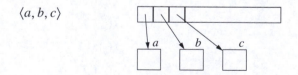

The *push* operation places a reference to the new entry in the first free position and increments a count of the number of entries:

$\langle a, b, c, d \rangle$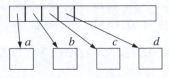

The *pop* operation just decrements this count. Again, all operations have $O(1)$ cost, except that, on the rare occasions when the array is full, *push* must first resize it before performing the insertion.

Both implementations are so simple and efficient that it is difficult to find good reasons for preferring one to the other. An array has no memory overhead when full so is a good choice when there are many very small entries. The linked implementation is used for activation records (compiler writers call these links *dynamic pointers*), although memory for the records is allocated contiguously in a way reminiscent of the array implementation.

## 5.3 Queues

Queues are used in computing as they are in real life, to ensure fair access to some scarce resource, such as a bank teller, a supermarket checkout, or the central processing unit of a computer. If there is no reason to give priority to one claimant over another, the time-honored 'first come first served' rule applies, and queues provide it.

There are also applications where queues are used for reasons other than fairness. These include merge sorting (Section 9.3), radix sorting (Section 9.5), and breadth-first search in graphs (Section 11.5).

Traditionally, to join the back of a queue is to be *enqueued*, and to leave the front is to be *dequeued*. These two operations characterize the Queue ADT (Figure 5.4). The *append* operation is not normally considered to belong to this ADT, but several applications turn out to require it, and it can be efficiently implemented, so it has been included. Abstract values are sequences, with *enqueue* inserting at the right, and *dequeue* deleting at the left:

| Operation | Abstract value |
|---|---|
| | $\langle \rangle$ |
| *enqueue(a)* | $\langle a \rangle$ |
| *enqueue(b)* | $\langle a, b \rangle$ |
| *enqueue(c)* | $\langle a, b, c \rangle$ |
| *dequeue* | $\langle b, c \rangle$ |
| *enqueue(d)* | $\langle b, c, d \rangle$ |
| *enqueue(e)* | $\langle b, c, d, e \rangle$ |
| *dequeue* | $\langle c, d, e \rangle$ |

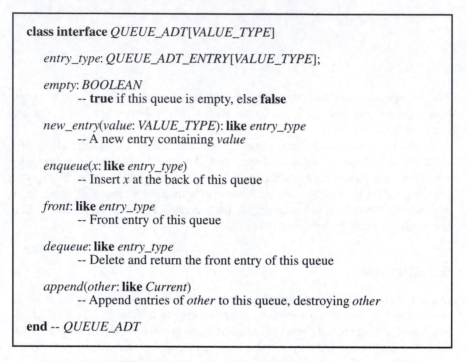

**class interface** *QUEUE_ADT[VALUE_TYPE]*

    *entry_type*: *QUEUE_ADT_ENTRY[VALUE_TYPE]*;

    *empty*: *BOOLEAN*
        -- **true** if this queue is empty, else **false**

    *new_entry(value*: *VALUE_TYPE)*: **like** *entry_type*
        -- A new entry containing *value*

    *enqueue(x*: **like** *entry_type)*
        -- Insert *x* at the back of this queue

    *front*: **like** *entry_type*
        -- Front entry of this queue

    *dequeue*: **like** *entry_type*
        -- Delete and return the front entry of this queue

    *append(other*: **like** *Current)*
        -- Append entries of *other* to this queue, destroying *other*

**end** -- *QUEUE_ADT*

**Figure 5.4** Specification of the Queue ADT.

and so on. This ensures that the entries emerge in the order they were inserted. Queues are often called *fifo queues* or *first-in-first-out queues* to distinguish them from the priority queues of Chapter 8, and to contrast their behavior with the last-in-first-out behavior of stacks.

## Implementation of the Queue ADT

Since the operations of the Queue ADT are essentially a subset of the operations of List, once again a doubly linked list may be used to implement the Queue ADT. As with stacks, however, the simpler operations of Queue open the way for simpler implementations.

    The best linked implementation is a circular singly linked list with a header containing a reference to the last entry:

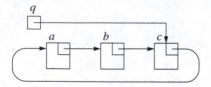

This clever arrangement allows access to the back and front in $O(1)$ time in a way that is very economical in space. A dequeue in the above structure yields

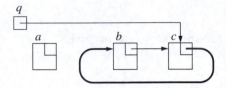

Only one reference (shown in bold) has changed. An enqueue now produces

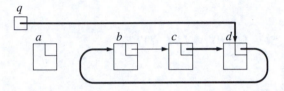

in which the three emboldened references have been changed. An empty queue is represented by a header containing a void reference, and the implementation must treat it as a special case.

The code for this implementation of the Queue ADT appears in Figure 5.5. It contains no loops and no recursion, and so all operations, including *append*, have $O(1)$ time complexity.

There is also a very efficient array implementation of Queue, but again some cleverness is needed. Enqueueing is as easy as pushing in stacks:

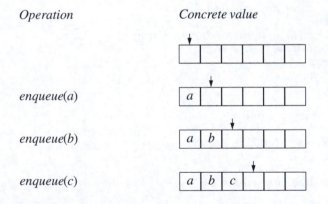

However, *dequeue* must remove the leftmost entry, and this leaves a very awkward empty space at the left:

```
class QUEUE_SLL[VALUE_TYPE]

inherit

    QUEUE_ADT[VALUE_TYPE] redefine entry_type, out end;


feature { QUEUE_SLL }

    last: like entry_type;

feature

    entry_type: QUEUE_SLL_ENTRY[VALUE_TYPE];

    empty: BOOLEAN is
        do
            Result := (last = Void)
        end;

    new_entry(v: VALUE_TYPE): like entry_type is
        do
            !!Result.make(v)
        end;

    enqueue(x: like entry_type) is
        do
            if last = Void then
                x.put_next_entry(x);
            else
                x.put_next_entry(last.next_entry);
                last.put_next_entry(x);
            end;
            last := x;
        end;

    front: like entry_type is
        do
            Result := last.next_entry
        end;

    dequeue: like entry_type is
        do
            Result := last.next_entry;
            if last.next_entry = last then
                last := Void
            else
                last.put_next_entry(last.next_entry.next_entry)
            end;
        end;
```

```
append(other: like Current) is
    local
        other_first: like entry_type;
    do
        if last = Void then
            last := other.last
        elseif other.last = Void then
            -- do nothing
        else
            other_first := other.last.next_entry;
            other.last.put_next_entry(last.next_entry);
            last.put_next_entry(other_first)
            last := other.last;
        end
    end;

end -- QUEUE_SLL
```

**Figure 5.5** Implementation of the Queue ADT using a circular singly linked list.

This space could be eliminated by shifting the remaining entries one step to the left, but since that would take $O(n)$ time, it is better to let the gap remain, and introduce a second array index marking the left-most entry:

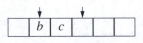

As further enqueues and dequeues occur, the interval between the indexes containing entries drifts to the right:

*enqueue(d)*

*enqueue(e)*

*dequeue*

*dequeue*

*enqueue(f)*

As shown, eventually the entries arrive at the right-hand end of the array.

One natural solution to the problem of what to do next is to shift all the entries back to the left end. Unfortunately, this is very bad when the array is almost full:

```
class QUEUE_ARRAY[VALUE_TYPE]

inherit

    QUEUE_ADT[VALUE_TYPE] redefine entry_type, out end;

creation

    make

feature { QUEUE_ARRAY }

    first, free: INTEGER;

    entries: ARRAY[like entry_type];

    array_size: INTEGER;

feature

    entry_type: QUEUE_ARRAY_ENTRY[VALUE_TYPE];

    initial_array_size: INTEGER is 100;

    make is
        do
            array_size := initial_array_size;
            !!entries.make(0, array_size − 1);
        end;

    empty: BOOLEAN is
        do
            Result := (first = free)
        end;

    new_entry(v: VALUE_TYPE): like entry_type is
        do
            !!Result.make(v)
        end;

    front: like entry_type is
        do
            Result := entries.item(first)
        end;

    dequeue: like entry_type is
        do
            Result := entries.item(first)
            first := (first + 1) \\ array_size;
        end;
```

```
enqueue(x: like entry_type) is
    local
        i, j: INTEGER;
    do
        entries.put(x, free);
        free := (free + 1) \\ array_size;
        if first = free then
            j := array_size – 1;
            array_size := array_size * 2;
            entries.resize(0, array_size – 1);
            from i := array_size – 1 until j < free loop
                entries.put(entries.item(j), i);
                i := i – 1;
                j := j – 1;
            end;
            first := i + 1;
        end;
    end;

append(other: like Current) is
    do
        from until other.empty loop
            enqueue(other.dequeue)
        end;
    end;

end -- QUEUE_ARRAY
```

**Figure 5.6** Implementation of the Queue ADT using a circular array of entries.

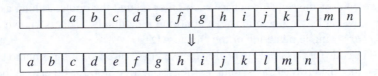

In this example, after just two more *enqueue* and *dequeue* operations, another shift becomes necessary. In general, with *n* entries and an array of size *m*, there will be one $O(n)$ shift every $m – n$ enqueues, which is unacceptable if $m – n$ is small.

The right solution, a very clever one, is to imagine that the array is bent into a circular shape so that the last slot is followed by the first:

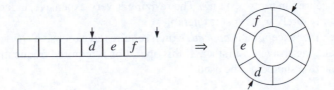

Now further operations are easy:

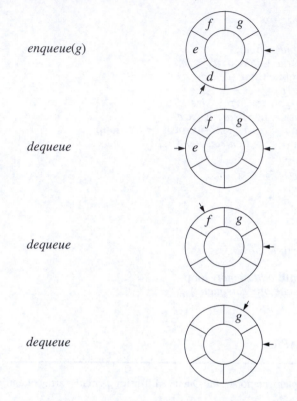

*enqueue(g)*

*dequeue*

*dequeue*

*dequeue*

The two ends of the sequence chase each other around the circle; as long as some space is available, the operations can continue indefinitely. This is known as the *circular array* implementation of the Queue ADT.

The code for this implementation appears in Figure 5.6. It turns out to be best to insist that the array always contain at least one free slot, for otherwise the case when the two indices (called *first* and *free* in the implementation) are equal could mean, curiously, either that the array is empty or that it is full. This condition is guaranteed by extending the array to twice its previous size whenever an *enqueue* operation threatens to consume the last free slot.

With two exceptions, the operations of the array implementation have $O(1)$ worst-case time complexity. The first exception is *enqueue* in the case where the operation causes an array resizing. The resizing is very expensive, in fact $O(n)$, but it occurs only rarely so its cost is tolerable.

The other exception is *append*, which requires an expensive $O(n)$ copy of the entries from one array into another. If this operation is required frequently, the array implementation should not be used.

## 5.4 Exercises

5.1    Perform an abstract trace (that is, showing sequences of entries, not any implementation) of the following operations from the List ADT:

> *l.make*;
> *a := l.new_entry("a")*;
> *b := l.new_entry("b")*;
> *c := l.new_entry("c")*;
> *d := l.new_entry("d")*;
> *e := l.new_entry("e")*;
> *l.insert_first(a)*;
> *l.insert_last(b)*;
> *l.insert_before(b, c)*;
> *l.insert_after(b, d)*;
> *l.insert_last(e)*;
> *l.delete(b)*;
> *l.insert_after(a, b)*;
> *x := l.first*;
> *x := l.next(x)*;
> *x := l.next(x)*;
> *x := l.next(x)*;
> *x := l.next(x)*;
> *x := l.next(x)*;
> *m := l.split(c)*;
> *l.append(m)*;

5.2    Complete the formal specification of the List ADT using preconditions and postconditions that was begun in Section 5.1.

5.3    Using the List ADT, write a program to find the largest element in a sequence of integers represented as a list of entries, each containing one integer.

5.4    Again using List, write a function

> *union(l1, l2: LIST_ADT): LIST_ADT*

which takes two sorted sequences of distinct integers, represented by lists, and returns a new sorted sequence which is the union of the two given lists. For example, given ⟨3, 6, 9⟩ and ⟨2, 4, 6, 8⟩, the result is to be ⟨2, 3, 4, 6, 8, 9⟩. The function should work correctly when one or both of the lists is empty, and it should not destroy its two parameters like *append* does.

5.5    Perform an abstract trace (that is, showing sequences of entries, not any implementation) of the following operations from the Stack ADT:

> *s.make*;
> *a := s.new_entry("a")*;
> *b := s.new_entry("b")*;

```
c := s.new_entry("c");
s.push(a);
s.push(b);
x := s.top;
x := s.pop;
s.push(c);
x := s.pop;
x := s.pop;
```

5.6    Give a formal specification of the Stack ADT using preconditions and postconditions as done for the List ADT in Section 5.1.

5.7    Use the Stack ADT in the implementation of a non-recursive program which prints a file of numbers in reverse order. For example, if the input is

   23 56 12 90 43

then the output should be

   43 90 12 56 23

5.8    Use the Stack ADT in the implementation of the algorithm for checking sequences of labeled parentheses that was described in Section 5.2.

5.9    Perform an abstract trace (that is, showing sequences of entries, not any implementation) of the following operations from the Queue ADT:

```
q.make;
a := q.new_entry("a");
b := q.new_entry("b");
c := q.new_entry("c");
d := q.new_entry("d");
e := q.new_entry("e");
f := q.new_entry("f");
s.enqueue(a);
s.enqueue(b);
x := s.dequeue;
s.enqueue(c);
x := s.dequeue;
s.enqueue(d);
s.enqueue(e);
x := s.dequeue;
s.enqueue(f);
x := s.dequeue;
x := s.dequeue;
x := s.dequeue;
```

Then perform a concrete trace of the same operation sequence using (a) the circular singly linked list implementation and (b) the circular array implementation with an array of size 4.

5.10   Give a formal specification of the Queue ADT using preconditions and postconditions as done for the List ADT in Section 5.1.

5.11   *Least-recently-used page replacement.* Virtual memory systems create an illusion of an unlimited main memory space by keeping pages (1024-byte segments of memory) on disk and moving them into main memory as needed. If main memory is full, some other page must be swapped out, and a good candidate is the least recently used page. Show how a List of pages can be used to keep track of which page is least recently used.

5.12   *Find-the-mouse.* Modern high-resolution display screens have *windows*: rectangular areas of the screen, each with the ability to carry out tasks independently of the others. There is a background window covering the whole screen, and windows may partly or totally hide it or other windows. Thus, every point on the screen lies inside at least one window; if it lies in several windows, it is deemed to belong to the window that is currently hiding the other windows at that point. A variety of commands for rearranging windows is provided:

> **class interface** *WINDOW_MANAGER*
>
> *new_window(x, y, xsize, ysize: INTEGER): WINDOW*;
> *bring_to_top(w: WINDOW)*;
> *change_window(w: WINDOW; x, y, xsize, ysize: INTEGER)*;
> *delete_window(w: WINDOW)*;
> *which_window(x, y: INTEGER): WINDOW*;
>
> **end** -- *WINDOW_MANAGER*

The *new_window* operation creates a new window with the given position and size, and returns an internal name for the window for use by later operations on that window. The *bring_to_top* operation brings a partially hidden window fully into view; *change_window* changes the position and size of a window, including a *bring_to_top* operation on it. The *delete_window* operation deletes a window. The last operation, *which_window*, is the most interesting one. It returns the name of the window to which the point $(x, y)$ currently belongs, and it is used to determine which window the mouse is currently pointing into. Since it is likely that there will be only a few windows, efficiency is of little concern in this application. Find a simple way to remember which windows are on top of which.

5.13   Define and implement an ADT for polynomials with one variable. Include addition, multiplication, and evaluation operations. Give a representation invariant and abstraction function for your implementation, and determine its worst-case time complexity.

5.14 *Sparse matrices.* The simplest way to implement matrices is to use a two-dimensional array. However, in many applications the matrices are *sparse*: very large, but with most of the entries equal to 0. In such cases, a linked representation may be more efficient:

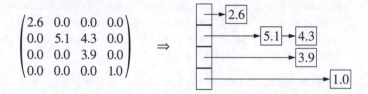

Define an ADT for matrices with addition, transposition, and multiplication operations (at least), and implement it using this linked representation. You may find transposition useful when implementing multiplication. How does your implementation's efficiency compare with the array implementation?

# Chapter 6

# Trees

The use of trees to organize information is far older than the computer. A table of contents, for example, is a tree:

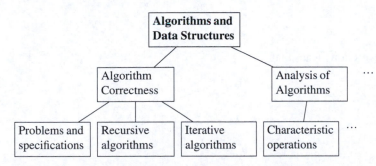

This structure permits related subjects to be grouped together and subdivided to any level of detail. It is also used to organize large numbers of people into a *hierarchy*. Armies, each with their general at the top and private soldiers at the bottom, are notable examples of hierarchies.

The structure of expressions in algebra is described naturally by trees:

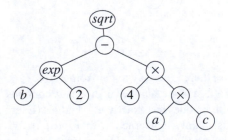

This shows the structure of the expression $\sqrt{b^2 - 4ac}$. More generally, *parse trees* are used in compiler construction and the theory of formal languages to describe the structure of a complex sequence of characters, such as a computer program.

Trees also arise when processes branch as time passes. Nature's trees are of this kind, as are family trees and evolutionary trees.

## 6.1 Definitions

A tree (also called a *free tree*) is formally defined to be a set of *vertices* (also called *nodes*) connected by *edges* (or *links*) so that there is exactly one way to get from any vertex to any other vertex:

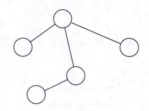

This restriction means that

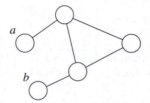

is not a tree because there are two ways to get from $a$ to $b$, and

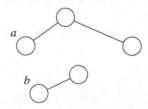

is not a tree because there is no way to get from $a$ to $b$.

The *size* of a tree is the number of nodes it contains. It turns out that every non-empty tree with $n$ nodes has exactly $n - 1$ edges (Exercise 6.1).

This book is mainly concerned with *rooted trees*, which are trees with a distinguished node called the *root*. Rooted trees have the advantage of a simple recursive definition:

A rooted tree consists of a *root node* and a finite set of *subtrees*, which are themselves rooted trees.

It is conventional to draw rooted trees with their root node at the top and the subtrees side by side below it:

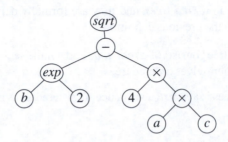

This diagram shows a rooted tree whose root node contains *sqrt*. This node has one subtree, whose root node contains −; that node has two subtrees, and so on.

In a rooted tree, every node has a unique *parent* (the node just above it in the tree), except the root which has no parent. The set of *ancestors* of a node *x* is recursively defined as *x* together with the ancestors of its parent, if any:

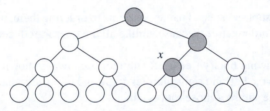

These nodes form a *path* from *x* up to the root of the tree. A *proper ancestor* of *x* is an ancestor of *x* other than *x* itself. The *children* of a node *x* are the roots of the subtrees of *x*, or equivalently those nodes whose parent is *x*. Two nodes are *siblings* if they share the same parent. The set of *descendants* of a node *x* consists of *x* together with all the descendants of its children:

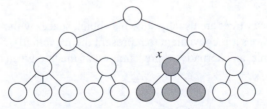

These nodes, together with the edges that join them, form the subtree whose root is *x*, denoted $T_x$. A *proper descendant* of *x* is a descendant of *x* other than *x* itself.

Often the order in which the subtrees of a tree are shown is important. This is true of expression trees, for example, since

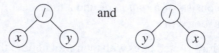

and

are certainly different: one represents $x/y$, the other represents $y/x$. Trees with this property are called *ordered trees*, and they are formally defined by replacing 'set' with 'sequence' in the previous definition:

> An ordered tree consists of a *root node* and a finite sequence of *subtrees*, which are themselves ordered trees.

A set of rooted trees is a *forest*; a sequence of ordered trees is an *ordered forest*.

## Binary trees

The binary tree is yet another variation on the theme, one with many applications:

> A *binary tree* is either empty or else it consists of a *root node* and two subtrees, called the *left subtree* and the *right subtree*, which are themselves binary trees.

Giving the two subtrees special names amounts to ordering them, but the binary tree is not a kind of ordered tree, because, unlike all the trees introduced above, a binary tree may be empty.

When drawing binary trees, left subtrees are always shown at the end of an edge slanting to the left, and right subtrees at the end of an edge slanting to the right. For example, the subtree whose root is $c$ in

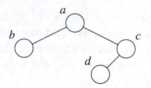

is a right subtree.

Empty binary trees are usually shown as blank spaces with no edge leading to them, but sometimes it is convenient to represent them explicitly, so that they can be seen. For example, an alternative representation of the tree given above is

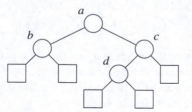

in which the empty subtrees appear as square nodes. The square nodes are also called *external nodes*, and the set of all external nodes of a binary tree $T$ is denoted $E(T)$. The square node version is sometimes called an *extended* binary tree. The round nodes are called *internal nodes*, and $I(T)$ denotes the set of internal nodes of $T$. A binary tree with $n$ internal nodes has $n + 1$ external nodes (Exercise 6.2). The extended version of the empty tree looks like this:

□

We often drop the word 'internal,' speaking, for example, of a tree with $n$ nodes, meaning $n$ internal nodes.

## 6.2 Operations on trees

The specification of a basic binary tree ADT appears in Figure 6.1. Its design may be called 'node-oriented,' meaning that the operations are performed on entries, which are either nodes of the tree or nil, rather than on subtrees. This seems to be the most convenient approach in practice for users of the ADT, and is most consistent with other standard ADTs such as List.

First come operations *new_entry(value)* and *new_nil_entry* for creating a new entry with a given value, and a new nil entry which has no value. The *nil_entry(x)* operation determines whether or not entry $x$ is a nil entry; if not, $x.value$ is its associated value.

The *empty* operation determines whether or not the entire tree is empty; *root* is the root of the tree, or nil if the tree is empty. The *put_root(x)* operation changes the root to $x$; in fact, it changes the entire tree to whatever tree has $x$ for its root.

The *left_child(x)* operation returns the left child of entry $x$; the result may be nil, but $x$ itself must not be nil. The *put_left_child(x, y)* operation changes the left child of $x$ to $y$; as with *put_root(x)*, this actually changes the entire left subtree to be whatever tree is rooted at $y$. If $y$ is nil this makes the left subtree empty. There are similar operations applying to the right child.

This ADT may be implemented very simply, and very economically in space, by storing two references in each entry, to the left and right child. The tree as a whole is represented by an object containing just a reference to the root, which will be nil if the tree is empty. Using this representation, the operations are trivial assignments and tests on these references, so the code is omitted.

The operations of this ADT have been limited to the most basic ones possible. The following subsections explore other operations which together constitute what might be called an extended binary tree ADT.

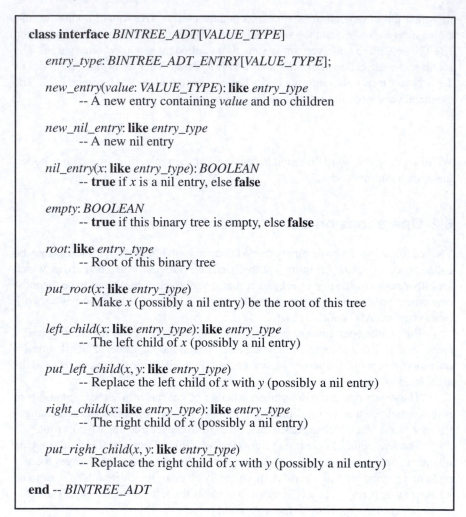

**class interface** *BINTREE_ADT[VALUE_TYPE]*

*entry_type*: *BINTREE_ADT_ENTRY[VALUE_TYPE]*;

*new_entry(value*: *VALUE_TYPE)*: **like** *entry_type*
    -- A new entry containing *value* and no children

*new_nil_entry*: **like** *entry_type*
    -- A new nil entry

*nil_entry(x*: **like** *entry_type)*: *BOOLEAN*
    -- **true** if *x* is a nil entry, else **false**

*empty*: *BOOLEAN*
    -- **true** if this binary tree is empty, else **false**

*root*: **like** *entry_type*
    -- Root of this binary tree

*put_root(x*: **like** *entry_type)*
    -- Make *x* (possibly a nil entry) be the root of this tree

*left_child(x*: **like** *entry_type)*: **like** *entry_type*
    -- The left child of *x* (possibly a nil entry)

*put_left_child(x, y*: **like** *entry_type)*
    -- Replace the left child of *x* with *y* (possibly a nil entry)

*right_child(x*: **like** *entry_type)*: **like** *entry_type*
    -- The right child of *x* (possibly a nil entry)

*put_right_child(x, y*: **like** *entry_type)*
    -- Replace the right child of *x* with *y* (possibly a nil entry)

**end** -- *BINTREE_ADT*

**Figure 6.1** Specification of the Binary Tree ADT.

## Traversal

To traverse a data structure is to travel over it, visiting each entry exactly once. This is more challenging in trees than in lists, because trees offer no natural linear sequence to follow. To avoid repetition, the traversal algorithms are presented for binary trees, and discussed briefly for rooted trees afterwards.

Of the many possible ways to traverse a binary tree, three are particularly important because they follow the recursive definition of the binary tree very closely. These three traversal algorithms are called *preorder*, *inorder*, and *postorder*:

*preorder_traversal(x*: **like** *entry_type*) **is**
     -- Traverse the subtree rooted at *x* in preorder
  **do**
    **if not** *nil_entry(x)* **then**
       *visit(x)*;
       *preorder_traversal(left_child(x))*;
       *preorder_traversal(right_child(x))*
    **end**
  **end**;

*inorder_traversal(x*: **like** *entry_type*) **is**
     -- Traverse the subtree rooted at *x* in inorder
  **do**
    **if not** *nil_entry(x)* **then**
       *inorder_traversal(left_child(x))*;
       *visit(x)*;
       *inorder_traversal(right_child(x))*
    **end**
  **end**;

*postorder_traversal(x*: **like** *entry_type*) **is**
     -- Traverse the subtree rooted at *x* in postorder
  **do**
    **if not** *nil_entry(x)* **then**
       *postorder_traversal(left_child(x))*;
       *postorder_traversal(right_child(x))*;
       *visit(x)*
    **end**
  **end**;

A binary tree may be empty, in which case there are no nodes to visit. Otherwise, the tree consists of a root node which must be visited, and two subtrees which must be traversed. The three algorithms do exactly this, differing only in the order of their steps: preorder visits the root first, postorder visits it last, and inorder visits it in between the two subtree traversals.

Here is an example of a binary tree with its nodes numbered in preorder:

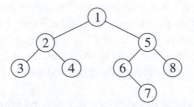

The root is visited first, and every node in the left subtree is visited before every node in the right subtree. This applies recursively to each subtree. Traversing the same tree in inorder produces this numbering:

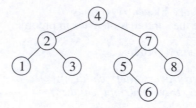

with the root visited after every node in the left subtree, but before every node in the right subtree; again, this applies recursively in both subtrees. In effect, the nodes are visited from left to right. Finally, postorder gives

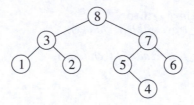

in which the root is visited last.

These traversals produce interesting results on expression trees:

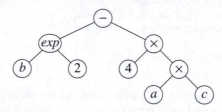

If visiting a node means printing its contents, a preorder traversal of this tree gives

$$- \; exp \; b \; 2 \times 4 \times a \; c$$

This is called the *prefix form* of the expression, because operators appear before the expressions they apply to. Prefix form has the curious property of being unambiguous despite the absence of parentheses, as can be shown by working from right to left: $\times a \; c$ can only mean $a \times c$, then $\times 4 \times a \; c$ can only mean $4 \times (a \times c)$, and so on. Prefix form is also the natural way to store trees in files, because there is a very simple recursive algorithm for reconstructing a rooted tree from its prefix form (Exercise 6.14).

Inorder traversal of the tree gives the familiar *infix form* of the expression:

$$b \; exp \; 2 - 4 \times a \times c$$

Of course, parentheses need to be added to resolve ambiguities. It is not difficult to print out suitable parentheses during the inorder traversal (Exercise 6.13):

$$((( \, b \, ) \, exp \, ( \, 2 \, )) - (( \, 4 \, ) \times (( \, a \, ) \times ( \, c \, ))))$$

Printing only the essential parentheses is a more difficult problem.

Postorder traversal gives *postfix form*:

$b \; 2 \; exp \; 4 \; a \; c \times \times -$

This is a suitable order in which to visit the nodes when evaluating the expression. For example, the − operation clearly must be done last; and in general any operation can be done only after the values of its operands have been calculated. This amounts to visiting each node after traversing its subtrees, which postorder does.

Preorder and postorder apply naturally to rooted trees: preorder visits the root then traverses each subtree, postorder traverses the subtrees then visits the root. The basic idea even applies to arbitrary graphs, where it is known as depth-first search (Section 11.6). Inorder does not extend so naturally to rooted trees, although one can visit the root repeatedly, between each pair of subtree traversals.

### Non-recursive traversals

Although preorder, inorder, and postorder traversals are defined recursively, it is often more convenient to implement them iteratively, in the style of the *first* and *next* operations from the List ADT:

> **from** $x := t.inorder\_first$ **until** $t.nil\_entry(x)$ **loop**
> $\quad visit(x);$
> $\quad x := t.inorder\_next(x)$
> **end**

The *inorder_first* operation must find the first node visited by the inorder traversal of tree $t$, and *inorder_next(x)* must find the node visited next after $x$. Similar operations may be defined for preorder and postorder. This form of traversal may easily be started or stopped halfway through, done simultaneously on two trees of different shapes, and so on.

A larger example helps to understand these operations:

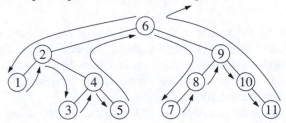

The arrows show each step of the traversal.

Of course, *inorder_first* is easy to implement since it just finds the leftmost node. If the tree is empty, there is no first node and the result of *inorder_first* is a nil entry. Implementing *inorder_next(x)* is harder, since the pattern is not easy to see at first. If $x$ has a right child, then an inorder traversal must go that way, and the next node is the leftmost in $x$'s right subtree:

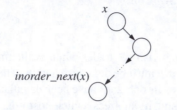

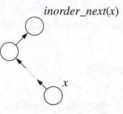

There may be zero or more left steps after the right step. If $x$ has no right child, some thought shows that the next node is reached by going upwards to the first right-moving upward step:

There may be zero or more left-moving steps before the right-moving step, which itself will not occur the very last time. See Figure 6.2 for an implementation. The *inorder_next(x)* operation needs to move upwards from $x$ in the case when $x$ has no right child, and the code accomplishes this by means of a *parent(x)* operation which returns the parent of $x$. Since this is not implementable in any reasonable time with the basic binary tree ADT, it is natural at this point to define an Extended Binary Tree ADT which includes a *parent* operation, the above and perhaps other traversal operations, and the *delete* operation presented next. The formal definition of this ADT is omitted; the implementation is easily accomplished by means of a third reference in each entry, to the parent.

## Deletion

Deletion of the subtree rooted at some node $x$ is of course quite trivial, but the problem considered here is to delete a node but not its subtrees. Even this would be simple enough if the remaining fragments could be linked together into any tree at all. However, in practice it is usually expected that the remaining nodes preserve their inorder sequence, and this complicates the problem.

If the node $x$ to be deleted has no children, it can simply be removed:

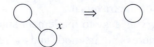

```
inorder_first: like entry_type is
    do
        if empty then
            Result := Void
        else
            from Result := root until left_child(Result) = Void loop
                Result := left_child(Result)
            end
        end
    end;

inorder_next(x: like entry_type): like entry_type is
    do
        if right_child(x) /= Void then
            from Result := right_child(x) until left_child(Result) = Void loop
                Result := left_child(Result)
            end
        else
            from Result := x until
                Result = root or else left_child(parent(Result)) = Result
            loop
                Result := parent(Result)
            end;
            if Result = root then
                Result := Void
            else
                Result := parent(Result)
            end
        end
    end;
```

**Figure 6.2** Implementation of the *inorder_first* and *inorder_next* operations from the Extended Binary Tree ADT.

If *x* has one child, remove *x* and make its child the child of *x*'s parent:

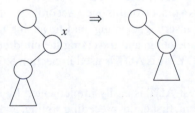

A moment's thought shows that the inorder sequence of the remaining nodes is not disturbed in either case.

If *x* has two children, there are several possible approaches. For efficiency of subsequent operations it is desirable not to increase the depth of any node. The usual way to accomplish this begins by finding $x$'s inorder predecessor $y$, which (since $x$ has a left child) must be the rightmost node of $x$'s left subtree. This node is then deleted; since it has no right child, this involves applying one of the first two cases above. Finally, $y$ is substituted for $x$ and $x$ is removed. For example, this is what happens when the node containing $j$ is deleted from this tree:

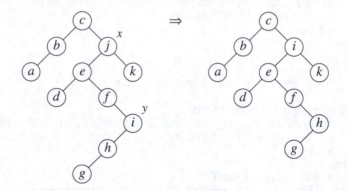

The inorder predecessor of $j$ is $i$. The implementation of this algorithm (Figure 6.3) is rather messy and error-prone; not only are there the three cases just given, but the third case itself includes the special case of $y$ being the left child of $x$. The parent of $x$ must be known, and this requires parent references, so *delete* is placed most naturally in the Extended Binary Tree ADT introduced earlier in this section. Alternatively, in some circumstances, such as the binary search trees of Section 7.4, it may be possible to find the parent of $x$ with a search downwards from the root.

## Operations on ordered trees

We close this section with a glance at one ADT that might be used with ordered trees. In fact, the ADT presented in Figure 6.4 is for an ordered forest (a sequence of ordered trees). Since the roots form a sequence of arbitrary length, and the children of any node also form a sequence of arbitrary length, it is natural to use the List ADT from Section 5.1 as a model for this one. Accordingly, the Ordered Forest ADT contains operations for inserting, deleting, and traversing the roots of the forest's trees, and for inserting, deleting, and traversing the children of any node, in ways copied from the List ADT. This ADT is used in Section 8.6 in the implementation of Fibonacci heaps.

The Ordered Forest ADT is easily implemented by storing four references in each entry, to the parent, first child, preceding sibling, and following sibling. All operations may be implemented so as to have $O(1)$ time complexity. It is convenient to make the sequence of roots, and the sequence of children of each node, into Lists (Section 5.1), for then most of the work can be done by List operations. The code for this implementation is very simple and is omitted.

```
put_left(x, y: like entry_type) is
    do
        x.put_left_child(y);
        if y /= Void then y.put_parent(x) end
    end;


put_right(x, y: like entry_type) is
    do
        x.put_right_child(y);
        if y /= Void then y.put_parent(x) end
    end;


delete(x: like entry_type) is
    local
        y, t: like entry_type;
    do

        -- find y, the new (possibly nil) root, and fix up its subtree
        if x.left_child = Void then
            y := x.right_child
        elseif x.right_child = Void then
            y := x.left_child
        elseif x.left_child.right_child = Void then
            y := x.left_child;
            put_right(y, x.right_child)
        else
            y := inorder_prev(x);
            delete(y);
            put_left(y, x.left_child);
            put_right(y, x.right_child)
        end

        -- replace x by y as the child of its parent
        if x = root then
            root := y;
            if y /= Void then y.put_parent(Void) end
        elseif x.parent.left_child = x then
            put_left(x.parent, y)
        else
            put_right(x.parent, y)
        end;
        put_left(x, Void);
        put_right(x, Void)
    end;
```

**Figure 6.3** Implementation of the *delete* operation from the Extended Binary Tree ADT.

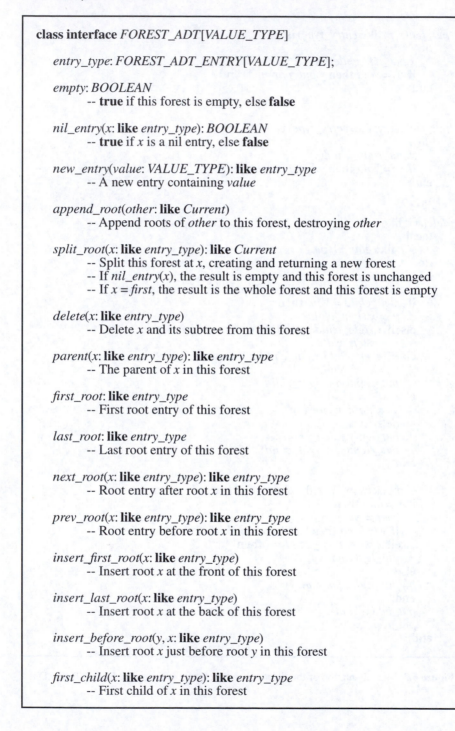

**class interface** *FOREST_ADT[VALUE_TYPE]*

*entry_type*: *FOREST_ADT_ENTRY[VALUE_TYPE]*;

*empty*: *BOOLEAN*
-- **true** if this forest is empty, else **false**

*nil_entry(x*: **like** *entry_type)*: *BOOLEAN*
-- **true** if *x* is a nil entry, else **false**

*new_entry(value*: *VALUE_TYPE)*: **like** *entry_type*
-- A new entry containing *value*

*append_root(other*: **like** *Current)*
-- Append roots of *other* to this forest, destroying *other*

*split_root(x*: **like** *entry_type)*: **like** *Current*
-- Split this forest at *x*, creating and returning a new forest
-- If *nil_entry(x)*, the result is empty and this forest is unchanged
-- If *x = first*, the result is the whole forest and this forest is empty

*delete(x*: **like** *entry_type)*
-- Delete *x* and its subtree from this forest

*parent(x*: **like** *entry_type)*: **like** *entry_type*
-- The parent of *x* in this forest

*first_root*: **like** *entry_type*
-- First root entry of this forest

*last_root*: **like** *entry_type*
-- Last root entry of this forest

*next_root(x*: **like** *entry_type)*: **like** *entry_type*
-- Root entry after root *x* in this forest

*prev_root(x*: **like** *entry_type)*: **like** *entry_type*
-- Root entry before root *x* in this forest

*insert_first_root(x*: **like** *entry_type)*
-- Insert root *x* at the front of this forest

*insert_last_root(x*: **like** *entry_type)*
-- Insert root *x* at the back of this forest

*insert_before_root(y, x*: **like** *entry_type)*
-- Insert root *x* just before root *y* in this forest

*first_child(x*: **like** *entry_type)*: **like** *entry_type*
-- First child of *x* in this forest

*last_child(x*: **like** *entry_type*): **like** *entry_type*
    -- Last child of *x* in this forest

*next_child(y, x*: **like** *entry_type*): **like** *entry_type*
    -- Child of *y* after *x* in this forest

*prev_child(y, x*: **like** *entry_type*): **like** *entry_type*
    -- Child of *y* before *x* in this forest

*insert_first_child(y, x*: **like** *entry_type*)
    -- Insert entry *x* as the first child of *y* in this forest

*insert_last_child(y, x*: **like** *entry_type*)
    -- Insert entry *x* as the last child of *y* in this forest

*insert_before_child(y, z, x*: **like** *entry_type*)
    -- Insert entry *x* as the child of *y* before *z* in this forest

*insert_after_child(y, z, x*: **like** *entry_type*)
    -- Insert entry *x* as the child of *y* after *z* in this forest

**end** -- *FOREST_ADT*

**Figure 6.4** Specification of the Ordered Forest ADT.

## 6.3 Mathematical properties of trees

Two trees of equal size (number of nodes) may differ dramatically in shape, in ways that are important to understand because of their effects on the time complexity of algorithms. This section explores the shape of trees.

The *height* $h(x)$ of a node *x* in a rooted tree is the number of nodes on the longest path leading downwards from *x*, including *x* itself. In a binary tree, the external nodes are defined to have height 0. For example, the following binary tree has heights written inside its nodes:

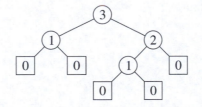

The height $h(T)$ of a rooted or binary tree *T* is the height of its root.

There is a natural association between the height of a tree and the worst-case time complexity of some operations on it. For example, if the tree above were a binary search tree (Section 7.4), the worst-case time complexity of a search in it would be $h(T)$, or three comparisons between keys.

The *depth* $d(x)$ of a node $x$ is the number of edges on the path from the root to $x$. Alternatively, it is the number of nodes on this path, excluding $x$ itself. For example, the following binary tree has depths written inside its nodes:

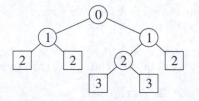

The *internal path length* $i(T)$ of a rooted tree $T$ is the sum of the depths of the internal nodes of $T$:

$$i(T) = \sum_{x \in I(T)} d(x)$$

The *external path length* $e(T)$ of a binary tree $T$ is the sum of the depths of the external nodes of $T$:

$$e(T) = \sum_{x \in E(T)} d(x)$$

For example, the binary tree above has $i(T) = 4$ and $e(T) = 12$. Internal and external path length are often connected with average complexity. They are closely related, as the following theorem shows.

**Theorem 6.1:** Let $T$ be a binary tree with $n$ internal nodes, where $n \geq 0$. Then $e(T) = i(T) + 2n$.
**Proof:** by induction on $n$.
**Basis step:** $n = 0$. Then $T$ is empty, $e(T) = i(T) = 0$, and the theorem holds.
**Inductive step:** Assume the theorem holds for all binary trees with $j$ nodes, for all $j$ such that $0 \leq j \leq k$. Let $T$ be an arbitrary binary tree with $k + 1$ nodes. Since $T$ is non-empty, it has the form

$T =$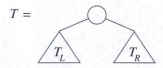

where $T_L$ has $i$ nodes (say), and so $T_R$ has $k - i$ nodes. Since $0 \leq i \leq k$,

$$e(T_L) = i(T_L) + 2i \tag{6.3.1}$$

by the inductive hypothesis applied to $T_L$; and since $0 \leq k - i \leq k$,

$$e(T_R) = i(T_R) + 2(k - i) \tag{6.3.2}$$

by the inductive hypothesis applied to $T_R$. Now every external node is one level deeper in $T$ than it is in $T_L$ or $T_R$. Since there are $k + 2$ external nodes in $T$,

$$e(T) = e(T_L) + e(T_R) + k + 2 \tag{6.3.3}$$

Similarly, the $k$ internal nodes of $T_L$ and $T_R$ are each one level deeper in $T$, and the root of $T$ has depth 0, so

$$i(T) = i(T_L) + i(T_R) + k \tag{6.3.4}$$

Putting these four identities together gives

$$e(T) = e(T_L) + e(T_R) + k + 2$$

by (6.3.3),

$$= i(T_L) + 2i + i(T_R) + 2(k - i) + k + 2$$

by (6.3.1) and (6.3.2),

$$= i(T_L) + i(T_R) + 3k + 2$$

and finally

$$= i(T) + 2(k + 1)$$

by (6.3.4), so the theorem holds for all binary trees with $k + 1$ nodes. $\qquad\square$

## Skew trees

Among all binary trees with $n$ nodes, there will be some whose internal path length is maximal. These are called *skew trees*. By Theorem 6.1, these trees will also have maximal external path length. This definition can be made more concrete as follows:

**Theorem 6.2:** A binary tree is a skew tree if and only if every node in it has at most one internal node among its children.

**Proof:** First, we must prove that if $T$ is a skew tree, then every node $x$ in it has at most one internal node among its children. An equivalent statement is the contrapositive: if node $x$ of tree $T$ has more than one internal node among its children, then $T$ cannot be a skew tree. Let $x$ be such a node, and let $y$ be any external node lying in the right subtree of $x$:

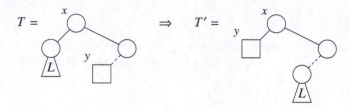

Exchanging $y$ with $L$, the left subtree of $x$, produces a new tree $T'$ as shown. In $T'$, the internal nodes of $L$ are deeper than they were in $T$; all other internal nodes are at the same depth in both trees. Therefore $i(T) < i(T')$, so $T$ is not a skew tree.

Conversely, we must prove that if every node of $T$ has at most one internal node among its children, then $T$ is skew. Consider the set $S$ of all trees $T$ with the property that every node of $T$ has at most one internal node among its children. For example,

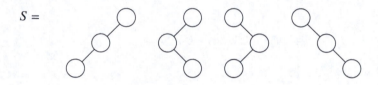

when $n = 3$. By the first part of this proof, the skew trees must lie in $S$. But the trees in $S$ all have equal internal path length: $i(T) = 0 + 1 + \cdots + n - 1 = n(n - 1)/2$, so they all have maximal internal path length, and they are all skew. $\square$

Skew trees also have maximal height, namely $h(T) = n$ (Exercise 6.4).

## Complete trees

At the other extreme, among all binary trees with $n$ nodes there will be some whose internal path length (and hence external path length) is minimal. These are called *complete trees*, and they can be characterized as follows:

**Theorem 6.3:** A binary tree is a complete tree if and only if there exists a number $q$ such that every external node in the tree has depth $q$ or $q + 1$.

**Proof:** First, it must be shown that if $T$ is a complete tree, then the number $q$ exists. We prove the contrapositive: if no $q$ exists, then $T$ is not complete.

If $q$ does not exist, then there must be at least two external nodes $x$ and $y$ whose depths differ by at least two. Assuming without loss of generality that $d(x) < d(y)$, we exchange $x$ with $y$'s parent, yielding a new tree $T'$:

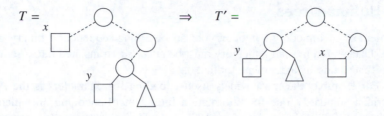

The only internal nodes affected are the descendants of $y$'s parent. These nodes all rise at least one level, so $i(T) > i(T')$, which proves that $T$ is not a complete tree.

Conversely, we must prove that, if a number $q$ exists such that every external node of $T$ has depth $q$ or $q + 1$, then $T$ is complete. This follows as in Theorem 6.2 from the fact that the external path lengths of all such trees are equal. $\quad\square$

For example, here are two complete trees ($n = 10$):

It is clear that all complete trees $T$ with $n$ nodes have equal height. Examination of examples reveals that when $n = 2^k - 1$, $h(T) = k$; while when $n = 2^k$, $h(T)$ jumps to $k + 1$. The appropriate formula is therefore $h(T) = \lceil \log_2(n + 1) \rceil$, which holds for $n \geq 0$. It can be shown that all binary trees $T$ with $n$ nodes have height $h(T) \geq \lceil \log_2(n + 1) \rceil$ (Exercise 6.5), so complete trees have minimal height as well as minimal path length.

The exact formula for the external path length of a complete tree is rather messy (Exercise 6.6), but the following approximation is good enough for most purposes. For all external nodes $x$, $h(T) - 1 \leq d(x) \leq h(T)$, and summing this over the $n + 1$ external nodes of $T$ yields

$$(n + 1)(\lceil \log_2(n + 1) \rceil - 1) \leq e(T) \leq (n + 1)\lceil \log_2(n + 1) \rceil$$

The following theorem summarizes the results of this section.

**Theorem 6.4:** For any binary tree $T$ with $n \geq 0$ internal nodes, or equivalently with $n + 1$ external nodes,

$$\lceil \log_2(n + 1) \rceil \leq h(T) \leq n$$
$$(n + 1)(\lceil \log_2(n + 1) \rceil - 1) - 2n \leq i(T) \leq n(n - 1)/2$$
$$(n + 1)(\lceil \log_2(n + 1) \rceil - 1) \leq e(T) \leq n(n - 1)/2 + 2n$$

$\quad\square$

## 6.4 Huffman trees

The memory of a modern computer consists of a long sequence of binary values (bits). Data stored in such a memory must be *encoded*: translated into a sequence of bits that stands, by agreement, for that data.

For example, the most widely used encoding for characters is the ASCII (American Standard Code for Information Interchange) encoding, in which $a$ is encoded as 1100001, $b$ is encoded as 1100010, and so on. Every code sequence is 7 bits long, so ASCII can encode up to $2^7 = 128$ distinct characters.

By choosing an encoding other than ASCII it is possible to reduce the amount of computer memory needed to store a file (sequence of characters) considerably. This idea is called *data compression*, and the best known data compression technique is *Huffman coding*, the subject of this section.

In a Huffman code the bit sequences assigned to the characters may vary in length. The best way to see that this can be done without confusion is to represent the encoding as a whole by a binary tree called the *encoding tree*. For example, here is part of the ASCII encoding tree:

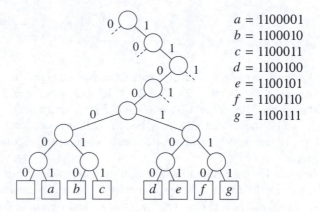

$a = 1100001$
$b = 1100010$
$c = 1100011$
$d = 1100100$
$e = 1100101$
$f = 1100110$
$g = 1100111$

Left branches are labeled 0, right branches are labeled 1, and each external node contains the character whose code labels the path from the root to that node, if any. For example, the path to $a$ in the tree above is labeled 1-1-0-0-0-0-1, which is the ASCII code for $a$.

Now consider this encoding:

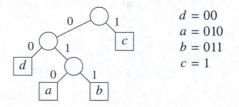

$d = 00$
$a = 010$
$b = 011$
$c = 1$

For example, *add* would be encoded as 0100000 using this encoding. To decode this bit sequence, start at the root of the tree. Since the first bit is 0, go left. Since the second bit is 1, go right. After three bits we arrive at the external node containing *a*, so declare the first character to be *a*, return to the root, and repeat. An encoding which can be represented by an encoding tree in this way is called a *prefix encoding*, because no code is a prefix (initial subsequence) of any other code.

In a prefix encoding, the length of an encoded sequence of characters depends only on how many times each character appears. For example, in the sequence *cdabcddcccc*, *d* occurs three times and its code has length 2 (using the encoding just above), so $3 \times 2$ bits are contributed by *d* characters, and altogether the length is $3 \times 2 + 1 \times 3 + 1 \times 3 + 5 \times 1 = 17$ bits.

In general, let $S$ be the sequence of characters to be encoded, let $w(x)$ be the number of occurrences of the character $x$ in $S$, and let $d(x)$ be the depth in the encoding tree $T$ of the external node containing $x$. Then the length in bits of the encoded sequence is

$$L = \sum_{x \in E(T)} w(x)d(x)$$

For a given fixed sequence of characters $S$, the *optimal prefix encoding problem* is to find the encoding tree $T$ that minimizes $L$.

This problem can be reformulated in a way that is independent of the particular application to optimal encodings. Let $T$ be a binary tree, and attach a *weight* (non-negative real number) $w(x)$ to each external node $x$. Define $wepl(T)$, the *weighted external path length of* $T$, by

$$wepl(T) = \sum_{x \in E(T)} w(x)d(x)$$

For a fixed multiset of $n \geq 1$ weights, it can be asked which trees with those weights attached have minimum weighted external path length. For example, if the weights are $\{1, 1, 3, 5\}$, then

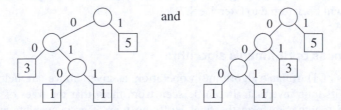

both have minimum weighted external path length, namely 17. Trees of minimum weighted external path length are called *Huffman trees*, after the discoverer of the algorithm given below. Notice that if the weights are all 1 then $wepl(T) = e(T)$, and the Huffman trees are exactly the complete trees.

The algorithm due to Huffman (1952) for finding trees of minimum weighted external path length is a miracle of simplicity. At the heart of the algorithm is a *forest* (set of trees) $F$, which is initially composed entirely of external nodes, one for each given weight. Each tree $T$ in $F$ has a weight $w(T)$ associated with it, which is just the sum of the weights of the external nodes of $T$. This weight is conventionally written in the root of $T$. The algorithm selects two trees of minimum weight from $F$ and combines them into one. This step is repeated until only one tree is left.

For example, given the weights $\{3, 1, 1, 5\}$, the forest at the start of each iteration of the loop is

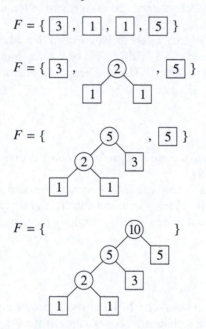

and the algorithm has produced one of the Huffman trees we saw earlier. This algorithm uses the Priority Queue ADT of Chapter 8, so its implementation and analysis will be deferred to Exercise 8.7.

## Correctness of Huffman's algorithm

Examples of Huffman's algorithm in operation, as given above, are helpful when guessing its loop invariant. It can be seen from them that the trees of $F$ can be combined together to form the final Huffman tree. Ties in weights are broken arbitrarily by the algorithm, so the final tree is not unique. This leads to

'The trees of $F$ can be combined into a Huffman tree for the weights $\{w_1, w_2, \ldots, w_n\}$'

for the loop invariant. This is clearly true initially, and when the loop terminates, it implies that the sole remaining tree is a Huffman tree. So it is a promising choice, and we are further encouraged by the realization that, if correct, this loop invariant would show that Huffman's algorithm is an incremental algorithm of the second kind (Section 4.2).

Call $F$ a *fringing forest* for $T$ whenever, by a sequence of zero or more combinings of the kind done by Huffman's algorithm, the trees of $F$ may be converted into $T$. Here is a proof that the proposed loop invariant is correct. The correctness of Huffman's algorithm follows immediately.

**Theorem 6.5 (Loop invariant of Huffman's algorithm):** At the beginning of the $k$th iteration of the loop in Huffman's algorithm, $F$ is a fringing forest for some Huffman tree for the weights $w_1, w_2, \dots, w_n$.
**Proof:** by induction on $k$.
**Basis step:** At the beginning of the first iteration, $F = \{\boxed{w_1}, \boxed{w_2}, \dots, \boxed{w_n}\}$, which is certainly a fringing forest for some Huffman tree for the weights $w_1, w_2, \dots, w_n$; in fact, it is a fringing forest for every tree with these weights.
**Inductive step:** The inductive hypothesis is that, at the beginning of the $k$th iteration of the loop of Huffman's algorithm, $F = \{T_1, T_2, \dots\}$ is a fringing forest for some Huffman tree $T$ for the weights $w_1, w_2, \dots, w_n$. It must be shown that this is true of the forest (call it $F'$) at the beginning of the next iteration of the loop.

Let $z$ be any internal node of $T$, excluding the nodes of $F$, such that $z$ has maximal depth. Then the two children of $z$ must be roots of trees in $F$, so

$T =$

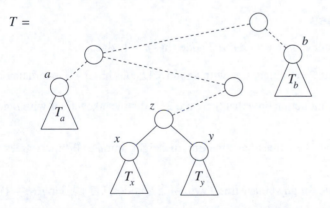

where $T_a$, $T_b$, $T_x$, and $T_y$ are all in $F$, and $T_a$ and $T_b$ are the trees selected from $F$ by Huffman's algorithm.

Since $z$ is of maximal depth outside $F$, $d(a) \le d(x)$; since $T_a$ was chosen by Huffman's algorithm, $w(T_a) \le w(T_x)$. These two conditions imply that $T_a$ and $T_x$ may be exchanged without increasing $wepl(T)$ (nor decreasing it, since $wepl(T)$ is minimum by assumption). Similarly, $T_b$ may be exchanged with $T_y$, and so the tree

$T' =$

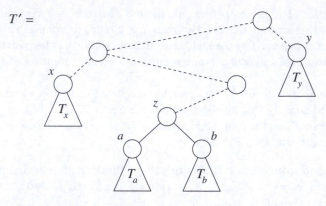

has $wepl(T') = wepl(T)$. This proves that $T'$ is also a Huffman tree for the weights $w_1, w_2, \ldots, w_n$. But

$F' = \{$ 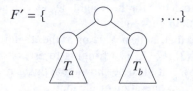 $, \ldots\}$

is a fringing forest for $T'$, so the theorem is true for $F'$.  □

## 6.5 Exercises

6.1 Prove that every tree with $n \geq 1$ nodes has $n - 1$ edges.

6.2 Prove that every binary tree with $n$ internal nodes has $n + 1$ external nodes.

6.3 Prove by induction on $n$ that there are $2^{n-1}$ distinct skew trees with $n$ nodes, for $n \geq 1$.

6.4 Prove that skew trees have maximum height among all binary trees with $n$ nodes.

6.5 Prove that, for any binary tree $T$ with $n \geq 0$ nodes, $h(T) \geq \lceil \log_2(n + 1) \rceil$.

6.6 Develop an exact formula for the external path length of a complete binary tree with $n$ nodes.

6.7 Show $i(T) = \sum_{x \in I(T)} s(x)$, where $s(x)$ is the size of the subtree rooted at $x$.

6.8 There are algorithms, such as those used with the AVL trees introduced by Adel'son-Vel'skii and Landis (1962) and with splay trees (Section 7.5), that attempt to keep binary trees balanced by performing *rotations* on them. A *Type I rotation* does this:

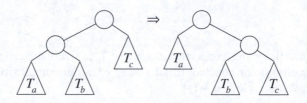

A *Type II rotation* does this:

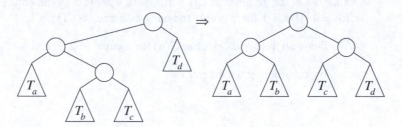

Both forms have mirror images that need not be considered further. In these diagrams, the subtrees may be empty, but the nodes shown must exist. When will a Type I rotation reduce the internal path length? When will a Type II rotation reduce it? Give the simplest conditions that you can.

6.9   Define the *size balance* of a node $x$ in a binary tree to be the size of its right subtree minus the size of its left subtree. For example, the following tree has size balances written inside its nodes:

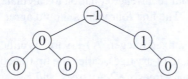

A binary tree is said to be *size-balanced* if the size balance of every node is either $-1, 0$, or $1$. Show that every size-balanced binary tree is complete, and that the converse does not hold.

6.10   There is a strong connection between the binary search of an array of $n$ elements, such as

| 2.5 | 3.7 | 5.9 | 6.1 | 6.3 | 9.8 |
|-----|-----|-----|-----|-----|-----|

and a certain binary tree $T_n$, which in this example is

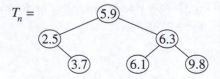

$$T_n =$$

Investigate this connection, show that $T_n$ is size-balanced (see the previous question), and conclude that the worst-case time complexity of binary search is $W(n) = \lceil \log_2(n + 1) \rceil$.

6.11 This question aims to find out how many distinct binary trees there are with $n$ nodes. Let this number be $C(n)$. If $n = 0$, there is only the empty tree, so $C(0) = 1$. If $n = 1$, there is only the one-node tree, so $C(1) = 1$.

(a) Draw all trees and calculate $C(n)$ for $n$ equal to 2, 3, and 4.

(b) By considering the diagram

$$T =$$

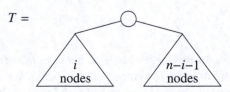

find a recurrence equation for $C(n)$. Its solution is beyond the scope of this book. The numbers $C(n)$ are called *Catalan numbers*; they are a standard example of the solution of recurrence equations by generating functions.

(c) Use your recurrence equation to calculate $C(n)$ for $n$ equal to $1, 2, 3, 4,$ and 5. The first four values should agree with the values above.

6.12 Let $t \geq 2$ be a fixed integer. A $t$-ary tree is either empty or else it consists of a root node and $t$ $t$-ary trees, called the first, second, ..., and $t$th subtrees. For example, binary trees are 2-ary trees, and

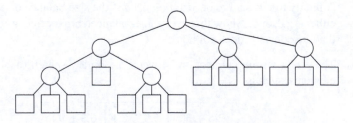

is a 3-ary tree. Develop a version of Theorem 6.4 for $t$-ary trees.

6.13 Adapt the inorder traversal algorithm from Section 6.2 to print out a binary expression tree in inorder, with parentheses to make the grouping clear. Given precedences for the various operations, can you find a way to print only the essential parentheses?

6.14 Design a simple recursive algorithm to read in a tree from a file, assuming that the tree was stored, without parentheses, in prefix order, and that the number of children of each node can be deduced easily from the node (for example, in an expression tree, a '+' node has two children, and a 'sqrt' node has one child).

6.15 *Level-order* is a useful tree traversal method, not discussed in the text, which first visits the root, then each of its children, then their children, and so on, visiting the nodes in order of increasing depth. It applies to any rooted tree. Use the Queue ADT in the design of an algorithm which visits all the nodes of a rooted tree in level-order.

6.16 In many applications of trees, the nodes are generated as the tree is traversed, rather than being fixed in advance. For example, game trees that record all possible moves in a game such as chess are generated by game playing programs in this way.

Such trees may have infinite depth, which creates problems for pre-order, inorder, and postorder traversals. However, level-order (Exercise 6.15) fares better, because although the traversal is still infinite, at least level-order is guaranteed to reach any nominated vertex in a finite amount of time.

However, even level-order will lose this important property if some nodes have infinitely many children. Implement a 'diagonal' traversal algorithm which at any moment has explored the first subtree of any node to depth at most $k$, the second to depth at most $k - 1$, the third to depth at most $k - 2$, and so on. Use it to list the set of all pairs of positive integers, and then the set of all sequences of zero or more positive integers, in such a way that any nominated pair or sequence is guaranteed to appear in a finite amount of time.

6.17 At each stage of Huffman's algorithm, a tree is constructed by combining two previously constructed trees. Let the tree constructed during the $i$th loop iteration be $T_i$, for $1 \leq i \leq n - 1$. Prove that

$$w(T_i) \leq w(T_{i+1})$$

$(1 \leq i < n - 1)$; that is, that the trees have monotone increasing weight.

6.18 Using the previous question, find an $O(n)$ implementation of Huffman's algorithm, assuming that the initial weights are given in sorted order.

# Chapter 7

# Symbol Tables

The Symbol Table ADT, which is the subject of this chapter, takes its name from program compilation, where it is used to record the variables of a program, together with their type, address, and so on. Symbol table operations are also fundamental to database systems, and the hash table and B-tree data structures discussed here are among the most popular for implementing databases on external storage devices.

## 7.1 Specification

A *symbol table* is an ADT whose mathematical entity is a set of *entries*, each containing a *key* and a *value*. Each key uniquely identifies its entry (in other words, the keys alone form a set).

Figure 7.1 contains a specification. First come two operations which apply to individual entries. The *new_entry(key, value)* operation returns a new entry with the given key and value. Given an entry $x$, the key and value may be obtained at any time by *x.key* and *x.value*. The second operation, *nil_entry(x)*, determines whether $x$ is the special nil entry, in which case it has no key or value.

After these come the four operations which characterize this ADT: *make*, which initializes the symbol table to empty; *insert(x)*, which inserts an entry into the symbol table; *retrieve(key)*, which retrieves the entry whose key is *key* from the symbol table; and *delete(x)*, which deletes entry $x$. Note that *retrieve(key)* does not delete the entry it retrieves; also, if there is no entry with the given key, *retrieve(key)* returns the special nil entry instead.

A symbol table can also be viewed as a mapping (function) from keys to values. The mapping is changed by insertions and deletions, and accessed by retrievals.

Occasionally additional operations are needed, based on an ordering of the keys. There are a variety of possible operations of this type; Figure 7.2 contains

130

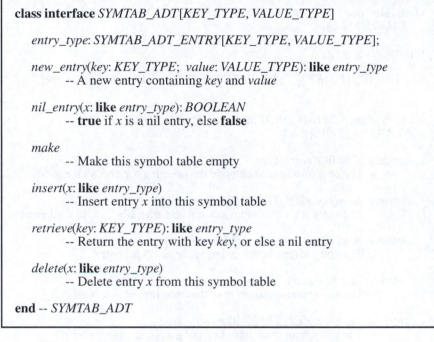

**Figure 7.1** Specification of the Symbol Table ADT.

six typical ones. The *retrieve_first* operation retrieves the entry with minimum key; *retrieve_from(key)* retrieves the entry with minimum key not less than the given key; and *retrieve_next(x)* retrieves the entry whose key is next in order to the key of *x*. The other three operations are similar but work in reverse order. All these operations return a nil entry if the desired entry does not exist.

As an example of the use of these operations, the following code retrieves from symbol table *s* all entries *x* whose keys lie in the range $a \leq key \leq b$:

```
from x := s.retrieve_from(a) until s.nil_entry(x) or else x.key > b loop
    visit(x);
    x := s.retrieve_next(x)
end
```

A symbol table with extra operations like these is called an *ordered symbol table*.

## 7.2 Linked lists

When it is known that the symbol table will always be small (say, containing no more than about 20 entries), it is not worthwhile to use the elaborate implementations that appear in the following sections. A simple list of entries is sufficient:

---

**class interface** *SYMTAB_ORDERED_ADT[KEY_TYPE -> COMPARABLE,*
 *VALUE_TYPE]*

**inherit**

 *SYMTAB_ADT[KEY_TYPE, VALUE_TYPE]* **redefine** *entry_type* **end**;


 *entry_type*: *SYMTAB_ORDERED_ADT_ENTRY[KEY_TYPE,*
  *VALUE_TYPE]*;

 *retrieve_first*: **like** *entry_type*
   -- The first (minimum) entry in the ordering, or else a nil entry

 *retrieve_from(key*: *KEY_TYPE)*: **like** *entry_type*
   -- The entry with minimum key not less than *key*, or else a nil entry

 *retrieve_next(x*: **like** *entry_type)*: **like** *entry_type*
   -- The entry after *x* in the ordering, or else a nil entry

 *retrieve_last*: **like** *entry_type*
   -- The last (maximum) entry in the ordering, or else a nil entry

 *retrieve_upto(key*: *KEY_TYPE)*: **like** *entry_type*
   -- The entry with maximum key not greater than *key*, else nil

 *retrieve_prev(x*: **like** *entry_type)*: **like** *entry_type*
   -- The entry before *x* in the ordering, or else a nil entry

**end** -- *SYMTAB_ORDERED_ADT*

---

**Figure 7.2** Specification of the Ordered Symbol Table ADT. The **inherit** clause means that this ADT contains all of the features of the Symbol Table ADT plus these additional ones. The notation *KEY_TYPE -> COMPARABLE* means that implementations may assume that keys may be compared using '<'.

The entries could be in sorted order, but since this complicates the code slightly and has no significant effect on efficiency, sorting is not recommended unless ordered symbol table operations are required.

The operations are easily implemented using the List ADT from Section 5.1, so they will not be given here in any detail. For the record, however, here is *retrieve(key)*:

*retrieve*(*key*: *KEY_TYPE*): **like** *entry_type* **is**
   **do**
      **from**
         *Result* := *list.first*
      **until**
         *list.nil_entry*(*Result*) **or else** *Result.key* = *key*
      **loop**
         *Result* := *list.next*(*Result*)
      **end**
   **end**

Retrieval clearly has $O(n)$ complexity, making this implementation unsuitable for all but small tables, containing perhaps twenty or thirty entries at most. The next section describes an interesting variant of the method.


## 7.3  Locality of reference and self-adjusting lists

In the context of symbol tables, *locality of reference* is the name given to the tendency for retrievals of a given symbol to cluster together in the operation sequence.

Locality of reference is hard to quantify, but it is very common. For example, when a compiler encounters the statement $n := n + 1$, two retrievals of the symbol $n$ will be generated, one immediately following the other. Customers of a bank may request two or three transactions on their accounts within a minute or two, then not visit the bank again for a week.

If significant locality of reference is expected, it may be worthwhile to adapt the implementation to take advantage of it. One simple way to do this, which applies to any data structure, is to remember the most recently accessed entry (an *access* is an insertion or retrieval). The first step in a retrieval is to compare the key being searched for with the key of the remembered entry. If they are equal, a search of the data structure has been avoided. Several entries could be remembered, and a check made of all of them before searching the data structure. A computer's memory is generally organized in this way; the set of remembered entries is called a *cache memory* by computer architects, and it is very effective in reducing the average cost of accessing memory.

Operation sequences are not obliged to exhibit locality of reference, so in the worst case no advantage is gained from this scheme, and in fact we are slightly worse off. Our interest in it arises from our conviction that, if a probability model of operation sequences which incorporated the locality of reference that occurs in real sequences could be constructed, then the average complexity analysis would show that the method has value. Of course, the usual problems of finding credible probability models may prevent this analysis from being done; but there might be empirical evidence to support our conviction. Methods like 'remember the most recently accessed entry,' whose advantages seem real but not readily quantifiable, are called *heuristics*.

These ideas will now be applied to the unsorted linked list.  For example:

In practice, every insertion is preceded by a retrieval which checks that no entry with the new key is present, and it will be convenient to include this check in the cost of the insertion by making the insertion at the back of the list (in the example above, after *pop*), after scanning along it to make the check.  The cost of this insertion will be taken to be $n + 1$, although only $n$ comparisons between keys are made.

To retrieve an entry, search along the list.  The cost of retrieving the $i$th entry is $i$ comparisons between keys.

It is not hard to think of a variety of plausible heuristics for improving the performance of this data structure; research has concentrated on three:

*Move-to-front (MF)*:  After accessing an entry, move it to the front of the list.

*Transpose (T)*:  After accessing an entry, if it is not the first entry then exchange it with its predecessor in the list.

*Frequency count (FC)*:  Record in each entry the number of times it has been accessed, and keep the list sorted into non-increasing order of this number.

The rationale for each of these heuristics should be clear.  Move-to-front expects the accessed entry to be accessed again very soon; if this happens immediately, the second access will cost only 1.  Transpose has similar ideas, but is more timid about disturbing the status quo.  Frequency count expects some entries to be accessed more often than others, but bases its decisions on the entire history of the operation sequence, rather than on the hope of exploiting locality of reference.  A linked list with a heuristic like these is called a *self-adjusting* (or *self-organizing*) list.

All self-adjusting lists have a worst-case complexity of $O(n)$ per operation, for the simple reason that, no matter how cleverly the list is reordered, there is always an entry at the back, and it could be the one that is accessed next.  (This type of observation is called an *adversary argument*, and is studied in Section 13.2.)  Self-adjusting lists are therefore unsuitable as symbol table implementations in their own right, but they can be used to improve the performance of the lists in a chained hash table (Section 7.7).

## Analysis of self-adjusting lists

An interesting way to compare the performance of these heuristics has been found by Sleator and Tarjan (1985a).  Their analysis suggests that move-to-front may well be the best choice.

A self-adjusting list heuristic is said to be *admissible* if it takes the form, 'after accessing an entry, move it zero or more places forward in the list.'  No restriction is placed on how the amount of movement is determined, so move-to-front, transpose, and frequency count are all admissible; in fact, it is hard to imagine how any reasonable heuristic could fail to be admissible. The movement of an entry one step forward in the list is called an *exchange*.

For any heuristic $H$ and sequence of symbol table operations $p$, let $C_H(p)$ be the total cost of the sequence when applied to a self-adjusting list with heuristic $H$. Similarly, let $E_H(p)$ be the total number of exchanges made.

**Theorem 7.1:** For any admissible heuristic $H$, and any sequence $p$ of $m$ insertions and successful retrievals, starting with the empty list,

$$C_{MF}(p) \le 2C_H(p) - E_H(p) - m$$

That is, the total cost under the move-to-front heuristic is never more than twice the cost under any other admissible heuristic.

**Proof:** The idea behind this proof is to run *MF* and *H* side by side on $p$, comparing the costs incurred on each operation. At each intermediate moment, the two lists will contain the same entries, but in different orders. For example, if $H$ is Transpose:

|  | *MF* | *T* |
| --- | --- | --- |
| *insert(a)* | $a$ | $a$ |
| *insert(b)* | $b \to a$ | $b \to a$ |
| *insert(c)* | $c \to b \to a$ | $b \to c \to a$ |
| *insert(d)* | $d \to c \to b \to a$ | $b \to c \to d \to a$ |
| *retrieve(d)* | $d \to c \to b \to a$ | $b \to d \to c \to a$ |
| *retrieve(a)* | $a \to d \to c \to b$ | $b \to d \to a \to c$ |
| *retrieve(a)* | $a \to d \to c \to b$ | $b \to a \to d \to c$ |

The total costs are

$$C_{MF}(p) = 1 + 2 + 3 + 4 + 1 + 4 + 1 = 16$$

and

$$C_T(p) = 1 + 2 + 3 + 4 + 3 + 4 + 3 = 20$$

Transpose makes $E_T(p) = 0 + 1 + 1 + 1 + 1 + 1 + 1 = 6$ exchanges, and there are seven operations, so the theorem states that $16 \le 2 \times 20 - 6 - 7$.

If the entries happen to be in the same order in both lists, the cost of the next operation will be the same for both heuristics. The situation becomes unbalanced when the orders become very different. An *inversion* is a pair of distinct entries $\{x, y\}$ such that $x$ precedes $y$ in one list and $y$ precedes $x$ in the other. For example, the two final lists above yield the inversions $\{a, b\}$, $\{d, b\}$, and $\{c, b\}$. The total number of inversions, which in this example is three, is a measure of how differently the entries are ordered in the two lists.

The total amortized complexity of $p$ under the move-to-front heuristic will now be calculated. This will be an upper bound on $C_{MF}(p)$. The potential function used will be the total number of inversions between $MF$'s list and $H$'s list.

Suppose the $i$th operation is *retrieve*$(x)$, and $x$ is the $j$th element of $MF$'s list and the $k$th element of $H$'s list. For convenience, the two lists are shown as arrays:

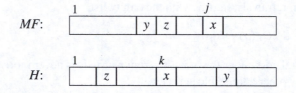

The actual complexity of the retrieval is $j$. Following it, $x$ is moved to the front of $MF$'s list, and moved forward $e_i$ places (say) on $H$'s list. The change in potential that these movements cause must be calculated.

First consider the effect on the potential of moving $x$ to the front of $MF$'s list; $x$ passes over $j - 1$ entries during this move. An entry like $y$ in the example above, which formed an inversion with $x$ before the move, no longer does so afterwards; while an entry like $z$, which did not form an inversion with $x$ before the move, does form one afterwards. Let $c$ be the number of entries preceding $x$ in $MF$'s list that form an inversion with $x$ before the move. Then $c$ inversions are destroyed by the move, and $j - 1 - c$ inversions are created.

With $x$ now at the front of $MF$'s list, every entry that precedes $x$ in $H$'s list forms an inversion with $x$. So when $x$ moves forward $e_i$ places in $H$'s list, exactly $e_i$ inversions are destroyed. Therefore the amortized complexity of the retrieval is

$$a_i = t_i + \Phi(S_i) - \Phi(S_{i-1})$$

$$= j - c + j - 1 - c - e_i$$

$$= 2(j - 1 - c) - e_i + 1$$

Here is a clever observation: $j - 1 - c$ was the number of entries preceding $x$ on $MF$'s list which did not form an inversion with $x$. Therefore, these $j - 1 - c$ entries must also have preceded $x$ on $H$'s list, so $j - 1 - c \leq k - 1$, and

$$a_i \leq 2(k - 1) - e_i + 1$$

$$= 2k - e_i - 1$$

The analysis of insertions is very similar: begin by adding $x$ to the back of both lists, which does not change the potential, and then proceed as for a retrieval. Since $k$ is the cost of the operation to $H$, summing the above over all operations gives

$$C_{MF}(p) = \sum_{i=1}^{m} t_i$$

$$\leq \sum_{i=1}^{m} a_i$$

$$\leq \sum_{i=1}^{m} [2k - e_i - 1]$$

$$= 2C_H(p) - E_H(p) - m$$

and the theorem is proved. □

## 7.4 The binary search tree

In this well-known implementation of the Ordered Symbol Table ADT, the entries are stored, one per node, in a binary tree. Their keys obey the *binary search tree invariant*: the key of any node is greater than the keys of all the nodes in its left subtree, and less than the keys of all the nodes in its right subtree. For example,

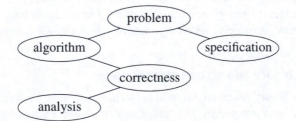

is a binary search tree. The keys are in alphabetical order, and values are not shown. An inorder traversal (Section 6.2) will visit the nodes in increasing key order, which makes the order-dependent operations easy to implement.

The symbol table as a whole is implemented by a header containing just a reference to the root of the tree. An entry is implemented by a reference to a node, and the special nil entry is a void reference.

Binary search tree operations are naturally expressed recursively. For example, to retrieve the entry with a given key, the algorithm first compares that key with the key in the root. If they are equal, the entry has been found; if the given key is smaller, the entry must lie in the left subtree if it exists at all; otherwise it must lie in the right subtree if it exists at all. These last two cases may be implemented recursively:

```
search_subtree(x: like entry_type; key: KEY_TYPE): like entry_type is
    do
        if x = Void then
            Result := Void
        elseif key = x.key then
            Result := x
        elseif key < x.key then
            Result := search_subtree(t.left_child(x), key)
        else
            Result := search_subtree(t.right_child(x), key)
        end
    end
```

The *retrieve(key)* operation proper is then just *search_subtree(root, key)*. This works correctly even when the tree is empty. Figure 7.3 contains non-recursive implementations of the operations, since recursion has some cost and is somewhat inconvenient to code when the tree has a header.

Deletion of a node $x$, preserving the binary search tree invariant, may be accomplished using the deletion algorithm presented in Section 6.2. The *retrieve_first*, *retrieve_next(x)*, *retrieve_last*, and *retrieve_prev(x)* operations are based on traversal operations from Section 6.2.

The worst-case complexity of each operation on a binary search tree $T$ is easily seen to be $h(T)$, the height of the tree, since the operations are all confined to a single path from the root to some leaf. The height is maximized when $T$ is skew, when its value is $n$. This poor $O(n)$ worst case would occur, for example, if entries were inserted in increasing order; in effect, the tree degenerates into a list.

On average, the binary tree can be expected to do much better. It is shown below that, speaking loosely, the average complexity is $O(\log n)$ per operation.

### Analysis of binary search tree insertions

Intuitively, the binary search tree should perform much better than indicated by the worst-case analysis just given. This suggests that an average complexity analysis should be performed. Unfortunately, to do a practically useful average complexity analysis of the binary search tree implementation of the symbol table as a whole is impossible, because meaningful probabilities for the instances cannot be found.

Instead, we choose to analyze the average complexity of a sequence of $n$ insertions into an initially empty tree:

```
build(entries: ARRAY[like entry_type]) is
    do
        make;
        from i := 1 until i > n loop
            insert(entries.item(i));
            i := i + 1
        end
    end
```

The average complexity of *build* will give some insight into the average behavior of the binary search tree, avoiding the intractable problems of the full analysis.

A sequence of keys like ⟨*problem, specification, correctness, analysis*⟩ might just as well be ⟨3, 4, 2, 1⟩, since *build* treats the two identically. So the instances of *build* are the $n!$ permutations of $1, 2, \ldots, n$. For example, if $n = 3$ there are six permutations. Denoting by $B(a)$ the tree produced by *build(a)*, we have

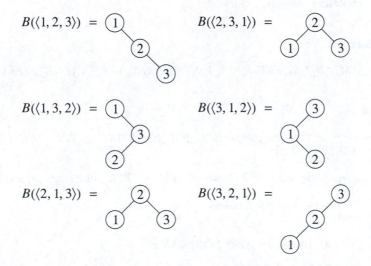

The cost of inserting a node $x$ is equal to its depth in $B(a)$, since $x$ is compared once with each of its proper ancestors during its insertion. Summing over all nodes, the total cost of *build(a)* is the internal path length $i(B(a))$ (Section 6.3). For example, the cost of building $B(\langle 2, 1, 3\rangle)$ is $0 + 1 + 1 = 2$. Since skew trees have maximal internal path length, namely $n(n-1)/2$, the worst-case complexity of *build(a)* is $W(n) = n(n-1)/2$.

For the average complexity analysis, it may as well be assumed that $a$ is equally likely to be any element of the set $S_n$ of permutations of $1, 2, \ldots, n$. Averaging over these $n!$ instances gives

$$A(n) = \sum_{a \in S_n} \frac{1}{n!} i(B(a))$$

For example, $A(3) = [3 + 3 + 2 + 2 + 3 + 3]/6 = 8/3$.

This difficult sum for $A(n)$ can be converted into a recurrence equation. Clearly $A(0) = 0$. For $n > 0$, let

$B(a) =$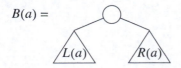

```
class SYMTAB_ORDERED_BST[KEY_TYPE -> COMPARABLE,
VALUE_TYPE]

inherit

    SYMTAB_ORDERED_ADT[KEY_TYPE, VALUE_TYPE]
        redefine entry_type, out end;


feature { NONE }

    t: SYMTAB_ORDERED_BST_BINTREE[KEY_TYPE, VALUE_TYPE]


feature

    entry_type: SYMTAB_ORDERED_BST_ENTRY[KEY_TYPE,
    VALUE_TYPE];

    new_entry(key: KEY_TYPE;  value: VALUE_TYPE): like entry_type is
        do
            !!Result.make(key, value)
        end;

    nil_entry(x: like entry_type): BOOLEAN is
        do
            Result := (x = Void)
        end;

    make is
        do
            !!t;
        end;

    retrieve(key: KEY_TYPE): like entry_type is
        do
            from
                Result := t.root
            until
                t.nil_entry(Result) or else Result.key.is_equal(key)
            loop
                if key < Result.key then
                    Result := t.left_child(Result)
                else
                    Result := t.right_child(Result)
                end
            end
        end;
```

```
insert(x: like entry_type) is
    local
        finished: BOOLEAN;
        y: like entry_type;
    do
        if t.root = Void then
            t.put_root(x)
        else
            from y := t.root; finished := false until finished loop
                if x.key < y.key then
                    if t.nil_entry(t.left_child(y)) then
                        t.put_left_child(y, x);
                        finished := true;
                    else
                        y := t.left_child(y);
                    end
                else
                    if t.nil_entry(t.right_child(y)) then
                        t.put_right_child(y, x);
                        finished := true;
                    else
                        y := t.right_child(y);
                    end
                end
            end
        end;
        t.put_left_child(x, Void);
        t.put_right_child(x, Void)
    end;

    delete(x: like entry_type) is
        do
            t.delete(x)
        end;

    -- retrieve_first and other ordered symbol table operations omitted

end -- SYMTAB_ORDERED_BST
```

**Figure 7.3** Non-recursive implementation of the Ordered Symbol Table ADT using binary search trees. This class contains just one attribute, $t$, which is an instance of the Extended Binary Tree ADT (the binary tree extended with parent references, traversal operations, and deletion; see Section 6.2) with its *entry_type* adapted as appropriate.

Now $i(B(a)) = n - 1 + i(L(a)) + i(R(a))$, from the proof of Theorem 6.1, so

$$A(n) = \frac{1}{n!} \sum_{a \in S_n} i(B(a))$$

$$= \frac{1}{n!} \sum_{a \in S_n} [n - 1 + i(L(a)) + i(R(a))]$$

$$= n - 1 + \frac{1}{n!} \sum_{a \in S_n} i(L(a)) + \frac{1}{n!} \sum_{a \in S_n} i(R(a))$$

$$= n - 1 + \frac{2}{n!} \sum_{a \in S_n} i(L(a))$$

This last step is by symmetry: on the average, it costs the same to build right subtrees as it does to build left ones.

Let $S_n^j$ be the set of permutations $a$ of $1, 2, \ldots, n$ such that the root of $B(a)$ contains $j$. This is equivalent to saying that the first element of $a$ is $j$, since the first element always occupies the root. For example, here is an element of $S_8^6$:

The example shows that, if $a \in S_n^j$, $L(a)$ is determined by the order in which the numbers $1, 2, \ldots, j - 1$ appear within $a$. Since there are $(j - 1)!$ possible orderings (permutations) of $1, 2, \ldots, j - 1$, all equally likely to occur within $S_n^j$, and since $S_n^j$ has $(n - 1)!$ elements, each permutation of $1, 2, \ldots, j - 1$ must occur exactly $(n - 1)!/(j - 1)!$ times within $S_n^j$. As far as its effect on left subtrees is concerned, $S_n^j$ is just $(n - 1)!/(j - 1)!$ copies of $S_{j-1}$. Therefore,

$$\sum_{a \in S_n^j} i(L(a)) = \frac{(n - 1)!}{(j - 1)!} \sum_{a \in S_{j-1}} i(B(a)) = (n - 1)! A(j - 1)$$

by the definition of $A(n)$. Immediately then,

$$A(n) = n - 1 + \frac{2}{n!} \sum_{a \in S_n} i(L(a))$$

$$= n - 1 + \frac{2}{n!} \sum_{j=1}^{n} \sum_{a \in S_n^j} i(L(a))$$

$$= n - 1 + \frac{2}{n!} \sum_{j=1}^{n} (n - 1)! A(j - 1)$$

and so, as promised, this gives a recurrence equation for $A(n)$:

$$A(0) = 0$$

$$A(n) = n - 1 + \frac{2}{n} \sum_{j=1}^{n} A(j - 1)$$

There is a less formal derivation of this formula, which runs as follows. To build an 'average' tree, the root must be inserted, then $n - 1$ comparisons must be made between the root and the other keys as they pass through the root on their way to the left and right subtrees:

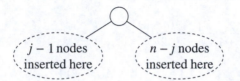

To build an average left subtree containing $j - 1$ nodes costs $A(j - 1)$ comparisons, and, since the root is equally likely to contain any one of the numbers $1, 2, \ldots, n$, the left subtree is equally likely to contain $0, 1, \ldots, n - 1$ nodes. On the average, then, the cost of building the left subtree must be

$$\frac{1}{n} \sum_{j=1}^{n} A(j - 1)$$

and, by symmetry, the average right subtree has the same cost, giving

$$A(n) = n - 1 + \frac{2}{n} \sum_{j=1}^{n} A(j - 1)$$

for the cost of *build*, as before. This derivation should be treated with caution: it glosses over points that are more carefully handled in the first derivation.

The first step in solving the recurrence equation is to eliminate the summation, which is done by a clever trick. Multiplying by $n$,

$$nA(n) = n(n - 1) + 2 \sum_{j=1}^{n} A(j - 1)$$

and substituting $n - 1$ for $n$ gives

$$(n - 1)A(n - 1) = (n - 1)(n - 2) + 2 \sum_{j=1}^{n-1} A(j - 1)$$

Now if the second equation is subtracted from the first, the summation disappears:

$$nA(n) - (n - 1)A(n - 1) = n(n - 1) - (n - 1)(n - 2) + 2A(n - 1)$$

and so

$$nA(n) = 2(n-1) + (n+1)A(n-1)$$

It is possible to divide by $n$ and apply repeated substitution now, but the algebra is simplified by first dividing by $2n(n+1)$:

$$\frac{A(n)}{2(n+1)} = \frac{n-1}{n(n+1)} + \frac{A(n-1)}{2n}$$

By partial fractions, $(n-1)/n(n+1) = 2/(n+1) - 1/n$, so

$$\frac{A(n)}{2(n+1)} = \frac{2}{n+1} - \frac{1}{n} + \frac{A(n-1)}{2n}$$

$$= \frac{2}{n+1} - \frac{1}{n} + \left[ \frac{2}{n} - \frac{1}{n-1} + \frac{A(n-2)}{2(n-1)} \right]$$

$$= \frac{2}{n+1} - \frac{1}{n} + \left[ \frac{2}{n} - \frac{1}{n-1} + \left[ \frac{2}{n-1} - \frac{1}{n-2} \right] \right] + \frac{A(n-3)}{2(n-2)}$$

$$= \cdots$$

$$= \frac{2}{n+1} + \frac{2}{n} + \cdots + \frac{2}{n-(i-2)} - \frac{1}{n} - \frac{1}{n-1} - \cdots$$

$$- \frac{1}{n-(i-1)} + \frac{A(n-i)}{2(n-(i-1))}$$

and letting $i = n$,

$$\frac{A(n)}{2(n+1)} = \frac{2}{n+1} + \frac{2}{n} + \cdots + \frac{2}{2} - \frac{1}{n} - \frac{1}{n-1} - \cdots - \frac{1}{1} + 0$$

$$= \frac{2}{n} + \cdots + \frac{2}{2} + \left[ \frac{2}{1} - \frac{2}{1} \right] - \frac{1}{n} - \cdots - \frac{1}{1} + \frac{2}{n+1}$$

$$= \left[ \frac{2}{n} + \cdots + \frac{2}{2} + \frac{2}{1} \right] - \left[ \frac{1}{n} + \cdots + \frac{1}{1} \right] + \frac{2}{n+1} - \frac{2}{1}$$

$$= \left[ \frac{1}{n} + \cdots + \frac{1}{1} \right] + \frac{2 - 2(n+1)}{n+1}$$

$$= \sum_{i=1}^{n} 1/i - \frac{2n}{n+1}$$

and finally, multiplying through by $2(n+1)$ proves the following theorem.

**Theorem 7.2:** The average complexity of a sequence of $n$ insertions into an initially empty binary search tree, assuming that each of the $n!$ distinct permutations of $1, 2, \dots, n$ is equally likely to be an instance, is

$$A(n) = 2(n + 1)H_n - 4n$$

where $H_n = \sum_{i=1}^{n} 1/i$ is the $n$th *Harmonic number*. $\qquad\square$

The formula $\sum_{i=1}^{n} 1/i$ cannot be simplified any further, as far as anyone knows, but there is an approximation $H_n \simeq \ln n + \gamma$, where $\gamma \simeq 0.5572$ is Euler's constant. So $A(n)$ is about $1.38n\log_2 n$ for the $n$ insertions, which, speaking loosely, is $O(\log n)$ per insertion – considerably less than the worst case.

This analysis can be extended to include retrievals (Exercise 7.11), but it tells us nothing about the binary search tree when deletions occur, and in fact almost nothing is known, according to Knuth (1973b).

## 7.5 Splay trees

In Section 7.3 several heuristics were studied for adjusting a linked list to take advantage of locality of reference in the operation sequence. The most successful one was move-to-front: after accessing entry $x$, move it to the front of the list. This suggests that the analogous heuristic for binary search trees is worth trying: after accessing node $x$, move it to the root of the tree, where it will be found quickly by subsequent accesses.

A binary search tree is not as simple to adjust as a linked list, because it is necessary to preserve the binary search tree invariant (in other words, to ensure that the key in any node is always greater than all the keys in its left subtree, and smaller than all the keys in its right subtree). Nevertheless, there is a way.

Consider any internal node $y$ that has a left child $x$ that is also internal. A *right rotation at $y$* adjusts the tree so that $y$ becomes the right child of $x$:

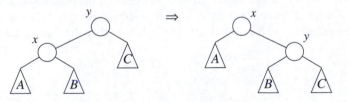

$A$, $B$, and $C$ are arbitrary subtrees, possibly empty. The tree after rotation has the same nodes as the original tree, and, most important, the binary search tree invariant is preserved. This is easily verified by traversing the two trees in inorder: both give the ordering $A, x, B, y, C$, which shows that if the invariant holds in one tree, it holds in the other.

A *left rotation* is similar, going the other way:

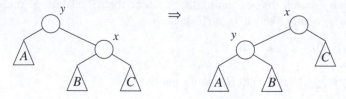

The binary search tree invariant is preserved once again. Rotations, invented by Adel'son-Vel'skii and Landis (1962), are frequently used to adjust binary trees.

Rotations are useful here because in each case the depth of node $x$ decreases by 1. Thus, a sequence of rotations at the parent of $x$ will move $x$ to the root:

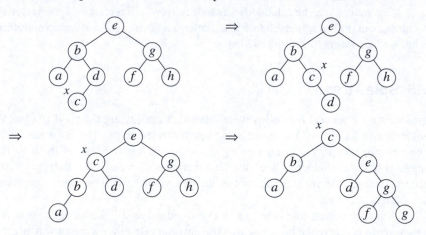

This gives a first heuristic for binary search trees: after accessing (that is, inserting or retrieving) a node $x$, move it to the root by a sequence of left and right rotations at its parent. This heuristic, which is called *move-to-root*, has been studied by Allen and Munro (1978) and by Bitner (1979).

Move-to-root should improve the performance of the binary search tree when there is locality of reference in the operation sequence, but it is not ideal. The final tree in the example above is marginally less balanced than the starting tree, and

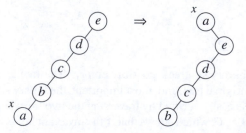

shows that move-to-root will not turn an unbalanced tree into a balanced one.

Sleator and Tarjan (1985b) have found a way to move $x$ to the root and simultaneously clean up an unbalanced tree. Their method performs the equivalent of two rotations at each *splaying step*:

*Case 1*

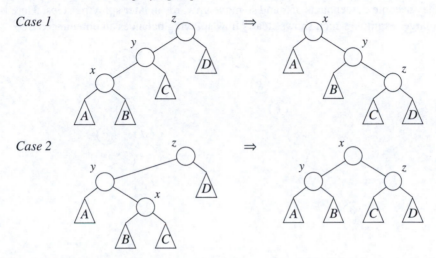

*Case 2*

Each case has a symmetric variant, not shown here. Altogether these cases account for the four possible places that $x$ could occupy as a grandchild of $z$. It is easy to verify that these transformations preserve the binary search tree invariant.

After these splaying steps have been performed as many times as possible, $x$ will be the root or a child of the root. If $x$ is a child of the root, a final rotation is performed to bring $x$ to the root:

*Case 3*

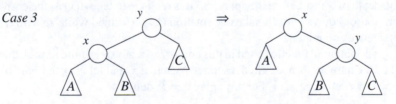

The whole process is a *splay at $x$*, and a binary tree with splaying is a *splay tree*.

It happens that Cases 2 and 3 do exactly what move-to-root would do in the same situation. However, applying move-to-root to Case 1 would yield

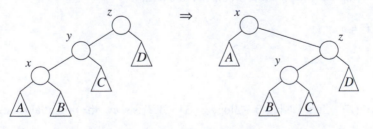

which is not the same. The crucial difference is that, while move-to-root leaves $B$ at its original depth, the splaying step moves both subtrees of $x$ up at least one level. Although subtrees $C$ and $D$ appear to lose out in splaying's Case 1 transformation, they become descendants of $x$ and so move upwards in later splaying steps. Here is a larger example which shows clearly how splaying balances an unbalanced tree:

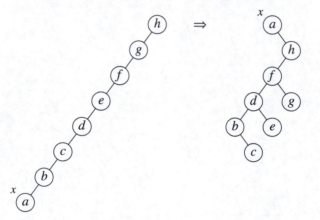

When implemented carefully, splay trees are very fast, according to Jones (1986).

## Amortized analysis of splay trees

The insertion or retrieval of a node $x$ has two stages: a search down some path, followed by splaying back up the path. Both stages have cost $O(d(x))$, where $d(x)$ is the depth of $x$ just before the splay. So it is realistic to take $d(x)$ as the cost of the operation, or equivalently, to take one rotation (as performed while splaying) as the characteristic operation.

The potential function used in this amortized analysis is quite remarkable. Let $s(x)$ be the number of nodes in the subtree rooted at $x$, and let $r(x)$, the *rank* of $x$, be defined by $r(x) = \log_2 s(x)$. For any splay tree $T$, define

$$\Phi(T) = \sum_{x \in T} r(x) = \sum_{x \in T} \log_2 s(x)$$

If $T$ is complete, the potential is small. For example,

$T =$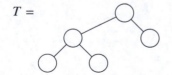

yields $\Phi(T) = \log_2 5 + \log_2 3 + 3\log_2 1 \approx 3.9$. If $T$ is skew, the potential is large:

$T =$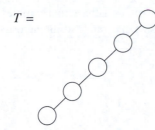

yielding $\Phi(T) = \log_2 5 + \log_2 4 + \log_2 3 + \log_2 2 + \log_2 1 \approx 5.9$. So $\Phi(T)$ is reminiscent of the internal path length $i(T)$, modified to have an $O(n\log n)$ maximum rather than $O(n^2)$. This connection with $i(T)$ is clarified by Exercise 6.7.

Now splaying at $x$ consists of a number of steps:

1      splaying step at $x$ (Case 1 or 2)
      ...
$m$      splaying step at $x$ (Case 1, 2 or 3)

The amortized complexity $a_i = t_i + \Phi(T_i) - \Phi(T_{i-1})$ will be calculated for each step. Then the total amortized complexity of all the steps will equal the amortized complexity of splaying at $x$, which is the cost of the insertion or retrieval.

**Lemma 7.1:** Let $\alpha$ and $\beta$ be real numbers such that $\alpha > 0$, $\beta > 0$, and $\alpha + \beta \leq 1$. Then $\log_2 \alpha + \log_2 \beta \leq -2$.
**Proof:** Since $\log_2 \alpha + \log_2 \beta = \log_2 \alpha\beta$, and the logarithm is a monotone increasing function, its value will be maximum when $\alpha\beta$ is maximum. In the given region, this clearly occurs when $\alpha = \beta = 1/2$, when $\log_2 \alpha + \log_2 \beta = -2$.      □

This $-2$ will be used to cancel out the actual complexity of 2 per splaying step. Here is the main theorem, named the 'Access Lemma' by its discoverers:

**Theorem 7.3 (Access lemma for splay trees):** Suppose that node $x$ has size $s_{i-1}(x)$ and rank $r_{i-1}(x)$ just before the $i$th splaying step, and that after the step its size and rank are $s_i(x)$ and $r_i(x)$. Then the amortized complexity of the $i$th splaying step is at most $3r_i(x) - 3r_{i-1}(x)$, unless it is the final step, in which case the amortized complexity is at most $1 + 3r_i(x) - 3r_{i-1}(x)$.
**Proof:** Consider first the amortized complexity of a Case 1 splaying step:

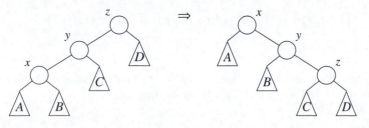

Since the characteristic operation we are using is one rotation, the actual complexity is two rotations. Now only $x$, $y$, and $z$ change in size and rank, so the amortized complexity of the step is

$$a_i = t_i + \Phi(T_i) - \Phi(T_{i-1})$$

$$= 2 + r_i(x) + r_i(y) + r_i(z) - r_{i-1}(x) - r_{i-1}(y) - r_{i-1}(z)$$

$$= 2 + r_i(y) + r_i(z) - r_{i-1}(x) - r_{i-1}(y)$$

This last line follows because $s_{i-1}(z)$, the size of the subtree rooted at $z$ before the step, equals $s_i(x)$, the size of the subtree rooted at $x$ after the step.

    Now before the step, $y$ is an ancestor of $x$, so $r_{i-1}(y) \geq r_{i-1}(x)$. After the step, $y$ is a descendant of $x$, so $r_i(y) \leq r_i(x)$. Substituting these values gives

$$a_i \leq 2 + r_i(x) + r_i(z) - 2r_{i-1}(x)$$

The lemma is now used to cancel the actual complexity of 2. Let $\alpha = s_{i-1}(x)/s_i(x)$, and let $\beta = s_i(z)/s_i(x)$. Clearly, $\alpha > 0$ and $\beta > 0$, but also,

$$\alpha + \beta = (s_{i-1}(x) + s_i(z))/s_i(x) \leq 1$$

This follows because, as the diagram above shows, $s_{i-1}(x)$ encompasses $A$, $x$, and $B$; $s_i(z)$ encompasses $C$, $z$, and $D$; and together these contain exactly one node less than $s_i(x)$. Therefore, by the lemma,

$$\log_2(s_{i-1}(x)/s_i(x)) + \log_2(s_i(z)/s_i(x)) \leq -2$$

so that

$$r_{i-1}(x) + r_i(z) - 2r_i(x) \leq -2$$

and then

$$2r_i(x) - r_{i-1}(x) - r_i(z) - 2 \geq 0$$

Since this quantity is non-negative, it may be added to the expression for $a_i$ derived above, giving

$$a_i \leq [2 + r_i(x) + r_i(z) - 2r_{i-1}(x)] + [2r_i(x) - r_{i-1}(x) - r_i(z) - 2]$$

$$= 3r_i(x) - 3r_{i-1}(x)$$

and the theorem is proved for Case 1. The other two cases are left as an exercise; Case 2 is similar to Case 1, and Case 3 is quite simple.       □

Now the total amortized complexity of an insertion or retrieval is

$$\sum_{i=1}^{m} a_i = \sum_{i=1}^{m-1} a_i + a_m$$

$$\leq \sum_{i=1}^{m-1} (3r_i(x) - 3r_{i-1}(x)) + 1 + 3r_m(x) - 3r_{m-1}(x)$$

$$= 1 + 3r_m(x) - 3r_0(x)$$

$$\leq 1 + 3r_m(x)$$

$$= 1 + 3\log_2 n$$

since after the final rotation, $x$ is the root, so that $s_m(x) = n$. Thus the amortized complexity of an insertion or retrieval is $O(\log n)$. Any sequence of $p$ of these splay tree operations will have $O(p\log n)$ worst-case complexity, which is much better than the $O(pn)$ worst-case complexity of the binary search tree.

## 7.6 B-trees

Previous sections have presented the binary search tree, which has $O(\log n)$ average complexity per operation, and the splay tree, which has $O(\log n)$ amortized complexity. It is now time to study a data structure of $O(\log n)$ complexity in the worst case: the *B-tree* of Bayer and McCreight (1972).

The B-tree is only one of a large class of tree structures which achieve this performance; the first was the AVL tree of Adel'son-Vel'skii and Landis (1962). The B-tree has been chosen because it is a popular method of implementing ordered symbol tables on disk units – that is, databases – and so is the most widely used of all the methods.

The first step is to generalize the binary search tree in the following way. A *multiway search tree* may have more than one entry in each node. For example,

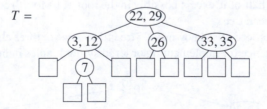

is a multiway search tree. The entries within each node are stored in sorted order. For each gap between two entries, there is a subtree containing all the entries whose keys lie between those two entries. To the left of the entry with the smallest key in the node is a subtree whose entries are all smaller than that entry; similarly there is a subtree containing large entries at the right end. Thus, the number of subtrees of any internal node is one greater than the number of entries in the node.

Searching and traversal in a multiway search tree are simple generalizations of the corresponding algorithms for binary search trees. For example, consider searching for a key $x$ in the tree shown above. If $x < 25$ the search goes left; if $25 < x < 29$ the search goes down; and if $29 < x$ the search goes right. Linear search within the node may be used if there are only a few entries in it, or binary search if there are many. The process is repeated recursively. Traversal in inorder is also quite simple: to traverse a tree $T$, traverse its first subtree, then visit the first entry of its root, then traverse the second subtree, then visit the second entry of its root, and so on, finishing with a traversal of the last subtree.

A *B-tree of order m* obeys the following representation invariant:

(1)    It is a multiway search tree.

(2)    The root is either external or else it has between 2 and $m$ children inclusive.

(3)    Every internal node (except possibly the root) has between $\lceil m/2 \rceil$ and $m$ children inclusive.

(4)    The external nodes all have equal depth.

For example, here are some B-trees of order $m = 4$:

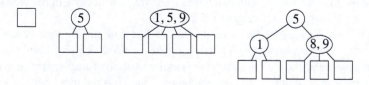

The second and third conditions make it possible to allocate a fixed amount of memory to each node (space for $m$ references to subtrees, $m - 1$ entries, and an integer count of the number of entries currently stored in the node), yet be sure of wasting less than half of it, except possibly in the root. The fourth condition ensures a very well-balanced tree.

B-trees of order 3 (also known as 2-3 trees) have two or three children per node, and are a good choice for implementing ordered symbol tables in internal memory:

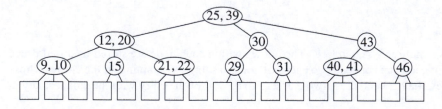

is a 2-3 tree. B-trees on disk units typically have $m = 256$ or more, chosen so that one node fits neatly into one disk block. This makes for a very shallow tree, which reduces the number of nodes examined (and hence the number of disk accesses) during searching. In such applications it is common to store only the keys in the internal nodes, keeping the values in the external nodes. This is done to make $m$ as large as possible.

The B-tree invariant is rather stringent, and it is not obvious that efficient insertion and deletion algorithms which preserve it exist. Let us begin by inserting 44 into the 2-3 tree tree given above:

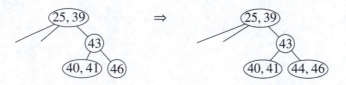

Insertions are always made in the first instance into internal nodes of maximum depth. If there is room there, any entries with larger keys are shuffled up and the insertion is made. If the node is full (for example, now insert 45), it is first inserted anyway, creating a 'problem node' with $m$ keys:

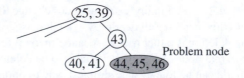

and then the problem node is split into three pieces: a node containing the first $\lceil m/2 \rceil - 1$ entries; a single entry, the $\lceil m/2 \rceil$th; and a node containing the remaining $m - \lceil m/2 \rceil$ entries:

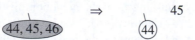

Then the isolated entry is inserted into the parent node:

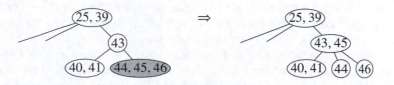

Notice that one reference in the parent is replaced by two references and one entry. These insertions into parents may propagate upwards if the parent is full. For example, if 42 is now inserted:

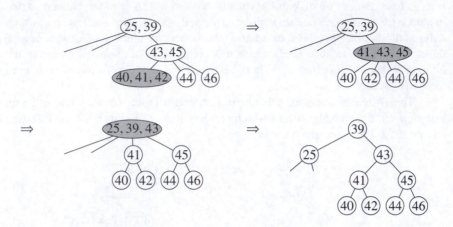

The B-tree's height increases by one in this example, because the root was split.

It is easy to see that the B-tree invariant is preserved by this insertion algorithm. All nodes end up with at most $m$ children, since otherwise they are split in two. All nodes except possibly the root end up with at least $\lceil m/2 \rceil - 1$ entries, since the two new nodes have $\lceil m/2 \rceil - 1$ and $m - \lceil m/2 \rceil$ entries respectively, and $m - \lceil m/2 \rceil \geq \lceil m/2 \rceil - 1$. Finally, external nodes change their depth only when the root is split, and this increases all depths by 1, so the last condition is maintained.

As usual, deletion is rather tricky. Assume that a reference to a node is given, plus the index in that node of the entry which is to be deleted. Also assume that the parent of the node can be found. The simplest way to obtain all this information is to begin the deletion with a retrieval.

First, if the entry $x$ to be deleted does not lie at the bottom level, find its inorder predecessor $y$ (which must exist) and overwrite $x$ with $y$. This reduces the problem to the deletion of an entry from the bottom level.

Remove the entry by shuffling its right neighbors to the left. If the node still contains at least $\lceil m/2 \rceil - 1$ entries (as it usually will), or if the node is the root, nothing further is required. Otherwise the node is not the root and it contains $\lceil m/2 \rceil - 2$ entries, one fewer than the representation invariant permits.

Examine the left or right sibling of this node (there must be at least one sibling, since the node is not the root). If the sibling contains more than $\lceil m/2 \rceil - 1$ entries, the entries can be redistributed between the two nodes so that both nodes have at least $\lceil m/2 \rceil - 1$ entries, and nothing further is required.

Otherwise the two sibling nodes contain $\lceil m/2 \rceil - 2$ and $\lceil m/2 \rceil - 1$ entries respectively. Together with the entry in the parent that separates these two nodes, this is $2\lceil m/2 \rceil - 2 \leq m - 1$ entries altogether. These entries can therefore be squeezed into one node, in a manner exactly inverse to the node splitting used by insertions. Since the parent has one fewer entry afterwards, the process may need to be repeated on the parent.

For example, consider deleting the entry whose key is 25 from the 2-3 tree

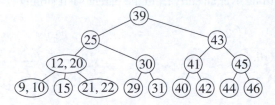

Since this entry does not lie at the bottom level, it must be overwritten with its inorder precedessor, 22, leaving

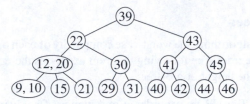

which satisfies the invariant. If now 20 is deleted, again since it is not at the bottom level its inorder predecessor 15 must overwrite it:

As shown, this leaves an underfull 'problem node' which may be corrected by shuffling over an entry from the left sibling:

Suppose now that 30 is deleted. Overwriting with the inorder predecessor leaves

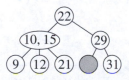

Now the underfull problem node has no sibling which can spare any entry, so it must be merged with its sibling and the entry separating them in the parent:

In this case this leaves a problem node in the parent, which, as it happens, can be corrected by shuffling over an entry from the parent's left sibling:

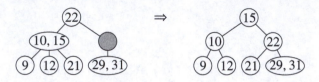

Subtrees also move in the shuffle. In other cases the problem node will have to be merged with its sibling and the entry separating them in the parent, and so on.

## Analysis of B-trees

As usual with tree algorithms, the worst-case complexity of each operation is related to the height of the tree. The following theorem expresses the crucial relationship between $n$, $m$ and the height of a B-tree:

**Theorem 7.4:** Let $T$ be a B-tree of order $m$, and suppose $T$ has height $h$ and contains $n \geq 1$ entries. Then

$$n \geq 2\lceil m/2 \rceil^{h-1} - 1$$

**Proof:** Construct the B-tree of order $m$ and height $h$ that contains the minimum possible number of entries, by assigning the minimum possible number to each node. The root has at least one entry, and the other nodes have at least $\lceil m/2 \rceil - 1$ entries each, so this tree is

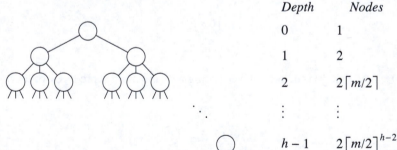

| Depth | Nodes |
|-------|-------|
| 0 | 1 |
| 1 | 2 |
| 2 | $2\lceil m/2 \rceil$ |
| $\vdots$ | $\vdots$ |
| $h-1$ | $2\lceil m/2 \rceil^{h-2}$ |
| $h$ | 0 |

Excluding the root, the number of nodes is

$$2 + 2\lceil m/2 \rceil + \cdots + 2\lceil m/2 \rceil^{h-2} = 2\frac{\lceil m/2 \rceil^{h-1} - 1}{\lceil m/2 \rceil - 1}$$

by the standard formula for the sum of a geometric progression. Each of these nodes contains $\lceil m/2 \rceil - 1$ entries, giving $2(\lceil m/2 \rceil^{h-1} - 1)$ entries altogether in these nodes. Plus one entry in the root gives a total of $2\lceil m/2 \rceil^{h-1} - 1$ entries. Since this was the minimum possible, the result follows. □

Manipulating this result to bring $h$ to the left-hand side, any B-tree $T$ of order $m$, containing $n \geq 1$ entries, has height

$$h(T) \leq \log_{\lceil m/2 \rceil}(\frac{n+1}{2}) + 1$$

The cost of searching a node is $O(\log m)$ using binary search, and the cost of shuffling entries up and down is $O(m)$. However, $m$ is a constant and so it is fair to consider both of these as $O(1)$. It follows that insertions, retrievals, and deletions are $O(\log n)$ in the worst case.

## 7.7 Hashing

*Hashing* is a radically different implementation of the Symbol Table ADT. It exploits the nature of random access memory to achieve $O(1)$ average complexity per operation, which is faster than any method based on trees. It does not implement the ordered symbol table operations efficiently, however, and its worst case is a poor $O(n)$ per retrieval. It is widely used in compilers and databases.

First, consider the special case where the keys are integers in the range 0 to $m - 1$, and $m$ is small enough for an array *entries.item*(0..*m*−1) of $m$ references to entries to be feasible. Then the symbol table operations can be implemented in $O(1)$ time each, by storing a reference to the entry whose key is $x$ in *entries.item*($x$).

In general, unfortunately, the number of possible keys is enormous, or even infinite (for example, there are infinitely many character strings). To reconcile this huge number with the limited size of the array *entries*, a *hash function*

$$f : \{ \text{All possible keys} \} \rightarrow \{0, 1, \ldots, m - 1\}$$

is introduced, and the entry whose key is $x$ is stored in *entries.item*($f(x)$).

For example, suppose that the keys are strings of letters, and that the concrete representation of the letter $a$ is the two-digit decimal number 01, of $b$ is 02, and so on. Then the string *fred* has concrete representation 06180509. Suppose $m = 10$ and the hash function is $f(x) = x \setminus\setminus m$, where the Eiffel expression $x \setminus\setminus m$ returns the remainder of the integer division of $x$ by $m$. Then

$$f(fred) = 06180504 \setminus\setminus 10 = 4$$
$$f(inc) = \quad 091403 \setminus\setminus 10 = 3$$
$$f(put) = \quad 162120 \setminus\setminus 10 = 0$$

since $x \backslash\backslash 10$ returns the last decimal digit of $x$. Entries with these keys may be inserted into *entries.item*(0..9):

|   | 0 | 1 | 2 | 3 | 4 | 5 | 6 | 7 | 8 | 9 |
|---|---|---|---|---|---|---|---|---|---|---|
| A | put |  |  | inc | fred |  |  |  |  |  |

Retrieval is easy. For example, to retrieve the entry whose key is *inc*, calculate $f(inc) = 3$, and examine *entries.item*(3).

Since $f$ maps from a large set to a small one, it is inevitable that *collisions*, in which two keys hash to the same position, will occur. For example, $f(hd) = 4$, but *entries.item*(4) is occupied. Strategies for resolving collisions are studied below.

Although collisions are inevitable, their frequency can be reduced by choosing a hash function which spreads the entries uniformly through the table. A good hash function will be affected by all parts of the key, in an unpredictable way. For example, $x \backslash\backslash 256$ would not be a good choice on a binary computer, because it depends only on the last 8 bits of $x$. Choosing the middle $k$ bits of $x^2$ is also poor, since it will yield 0 whenever $x$ is small.

How then can the quality of a hash function be determined? In practice, this is done by checking that it does not have problems like those just seen, and then testing it empirically. One simple function that has been found to work very well is

$$f(x) = x \backslash\backslash m$$

provided $m$ is a prime number not close to a power of 2. Knuth (1973b) discusses this hash function and several others. Unless the hash function is to be implemented on hardware where division is unusually slow, there is no need to look further.

If the key is larger than a single machine word (for example, if it is a string of characters), it must first be compressed. This is most easily done by treating each element as an integer and adding them together. Of course, permutations like *abc* and *cba* will collide.

## Resolving collisions

No matter how carefully the hash function is chosen, there will always be collisions, and the technical literature abounds with ingenious ways to resolve them. A strategy called *chaining* is usually preferred; but before discussing chaining, here are two other strategies that are occasionally useful.

*Linear probing* should be considered when memory is scarce. The entries are stored directly in the array. When a collision occurs, the array is searched to the right for a free slot to accommodate the new entry:

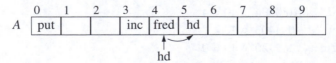

The search is circular: *entries.item*(0) follows *entries.item*(*m*–1). A retrieval must follow the same path, stopping either at the desired entry, or at the first free slot (in which case the entry is not present).

The worst-case time complexity is clearly $O(n)$ per operation; the average complexity analysis is beyond the scope of this book (however, see Exercise 7.26). Deletion is notoriously difficult to implement correctly (Exercise 7.24).

*Buckets* are used on disk units when fast retrieval is more important than efficient use of space. The idea is to allow space for several entries at each position:

| | 0 | 1 | 2 | 3 | 4 | 5 | 6 | 7 | 8 | 9 |
|---|---|---|---|---|---|---|---|---|---|---|
| A | put | | | inc | fred | | | | | |
| | | | | | hd | | | | | |
| | | | | | | | | | | |

Typically, one bucket occupies one disk block, and since the entry with key $x$ is almost always in bucket *entries.item*($f(x)$), a retrieval should require only about one disk block read on average. Bucket overflows may be handled by chaining or linear probing; a formal analysis is again beyond our scope.

The simplest collision resolution strategy, and usually the best, is *chaining*. Each element of the hash table is a reference to a linked list of entries:

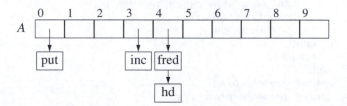

To retrieve an entry, its key is hashed and the appropriate list is searched. If the entries are well spread through the table, this list should contain only a few entries, so they may be kept in no particular order. Alternatively, the move-to-front list adjusting heuristic from Section 7.3 could be used. In fact, so could any of the symbol table data structures of this chapter, although the complex ones are not recommended, since the number of entries that hash to one location should be small.

A complete implementation of the Symbol Table ADT using a chained hash table is given in Figure 7.4. It includes a private *rehash* operation, which is used by *insert* to double the table size when the average list length exceeds 2.

## Analysis of chaining

The remainder of this section is devoted to an analysis of chaining, as implemented in Figure 7.4. As usual, one comparison between keys is taken as the characteristic operation, except for *delete*, where one test of the form '*y.hash_next = x*' is used.

```
class SYMTAB_HASHCHAINS[KEY_TYPE -> HASHABLE, VALUE_TYPE]

inherit

    SYMTAB_ADT[KEY_TYPE, VALUE_TYPE]

feature { NONE }

    entries: ARRAY[like entry_type];
    array_size: INTEGER;
    count: INTEGER;

    rehash(new_array_size: INTEGER) is
        local
            i, j: INTEGER;
            x: like entry_type;
            new_entries: ARRAY[like entry_type];
        do
            !!new_entries.make(0, new_array_size - 1);
            from i := 0 until i >= array_size loop
                from x := entries.item(i) until x = Void loop
                    entries.put(x.hash_next, i);
                    j := x.key.hash_code \\ new_array_size;
                    x.put_hash_next(new_entries.item(j));
                    new_entries.put(x, j);
                    x := entries.item(i);
                end;
                i := i + 1;
            end;
            entries := new_entries;
            array_size := new_array_size;
        end;


feature

    entry_type: SYMTAB_HASHCHAINS_ENTRY[KEY_TYPE,
        VALUE_TYPE];

    initial_array_size: INTEGER is 307;

    new_entry(key: KEY_TYPE;  value: VALUE_TYPE): like entry_type is
        do
            !!Result.make(key, value)
        end;

    nil_entry(x: like entry_type): BOOLEAN is
        do
            Result := (x = Void)
        end;
```

```
make is
    do
        array_size := initial_array_size;
        !!entries.make(0, array_size – 1);
        count := 0;
    end;

insert(x: like entry_type) is
    local
        i: INTEGER;
    do
        i := x.key.hash_code \\ array_size;
        x.put_hash_next(entries.item(i));
        entries.put(x, i);
        count := count + 1;
        if count > 2*array_size then rehash(2*array_size – 1) end;
    end;

retrieve(key: KEY_TYPE): like entry_type is
    do
        from
            Result := entries.item(key.hash_code \\ array_size)
        until
            Result = Void or else Result.key.is_equal(key)
        loop
            Result := Result.hash_next
        end
    end;

delete(x: like entry_type) is
    local
        i: INTEGER;
        y: like entry_type;
    do
        i := x.key.hash_code \\ array_size;
        if entries.item(i) = x then
            entries.put(x.hash_next, i)
        else
            from y := entries.item(i) until y.hash_next = x loop
                y := y.hash_next;
            end;
            y.put_hash_next(x.hash_next);
        end;
        count := count – 1;
    end;

end -- SYMTAB_HASHCHAINS
```

**Figure 7.4**  The chained hash table implementation of the Symbol Table ADT.

In the worst case, the $n$ entries all hash to the same position, and the analysis reduces to that of an unsorted linked list. Insertions go at the front of the list so are $O(1)$, except for the rare case where the table must be resized (Exercise 7.27); retrievals and deletions must search this list, so have $O(n)$ worst-case complexity.

There is a remarkable average complexity analysis of chaining – remarkable, because for once it is possible to assign meaningful probabilities to the instances, and analyze the ADT as a whole. Let the size of the hash table array be $m$ (indexed from 0 to $m - 1$), and let the number of entries be $n$. Nothing is assumed about where in the table these $n$ entries are.

The *insert(x)* operation is of course $O(1)$ on average as well as in the worst case. Consider an unsuccessful *retrieve(key)* operation. It may be assumed that *key* is equally likely to hash to any one of the $m$ table positions, and *retrieve(key)* must search the entire list at that position, giving the average complexity table

| $i$ | Instance | $p_i$ | $T_i(n)$ |
|-----|----------|-------|----------|
| 1 | $f(key) = 0$ | $1/m$ | Length of list 0 |
| 2 | $f(key) = 1$ | $1/m$ | Length of list 1 |
| | ... | | |
| $m$ | $f(key) = m - 1$ | $1/m$ | Length of list $m - 1$ |

So the average complexity of an unsuccessful retrieval is

$$A(n) = \sum_{i=1}^{m} p_i T_i(n)$$

$$= \frac{1}{m} \sum_{i=0}^{m-1} [\text{Length of list } i]$$

$$= n/m,$$

since the total length of all lists is just the total number of entries in the table, $n$. This analysis shows that, if $m \simeq n$, $A(n) = O(1)$.

When analyzing successful retrievals, it is not correct to assume that each table position is equally likely to be the outcome of the hash. If the corresponding list is empty, for example, then clearly no successful retrieval will ever search it. A better assumption is that each of the $n$ entries is equally likely to be the outcome of the retrieval. Here is an analysis from Knuth (1973b) based on this assumption. The analysis is not very rigorous, but it is simple and it gives the right answer.

Number the entries from 1 to $n$ in reverse order of insertion: let $x_1$ be the last entry inserted, $x_2$ be the second last, and so on until $x_n$ is the first entry inserted.

The cost of a successful retrieval of entry $x_j$ is one plus the number of entries preceding $x_j$ in its list. Since insertions are made at the front, only entries inserted after $x_j$ can precede $x_j$ in its list; that is, only entries from the set $\{x_1, \ldots, x_{j-1}\}$.

Since $x_j$ is equally likely to be inserted into any list, the average number of entries preceding $x_j$ in its list is equal to the average length of a list in a hash table containing the entries $\{x_1, \dots, x_{j-1}\}$. The previous analysis of unsuccessful retrievals showed this to be $(j - 1)/m$.

Retrieving $x_j$ costs $(j - 1)/m + 1$, so averaging over the $n$ entries gives

$$A(n) = \frac{1}{n} \sum_{j=1}^{n} [(j - 1)/m + 1]$$

$$= \frac{1}{nm} \sum_{j=1}^{n} (j - 1) + \frac{1}{n} \sum_{j=1}^{n} 1$$

$$= \frac{1}{nm} \cdot \frac{n(n - 1)}{2} + \frac{1}{n} \cdot n$$

$$= \frac{n - 1}{2m} + 1$$

for the average cost of a successful retrieval. Not surprisingly, this is about half the average cost of an unsuccessful retrieval, and is again $O(1)$ if $m \simeq n$. It is interesting to interpret this formula for the cases $n = 1$ and $n = 2$.

Finally, deletion as implemented in Figure 7.4 has the same cost as a successful retrieval, so if the deletion is equally likely to be applied to any entry, its average complexity is also $(n - 1)/2m + 1$. This could be reduced to $O(1)$ in the worst case by using a doubly linked list.

The fundamental reason why an average complexity analysis is justifiable for this ADT implementation is that any lack of randomness in the input (for example, in the values of the keys) is compensated for by the randomizing effect of the hash function. Observing this, researchers have designed *randomized algorithms* which introduce randomly generated numbers into the calculations so as to be able to use this kind of analysis even when the input itself cannot be assumed to be random.

## 7.8 The Indexed List ADT

This section takes up a thread that was dropped in Section 5.1, where the operation of finding the $i$th entry was omitted from the List ADT because of concerns over efficiency. The Indexed List ADT (Figure 7.5) is the List ADT with three additional operations: *size* returns the number of entries in the list, *find(i)* returns the $i$th entry if $1 \le i \le size$ and a nil entry otherwise, and *index_of(x)* returns the index of entry $x$, which is assumed to lie in the list.

The Indexed List ADT is appropriate for the sequence of lines of a file within a text editor. Text editors require all the usual operations of the List ADT, including insertion, deletion, and traversal, but they also provide direct access to the $i$th line.

---

**class interface** *LIST_INDEXED_ADT[VALUE_TYPE]*

**inherit**

  *LIST_ADT[VALUE_TYPE]* **redefine** *entry_type* **end**


  *entry_type*: *LIST_INDEXED_ADT_ENTRY[VALUE_TYPE]*

  *size*: *INTEGER*
      -- The number of entries in this indexed list

  *find*(*i*: *INTEGER*): **like** *entry_type*
      -- The *i*th entry of this list

  *index_of*(*x*: **like** *entry_type*): *INTEGER*
      -- The index of entry *x* in this list

**end** -- *LIST_INDEXED_ADT*

---

**Figure 7.5** Specification of the Indexed List ADT. The **inherit** clause means that the ADT contains all the operations of the List ADT as well as these additional ones.

  Since *find*(*i*) is reminiscent of *retrieve* in symbol tables, a natural first thought is to use the Ordered Symbol Table ADT with index numbers for keys. This fails because an insertion or deletion changes the index number of every entry after the point where it occurs. However, it turns out that all the tree implementations of the ordered symbol table can be adapted to the indexed list. This adaptation will be done here for the binary search tree and splay tree.

  The data structure to be described is widely known but not often discussed, and seems to have no standard name; it will be called the *binary indexing tree* here. The list entries are nodes of a binary tree, arranged so that an inorder traversal (Section 6.2) gives the correct sequence. In addition to the usual *left_child*, *right_child*, and *parent* attributes, each node contains a *size* attribute which holds the size of the subtree rooted at that node:

*Abstract value*  $\langle a, b, c, d, e, f, g \rangle$

*Concrete value*

The *size* fields replace the *key* fields of the binary search tree. Any shape of tree is acceptable, provided an inorder traversal gives the entries in the correct order.

As will be seen in a moment, it is not difficult to find implementations for all the Indexed List operations. The key point is that each traverses a single path from the root to a leaf (or vice versa), and so is potentially very fast.

The front of the sequence is at the extreme left, so *insert_first* simply adds a node there. It turns out that *insert_after(x)* is also very easy: if *x* has no right child, the insertion goes there, otherwise it goes at the bottom left of *x*'s right subtree:

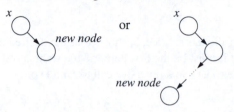

The nature of inorder traversal (Section 6.2) shows that the new node will then come immediately after *x* in the inorder traversal, as required. After the insertion it is necessary to set the size field of the new node to 1, and to add 1 to the size field of every proper ancestor of the new node.

The same ideas, reversing left and right, take care of *insert_last* and *insert_before(x)*. The deletion algorithm for binary trees works here too, although again there are *size* fields to be updated. The traversal operations *first* and *next(x)* are just *inorder_first* and *inorder_next(x)* from Section 6.2, and *last* and *prev(x)* are the same with left and right reversed. Two binary trees may be appended by deleting the rightmost node from the first tree and making it the root of the result:

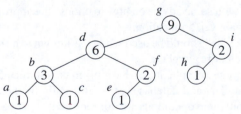

Of course, if either tree is empty *append* is trivial. The *split(x)* operation is quite tricky, and if it is required it is probably best to use splay trees (see below).

Since that is all the List operations, and *size* is trivial because the *size* field of the root holds the total size, the only remaining operations are *find(i)* and *index_of(x)*. Consider executing *find(5)* on this tree:

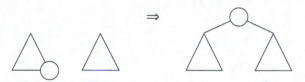

The *size* field of the root shows that a fifth entry does exist, but it is not otherwise helpful. However, the *size* field of its left child, 6, shows that the fifth entry of the whole tree is also the fifth entry of the left subtree, so the next step is to execute *find*(5) recursively on that subtree:

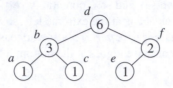

This time the size of the left subtree, 3, shows that the desired entry must lie in the right subtree; in fact it must be the first entry of the right subtree $(5 - (3 + 1) = 1,$ where + 1 counts the root). So a recursive call to *find*(1) on

will complete the task by returning *e*. The *index_of*(*x*) operation can be done by a single scan from *x* up to the root, or more simply in splay trees (see below).

The Indexed List ADT is highly prone to insertion sequences that produce skew trees: consider the common text editing situation where lines are added at the end of the file. So some kind of tree balancing scheme is certainly needed. Splay trees (Section 7.5) are particularly appropriate here because splaying exploits locality of reference (Section 7.3), which is highly likely to arise in indexed lists, and because *split*(*x*) and *index_of*(*x*) are trivial to implement in splay trees. A splay at *x* will bring *x* to the root, where a split is very easy:

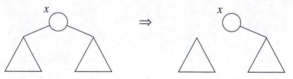

and when *x* is the root, *index_of*(*x*) is just the size of its left subtree plus one.

## 7.9 Choosing a symbol table implementation

This chapter closes with some advice on how to choose the appropriate symbol table implementation for a given application.

The basic linked list should be used when *n* is known to be small ($n \leq 20$, say); however, it is inefficient for larger *n*.

The $O(1)$ average complexity of hashing makes it very attractive, and it is widely used in compilers and databases. It will usually be the appropriate choice when ordered symbol table operations are not required.

If hashing is chosen, the simplicity and efficiency of chaining generally make it the method of choice. Only if the entries are very small, on the order of the size of one reference, would the space overhead of the links suggest a change to linear probing. In a chained hash table, the move-to-front heuristic is very cheap to implement and will be worthwhile whenever there is locality of reference in the operation sequence. Hash tables on disk generally employ a number of hardware-dependent optimizations: the use of buckets, for example.

If hashing is not suitable, some kind of search tree must be used. On disk, some balanced multiway search tree like the B-tree would always be chosen, and optimized to minimize the number of disk block reads as described in Section 7.6. In memory, the binary search tree is often used: it provides good average complexity for the ordered symbol table operations, and is quite simple to implement. If greater efficiency is required, the more complex splay tree has $O(\log n)$ amortized complexity per operation and in practice seems to run very fast. If $O(\log n)$ worst-case performance is required, a variety of balanced tree methods is available; 2-3 trees are as simple as any, although some of the others, for example the red-black trees (closely related to B-trees of order 4) described in Sedgewick (1988), offer the convenience of one entry per node.

The reader interested in further study of symbol table implementations will find many in Knuth (1973b) that lack of space and a desire to concentrate on the most practically useful methods have excluded from this chapter. Knuth's treatment of hashing is particularly interesting, containing descriptions and analyses of a large number of ingenious variants.

## 7.10 Exercises

7.1     Perform an abstract trace (showing sets of entries, each containing a key and a value) of the following sequence of Symbol Table operations:

> *s.make*;
> *a := s.new_entry("a", 0)*;
> *b := s.new_entry("b", 0)*;
> *c := s.new_entry("c", 0)*;
> *d := s.new_entry("d", 0)*;
> *e := s.new_entry("e", 0)*;
> *f := s.new_entry("f", 0)*;
> *s.insert(e)*;
> *s.insert(c)*;
> *x := s.retrieve("e")*;
> *y := s.retrieve("d")*;
> *s.insert(a)*;
> *s.insert(d)*;
> *y := s.retrieve("d")*;
> *z := s.retrieve("a")*;
> *s.delete(c)*;

7.2     Give a formal specification of the Symbol Table ADT using preconditions and postconditions as in Section 3.2. The mathematical entity is a set of entries, each containing a key and a value.

7.3     Trace the three list adjusting heuristics using the sequence of operations given in Question 7.1.

7.4     How does the move-to-front list adjusting heuristic compare with making no adjustment at all?

7.5     Using the potential function given in the text, find the amortized complexity of a deletion in a linked list employing the move-to-front heuristic. Assume that the list must be scanned to find the deletion point.

7.6     Suppose there is given, for each entry $x_i$ in a symbol table, a fixed probability $p_i$ that $x_i$ will be retrieved next. If the entries are kept in an unsorted linked list, in what order should they appear so as to minimize the average complexity of the next retrieval? Prove your result.

7.7     Trace the binary search tree implementation of the Symbol Table ADT on the operations given in Question 7.1. The ordering is lexicographical (that is, alphabetical).

7.8     It is clear that the implementation of *delete*(x) in a binary tree requires that we know the value of the parent of node $x$, since the reference to $x$ in the parent must be changed. In a binary search tree, there are at least two viable ways to get this information: keep a reference to the parent in every node, or begin the deletion with a retrieval so as to approach $x$ from above. Investigate their relative advantages and disadvantages.

7.9     Let $T$ be a fixed binary search tree containing $n$ nodes. Show that, under reasonable assumptions, the average complexity of a successful retrieval in $T$ is $i(T)/n$, and of an unsuccessful retrieval is $e(T)/(n + 1)$, where $i(T)$ and $e(T)$ are the internal and external path lengths of $T$.

7.10    What is the average complexity of the last insertion of a sequence of $n$ insertions into an initially empty binary search tree?

7.11    Consider a sequence of $n$ insertions into an initially empty binary search tree, followed by a single retrieval. What is the average complexity of the retrieval, if (a) it is successful (that is, an entry with the given key is present)? and (b) it is unsuccessful?

7.12    *Right-threaded binary search trees.* This question is devoted to a method of implementing the Ordered Symbol Table ADT using binary search trees, due to Perlis and Thornton (1960), which avoids most of the space overhead of parent references. Each node contains an additional boolean field called *right_thread*. In nodes $x$ that have a non-void right child, $x.right\_thread$ is **false** and $x.right\_child$ points to the right child in the usual way. However, in nodes where $x.right\_child$ would normally be void, $x.right\_thread$ is **true** and $x.right\_child$ points to the inorder successor of $x$, or is void if $x$ has no successor. These extra references are called *right threads*, and they are conventionally shown as dashed arrows:

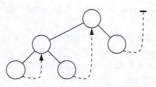

It is surprisingly easy to insert a new node while maintaining the threads correctly. If the new node is a left child, the insertion is done like this:

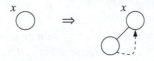

If the new node is a right child, it is done like this:

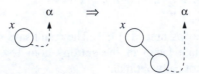

with one thread copied into the new node. Implement the Ordered Symbol Table ADT (right-moving traversals only) using right-threaded trees.

7.13 Perform a splay at $e$ in this tree:

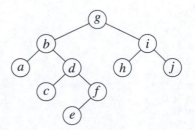

7.14 Complete the proof of the Access Lemma for splay trees (Theorem 7.3) by verifying the statements made about the amortized complexity of the Case 2 and Case 3 splaying steps.

7.15 Adopt the following more general potential function for splay trees. Assign to each node $x$ an arbitrary positive number $w(x)$. Let $W = \Sigma w(x)$ be the total weight. Let

$$s(x) = \sum_{y \in T_x} w(y)$$

where $T_x$ is the subtree rooted at $x$; and let $r(x) = \log_2 s(x)$ as usual.

(a) Verify that the original potential function is a special case of this.

(b) Modify the Access Lemma and its proof appropriately.

(c) Consider a splay tree with some fixed number of nodes. Initially the tree could have any shape. Show that, for any sequence of retrievals whatsoever, the change in potential cannot exceed

$$\sum_{x \in T} \log_2(W/w(x))$$

Hence show that, if $s$ is any sequence of $m$ retrievals, and $q(x)$ is the number of times $x$ is retrieved in $s$, then the total cost of the sequence is of the order of

$$m + \sum_{x \in T} q(x)\log_2(m/q(x))$$

You may assume $q(x) \geq 1$. The result says that splay trees are within a constant factor of the entropy bound (Section 13.4), and so are asymptotically optimal.

7.16 Trace the following operation sequence on the 2-3 tree implementation of the Symbol Table ADT. Note that '59' is shorthand for an entry whose key is 59, and so on.

*s.make*;
*s.insert*(59);
*s.insert*(25);
*s.insert*(41);
*s.insert*(12);
*s.insert*(34);
*s.insert*(63);
*s.insert*(76);
*s.insert*(88);
*s.delete*(59);
*s.insert*(59);
*s.delete*(25);
*s.delete*(34);

7.17 Trace the operation sequence

> *s.insert*(11);
> *s.insert*(12);
> *s.insert*(13);
> *s.insert*(14);
> *s.insert*(15);

on the following B-tree of order 5:

7.18 What is the maximum number of entries that will fit into a B-tree of order *m* and height *h*?

7.19 If you had a file of 500 000 entries stored as a B-tree of order *m*, and only the root could be fitted into main memory, how large would *m* have to be to guarantee that every entry could be found in at most two disk accesses? Assume that it takes one access per node regardless of *m*.

7.20 The cost of splitting a B-tree node into two is $O(m)$. This question aims to show that splittings happen so rarely that their overall cost is negligible.

(a) Show that a B-tree of order *m*, containing *n* entries, cannot have more than $(n - 1)/(\lceil m/2 \rceil - 1) + 1$ nodes.

(b) Use this to show that, over the course of *n* insertions into an initially empty B-tree, the number of node splittings per insertion is at most $1/(\lceil m/2 \rceil - 1)$. The creation of a new root is not a node splitting.

7.21 B-trees were introduced in order to get $O(\log n)$ worst-case performance per operation. There are several other data structures that achieve this; one well-known one is the *AVL tree*, named after its originators, Adel'son-Vel'skii and Landis (1962). An AVL tree is a binary tree which is *height-balanced*: that is, for any internal node *x* of *T*, the heights of *x*'s left and right subtrees may differ by at most 1. For example, $T_1$ below is height-balanced but $T_2$ is not, because the node marked with a * violates the requirement:

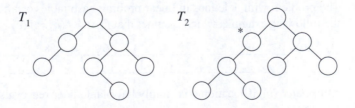

Let $N(h)$ be the minimum possible number of external nodes in a height-balanced tree of height $h$. Show that

$$N(0) = 1$$
$$N(1) = 2$$
$$N(h) = N(h-1) + N(h-2)$$

From this, it follows that $N(h) = F(h+2) \geq \phi^h$, where $\phi \approx 1.6180339$ (see Exercise 2.6). For any height-balanced tree $T$ with $n$ internal nodes, therefore, $h(T) \leq \log_\phi(n+1)$, and operations that are confined to one path from the root to a leaf will have $O(\log n)$ worst-case time complexity.

7.22　Trace the following operation sequence on a hash table of size 10 with (a) chaining and (b) linear probing. Use hash function $f(x) = x \setminus\setminus 10$. Note that '59' within *insert* is shorthand for an entry whose key is 59, and so on.

> *s.make*;
> *s.insert*(59);
> *s.insert*(41);
> *s.insert*(25);
> *s.insert*(12);
> *s.insert*(91);
> *s.insert*(34);
> *s.retrieve*(91);
> *s.insert*(63);
> *s.insert*(75);
> *s.insert*(85);
> *s.insert*(99);
> *s.insert*(23);
> *s.retrieve*(34);

7.23　Using the two-digit decimal character set $a = 01, \ldots, z = 26$, and letting $//$ be integer division and $\setminus\setminus$ be integer remainder, find three identifiers that hash to the same location when the hash function is

(a)　$f(x) = x \setminus\setminus 53$

(b)　$f(x) = (x.item(1) * x.item(2)) \setminus\setminus 100$

(c)　$f(x) = (x^2 // 100) \setminus\setminus 100$

7.24　The problem with deletions in linear probing hash tables can be seen from the following example, which assumes that $f(a) = f(b) = f(c) = 3$:

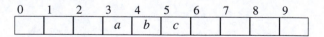

After *delete*(b), if location 4 is simply left blank, later retrievals will fail to find *c*. Devise a deletion algorithm that overcomes this; but be warned this is a very tricky problem.

7.25 Implement the Symbol Table ADT using a hash table with linear probing. Be careful with deletions (see the preceding question), and also with correct termination of the insertion and retrieval algorithms. A good plan is to keep a count of the number of entries present, and use it to ensure that there is always at least one empty slot.

7.26 Let $p_1, p_2, \ldots, p_m$ be any sequence of symbol table operations beginning with *make*, and containing no deletions. Consider two hash tables, one employing linear probing and the other employing chaining, but both using the same hash function. Show that, for all *i*, the cost of $p_i$ in the linear probing table is at least as great as its cost in the chained hash table.

7.27 The chained hash table implementation in Figure 7.4 includes a private *rehash* operation. Whenever *n* comes to exceed 2*m*, a rehash is performed which switches to a new table of size 2*m* − 1. This is expensive, since every entry must be transferred. Show that the total complexity of all rehashes is $O(n)$, where *n* is the maximum number of entries in the table, and conclude that rehashing does not dominate the overall cost.

7.28 Suppose you know in advance what all the keys in some symbol table will be. For example, the symbol table might hold just the reserved words of a programming language (**class, do**, and so on). Can you invent a hash function which will guarantee that no two keys will collide?

7.29 *Best-fit memory allocation*. A computer's internal memory is a valuable resource, and one of the tasks of an operating system is to keep track of which parts of the memory are in use, and which are available. Processes wishing to acquire a slice of memory do so via the following ADT:

> **class interface** *MEMORY_ALLOCATOR*
>
> *start_address*(*s*: *MEMORY_SLICE*): *MEMORY_ADDRESS*
> -- The address of memory slice *s*
>
> *slice_size*(*s*: *MEMORY_SLICE*): *INTEGER*
> -- The size in bytes of memory slice *s*
>
> *allocate*(*size*: *INTEGER*): *MEMORY_SLICE*
> -- A newly allocated memory slice of size *size*
>
> *deallocate*(*s*: *MEMORY_SLICE*)
> -- Free the memory consumed by slice *s* for other uses
>
> **end** -- *MEMORY_ALLOCATOR*

A *memory slice s* is a record describing a contiguous block of memory, which begins at *start_address(s)* and contains *slice_size(s)* bytes of memory. A process requests a slice of a certain size by calling *s := allocate(size)*; when this memory is no longer required by the process, it returns it to the operating system by the call *deallocate(s)*.

The memory allocator views the entire memory as a sequence of slices, some free and some allocated:

The allocated memory is fragmented in this way because of the unpredictable way in which slices are allocated and deallocated.

A *best-fit memory allocator* responds to *allocate(size)* by finding a smallest free slice whose size is at least as large as *size*. This is split into two slices; the first is of size *size* and is returned to the caller; the second holds the rest and remains free. When a slice is deallocated, it must be joined with neighboring free slices to prevent the memory from fragmenting into many small adjacent free slices.

Find an efficient implementation of this ADT. Aim for $O(\log n)$ worst-case complexity per operation, where $n$ is the number of *free* slices.

7.30 *The block cache.* Most of the information stored inside a computer is held on disk, where it is organized into *blocks*, each typically holding 1024 bytes. Two operations, *read_block(i: INTEGER; p: MEMORY_ADDRESS)* and *write_block(i: INTEGER; p: MEMORY_ADDRESS)* are provided for copying the block whose number is *i* into or out of the main memory of the computer, starting at address *p*. These operations are slow, and so it is worthwhile to keep copies of blocks in main memory. The copies may be accessed much more cheaply than the actual blocks, and even if there is room for only a few block copies in main memory, the method will be worthwhile whenever block accesses exhibit locality of reference.

In order to take advantage of these ideas, an operating system provides the following ADT:

**class interface** *BLOCK_HANDLER*

    *start_address(b: BLOCK_COPY): MEMORY_ADDRESS*
      -- The address in memory of block copy *b*

    *open_block(i: INTEGER): BLOCK_COPY*
      -- A memory copy of block *i*

    *close_block(b: BLOCK_COPY)*
      -- Indicate that block copy *b* is no longer required

**end** -- *BLOCK_HANDLER*

Programs call on this ADT instead of calling *read_block* and *write_block* directly. A *BLOCK_COPY* is a reference to a record containing information private to the ADT, plus one 1024-byte field, whose address is *start_address(b)*, holding the copy of the block. A program gains access to a copy *b* of block number *i* by calling *b* := *open_block(i)*, and it informs the operating system that it is finished with the block by calling *close_block(b)*. Several programs may share the same block; a copy must remain in main memory until all are finished with it.

The ADT manages a set of block copies, whose total number cannot exceed some fixed number *M* determined by the amount of main memory available. If *M* block copies are currently in use and a new block must be opened, it is first necessary to make room for it by writing out a closed block, which should be the one least recently closed, since it is reasonable to assume that that block is unlikely to be needed again. If all *M* blocks are open, the correct action is to wait until a block closes; but, since concurrent programming is beyond the scope of this book, it is sufficient for the purposes of this question to signal in some way that this situation has arisen. Find an efficient implementation of this ADT.

7.31   The symbol table in a compiler for a block-structured programming language is defined by the following ADT:

> **class interface** *BLOCKTAB[KEY_TYPE, VALUE_TYPE]*
>
> *entry_type*: *BLOCKTAB_ENTRY[KEY_TYPE, VALUE_TYPE]*
>
> *make*
>     -- Make a new, empty table
>
> *insert(x*: **like** *entry_type)*
>     -- Insert *x* into the current block
>
> *retrieve(key*: *KEY_TYPE)*
>     -- Retrieve an entry with key *key*
>
> *enter_block*
>     -- Enter a new block of symbols
>
> *leave_block*
>     -- Leave the most recent block of symbols
>
> **end** -- *BLOCKTAB*

The *enter_block* operation is called when the compiler reaches the beginning of a block (for example, the start of a class or routine definition), and the *leave_block* operation is called when the compiler reaches the end of the block, at which point all entries inserted since the corresponding *enter_block* must be deleted, since they are no longer visible in the program text. For example, in the sequence

> *s.make*;
> *s.enter_block*;
> *s.insert(p)*;
> *s.enter_block*;
> *s.insert(q)*;
> *s.insert(r)*;
> *s.leave_block*;
> *s.leave_block*;

entries *q* and *r* are deleted by the first *leave_block*, and *p* by the second.

Another complication is that it is possible for entries to have the same key, provided that they are inserted in different blocks. In such cases, *retrieve* is to return the innermost (most recently inserted) of the entries.

Devise an implementation of this ADT based on hashing.

# Chapter 8

# Priority Queues

The Priority Queue abstract data type, whose implementations are studied in this chapter, appears in more algorithms than any other ADT. In this book, it may be found in algorithms for Huffman coding, selection sorting, minimum spanning trees, and shortest path spanning trees. Its name comes from an application in operating systems: the maintenance of a queue of processes, to be run according to their priorities. And it lies at the heart of one of the most time-consuming of all applications of computing: the simulation of processes evolving over time.

## 8.1 Specification

A *priority queue*, like a symbol table, is a set of entries, each containing a key and a value. However, a given key may appear in more than one entry, there is always an ordering on the keys, and the operations, shown in Figure 8.1, are somewhat different. As usual, the *new_entry(key, value)* operation returns a new entry with the given key and value. There seems to be no need for a nil entry. The five priority queue operations initialize a priority queue to empty, test whether a priority queue is empty, insert an entry, retrieve (but not delete) an entry with minimum key, and delete (but not destroy) and return an entry with minimum key.

As an example of the use of priority queues, consider the simulation of a supermarket checkout line. The aim is to determine experimentally the average time that a customer can expect to wait for service, given certain assumptions about the rate at which customers arrive, and the time it takes to serve one customer.

The customer's experience of the supermarket line can be described as a sequence of *events*, which occur over time:

---

**class interface** *PRIQUEUE_ADT[KEY_TYPE -> COMPARABLE, VALUE_TYPE]*

*entry_type*: *PRIQUEUE_ADT_ENTRY[KEY_TYPE, VALUE_TYPE]*;

*new_entry(key*: *KEY_TYPE*; *value*: *VALUE_TYPE*): **like** *entry_type*
     -- A new entry containing *key* and *value*

*make*
     -- Initialize this priority queue to empty

*empty*: *BOOLEAN*
     -- **true** if this priority queue is empty, else **false**

*insert(x*: **like** *entry_type)*
     -- Insert *x* into this priority queue

*find_min*: **like** *entry_type*
     -- An entry of this priority queue whose key is minimum

*delete_min*: **like** *entry_type*
     -- Delete and return the entry that would be returned by *find_min*

**end** -- *PRIQUEUE_ADT*

---

**Figure 8.1** Specification of the Priority Queue ADT. The Eiffel notation *KEY_TYPE -> COMPARABLE* means that implementations may compare keys using '<'.

The simulation as a whole must keep track of many customers, arriving at random times, so hundreds or thousands of events can be expected.

Suppose that the event 'customer $C$ is served' occurs at time $t$. Assuming that it takes between 30 and 300 seconds to serve one customer, a random number generator may be used to decide that at time $t + 227$, say, the customer will leave. This defines a new event, 'customer $C$ leaves,' which must happen at time $t + 227$: a *pending event*.

A pending event is represented by an entry whose key equals the time at which the event will occur, and whose value describes the nature of the event. If these entries are stored in a priority queue, the simulation can then proceed as follows. First, use *delete_min* to determine which event will happen next. Declare that the event has happened, and perform whatever action is needed to simulate its occurrence. For example, the action for the event 'customer $C$ is served' is the insertion of a new event 'customer $C$ leaves,' with time $t + 227$ or whatever, into the priority queue. The action for 'customer $C$ leaves' is the insertion of 'customer $D$ is served' with time 5 seconds from now, where customer $D$ is the customer next in line, as recorded in some auxiliary data structure (which in this case would be a fifo queue).

In outline, then, the simulation algorithm is

!!*q.make*;
**from** *q.insert(some_initial_event)* **until** *q.empty* **loop**
  *event := q.delete_min*;
  *execute(event)*
**end**

where *execute(event)* may include insertions into the queue. A variety of observations would be recorded as the simulation proceeds, so that statistics such as the average wait can be calculated after the simulation ends.

Although the ordered symbol table implementations of Chapter 7 can be used for priority queues (suitably modified to permit non-unique keys), there are simpler ways to achieve $O(\log n)$ worst-case complexity per operation. And there are some more exotic operations, which make up what will be called the Extended Priority Queue ADT (Figure 8.2), which are not all so amenable to efficient implementation with an ordered symbol table. These extra operations are *delete(x)*, which deletes entry $x$, *meld(other)*, which merges all the entries of some other priority queue into this one (similarly to *append* for lists), and *decrease_key(x, newkey)*, which takes entry $x$ and alters the value of its key to *newkey*, which must be no larger than the old key. This naturally requires the position of $x$ within the priority queue ranking to be changed. It is a particularly exotic operation, admittedly, but it happens to be required by some of the graph algorithms of Chapter 12, so it is included here.

## 8.2 Heap-ordered trees

The data structures of this chapter are all based on the idea of heap-ordered trees. A *heap-ordered* (or *partially ordered*) tree is a rooted tree in which each non-root node obeys the *heap invariant*: its key is greater than or equal to the key of its parent. For example,

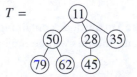

is heap-ordered. The root holds a minimum key, and the keys increase going down any path. The second minimum could lie in any child of the root. A node may have any number of children; $c(x)$ is defined to be the number of children of node $x$.

**class interface** *PRIQUEUE_EXTENDED_ADT[KEY_TYPE ->*
  *COMPARABLE, VALUE_TYPE]*

**inherit**

  *PRIQUEUE_ADT[KEY_TYPE, VALUE_TYPE]* **redefine** *entry_type* **end**;

  *entry_type*: *PRIQUEUE_EXTENDED_ADT_ENTRY[KEY_TYPE,*
    *VALUE_TYPE]*;

  *delete(x*: **like** *entry_type)*
        -- Delete *x* from this priority queue

  *meld(other*: **like** *Current)*
        -- Insert all entries of *other* into this priority queue

  *decrease_key(x*: **like** *entry_type; newkey: KEY_TYPE)*
        -- Decrease the key of *x* to *newkey*

**end** -- *PRIQUEUE_EXTENDED_ADT*

**Figure 8.2** Specification of the Extended Priority Queue ADT. The **inherit** clause means that the Extended Priority Queue ADT includes all of the operations of the Priority Queue ADT as well as the additional ones given here.

## Adding a leaf

There are two ways to build a heap-ordered tree of a given shape. The first is based on an operation called *add_leaf*, which attaches one node to a given node of the tree (or, if the tree is empty, it is replaced by the new node). For example, given the tree

*add_leaf* may be used to attach a new node containing 50 to the node containing 62. The new node is not known to satisfy the heap invariant, and this will be indicated by a dashed link:

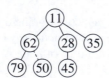

The *add_leaf* operation compares 50 with 62, discovers that they are out of order, and exchanges the entries:

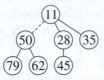

Now 50 is not known to obey the heap invariant with its parent 11, so *add_leaf* compares them, discovers that the invariant is in fact satisfied, and halts:

The new entry moves up the path towards the root, stopping when the heap invariant holds. The new key is only compared with keys on this path: since it is smaller than each key it replaces, it can only be out of order with its parent, not its children.

In the worst case, the new key is compared once with each of its proper ancestors, giving a cost of $d(x)$, where $d(x)$ is the depth of the new node. An entire tree $T$ with $n$ nodes can be built by repeated *add_leaf* operations; the worst-case complexity of building $T$ in this way is

$$W(n) = \sum_{x \in I(T)} d(x)$$

$$= i(T)$$

the internal path length of $T$.

## Adding a root

The second way to build a heap-ordered tree of a given shape is based on an operation that will be called *add_root*. Suppose there is a non-empty tree

$T =$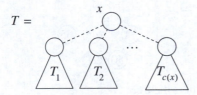

where $T_1, T_2, \ldots, T_{c(x)}$ are heap-ordered trees, but nothing is known about their relationship with the key of $x$. The task of *add_root* is to make $T$ heap-ordered.

If $x$ has no children, $T$ is clearly heap-ordered, so *add_root* has nothing to do. Otherwise, find a minimum child $y$ of $x$. If the key of $y$ is not smaller than the key of $x$, then the key of $x$ must be equal to or smaller than all the keys in $T$, so again there is nothing more to do. Otherwise, the key of $y$ is the smallest in the whole tree, and it belongs in the root. So swap $x$'s entry with $y$'s entry. Now the subtree rooted at $y$ may not be heap-ordered, so apply *add_root* recursively to it.

Here is an example of this algorithm. As usual, links not known to obey the heap invariant are shown dashed. In the initial tree shown below, the minimum child of the root contains 11, which is smaller than 62, so a swap is needed:

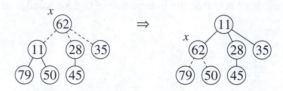

Now *add_root* must be applied recursively. The minimum child of the node now containing 62 contains 50, so swap again:

Now the node containing 62 has no children, so it is time to stop.

The new root moves down some path until its children all satisfy the heap invariant, or there are no children. Since the entry of $x$ is replaced by the entry of its minimum child $y$, after the swap all the children of $x$ satisfy the heap invariant. But the key of $y$ is increased by the swap, so the heap invariant may be violated by some of its children – hence the recursive call.

To build a heap-ordered tree $T$ using *add_root* operations, begin with the keys of $T$ in no particular order. The nodes with no children already constitute heap-ordered trees, so work upwards from them, using the dynamic programming principle of ensuring that all the subtrees of $x$ are heap-ordered before calling *add_root*($x$):

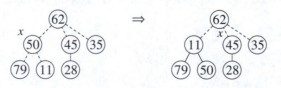

Applying *add_root*($x$) twice more heap-orders the tree:

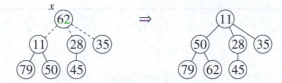

It takes $c(x) - 1$ comparisons between keys to determine the minimum child $y$ of $x$ (a find-the-minimum on the $c(x)$ children of $x$), plus one comparison of $x$ with $y$, for a total of $c(x)$ comparisons to move the root down one level. In the worst case, the new entry propagates all the way down. The longest possible such path contains $h(x)$ nodes, by the definition of the height $h(x)$, but the last node has no children, so it contributes nothing to the cost. So the maximum number of nodes on the path may be taken to be $h(x) - 1$. Letting $C = \max_{x \in I(T)} c(x)$, it is clear that $C[h(x) - 1]$ is an upper bound on the cost of *add_root(x)*, and the worst-case complexity of building an $n$-node tree by repeated *add_root* operations is

$$W(n) \le C \sum_{x \in I(T)} [h(x) - 1]$$

where $I(T)$, as usual, is the set of internal nodes of $T$. Such a sum of heights has not been encountered before, so it is not clear how this method of building a heap compares with the method of repeated *add_leaf* operations.

## 8.3 The heap

Since it is possible to build a heap-ordered tree of any shape, it is natural to consider building a complete binary tree. It is also possible to insist that the nodes at the bottom level be *left-justified*:

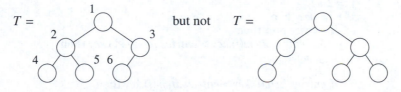

The advantage of this is that, by numbering the nodes from top to bottom and left to right (as shown above), the children of node $i$ are $2i$ and $2i + 1$ if they exist, and the parent of node $i$ is $\lfloor i/2 \rfloor$ if it exists. $T$ may be stored in an array:

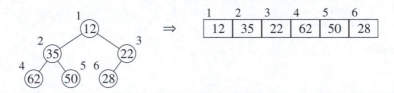

```
class PRIQUEUE_HEAP[KEY_TYPE -> COMPARABLE, VALUE_TYPE]

inherit

   PRIQUEUE_ADT[KEY_TYPE, VALUE_TYPE]

feature { NONE }

   entry_type: PRIQUEUE_HEAP_ENTRY[KEY_TYPE, VALUE_TYPE]

   entries: ARRAY[like entry_type]

   size: INTEGER

   add_leaf(pos: INTEGER) is
         -- Add leaf at position pos
      local
         i, j: INTEGER; x: like entry_type
      do
         from x := entries.item(pos);  i := pos;  j := i // 2
         until j <= 0 or else  entries.item(j).key <= x.key loop
            entries.put(entries.item(j), i)
            i := j;  j := i // 2
         end;
         entries.put(x, i)
      end -- add_leaf

   add_root(i: INTEGER) is
         -- Add a new root at position i
      local
         j: INTEGER;  x: like entry_type;
      do
         j := 2 * i;
         if j <= size then
            if j < size and then
                  entries.item(j).key > entries.item(j+1).key then
               j := j + 1
            end;
            if entries.item(i).key > entries.item(j).key then
               x := entries.item(i);
               entries.put(entries.item(j), i);
               entries.put(x, j);
               add_root(j)
            end
         end
      end; -- add_root

feature
```

```
new_entry(k: KEY_TYPE; v: VALUE_TYPE): like entry_type is
    do
        !!Result.make(k, v);
    end;

make is
    do
        !!entries.make(1, 100);
        size := 0;
    end; -- make

empty: BOOLEAN is
    do
        Result := (size = 0)
    end;

insert(x: like entry_type) is
    do
        if size = entries.upper then
            entries.resize(1, size * 2)
        end;
        size := size + 1;
        entries.put(x, size);
        add_leaf(size)
    end; -- insert

find_min: like entry_type is
    do
        Result := entries.item(1)
    end; -- find_min

delete_min: like entry_type is
    do
        Result := entries.item(1);
        size := size - 1;
        if size > 0 then
            entries.put(entries.item(size + 1), 1);
            add_root(1);
        end;
    end; -- delete_min

end -- class PRIQUEUE_HEAP
```

**Figure 8.3** Implementation of the Priority Queue ADT, using the heap data structure. The extended priority queue operations have been omitted; *delete* and *decrease_key* require back indexes in the entries (so that from each entry it is possible to find its index in the array) if they are to be implemented efficiently, and *meld* cannot be efficient in any case.

No links are needed: to move about in the tree, simply calculate the indices of parents and children. A heap-ordered left-justified complete binary tree stored in an array like this is called a *heap*.

The insertion of a new entry into a heap of size $n$ can be implemented easily by an *add_leaf* to position $n + 1$. The code for this appears in Figure 8.3.

The analysis is also quite simple, given a number of results that have been developed previously. Let $n$ be the size of the ADT just before the insertion takes place, or in other words, the number of entries in the heap. It was shown in the last section that the cost of this *add_leaf* operation is equal to $d(x)$, the depth of the new node. Since this new node $x$ is an internal node of maximum depth in the $(n + 1)$-node complete tree $T$ which is the result of this operation, the worst-case complexity of *insert* is

$$W(n) = h(T) - 1$$

$$= \lceil \log_2(n + 2) \rceil - 1$$

by Theorem 6.4.

The *delete_min* operation has no problem locating a minimum entry, since the root contains one, but when it is deleted the remainder has to be re-formed into a heap. This is done by moving the last entry to the root and calling *add_root*:

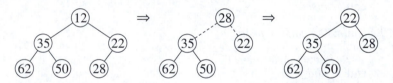

See Figure 8.3 for an implementation.

Again, let $n$ be the number of entries in the heap just before the *delete_min* operation. If $n = 1$, no call to *add_root* is made and the complexity of *delete_min* is $W(1) = 0$. Otherwise, the complexity is equal to the cost of *add_root(x)*, where $x$ is the root of the $(n - 1)$-node complete tree $T$ which is the result of the operation. Therefore, the worst-case complexity of *delete_min* is

$$W(n) \leq 2[h(x) - 1]$$

$$= 2(\lceil \log_2 n \rceil - 1)$$

by the formula for the complexity of *add_root* given in the preceding section, and by Theorem 6.4.

To summarize, the heap is an efficient implementation of the priority queue ADT which provides $O(\log n)$ worst-case complexity for *insert* and *delete_min*, and $O(1)$ worst-case complexity for *make*, *empty*, and *find_min*. This is achieved without any overhead in space, and with code of modest length.

## 8.4 Heapsort

Before leaving the subject of heaps, it is worth deviating a little to discuss a sorting algorithm based on them. It is already clear that $n$ entries may be sorted using a heap by performing $n$ *insert* operations followed by $n$ *delete_min* operations, for a cost of about $3n\log_2 n$ comparisons between keys in the worst case; but we are going to produce a more highly tuned, rather clever in-place sorting algorithm.

Let *entries.item*(1..$n$) contain the entries. Maximum elements will be needed, not minimum ones, so here is a new *add_root*, with its comparisons reversed:

```
add_root(i, n: INTEGER) is
    local j: INTEGER;
    do
        j := 2 * i;
        if j <= n then
            if j < n and then entries.item(j).key < entries.item(j+1).key then
                j := j + 1
            end;
            if entries.item(i).key < entries.item(j).key then
                swap(entries, i, j);
                add_root(j, n)
            end
        end
    end
```

The first optimization is to use *add_root* operations instead of repeated insertions to build the heap. That is, begin with the $n$ entries in arbitrary order and call

```
build_heap(n: INTEGER) is
    local i: INTEGER;
    do
        from i := n // 2 until i < 1 loop
            add_root(i, n);
            i := i - 1
        end
    end
```

to build the heap. The second optimization is to store the extracted maximum entries at the top of *entries* as the heap shrinks. Altogether, this is Heapsort:

```
heapsort(n: INTEGER) is
    local i: INTEGER;
    do
        build_heap(n);
        from i := n until i < 2 loop
            swap(entries, 1, i);
            add_root(1, i - 1);
            i := i - 1
        end
    end
```

It is due to Williams (1964) and Floyd (1964). For example, starting with a heap with six elements, the first two iterations produce

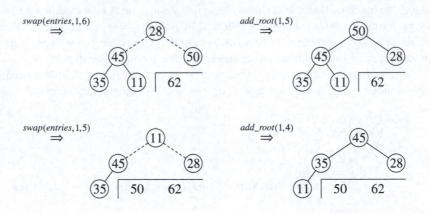

and this continues until the array is sorted.

## Analysis of Heapsort

The case $n = 0$ in Heapsort is special, because the loop is executed zero times, not $b - a + 1$ times in the terminology of Section 2.3. Clearly $W(0) = 0$, so the remainder of this analysis will assume that $n \geq 1$. According to Section 8.2, the complexity of *build_heap(n)* is

$$W(n) \leq 2 \sum_{x \in I(T)} [h(x) - 1]$$

where $T$ is the final tree. Letting $h(T) = h$, the following situation holds:

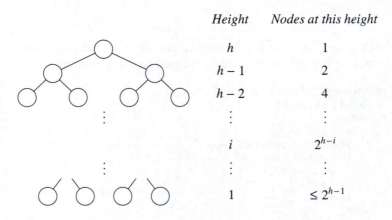

| | Height | Nodes at this height |
|---|---|---|
| | $h$ | 1 |
| | $h - 1$ | 2 |
| | $h - 2$ | 4 |
| | ⋮ | ⋮ |
| | $i$ | $2^{h-i}$ |
| | ⋮ | ⋮ |
| | 1 | $\leq 2^{h-1}$ |

The bottom level may not be full, so $2^{h-1}$ is only an upper bound on the number of nodes it contains. Since there are at most $2^{h-i}$ internal nodes at height $i$,

$$W(n) \leq 2 \sum_{x \in I(T)} [h(x) - 1]$$

$$\leq 2 \sum_{i=1}^{h} 2^{h-i}(i-1)$$

$$= 2 \sum_{i=0}^{h-1} i2^{h-i-1}$$

$$= 2^h \sum_{i=0}^{h-1} i2^{-i}$$

$$\leq 2 \times 2^h$$

using the standard formula $\sum_{i=0}^{\infty} i2^{-i} = 2$. Since $n \geq 2^{h-1}$, it follows that

$$W(n) \leq 4n$$

This startling result says that a heap may be built in linear time. In fact, a more careful analysis shows that $W(n) \leq 2(n-1)$: a non-empty heap may be built with just twice as many comparisons as it takes to find the minimum (Exercise 8.3).

The cost of $add\_root(1, i-1)$ is at most $2(h(x) - 1)$, where $h(x)$ is the height of the root in a complete tree containing $i - 1$ nodes, which by Theorem 6.4 is $\lceil \log_2 i \rceil$. Therefore the worst-case time complexity of $heapsort(n)$ is

$$W(n) = \text{cost of } build\_heap(n) + \sum_{i=2}^{n} \text{cost of } add\_root(1, i-1)$$

$$\leq 2(n-1) + \sum_{i=2}^{n} 2(\lceil \log_2 i \rceil - 1)$$

$$= 2 \sum_{i=2}^{n} \lceil \log_2 i \rceil$$

$$\leq 2(n-1)\lceil \log_2 n \rceil$$

provided $n \geq 1$. The average complexity of Heapsort was unknown for many years, but it has recently been shown to differ from the worst case by only $O(n)$.

## 8.5 Binomial queues

The subject of this section is a data structure, the *binomial queue* of Vuillemin (1978), which was the first priority queue implementation to offer efficient melding (that is, the merging of two priority queues into one). Binomial queues also form a stepping stone to the Fibonacci heaps of the next section.

Binomial queues are based on an interestingly shaped tree. The *binomial tree* $B_r$ is defined inductively by

$$B_0 = \bigcirc$$

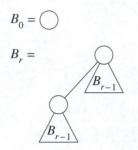

$$B_r =$$

This recurrence equation means that the tree $B_r$ is created by linking together two copies of $B_{r-1}$. For example,

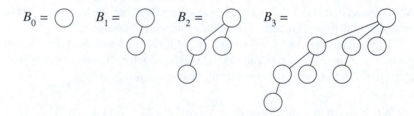

$$B_0 = \qquad B_1 = \qquad B_2 = \qquad B_3 =$$

It is easy to prove by induction on $r$ that $B_r$ has $2^r$ nodes, that $h(B_r) = r + 1$, and that the root of $B_r$ has exactly $r$ children. Other interesting properties of the binomial trees include

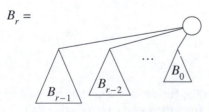

$$B_r =$$

and (for readers familiar with binomial coefficients) the fact that $B_r$ contains exactly $\binom{r}{i}$ nodes of depth $i$, which explains why these trees bear the name they do. From this it can easily be shown that the internal path length $i(B_r)$ is $r2^{r-1}$.

There is an efficient way to link two heap-ordered binomial trees $B_r$ together, to form a heap-ordered binomial tree $B_{r+1}$:

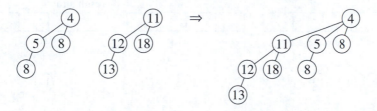

Simply compare the keys of the two roots, and make the larger the first child of the smaller. This costs just one comparison between keys.

A *binomial queue* is a forest of heap-ordered binomial trees. For convenience of presentation, references to the roots of these trees will be stored in an array, although a linked list would do as well. The tree sizes are determined by the binary representation of $n$, the number of nodes that the forest is to have; for example, if $n = 9 = 1001_2$, one $B_3$ and one $B_0$ are needed:

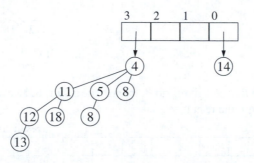

Notice that if the binomial queue as a whole contains $n$ nodes, the largest $B_r$ that it can possibly contain has $r = \log_2 n$, since a larger tree than this would have more than $n$ nodes. Since a binomial queue never contains two copies of $B_r$ for any $r$, it follows that there can be at most $\log_2 n$ trees in any binomial queue containing $n$ nodes.

Two binomial queues may be melded together into one. For example, suppose these two binomial queues are given:

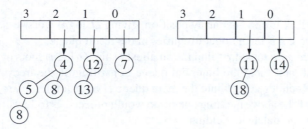

The melding is analogous to the binary addition $0111 + 0011 = 1010$. The first step is to link the two $B_0$ trees together, giving no $B_0$ trees and a carry of one $B_1$:

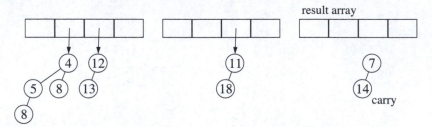

Now there are three $B_1$ trees. Insert any one into the result array and link the other two into a carry of one $B_2$:

Now link the two $B_2$ trees, giving no $B_2$ trees in the result, and a carry of one $B_3$ which can be inserted into the result:

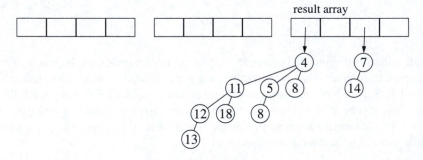

At most one link is done per array position, giving $O(\log n)$ worst-case complexity per meld, where $n$ is the number of entries in the result queue.

A *delete_min* must first find the smallest of the $O(\log n)$ roots of all the trees, then delete it, and meld the binomial queue consisting of the trees rooted at the deleted node's children back into the main queue. For example, *delete_min* applied to the result of the above melding operation would proceed as follows. First find the smallest root and delete it, yielding

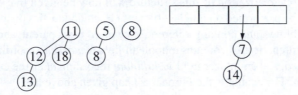

Then meld these fragments back into the queue:

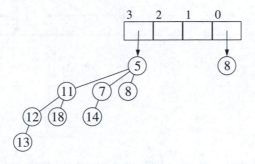

This operation is clearly also $O(\log n)$.

An insertion is just a meld of one queue with a singleton queue. Deletion of an arbitrary node is more complicated, requiring a dissection of the tree where the deletion occurred into binomial fragments and their meld back into the queue, but Vuillemin has shown that it also can be accomplished in $O(\log n)$ time.

## 8.6 Fibonacci heaps

The *Fibonacci heap* is the most efficient implementation of the full complement of priority queue operations that is currently known. It was developed by Fredman and Tarjan (1987) from the binomial queue of Section 8.5.

A Fibonacci heap is a forest of heap-ordered trees, which need not be any particular shape or size. Some nodes may be *marked*, which will be shown with an asterisk. A root node is never marked. A reference to a root node containing a minimum entry is maintained. For example,

is a Fibonacci heap with two marked nodes, and minimum reference pointing to the node containing 4.

A concrete realization of this structure will now be given that enables all the operations to be performed on it to be efficient. Each node *x* lies on a doubly linked list with its siblings, and contains references *x.parent* to its parent, and *x.children* to its list of children. It also contains a boolean field *x.marked* recording whether or not it is marked, and an integer field *x.childnum* recording $c(x)$, the current number of its children. For example, the Fibonacci heap given above has

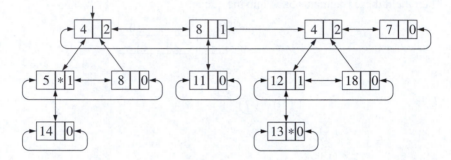

for its implementation. Observe that the roots of the trees are linked together as though they were siblings, and that the Fibonacci heap as a whole is accessed via a reference to the first root on the list. Furthermore, this first root always holds a minimum entry.

Whenever the *meld* operation is used, there must be several priority queues in existence. In such circumstances it is better to regard the ADT as a set of disjoint priority queues; the *make* operation adds a new, empty priority queue to this set, and each priority queue is implemented by one Fibonacci heap. For a reason that will become clear during the implementation of *delete_min*, an *accumulator a*, which is an array of $M + 1$ references to nodes, will be considered part of the concrete state. $M$ is some upper bound on the number of children of any node, and will be determined later. Initially, these references are all void. The picture of a typical concrete state of the ADT is thus

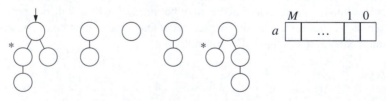

The potential of this state is defined to be

$$\Phi(S) = 3 \times \textit{the number of marked nodes} +$$
$$2 \times \textit{the number of roots} +$$
$$1 \times \textit{the number of non-void elements of a}$$

Thus, the structure is poorly balanced when there are many marked nodes, many roots, or $a$ is in use (in fact, $a$ will be used only by the *delete_min* operation). For example, the structure shown above has potential $\Phi(S) = 3 \times 2 + 2 \times 5 + 0 = 16$.

The *make* operation returns an empty list of roots; the *empty* operation checks whether the list is empty. Both have $O(1)$ actual complexity, and since they cause no change in potential, they have $O(1)$ amortized complexity also.

The *meld* operation appends the two lists of roots together, in such a way as to ensure that the smallest root comes first. This requires one comparison between the keys of the two first roots, followed by a list append, so it clearly has $O(1)$ actual complexity. There is no change in potential, since, although the trees are regrouped, their number does not change. Therefore the amortized complexity of the *meld* operation is also $O(1)$.

To implement *insert(x)*, convert $x$ into a one-element Fibonacci heap and meld it with the main heap. The new node causes a potential increase of 2, so *insert* also has $O(1)$ amortized complexity. A *find_min* operation merely returns a reference to the distinguished root node, without changing the potential, so its worst-case and amortized cost are both $O(1)$.

The *delete_min* operation is rather messy. It begins by removing the minimum node, making its children into the roots of isolated trees. For example, starting with the Fibonacci heap

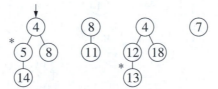

this first step produces

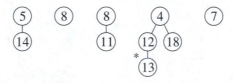

Any marked children of the deleted node are made unmarked, in line with the policy of having no marked root nodes.

The next step is to feed these trees one by one into the accumulator, which links them together in the same way as was done for binomial queues in Section 8.5. In a binomial queue, one $B_r$ is always linked with another $B_r$; since the root of $B_r$ has exactly $r$ children, the nearest equivalent in a Fibonacci heap is to link trees whose roots have the same number of children:

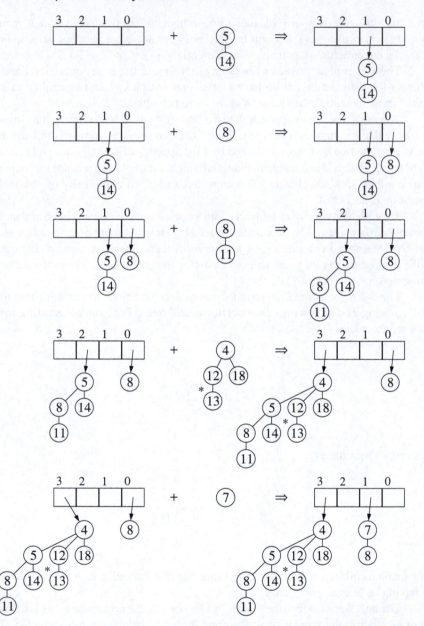

Recall that $c(x)$, the number of children of $x$, is stored in each node $x$, so it is available to index the accumulator array. The final step is a scan through the accumulator, collecting the resulting trees and simultaneously finding the root with minimum key:

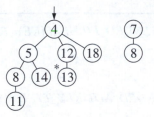

This is the final result of *delete_min*.

The analysis of *delete_min* will follow the implementation given in Figure 8.4. The characteristic operation will be one comparison of *a.item(i)* with *Void*; this is clearly realistic. Since the number of marked nodes cannot increase during *delete_min*, the potential function may be simplified to

$$\Phi(S) = 2 \times \textit{the number of roots} + 1 \times \textit{the number of non-void elements of a}$$

Let $k$ be the number of root nodes just before the operation, and $k'$ be the number of root nodes just afterwards. Clearly the first part of $\Phi(S)$ contributes $2(k' - k)$ to the change in potential. From now on it is necessary to keep track of only the second part of $\Phi(S)$: the number of non-void elements of $a$.

The cost of the first loop will be ignored in this analysis, since each iteration contributes one entry to the list of roots scanned in the second loop, and hence the first loop cannot exceed the second in cost.

The body of the second loop is executed once for each root. The list of roots contains the $k$ initial roots, minus the minimum root *Result*, plus the $c(\textit{Result})$ children of *Result*; so the body of the second loop is executed $k - 1 + c(\textit{Result})$ times. Whenever the test $a.item(i) = \textit{Void}$ is executed inside this loop, an actual cost of 1 is incurred. But if the test succeeds, its cost is cancelled by the change in potential of $-1$ caused by the assignment *a.put(Void, i)* within the inner loop. The total amortized cost of one iteration of the outer loop therefore reduces to 1 for the concluding test $a.item(i) = \textit{Void}$ that fails, plus an increase in potential of 1 caused by the assignment *a.put(carry, i)*, for a total of $2(k - 1 + c(\textit{Result}))$ for the loop.

The third loop has actual complexity $M + 1$, but the operation *a.put(Void, i)* is performed $k'$ times, giving an amortized complexity of $M + 1 - k'$.

Putting the pieces together, the amortized complexity of *delete_min* is

$$a_i = 2(k' - k) + 2(k - 1 + c(\textit{Result})) + (M + 1 - k')$$

$$= k' + 2c(\textit{Result}) + M - 1$$

$$\leq 4M,$$

since $k' \leq M + 1$ (there cannot be more final trees than positions in $a$), and $c(\textit{Result}) \leq M$ ($M$ is an upper bound on the number of children of any node).

```
class PRIQUEUE_EXTENDED_FIBHEAP[KEY_TYPE -> COMPARABLE,
  VALUE_TYPE]

inherit

  PRIQUEUE_EXTENDED_ADT[KEY_TYPE, VALUE_TYPE]

feature { PRIQUEUE_EXTENDED_FIBHEAP }

  entry_type: PRIQUEUE_EXTENDED_FIBHEAP_ENTRY[KEY_TYPE,
    VALUE_TYPE]

  nodes: PRIQUEUE_EXTENDED_FIBHEAP_FOREST[KEY_TYPE,
    VALUE_TYPE];

  array_size: INTEGER is 50;

  add_node(x: like entry_type) is
    do
      if nodes.empty or else x.key <= nodes.first_root.key then
        nodes.insert_first_root(x)
      else
        nodes.insert_last_root(x)
      end
    end;

  link(f1, f2: like nodes): like nodes is
    local
      x, y: like entry_type
    do
      x := f1.first_root;
      y := f2.first_root;
      if x.key <= y.key then
        f1.insert_first_child(x, y);
        x.put_childnum(x.childnum + 1);
        Result := f1;
      else
        f2.insert_first_child(y, x);
        y.put_childnum(y.childnum + 1);
        Result := f2;
      end
    end;
```

```
cascade_cut(x: like entry_type) is
    local
        y: like entry_type;
    do
        y := nodes.parent(x);
        nodes.delete(x);
        x.put_marked(false);
        y.put_childnum(y.childnum − 1);
        add_node(x);
        if y.marked then
            y.put_marked(false);
            cascade_cut(y);
        elseif nodes.parent(y) /= Void then
            y.put_marked(true)
        end
    end;


feature

    new_entry(k: KEY_TYPE;  v: VALUE_TYPE): like entry_type is
        do
            !!Result.make(k, v);
        end;

    make is
        do
            !!nodes;
        end;

    empty: BOOLEAN is
        do
            Result := nodes.empty;
        end;

    insert(x: like entry_type) is
        local
            other: like Current;
        do
            x.put_marked(false);
            x.put_childnum(0);
            add_node(x);
        end;

    find_min: like entry_type is
        do
            Result := nodes.first_root
        end;
```

```
delete_min: like entry_type is
    local
        i: INTEGER;
        x: like entry_type;
        a: ARRAY[like nodes];
        carry: like nodes;
    do

        -- detach the minimum entry from the queue and from its children
        Result := nodes.first_root;
        from x := nodes.first_child(Result) until nodes.nil_entry(x) loop
            nodes.delete(x);
            x.put_marked(false);
            nodes.insert_last_root(x);
            x := nodes.first_child(Result);
        end;
        nodes.delete(Result);

        -- insert each tree into a, linking as we go
        !!a.make(0, array_size);
        from until nodes.empty loop
            x := nodes.first_root;
            nodes.delete(x);
            x.put_marked(false);
            !!carry;
            carry.insert_first_root(x);
            from i := x.childnum until a.item(i) = Void loop
                carry := link(carry, a.item(i));
                a.put(Void, i);
                i := i + 1;
            end;
            a.put(carry, i);
        end;

        -- reassemble the trees of a into the heap
        from i := 0 until i > array_size loop
            if a.item(i) /= Void then
                add_node(a.item(i).first_root);
                a.put(Void, i)
            end;
            i := i + 1;
        end;

    end;
```

```
delete(x: like entry_type) is
    local
        junk: like entry_type
    do
        if nodes.first_root = x then
            junk := delete_min;
        else
            if nodes.parent(x) /= Void then
                cascade_cut(x)
            end;
            from until nodes.nil_entry(nodes.first_child(x)) loop
                cascade_cut(nodes.first_child(x))
            end;
        end
    end;

meld(other: like Current) is
    do
        if empty then
            nodes := other.nodes
        elseif other.empty then
            -- do nothing
        elseif nodes.first_root.key <= other.nodes.first_root.key then
            nodes.append_root(other.nodes)
        else
            other.nodes.append_root(nodes);
            nodes := other.nodes;
        end
    end;

decrease_key(x: like entry_type; newkey: KEY_TYPE) is
    do
        x.put_key(newkey);
        if nodes.parent(x) /= Void then
            cascade_cut(x)
        else
            nodes.delete(x);
            add_node(x)
        end
    end;

end -- class PRIQUEUE_EXTENDED_FIBHEAP
```

**Figure 8.4** Implementation of the Extended Priority Queue ADT, including *delete*, *meld*, and *decrease_key*, using Fibonacci heaps. The *nodes* attribute is the actual forest; it inherits from the *FOREST* ADT from Section 6.1, with entries suitably modified; this ADT supplies the basic forest operations of inserting and deleting nodes and so on.

If the operations on a set of Fibonacci heaps are restricted to *make, empty, insert, find_min, delete_min,* and *meld*, it is easy to prove by induction on the length of the operation sequence that every tree is a binomial tree. The *make, empty, find_min,* and *meld* operations introduce no new trees; *insert* introduces a new $B_0$ tree. The trees linked together during *delete_min* have the same number of children, $r$ say, and since both are binomial trees by the inductive hypothesis, both must be $B_r$, and hence the result is a binomial tree.

Since a binomial tree whose root has $r$ children has exactly $2^r$ nodes, every node of a binomial tree can have at most $\lfloor \log_2 n \rfloor$ children. When the set of operations is restricted to *make, empty, insert, find_min, delete_min,* and *meld*, then, it is permissible to take $M = \lfloor \log_2 n \rfloor$ in the analysis above, and this shows that *delete_min* has $O(\log n)$ amortized complexity. Each of the other operations has $O(1)$ amortized complexity.

Up to this point, a Fibonacci heap is just a binomial queue with the linking operations postponed until the next *delete_min*. It is in the implementation of the two remaining operations, *decrease_key* and *delete*, that new ideas emerge.

The problem with *decrease_key* and *delete* is that they move away from the realm of binomial trees, with the result that it is no longer permissible to take $M = \lfloor \log_2 n \rfloor$, and there is a danger of losing, not the analysis of *delete_min*, which applies for all $M$, but the quality of the bound it gives. Specifically, if many grandchildren of a node $x$ are deleted, $c(x)$ is unaffected, but $s(x)$, the number of nodes in the subtree rooted at $x$, may drop as low as $c(x) + 1$, which would force the choice $M = n - 1$. Fibonacci heaps solve this problem by insisting that if a node loses more than a few grandchildren, it must lose a child as well.

This strategy is based on an operation called *cascade_cut(x)*, which is defined for any non-root node $x$. The link between $x$ and its parent is broken (this is called a *cut*), and $T_x$ becomes an independent tree. If the parent is marked when the cut occurs, the parent is itself cut from its parent, and so on. Otherwise the cut places a mark in the parent:

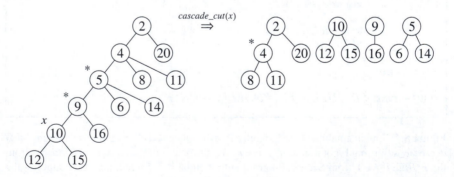

In this example of *cascade_cut(x)*, the first two proper ancestors of $x$ are marked, and this leads to a cascade of three cuts.

A cut has actual complexity 1 (say), but adds a new root to the Fibonacci heap, which increases the potential by 2. If the cut is not the last one in the cascade, the new root goes from marked to unmarked, which decreases the potential by 3. So every cut except the last one in the cascade is free, and the amortized complexity of *cascade_cut(x)* is at most 6: that is, 1 for the final cut, 2 for the last new root, and possibly 3 for the new mark created by the final cut. This is essentially the same accounting trick as the one used to control the cost of carry propagation in *delete_min*'s accumulator, and it explains why the components of the potential function are weighted as they are.

The *decrease_key* operation is now trivial to implement. To decrease the key of a non-root node $x$, modify the value and apply a cascade cut at $x$:

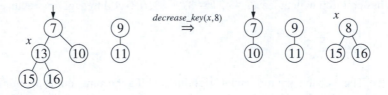

The task is even easier if $x$ is a root node; simply decrease the value and check whether it is the new overall minimum. The amortized complexity of *decrease_key* is at most 6. Note that, since the key of $x$ is known to decrease, $x$ cannot become out of order with any of its children. Deletion is similar; its amortized complexity turns out to be $O(M)$.

This analysis is drawing to a close. It remains to find an upper bound $M$ on the number of children of any node.

**Theorem 8.1:** Let $x$ be any node in a Fibonacci heap. Then $s(x)$, the size of the subtree rooted at $x$, obeys

$$s(x) \geq F_{c(x)+2}$$

where $F_k$ is the $k$th Fibonacci number, defined by the recurrence equation $F_0 = 0$, $F_1 = 1$, $F_k = F_{k-1} + F_{k-2}$.

**Proof:** Arrange the children of $x$ in the order they were linked to $x$, from earliest to latest (right to left in the implementations and diagrams). Let $y$ be the $i$th child of $x$ in this ordering. Consider the moment in the past just before $y$ was linked to $x$. Since $y$ is now $x$'s $i$th child, $x$ had at least $i - 1$ children at that moment (*at least*, because some of these children may have been removed by cuts since then). Since $y$ was linked to $x$, at that moment it must have been the case that $c(y) = c(x)$, and therefore that $c(y) \geq i - 1$.

Now back in the present, $y$ is still a child of $x$. If $y$ had lost more than one child through cuts, it would itself have been cut from $x$. It hasn't been cut from $x$, so at most one child has been lost, and $c(y) \geq i - 2$.

The $i$th child of $x$ has at least $i - 2$ children, so the general picture is

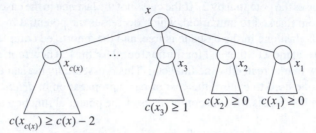

$$c(x_{c(x)}) \geq c(x) - 2$$

Now, what is the minimum possible value of $s(x)$, given that $c(x) = k$? Let this minimum be $S_k$. Trivially, $S_0 = 1$ and $S_1 = 2$. From the figure, a node $x$ with $k \geq 2$ children has children with at least $k - 2, k - 3, \ldots, 1, 0, 0$ children, giving recurrence

$$S_k = 2 + \sum_{j=0}^{k-2} S_j$$

($k \geq 2$). The 2 counts the root and its rightmost child; the sum counts the minimum possible number of nodes in the subtrees rooted at the remaining children. But now, by substituting $k + 1$ for $k$,

$$S_{k+1} = 2 + \sum_{j=0}^{k-1} S_j$$

Subtracting the two equations gives $S_{k+1} - S_k = S_{k-1}$, or $S_{k+1} = S_k + S_{k-1}$, so that the $S_k$ are just the Fibonacci numbers, with $S_0 = F_2 = 1$. Since $s(x) \geq S_k$, where $k = c(x)$, the result follows immediately. □

The properties of the Fibonacci numbers are well known; according to Exercise 2.6, $F_k \geq \phi^{k-2}$, where $\phi = (1 + \sqrt{5})/2 \simeq 1.6180$. Therefore

$$n \geq s(x) \geq F_{c(x)+2} \geq \phi^{c(x)}$$

and so $c(x) \leq \log_\phi n \simeq 1.44\log_2 n$. It is therefore permissible to take $M = \lfloor \log_\phi n \rfloor$ in the analysis above; the conclusion is that the amortized complexity of *make*, *empty*, *insert*, *find_min*, *meld*, and *decrease_key* is $O(1)$, and the amortized complexity of *delete_min* and *delete* is $O(\log n)$.

## 8.7  Choosing a priority queue implementation

This chapter closes with a comparison of the priority queue implementations, and some suggestions about when each should be used. To begin with, here is a table showing their complexities:

| | Unsorted doubly linked list | 2-3 tree | Heap | Binomial queue | Fibonacci heap (amortized) |
|---|---|---|---|---|---|
| make | $O(1)$ | $O(1)$ | $O(1)$ | $O(1)$ | $O(1)$ |
| empty | $O(1)$ | $O(1)$ | $O(1)$ | $O(1)$ | $O(1)$ |
| insert | $O(1)$ | $O(\log n)$ | $O(\log n)$ | $O(\log n)$ | $O(1)$ |
| find_min | $O(n)$ | $O(\log n)$ | $O(1)$ | $O(\log n)$ | $O(1)$ |
| delete_min | $O(n)$ | $O(\log n)$ | $O(\log n)$ | $O(\log n)$ | $O(\log n)$ |
| delete | $O(1)$ | $O(\log n)$ | $O(\log n)$ | $O(\log n)$ | $O(\log n)$ |
| meld | $O(1)$ | $O(n)$ | $O(n)$ | $O(\log n)$ | $O(1)$ |
| decrease_key | $O(1)$ | $O(\log n)$ | $O(\log n)$ | $O(\log n)$ | $O(1)$ |

Note that the times for Fibonacci heaps are amortized; an individual operation may be more expensive. The other complexities are all worst-case.

For completeness, the unsorted doubly linked list has been included. In operation sequences featuring *meld* and *decrease_key*, it has something to offer; and it would be preferred for small *n*.

Also included are 2-3 trees to represent the ordered symbol table implementations, although splay trees might be a better choice in practice. Ordered symbol table implementations are preferred when operations like *retrieve_next* are needed in addition to priority queue operations (Section 7.1).

The heap is the simplest efficient structure, and for the core operations *make*, *empty*, *insert*, *find_min*, and *delete_min*, which are all that are required in the majority of applications, it is generally the method of choice. If *decrease_key* and *delete* operations are needed, back indexes must be added to the entries (so that from each entry it is possible to find its index in the array); *meld* cannot be implemented efficiently in any case.

The binomial queue provides efficient melds. It also runs fast in practice, and the code for the five core operations plus *meld* is quite simple.

The complexity bounds shown above for the Fibonacci heap lead to asymptotically efficient implementations of several important graph algorithms, as will be seen in Chapter 12. Unfortunately, the space overhead per entry is rather high, and the operations are somewhat cumbersome to implement. Several alternative data structures have been proposed, by Fredman et al. (1986), Peterson (1987), and Driscoll et al. (1988). None of these combine the time complexity guarantees of Fibonacci heaps with efficiency in practice.

The paper by Jones (1986) is a good starting point for further study of priority queues. It contains descriptions and empirical comparisons of a number of implementations, including several not covered here. There is an alternative approach, in which the key is used to index an array in a manner roughly analogous to hashing. One interesting version may be found in Brown (1988).

## 8.8 Exercises

8.1 Give a formal specification of the Priority Queue ADT which accords with the informal one given in Section 8.1. Describe the priority queue as a set of entries, each containing a key and a value.

8.2 Trace the effect of the following operation sequence on the heap implementation of the priority queue ADT. Show the heap as a tree, not an array. Note that '59' is shorthand for an entry whose key is 59, and so on.

> *q.make*;
> *q.insert*(59);
> *q.insert*(41);
> *q.insert*(25);
> *q.insert*(12);
> *q.insert*(91);
> *q.find_min*;
> *q.delete_min*;
> *q.insert*(34);
> *q.insert*(63);
> *q.delete_min*;
> *q.insert*(75);
> *q.insert*(85);
> *q.delete_min*;

8.3 In Section 8.4, it is shown that for a heap $T$ with $n$ nodes,

$$\sum_{x \in I(T)} [h(x) - 1] \leq 2n$$

Show that, in fact,

$$\sum_{x \in I(T)} [h(x) - 1] \leq n - 1$$

8.4 The following variant of *add_root* has been attributed by Knuth (1973b) to R. W. Floyd. In the first phase, the roots of the two subtrees are compared and the smaller becomes the new root:

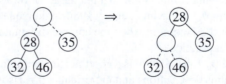

Then this process is repeated on the appropriate subtree; the effect is to move the 'hole' from the root to a leaf. In the second phase, *add_leaf* is used to insert an entry into this hole:

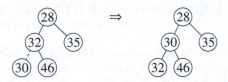

Compare the efficiency of this version of *add_root* with the one given in Section 8.2.

8.5 Eliminate tail recursion from procedure *add_root* of Section 8.4, and hence produce a tuned version of Heapsort that contains no procedure calls. Can you find any other ways to tune the algorithm?

8.6 There is a way to reduce the number of comparisons between keys made by *add_leaf* to far, far below $O(\log n)$. Can you find it?

8.7 Here is an implementation of Huffman's algorithm, as presented informally in Section 6.4. The *n* weights are initially stored in the List *weights*.

```
tree_type: BINTREE_LINKED[INTEGER];

huffman(weights: LIST_DLL[INTEGER]): like tree_type is
    local
        q: PRIQUEUE_HEAP[INTEGER, like tree_type];
        e: LIST_DLL_ENTRY[INTEGER];
        e1, e2: PRIQUEUE_HEAP_ENTRY[INTEGER, like tree_type];
        t: like tree_type;
    do
        !!q.make;
        from e := weights.first until weights.nil_entry(e) loop
            !!t;
            t.put_root(t.new_entry(e.value));
            q.insert(q.new_entry(e.value, t));
            e := weights.next(e)
        end;
        from e1 := q.delete_min until q.empty loop
            e2 := q.delete_min;
            !!t;
            t.put_root(t.new_entry(e1.key + e2.key));
            t.put_left_child(t.root, e1.value.root);
            t.put_right_child(t.root, e2.value.root);
            q.insert(q.new_entry(e1.key + e2.key, t));
            e1 := q.delete_min
        end;
        Result := e1.value
    end
```

Analyze this algorithm.

8.8 Invent a simple potential function for binomial queues and use it to find amortized bounds of $O(1)$ for *insert* and $O(\log n)$ for *delete_min*.

8.9 The implementation of Fibonacci heaps given in Section 8.6 requires four references, one integer, and one boolean per node. Can this large memory overhead be reduced without affecting the asymptotic amortized complexity of any operation?

8.10 Write a program to simulate a checkout queue. Make reasonable assumptions about service times, and determine experimentally the effect of customer arrival rate on waiting time.

8.11 In many operating systems, the priority of a process is an integer in some small, fixed range, say between 1 and 20. Show how to implement the Priority Queue ADT in $O(1)$ time per operation, when the keys are restricted to such a range.

8.12 A priority queue implementation is said to be *stable* if entries with equal keys are returned by *delete_min* in the order they were inserted. Stability has been a traditional requirement of discrete event simulations. What advice would you give to someone who is looking for an efficient, stable priority queue implementation?

# Chapter 9

# Sorting

A sorted sequence (one whose entries are arranged in non-decreasing order by key) has several advantages over an unsorted one: for example, it may be searched efficiently, and entries with equal keys are found together. Sorting is also the classical example of a problem where careful design produces algorithms of low complexity, whereas naive approaches are only marginally feasible. For these reasons it is not surprising that sorting is the most-studied and most-solved problem in the theory of algorithms.

## 9.1 Insertion sorting

The first sorting strategy is a very simple one. Build up the sorted sequence incrementally, by inserting one entry into it, in the appropriate place, at each stage:

| Instance | Result |
|----------|--------|
| $\{35, 62, 28, 50, 11, 45\}$ | $\langle\rangle$ |
| $\{62, 28, 50, 11, 45\}$ | $\langle 35\rangle$ |
| $\{28, 50, 11, 45\}$ | $\langle 35, 62\rangle$ |
| $\{50, 11, 45\}$ | $\langle 28, 35, 62\rangle$ |
| $\{11, 45\}$ | $\langle 28, 35, 50, 62\rangle$ |
| $\{45\}$ | $\langle 11, 28, 35, 50, 62\rangle$ |
| $\{\}$ | $\langle 11, 28, 35, 45, 50, 62\rangle$ |

In this example the first entry of the instance has always been chosen for insertion into the result, but any entry would do. In abstract terms, then, the algorithm is

```
insertion_sort(instance: like instance_type): like result_type is
    local
        x: like entry_type;
    do
        from
            !!Result.make;
        until instance.empty loop
            x := instance.delete_any;
            Result.insert(x)
        end
    end
```

The loop invariant, 'Result is a sorted permutation of the elements deleted from instance,' shows that insertion_sort is an incremental algorithm of the first kind, in the classification introduced in Section 4.2.

The operations on instance are easily implemented by the Simple Set ADT of Section 3.1, but the insertion of $x$ into its appropriate place in Result is more expensive, and suggests that Result should be implemented using an ordered symbol table, modified to accept equal keys. For example, suppose a binary search tree is used to implement Result. The analysis at the end of Section 7.4 shows that the $n$ insertions require $n(n-1)/2$ comparisons between keys in the worst case, and $2(n+1)H_n - 4n$ comparisons on average. Once the insertions are complete, an inorder traversal of the tree will visit the entries in non-decreasing order. This takes $O(n)$ time, which is negligible compared with the insertions. So the binary search tree sort has $O(n^2)$ worst-case complexity, and $O(n\log n)$ average complexity.

Alternatively, a 2-3 tree could be used to implement the ordered symbol table, giving $O(n\log n)$ complexity in the worst case.

The remainder of this section is devoted to a very simple implementation of insertion sort, known as *straight insertion*. Although straight insertion is not efficient, its simplicity makes it the method of choice for small instances (say, $n \le 10$), and it is also a good choice when the input is known to be almost sorted.

The entries appear in an array entries.item(a..b), and are sorted in place. The sorted sequence grows through the array from left to right, by engulfing the entry $x$ just to its right at each stage:

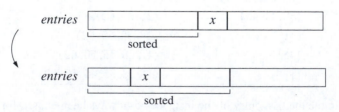

This is achieved by moving entries at the right of the sorted sequence one step to the right until a gap opens up at the place where $x$ belongs. It is assumed that a sentinel entry entries.item(a−1) exists which is no larger than the minimum element of entries.item(a..b). Here is the code:

```
straight_insertion_sort(a, b: INTEGER) is
    local
        i, j: INTEGER;
        x: like entry_type;
    do
        from i := a until i > b loop
            x := entries.item(i);
            from j := i until entries.item(j−1).key <= x.key loop
                entries.put(entries.item(j−1), j);
                j := j − 1
            end;
            entries.put(x, j);
            i := i + 1
        end;
    end
```

The outer loop's invariant is '*entries.item(a..i*−1) contains a sorted permutation of the original contents of *entries.item(a..i*−1).' Here is an example of the algorithm in operation, with *entries.item(a..i*−1) bracketed at each stage:

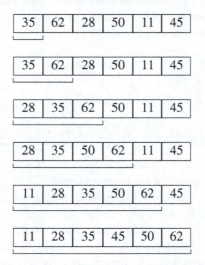

## Analysis of straight insertion sort

Most sorting algorithms are based on comparisons between keys, and the number of these comparisons is generally a realistic measure of complexity. Although two keys may be equal, the algorithms to be studied do not exploit this possibility, so for the purposes of analysis it may be assumed that the keys are distinct.

A sequence of keys like ⟨*problem, specification, correctness, analysis*⟩ might just as well be ⟨3, 4, 2, 1⟩, since any comparison-based sorting algorithm will treat the two sequences identically. This means that the instances of the sorting problem are

the $n!$ permutations of the numbers $1, 2, \dots, n$. In the absence of any further information it is reasonable to assume that each of these instances is equally likely to occur,
and the average complexity analyses of this chapter all make this assumption.

It is not hard to see that the worst-case complexity of straight insertion sort is
$O(n^2)$. Consider an initial array whose keys are in decreasing order. At each stage,
the entry $x$ to be inserted is smaller than all the entries in the sorted sequence to its
left, and so it must be compared with all of them and with the sentinel. If $x$ is the
$i$th entry, this makes $i$ comparisons to insert $x$, and so the total cost is

$$\sum_{i=1}^{n} i = \frac{n(n + 1)}{2}$$

comparisons between keys. This is clearly the worst case.

To go more deeply into the analysis of straight insertion sort, and similar
simple sorting algorithms containing two nested loops, *inversions* are needed. Let
$a = a_1, a_2, \dots, a_n$ be a permutation of $1, 2, \dots, n$. An inversion of $a$ is a pair $(a_i, a_j)$
such that $i < j$ and $a_i > a_j$, which means that $a_i$ and $a_j$ are out of order. The number
of inversions of $a$, denoted $I(a)$, is a measure of how disordered $a$ is. For example,
here are four permutations and their inversions:

| $a$ | *Inversions* | $I(a)$ |
|---|---|---|
| 1 3 4 2 5 | $(3, 2), (4, 2)$ | 2 |
| 3 5 2 1 4 | $(3, 2), (3, 1), (5, 2), (5, 1), (5, 4), (2, 1)$ | 6 |
| 1 2 3 4 5 | | 0 |
| 5 4 3 2 1 | $(5, 4), (5, 3), (5, 2), (5, 1), (4, 3), (4, 2), (4, 1), (3, 2), (3, 1), (2, 1)$ | 10 |

The permutation $n, n - 1, \dots, 1$ has $(n - 1) + (n - 2) + \cdots + 0 = n(n - 1)/2$ inversions. This is the maximum that any permutation of $1, 2, \dots, n$ can have, since $a_1$ can
be the first element of at most $n - 1$ inversions, namely $(a_1, a_2), \dots, (a_1, a_n)$; then $a_2$
can be the first element of at most $n - 2$ inversions; and so on.

There is a clever trick for finding the average number of inversions, assuming
that each of the $n!$ permutations of $1, 2, \dots, n$ is equally likely. Each permutation
$a$ has a *reflection* $a'$, which is $a$ written backwards. For all $a$, every inversion of
$n, n - 1, \dots, 1$ appears either in $a$ or in $a'$, as this example illustrates:

| $a$ | *Inversions* | $I(a)$ |
|---|---|---|
| 3 5 2 1 4 | $(3, 2), (3, 1), (5, 2), (5, 1), (5, 4), (2, 1)$ | 6 |
| 4 1 2 5 3 | $(4, 1), (4, 2), (4, 3), (5, 3)$ | 4 |

To see why this is so, consider any inversion, say $(5, 2)$. If $(5, 2)$ is an inversion of
$a$, then 5 appears before 2 in $a$; but then 5 appears after 2 in $a'$, and so $(5, 2)$ is not an
inversion of $a'$. Conversely, if $(5, 2)$ is not an inversion of $a$, then 5 appears after 2
in $a$, and $(5, 2)$ is an inversion of $a'$.

It follows that $I(a) + I(a') = n(n-1)/2$, for all $a$. Now by definition, the average number of inversions, $A(n)$, is

$$A(n) = \frac{1}{n!} \sum_{a \in S_n} I(a)$$

where $S_n$ is the set of all permutations of $1, 2, \ldots, n$. But as $a$ runs through $S_n$, so does $a'$. Therefore,

$$A(n) = \frac{1}{n!} \sum_{a \in S_n} I(a')$$

Adding these equations gives

$$2A(n) = \frac{1}{n!} \sum_{a \in S_n} [I(a) + I(a')]$$

$$= \frac{1}{n!} \sum_{a \in S_n} \frac{n(n-1)}{2}$$

$$= \frac{n(n-1)}{2}$$

and so the average number of inversions is $n(n-1)/4$.

Consider now the number of comparisons *entries.item(j–1).key <= x.key* in *straight_insertion_sort*$(1, n)$. Divide these comparisons into those that succeed and those that fail. Since success terminates the inner loop, it must happen once per iteration of the outer loop, which is exactly $n$ times. On the other hand, every failed comparison is between two keys *entries.item(j–1).key* and *x.key* that formed an inversion in the original input, since $j - 1 < i$ and *entries.item(j–1).key > x.key*; and every inversion shows up at some point as such a comparison. Therefore, for each permutation $a$ in $S_n$,

*Total number of comparisons = Total number of inversions + n*

and so $W(n) = n(n-1)/2 + n$ as before, and the average number of comparisons performed by straight insertion sort is

$$A(n) = \frac{n(n-1)}{4} + n$$

Observe that the complexity is closely related to the number of inversions. This means that it can vary dramatically with the input. In particular, if the input is known to be almost sorted (say, containing only $2n$ or $3n$ inversions), then straight insertion sort will be very efficient.

## 9.2 **Selection sorting**

*Selection sorting* is another simple strategy. Repeatedly extract an entry with minimum key from the instance, and append it to the result sequence:

| Instance | Result |
|---|---|
| $\{35, 62, 28, 50, 11, 45\}$ | $\langle\rangle$ |
| $\{35, 62, 28, 50, 45\}$ | $\langle 11\rangle$ |
| $\{35, 62, 50, 45\}$ | $\langle 11, 28\rangle$ |
| $\{62, 50, 45\}$ | $\langle 11, 28, 35\rangle$ |
| $\{62, 50\}$ | $\langle 11, 28, 35, 45\rangle$ |
| $\{62\}$ | $\langle 11, 28, 35, 45, 50\rangle$ |
| $\{\}$ | $\langle 11, 28, 35, 45, 50, 62\rangle$ |

The abstract implementation of this is

```
selection_sort(instance: like instance_type): like result_type is
    local
        x: like entry_type;
    do
        from
            !!Result.make
        until instance.empty loop
            x := instance.delete_min;
            Result.insert_last(x)
        end
    end
```

Although it is true that *Result* is always a sorted permutation of the entries deleted from *instance*, this is not the whole story: it is also necessary to say that these entries are the smallest elements of *instance*. The loop invariant of *selection_sort* is therefore quite different from the loop invariant of *insertion_sort*, and in fact it is '*Result* contains an initial part of a sorted permutation of the initial instance, consisting of the entries deleted from *instance*.' This shows that *selection_sort* is an incremental algorithm of the second kind, according to the classification introduced in Section 4.2.

*Result* may be a simple list, but the operations on *instance* suggest the use of a priority queue. The data structures of Chapter 8 provide a variety of $O(n\log n)$ implementations of selection sorting. One in particular stands out, as being an in-place sort of $O(n\log n)$ worst-case complexity, using no extra memory for references or anything else – a combination of advantages found in no other sorting algorithm. This is Heapsort, and it is presented in Section 8.4.

A very simple $O(n^2)$ implementation of selection sort, known as *straight selection*, is described and proved correct in Section 1.3.

## 9.3 Merging and Mergesort

Consider the problem of taking two sorted sequences of entries and *merging* them into a single sorted sequence. The primary motivation for this is a sorting algorithm, called Mergesort, which appears below; but merging has other applications as well, for example batch file update (Exercise 9.18).

When merging two sorted sequences $p$ and $q$, the first entry of the result will be the smaller of the first entries of the two sequences. After it is removed, the second entry will be the smaller of what remains, and so on. For example,

| $p$ | $q$ | *Result* |
|---|---|---|
| $\langle 28, 35, 50, 62 \rangle$ | $\langle 11, 45 \rangle$ | $\langle \rangle$ |
| $\langle 28, 35, 50, 62 \rangle$ | $\langle 45 \rangle$ | $\langle 11 \rangle$ |
| $\langle 35, 50, 62 \rangle$ | $\langle 45 \rangle$ | $\langle 11, 28 \rangle$ |
| $\langle 50, 62 \rangle$ | $\langle 45 \rangle$ | $\langle 11, 28, 35 \rangle$ |
| $\langle 50, 62 \rangle$ | $\langle \rangle$ | $\langle 11, 28, 35, 45 \rangle$ |

At this point, no more comparisons are needed, and the remaining elements of $p$ may be moved to the back of the result sequence.

In abstract terms, the Queue ADT of Section 5.3 is needed to implement this algorithm. It provides *p.dequeue*, which deletes and returns the entry at the front of $p$, and *Result.enqueue(x)*, which adds $x$ to the back of *Result*. Using this ADT, the code for *merge* is

```
merge(p, q: like queue_type): like queue_type is
   do
       from !!Result until p.empty or q.empty loop
           if p.front.key < q.front.key then
               Result.enqueue(p.dequeue)
           else
               Result.enqueue(q.dequeue)
           end
       end;
       Result.append(p);
       Result.append(q)
   end
```

This algorithm works correctly when either or both of $p$ and $q$ are empty. The loop invariant is '*Result* is an initial part of the sequence which is the original $p$ and $q$ merged,' making *merge* a simple example of an incremental algorithm of the second kind, in the terminology of Section 4.2.

The analysis of *merge* is easy. The Queue operations may be implemented in $O(1)$ time each, so it is realistic to take the number of comparisons between keys as the measure of complexity. Suppose that initially $p$ contains $m$ entries and $q$ contains $n$ entries. Each comparison between keys is followed by the movement of one entry to the result sequence, so while the loop is running the number of comparisons between keys is equal to the size of the result sequence. When the loop terminates, some unknown number of entries, say $k$, will remain on $p$ or $q$, and at that moment the size of the result sequence is $m + n - k$, which must therefore be the total number of comparisons made. This is maximized when $k$ is minimized. If both $p$ and $q$ are initially non-empty, $k \geq 1$, so the worst-case complexity of $merge(p, q)$ is

$$\begin{aligned} W(m, n) &= 0 && \text{if } m = 0 \text{ or } n = 0 \\ &= m + n - 1 && \text{otherwise} \end{aligned}$$

Incidentally, the corresponding formula for average complexity is

$$A(m, n) = m + n - \left[ \frac{n}{m + 1} + \frac{m}{n + 1} \right]$$

but the derivation requires expertise with binomial coefficients, so is beyond the scope of this book. If $m = n$, this is never less than $m + n - 2$, which is surprisingly close to $W(m, n)$.

## Mergesort

The Mergesort algorithm is a classic example of divide-and-conquer. To sort a set of entries, divide it into two halves and recursively sort each half separately; then merge them. For example, beginning with the set

$$\{35, 62, 28, 50, 11, 45\}$$

the first step is to break it into two halves:

$$\{35, 62, 28\} \text{ and } \{50, 11, 45\}$$

Next, these are sorted recursively, yielding two sorted sequences:

$$\langle 28, 35, 62 \rangle \text{ and } \langle 11, 45, 50 \rangle$$

Finally, these two sequences are merged into the result sequence:

$$\langle 11, 28, 35, 45, 50, 62 \rangle$$

This strategy is so simple, and so efficient (as will be seen shortly), that one could well ask why we bother with any other method. The problem here is that there seems to be no easy way to merge two adjacent sorted arrays together in place. (It is quite easy to do if the result may be built up in a separate array, but this idea will not be pursued any further here.) So each entry has to be made into a one-element queue, and the *merge* algorithm above used to perform the merging:

```
mergesort(a, b: INTEGER): like queue_type is
    local
        p, q: like queue_type;
        mid: INTEGER;
    do
        if a = b then
            Result := queues.item(a)
        else
            mid := (a + b) // 2;
            p := mergesort(a, mid);
            q := mergesort(mid + 1, b);
            Result := merge(p, q)
        end
    end;
```

This assumes that *queues*, the initial array of one-element queues, is not empty. No entries actually move; only the references do. If the entries are required to appear in the array in increasing order, Mergesort is probably inferior to Heapsort; alternatively, a tedious rearrangement of the entries is possible (Exercise 9.6).

## Analysis of Mergesort

Let $W(n)$ be the number of comparisons between keys made by $mergesort(1, n)$ in the worst case; since the algorithm assumes that the array is not empty, let $n \geq 1$. Clearly $W(1) = 0$, and for larger $n$ the code executed is

$$p := mergesort(1, \lfloor (n + 1)/2 \rfloor);$$
$$q := mergesort(\lfloor (n + 1)/2 \rfloor + 1, n);$$
$$Result := merge(p, q);$$

The total length of the $p$ and $q$ queues is $n$, so $merge(p, q)$ costs $n - 1$ comparisons in the worst case. The recurrence equation is therefore

$$W(1) = 0$$
$$W(n) = W(\lfloor (n + 1)/2 \rfloor) + W(n - \lfloor (n + 1)/2 \rfloor) + n - 1$$

The floor function can be eliminated by restricting $n$ to the form $n = 2^k$, for $k \geq 1$. Informally, this ensures that the array will break into two equal halves at each level of the recursion; algebraically, it gives

$$\lfloor (n + 1)/2 \rfloor = n - \lfloor (n + 1)/2 \rfloor = 2^{k-1}$$

Substituting these values into the recurrence equation gives

$$W(1) = 0$$
$$W(2^k) = 2W(2^{k-1}) + 2^k - 1$$

which can be solved by repeated substitution:

$$W(2^k) = 2W(2^{k-1}) + 2^k - 1$$

$$= 2[2W(2^{k-2}) + 2^{k-1} - 1] + 2^k - 1$$

$$= 2[2[2W(2^{k-3}) + 2^{k-2} - 1] + 2^{k-1} - 1] + 2^k - 1$$

$$= 2^3 W(2^{k-3}) + 3 \times 2^k - 2^2 - 2^1 - 2^0$$

$$= \dots$$

$$= 2^i W(2^{k-i}) + i2^k - \sum_{j=0}^{i-1} 2^j$$

Letting $i = k$ gives

$$W(2^k) = 2^k W(2^0) + k2^k - \sum_{j=0}^{k-1} 2^j$$

$$= 0 + k2^k - (2^k - 1)$$

using the standard formula for the sum of a geometric progression. But now $2^k = n$, $k = \log_2 n$, and so the worst-case complexity of *mergesort*$(1, n)$ is

$$W(n) = n\log_2 n - (n - 1)$$

when $n$ is a power of 2. This is the lowest of any sorting algorithm studied in this book, and (as will be proved in Chapter 13) is close to the best possible for any sorting algorithm based on comparisons between keys.

The average complexity analysis is beyond our scope, but it turns out that

$$A(n) \simeq n\log_2 n - 1.2645n$$

which is surprisingly close to the worst case. See Knuth (1973b).

## 9.4 Quicksort

The sorting algorithm presented in this section was named Quicksort by its inventor, Hoare (1962). Like Mergesort, it uses the divide-and-conquer strategy.

Quicksort is the method of choice for general-purpose sorting, because, when implemented carefully, its average running time is smaller than other algorithms. Unfortunately, its worst-case complexity is poor, and in practice it is necessary to take precautions which reduce the probability of a worst case occurring.

The idea of Quicksort is as follows. Choose any entry, the first say, and compare every other entry with it. Those that turn out to be smaller go into one subset, those that turn out to be larger go into another. These two sets are then sorted recursively; the final result is made by appending them, with the chosen entry, called the *pivot*, in between.

For example, suppose the initial set is

$$\{35, 62, 28, 50, 11, 45\}$$

and the first element, 35, is chosen as pivot. Then comparing all the others with it and dividing them into two sets gives

$$\{28, 11\} \quad 35 \quad \{62, 50, 45\}$$

After recursively sorting the two subsets, the situation is

$$\langle 11, 28 \rangle \quad 35 \quad \langle 45, 50, 62 \rangle$$

and an append of the three pieces gives the final result. The code for this, using a queue $q$ to hold both the initial unsorted set and the final sorted sequence, is:

```
quicksort(q: like queue_type) is
    local
        left, right: like queue_type;
        pivot, x: like entry_type;
    do
        if not q.empty then
            !!left.make;
            !!right.make;
            from pivot := q.dequeue until q.empty loop
                x := q.dequeue;
                if x.key < pivot.key then
                    left.enqueue(x)
                else
                    right.enqueue(x)
                end
            end;
            quicksort(left);
            quicksort(right);
            q.append(left);
            q.enqueue(pivot);
            q.append(right)
        end
    end
```

Notice that the pivot entry is taken from the front of the initial queue.

The analysis of Quicksort is based on an unexpected correspondence between it and binary search trees. For example, when partitioning

$$\{35, 62, 28, 50, 11, 45\}$$

35 is compared with each of the other $n - 1$ entries, to determine which side to put them, and the result is

$$\{28, 11\} \quad 35 \quad \{62, 50, 45\}$$

Now consider what happens when 35, 62, 28, 50, 11, and 45 are inserted into an initially empty binary search tree. The first element, 35, becomes the root, and there are $n - 1$ comparisons between it and the other elements, as they pass through the root on their way to the left or right subtree:

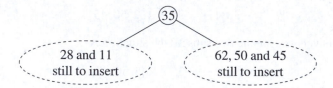

The costs are both $n - 1$ to this point, and the same argument applies recursively, so it follows that for every permutation $a$ in $S_n$, the set of all permutations of $n$ elements, the cost of Quicksort on $a$ is the same as the cost of inserting the elements of $a$ one by one into an initially empty binary search tree.

By the analysis at the end of Section 7.4, the worst-case complexity of Quicksort is $W(n) = n(n - 1)/2$ comparisons between keys. This occurs when the corresponding tree is skew, for example when the input is already sorted. The average complexity is

$$A(n) = 2(n + 1)H_n - 4n \simeq 1.38 n \log_2 n - 4n$$

which is about 38% more comparisons between keys than Mergesort makes in the worst case. In practice, however, the inner loops of the efficient implementation of Quicksort given below are faster than those of Mergesort, and this gives Quicksort the advantage.

In his original paper, Hoare suggested a variety of ways to improve the running time of Quicksort. One suggestion is to stop the recursion when $n \leq 10$ (say), and use some simple sort like straight insertion instead. This increases $A(n)$, but pays off in less overhead for recursion (Exercise 9.9). Another is to choose for pivot element the median of a small sample of the input. Choosing the median of the first, middle, and last elements for pivot, as suggested by Singleton (1969), will convert a sorted initial sequence from a worst case into a best case, and will approximately halve $W(n)$ (Exercise 9.13); also, Knuth (1973b) shows that it reduces $A(n)$ to about $1.16 n \log_2 n$. It also provides a sentinel for the partitioning algorithm given below. Both improvements are recommended.

## An efficient Quicksort using arrays

Quicksort derives much of its advantage from a very efficient implementation based on arrays. One entry of the array, the pivot entry, is moved to the place it will occupy when the sort is complete. At the same time, other entries are moved, to guarantee that all entries to the left of the pivot are no larger than the pivot, and all entries to the right are no smaller. For example,

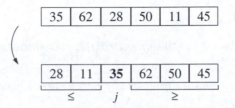

A method of doing this will be given in a moment. For now, assume the existence of a function *partition(a, b)* that rearranges *entries.item(a..b)* in this way and returns *j*, the index of the place where the pivot ended up. Then all that remains is to recursively sort *entries.item(a..j−1)* and *entries.item(j+1..b)*, and the whole array is sorted:

```
array_quicksort(a, b: INTEGER) is
    local
        j: INTEGER;
    do
        if b − a + 1 > 0 then
            j := partition(a, b);
            array_quicksort(a, j − 1);
            array_quicksort(j + 1, b)
        end
    end
```

There are several ways to implement *partition(a, b)*, but the following seems best. Starting at *entries.item(a+1)*, scan to the right, stopping at the first *i* such that *entries.item(i).key* ≥ *entries.item(a).key*. Then *entries.item(a+1..i−1)* are at their proper end, and need not be moved, but *entries.item(i)* belongs at the right-hand end. Now start at *entries.item(b)* and scan to the left, stopping at the first *j* such that *entries.item(j).key* ≤ *entries.item(a).key*. Then *entries.item(j+1..b)* are at their proper end, but *entries.item(j)* belongs at the left-hand end:

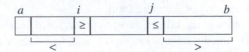

So swap *entries.item(i)* with *entries.item(j)*, and carry on from *entries.item(i+1)* and *entries.item(j−1)*. When *i* and *j* cross, it is time to stop, and a final swap of *entries.item(a)* with *entries.item(j)* brings the pivot in between the two subsets and completes the partitioning.

The version of *partition*(*a*, *b*) given below assumes that there is a sentinel entry *entries.item*(*b*+1) such that *entries.item*(*a*).*key* ≤ *entries.item*(*b* + 1).*key*, and this means that *array_quicksort*(1, *n*) assumes that *entries.item*(*n*+1) exists and that *entries.item*(*n*+1).*key* is at least as large as any element of *entries*. Here is the code for *partition*:

```
partition(a, b: INTEGER): INTEGER is
    local
        i, j: INTEGER;
    do
        from i := a + 1 until entries.item(i).key >= entries.item(a).key loop
            i := i + 1
        end;
        from j := b until entries.item(j).key <= entries.item(a).key loop
            j := j - 1
        end;
        from until i >= j loop
            swap(entries, i, j);
            from i := i + 1 until entries.item(i).key >= entries.item(a).key loop
                i := i + 1
            end;
            from j := j - 1 until entries.item(j).key <= entries.item(a).key loop
                j := j - 1
            end
        end;
        if a < j then swap(entries, a, j) end;
        Result := j
    end
```

This is a little longer than it needs to be, but it is more amenable to proof than other tuned implementations known to the author. The invariant of the main loop ('**until** $i >= j$ ...') is

$$entries.item(a + 1..i - 1).key \leq entries.item(a).key \leq entries.item(j + 1..b).key$$
$$\textbf{and } entries.item(i).key \geq entries.item(a).key$$
$$\textbf{and } entries.item(j).key \leq entries.item(a).key$$

The notation *entries.item*(*a* + 1..*i* − 1).*key* ≤ *entries.item*(*a*).*key* means that all the keys of *entries.item*(*a*+1..*i*−1) are less than or equal to *entries.item*(*a*).*key*. It is easy to see that the two initial loops establish this loop invariant, and that it holds at the beginning of each iteration of the main loop.

The inner loops will not allow *i* and *j* to cross, since *i* scans past keys that are strictly smaller than *entries.item*(*a*).*key*, and *j* scans past keys strictly larger than *entries.item*(*a*).*key*. Therefore, the farthest that *i* can get past *j* is *i* = *j* + 1, and this occurs when *i* = *j* − 1 at the beginning of the main loop of *partition*. It follows that at termination, either *i* = *j* or *i* = *j* + 1. If *i* = *j*, substituting *j* for *i* in the loop invariant gives

$$entries.item(a + 1..j - 1).key \leq entries.item(a).key \leq entries.item(j + 1..b).key$$
$$\textbf{and } entries.item(j).key = entries.item(a).key$$

and the final swap of *entries.item(a)* with *entries.item(j)* is unnecessary but correctly completes the partitioning. In the more usual case when $i = j + 1$, substituting $j + 1$ for $i$ in the loop invariant gives

$$entries.item(a + 1..j).key \leq entries.item(a).key \leq entries.item(j + 1..b).key$$

and again the final swap of *entries.item(a)* with *entries.item(j)* is correct.

This partitioning algorithm differs somewhat from the one employing queues analyzed at the beginning of this section. First, it makes one or two sentinel comparisons between keys in addition to the $n - 1$ comparisons counted in the analysis. They are best regarded as part of the general overhead. Second, it does not place entries into subarrays in the same order as they appeared in the original array (for example, 62 is moved to the right of 50 in the example partitioning above). This does not affect $W(n)$, since, if the array is sorted initially, no entries ever move; and Exercise 9.8 shows that it does not affect $A(n)$ either.

## 9.5 Radix sorting

The final sorting algorithm of this chapter, LSD Radixsort, is radically different from the others. Like hashing, it uses array indexing instead of comparisons to distinguish between keys.

Radix sorting assumes that the keys are $d$-digit numbers in base $r$ ($r$ is also called the *radix*). For example, if the keys are strings of lower-case letters of length 6, take $d = 6, r = 26$. The example below uses decimal keys in the range $0 \leq x \leq 999$, with $d = 3$ and $r = 10$. Any digit $x_i$ of a key satisfies $0 \leq x_i \leq r - 1$, and so may be used to index an array of $r$ linked lists.

The basic idea of radix sorting is to make one pass through the entries, placing each entry at the back of the $x_i$th linked list, where $x_i$ is the $i$th digit of the entry's key. This is called a *spread on the ith digit*.

The most natural way to sort using spreads is to begin with a sort on the first, or most significant digit. The resulting $r$ sublists are then sorted recursively (beginning with a spread on the second digit), and their concatenation is the final result – a kind of $r$-way divide-and-conquer. This algorithm is called *MSD Radixsort*. It suffers from fragmentation of its entries into many small sublists.

A less obvious strategy, *LSD Radixsort*, avoids this problem. It begins with a spread on the last, or least significant digit. For example, to sort

| 179 | ⊷ | 208 | ⊷ | 306 | ⊷ | 093 | ⊷ | 859 | ⊷ | 984 | ⊷ | 055 | ⊷ | 009 | ⊷ | 271 | ⊷ | 033 |

begin with a spread on the third digit:

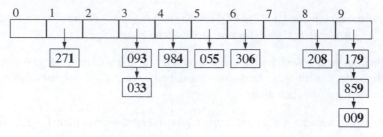

and then concatenate the lists, giving

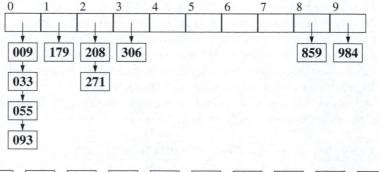

The entries are now in order, if all but the last digit of each key is ignored. This has been emphasized by emboldening these last digits. A second spread and concatenate, on the second last key, brings the entries into order if all but the last two digits of each key are ignored:

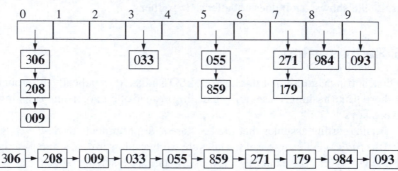

The last digits remain in order on each sublist, since entries are placed at the end of the sublist during the spread. Carrying on in this way, the final spread and concatenate on the most significant digit completes the sort:

The following implementation of LSD Radixsort uses the Queue ADT from Section 5.3 to supply the singly linked lists. Each key is an array of $d$ digits in base $r$.

```
radixsort(queue: like queue_type): like queue_type is
    local
        sublists: ARRAY[like queue_type];
        q: like queue_type;
        x: like entry_type;
        i, j: INTEGER;
    do

        -- initialize the array of sublists to be all empty
        !!sublists.make(0, radix − 1);
        from j := 0 until j = radix loop
            !!q.make;
            sublists.put(q, j);
            j := j + 1
        end;

        from i := 1 until i > digit_count loop

            -- spread on the ith digit
            from until queue.empty loop
                x := queue.dequeue;
                j := x.digits.item(i);
                sublists.item(j).enqueue(x)
            end;

            -- concatenate sublists
            from j := 0 until j = radix loop
                queue.append(sublists.item(j));
                !!q.make;
                sublists.put(q, j);
                j := j + 1
            end;

            i := i + 1
        end;
        Result := queue
    end;
```

The main loop's invariant is '*queue* is sorted if all but digits 1 to $i−1$ (the last $i − 1$ digits) of each key are ignored.' This makes LSD Radixsort an incremental algorithm of the first kind, in the terminology of Section 4.2.

The complexity of LSD Radixsort is a function of $n$, $d$, and $r$. The characteristic operation for the spread phase is the movement of one entry from the master list to a sublist, and this occurs $n$ times per spread. The characteristic operation for the concatenation phase is the append of a sublist to the new master list, and this occurs $r$ times per concatenate. Therefore the total cost of one spread and concatenate is $O(n + r)$, and since the whole sort consists of $d$ such phases, its complexity is $O(d(n + r))$ altogether.

For fixed $d$ and $r$, LSD Radixsort is $O(n)$. Note however that if the $n$ keys are distinct, then $d \geq \log_r n$. This is so because, given $d$ digits in base $r$, it is possible to represent at most $n = r^d$ distinct keys. So as $n$ increases, it may be necessary to increase $r$, if $O(n)$ complexity is to be maintained. Another problem with radix sorting is that the overhead $O(dr)$ is independent of $n$: if $n$ is small, a lot of time is wasted concatenating empty sublists.

## 9.6  Choosing a sorting algorithm

The sorting algorithms studied in this chapter may be summarized as follows (only the leading terms of the complexities are given):

|  | $W(n)$ | $A(n)$ |
|---|---|---|
| Straight insertion sort | $0.5n^2$ | $0.25n^2$ |
| Straight selection sort | $0.5n^2$ | $0.5n^2$ |
| Heapsort | $2.0n\log_2 n$ | $2.0n\log_2 n$ |
| Mergesort | $1.0n\log_2 n$ | $1.0n\log_2 n$ |
| Quicksort | $0.5n^2$ | $1.38n\log_2 n$ |
| LSD Radixsort | $O(d(n + r))$ | $O(d(n + r))$ |

Straight insertion is a good choice when $n$ is small, or when the input is known to be almost sorted. It is simple, and no extra memory for references is required.

Heapsort and Mergesort have similar characteristics: they offer $O(n \log n)$ complexity in the worst case, and in practice their running times are quite similar. The output of Heapsort is an array, and it has the advantage of requiring no extra memory. The principal advantage of Mergesort is that it accesses the entries sequentially, which makes it well adapted to sorting on external storage devices.

Quicksort is generally the method of choice. The partitioning algorithm can be highly tuned, and this, together with its low average complexity, makes Quicksort run faster than its competitors in practice. The improvements discussed in Section 9.4 offer some protection against the poor worst case.

LSD Radixsort has the potential to run in linear time, but several caveats apply. The keys must be composed of a fixed number $d$ of base $r$ digits. The result is a list, not a sorted array, and extra memory is needed for references. Most important, $n$ must be large, or else the $O(dr)$ part will dominate the complexity.

Many other sorting algorithms exist, and they have been comprehensively surveyed by Knuth (1973b). Knuth also discusses the methods employed when the data to be sorted are on external storage devices.

# 9.7 Exercises

9.1 A sorting algorithm is *stable* if it preserves the relative order of entries with equal keys. Are the following sorting algorithms stable, or can they easily be made so?

(a) Straight insertion sort

(b) Quicksort

(c) Mergesort

(d) Heapsort

(e) LSD Radixsort

9.2 The following implementation of insertion sort is known as *binary insertion sort*. It uses binary search to find the position of the next insertion:

```
binary_insertion_sort(a, b: INTEGER) is
    local
        i, j, pos: INTEGER;
        x: like entry_type;
    do
        from i := a + 1 until i > b loop
            x := entries.item(i);
            pos := binary_search(a, i − 1, x.key);
            from j := i − 1 until j = pos loop
                entries.put(entries.item(j), j + 1);
                j := j − 1
            end;
            entries.put(x, j + 1);
            i := i + 1
        end
    end
```

(a) Analyze *binary_insertion_sort*$(1, n)$, using one comparison between keys as the characteristic operation.

(b) Repeat (a), using the assignment *entries.put(entries.item(j), j + 1)* as the characteristic operation.

9.3 What is the time complexity of Mergesort when its input is already sorted?

9.4 Find a file of 8 elements that is a worst case for Mergesort, or in other words, one that takes $8\log_2 8 - 7 = 17$ comparisons to sort.

9.5 Use dynamic programming to eliminate the recursion from Mergesort. Does the method apply to Quicksort?

9.6 At the conclusion of Mergesort, the linked list gives the sorted ordering of the array elements, but they have not been moved:

Find an $O(n)$ algorithm for rearranging the entries into sorted order. Care must be taken when swapping 11 and 35, for example, to ensure that the data structure does not forget that 35 is the successor of 28.

9.7 *Median-finding.* Consider the problem of finding the $k$th smallest element of a set of numbers. For example, if $k = \lfloor (n + 1)/2 \rfloor$ this would be finding the median element. The obvious $O(n\log n)$ solution is to put the $n$ numbers into an array *entries.item*(1..$n$), sort the array, and return *entries.item*($k$). There are several algorithms in the literature which achieve $O(n)$ complexity in the worst case; the first was by Blum et al. (1973). They are unfortunately rather complicated to implement.

The following algorithm, based on Quicksort, is a good compromise because it is simple and turns out to have $O(n)$ average complexity:

```
select_k(a, b, k: INTEGER) is
    local
        j: INTEGER;
    do
        j := partition(a, b);
        if j < k then
            select_k(j + 1, b, k)
        else
            select_k(a, j – 1, k)
        end
    end
```

The precondition of this algorithm is $a \le k \le b$; its postcondition is

> *entries.item*($k$) contains the element of *entries.item*($a..b$) that it would contain if *entries.item*($a..b$) were sorted

It turns out that this algorithm is rather hard to analyze in general, so this question will look only at the special case of *select_k*(1, $n$, 1).

(a) Explain how *select_k*($a, b, k$) works. Include a diagram.

(b) What is the worst-case complexity of *select_k*(1, $n$, 1)?

(c) What is the average complexity of *select_k*(1, $n$, 1)? The analysis of Quicksort can be adapted to this problem.

9.8　Show that each permutation of $1, \ldots, j - 1$ is equally likely to occur in *entries. item*$(1..j{-}1)$ after $j := partition(1, n)$ is complete, where *partition* is the algorithm given at the end of Section 9.4. Conclude that the average complexity analysis of Quicksort holds for *array_quicksort*.

9.9　How many recursive calls to *quicksort*$(a, b)$ are made by *quicksort*$(1, n)$? If the recursion is stopped when $n \leq k$ (for example, $k = 10$), and some other sort is used on these small subarrays, what can be said about the number of recursive calls then?

9.10　This question concerns the amount of extra memory used by Quicksort.

(a)　Find a case which shows that the runtime stack which implements the recursion in Quicksort can grow to $O(n)$ in size.

(b)　Eliminate the recursion in the array version of Quicksort by storing the indices of the endpoints of unsorted subarrays in a stack. After *partition* produces two new subarrays, stack one and sort the other.

(c)　Show that, if the smaller of the two subarrays is stacked and the larger is sorted, then the size of the stack is always $O(\log_2 n)$.

9.11　Consider modifying the array version of Quicksort by choosing the pivot element at random from *entries.item*$(a..b)$.

(a)　How does the overhead of this method (that is, the cost of calling the random number generator) compare with the total cost of the sort?

(b)　In what sense is the worst case less likely to occur if this is done?

9.12　Produce a highly tuned version of Quicksort for production use. Implement median-of-three Quicksort, recursion elimination, stacking of smaller subarrays, and insertion sort of small subarrays (this requires a sentinel). A concluding single insertion sort applied to the whole array will be faster than many small sorts applied to small subarrays. Save procedure calls wherever possible by copying their bodies into the main program. Carefully test your implementation, then perform an empirical comparison of its performance against basic Quicksort. Was your effort worthwhile?

9.13　In the following implementation of median-of-three Quicksort, procedure *threesort*$(a, i, j, k)$ examines *a.item*$(i)$, *a.item*$(j)$, and *a.item*$(k)$, swapping the smallest into *a.item*$(i)$, the largest into *a.item*$(k)$, and the median of the three into *a.item*$(j)$. This takes three comparisons between keys. Function *partition*$(a, b)$ performs the usual partition of *entries.item*$(a..b)$ about *entries.item*$(a)$, taking $b - a$ comparisons.

```
threesort(a: ARRAY[like entry_type]; i, j, k: INTEGER) is
  do
    if a.item(i).key > a.item(j).key then swap(a, i, j) end;
    if a.item(i).key > a.item(k).key then swap(a, i, k) end;
    if a.item(j).key > a.item(k).key then swap(a, j, k) end
  end

median_quicksort(a, b: INTEGER) is
  local
    j, mid: INTEGER;
  do
    if b − a + 1 <= 1 then
      -- do nothing
    elseif b − a + 1 = 2 then
      if entries.item(a).key > entries.item(b).key then
        swap(entries, a, b)
      end;
    else
      mid := (a + b) // 2;
      threesort(entries, a, mid, b);
      if a + 1 /= mid then
        swap(entries, a + 1, mid)
      end;
      j := partition(a + 1, b − 1);
      median_quicksort(a, j − 1);
      median_quicksort(j + 1, b)
    end
  end
```

(a)  If $j$ is the value returned by *partition*, show that the number of comparisons between keys performed by *median_quicksort*$(1, n)$ is given by the recurrence

$$T(0) = 0$$
$$T(1) = 0$$
$$T(2) = 1$$
$$T(n) = n + T(j − 1) + T(n − j)$$

(b)  Assuming that the worst case occurs on the least balanced partition, use (a) to write down a recurrence equation for $W(n)$. Solve your recurrence for the case $n$ even, $n \geq 2$, and show that in this case $W(n) = n(n + 2)/4 − 1$.

9.14  LSD Radixsort has two characteristic operations: the movement of one entry from the master list to a sublist, and the concatenation of a sublist to the master list. In this question it is assumed that these two characteristic operations take equal time, so that the time complexity of Radixsort is $dn + dr$ characteristic operations.

Suppose that each key is $c$ bits in length and is divided into digits each $w$ bits in length. That is, $d = c/w$ and $r = 2^w$. For fixed $c$ and $n$, how sensitive is Radixsort to the choice of $w$? How can $w$ be chosen to minimize the number of characteristic operations performed?

9.15 If $r$ is large, Radixsort wastes time examining empty sublists when rebuilding the master. Can you find a way to examine only non-empty sublists?

9.16 It often happens that the keys to be sorted are strings of characters with the usual lexicographical ordering, for example *alp* < *alpha* < *beta*. Such keys are easily handled by comparison-based sorting algorithms, but the varying length is a problem for LSD Radixsort: the obvious approach, padding each string to a maximum length with blanks, is inefficient and inconvenient. Investigate ways to radix sort character strings, aiming for a complexity on the order of the total length of all the strings. Two ideas: look again at MSD Radixsort, and consider an initial sort of the strings by their length.

9.17 When many equal keys are expected, it may be worthwhile to adapt a sorting algorithm to take advantage of their presence. One method is to use a comparison with a three-way outcome (<, = or >). Then, when two keys are found to be equal, the two entries may be replaced with one 'super-entry' that henceforward represents both, effectively reducing the size of the instance by 1. For example, consider the following straight insertion sort:

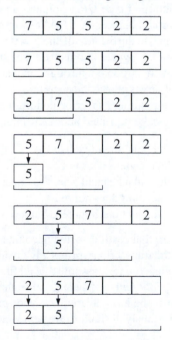

This idea can in principle be applied to any comparison-based sorting algorithm, but it will be more attractive if extra data structures, like the linked lists used above, can be avoided. Do any of the sorting algorithms of this chapter lend themselves to this?

9.18 A bank maintains a large file of account records, sorted by account number. During the day, many transactions occur on these accounts, but, since they are stored on a magnetic tape, the accounts cannot be updated as the transactions occur. When the bank's doors close at 4 p.m., the transactions are collected together, sorted by account number, and then merged with the account file to produce an updated account file:

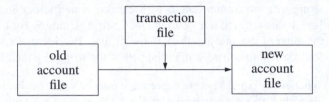

Each *ACCOUNT* object contains the account number, the current balance, and some other information of no relevance to this problem. Each *TRANS-ACTION* object contains the number of the account it applies to, the type of transaction it is (see below), and the amount of money involved.

A transaction of type *OPEN* creates a new account with the specified number and initial balance. A *CHANGE* transaction adds *amount* (which could be negative) to the balance of the given account. A *CLOSE* transaction closes an account, provided that its balance is 0. If there are no transactions for an account, it is copied through unchanged. There may be several transactions, of any type, on one account.

There are a number of error conditions that need to be detected. In each case, a message is printed and the offending transaction is ignored:

*OPEN*: account already exists
*CHANGE*: account does not exist
*CHANGE*: balance insufficient to cover withdrawal
*CLOSE*: account does not exist
*CLOSE*: account has non-zero balance

Write a program that reads a sorted accounts file and a sorted transactions file, performs the transactions, prints any error messages, and writes out the new accounts file. You may assume that all files are terminated with a record whose number is *infinity*, a special value that is larger than any account number. What is the loop invariant of your program? Be warned that this problem is notoriously difficult to solve correctly.

9.19 Consider the problem of writing a 'document analysis' program, which reads a file of text and reports the number of words in the file, the number of distinct words in the file, and the $k$ most frequent words in decreasing order of frequency, with ties broken arbitrarily. For example, a typical output might be

*File contains 2586 words, 931 distinct.*

*37 the*
*37 metempsychosis*
*32 and*
*31 a*

The value of $k$ is a parameter of the program. If there are fewer than $k$ distinct words, all are to be printed.

There are a number of solutions to this problem, of varying complexities. Aim to produce a solution that is efficient on the average. Determine the asymptotic complexity of your solution as a function of

$c$    the number of characters in the file
$m$    the number of words in the file
$n$    the number of distinct words in the file
$k$    the number of words printed at the end

These quantities satisfy $c \geq m \geq n \geq k$.

# Chapter 10

# Disjoint Sets

The subject of this chapter is the Disjoint Sets ADT. It is encountered much less frequently than symbol tables and priority queues, yet its applications are diverse: finding minimum spanning trees (Section 12.2); testing whether two finite automata are equivalent, for which see Aho et al. (1974); unifying logical predicates (attributed by Paterson and Wegman (1978) to G. Huet and G. Kahn, and independently to J. A. Robinson). It is a curious ADT, with implementations unlike any others.

## 10.1 Specification

A *disjoint sets structure* is a set of sets of entries. An entry may be in at most one set at any one time, which makes the sets disjoint. For example, if $a, b, \ldots, f$ are entries, then

$$\{\{a, b, c, d\}, \{e, f\}\}$$

is a disjoint sets structure.

Figure 10.1 contains a specification of the ADT built on this mathematical entity. The *new_entry(value)* operation creates a new entry, and *make_set(x)* places entry $x$ into a set by itself (a singleton set) and adds the set to the structure:

| | |
|---|---|
| *make* | $\{\}$ |
| *make_set(a)* | $\{\{a\}\}$ |
| *make_set(b)* | $\{\{a\}, \{b\}\}$ |
| *make_set(c)* | $\{\{a\}, \{b\}, \{c\}\}$ |
| *make_set(d)* | $\{\{a\}, \{b\}, \{c\}, \{d\}\}$ |
| *make_set(e)* | $\{\{a\}, \{b\}, \{c\}, \{d\}, \{e\}\}$ |
| *make_set(f)* | $\{\{a\}, \{b\}, \{c\}, \{d\}, \{e\}, \{f\}\}$ |

```
class interface DISJSETS_ADT[VALUE_TYPE]

    entry_type: DISJSETS_ADT_ENTRY[VALUE_TYPE];

    new_entry(value: VALUE_TYPE): like entry_type
            -- A new entry containing value

    make
            -- Make this disjoint sets structure empty

    make_set(x: like entry_type)
            -- Add a one-element set containing x to the sets

    same_set(x, y: like entry_type): BOOLEAN
            -- true if x and y lie in the same set, else false

    union(x, y: like entry_type)
            -- Replace the sets containing x and y by their union

end -- DISJSETS_ADT
```

**Figure 10.1** Specification of the Disjoint Sets ADT. Deletion and enumeration operations could be added (Exercise 10.5).

The *same_set(x, y)* operation determines whether entries $x$ and $y$ currently lie in the same set; in the example just given, the result will of course be false for any pair of entries. But the final operation, *union(x, y)*, replaces the two sets containing $x$ and $y$ by their union:

| | |
|---|---|
| *union(a, b)* | $\{\{a, b\}, \{c\}, \{d\}, \{e\}, \{f\}\}$ |
| *union(e, f)* | $\{\{a, b\}, \{c\}, \{d\}, \{e, f\}\}$ |
| *union(c, d)* | $\{\{a, b\}, \{c, d\}, \{e, f\}\}$ |
| *union(b, d)* | $\{\{a, b, c, d\}, \{e, f\}\}$ |

Now *same_set(c, a)* and *same_set(e, f)* are both **true**, for example.

The special cases *same_set(x, x)* and *union(x, x)*, where the two parameters are the same, may either be left undefined or else defined to be **true** for *same_set* and a null operation for *union*; such calls never occur in applications of this ADT anyway. If the disjoint sets structure has $n$ entries, a maximum of $n - 1$ *union* operations is possible before they all lie in one set.

This abstract data type arises whenever things which are initially separate are gradually joined together as time progresses. For example, consider the growth of the railway network of Britain and Ireland. In the year 1800, before the railway was invented, the cities of Britain and Ireland were unconnected by rail:

$D = \{\{London\}, \{Birmingham\}, \{Liverpool\}, \{Manchester\}, \{Edinburgh\},$
$\{Belfast\}, \{Dublin\}\}$

The first railway connected Liverpool and Manchester in the year 1830:

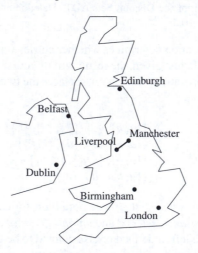

$D = \{\{London\}, \{Birmingham\}, \{Liverpool, Manchester\}, \{Edinburgh\}, \{Belfast\},$
$\{Dublin\}\}$

It is now easy to interpret the ADT operations. Using the disjoint sets structure shown, it is possible to determine whether cities $a$ and $b$ are connected by rail (either directly or via other cities) with the *same_set*($a$, $b$) operation. When a new railway is built between cities $a$ and $b$, *union*($a$, $b$) will update the structure accordingly. At the time of writing, the railway network is described by

$D = \{\{London, Birmingham, Liverpool, Manchester, Edinburgh\},$
$\quad \{Belfast, Dublin\}\}$

The disjoint sets ADT is also related to the concept of an *equivalence relation*, defined in Section 11.3. The sets are the equivalence classes of some equivalence relation $R$. The *same_set*$(x, y)$ operation determines whether $\langle x, y \rangle \in R$, that is, whether $x$ and $y$ are equivalent. The *union*$(x, y)$ operation informs the ADT that $x$ and $y$ are now to be considered equivalent; so clearly their classes must be united.

## 10.2 The Galler–Fischer representation

One simple way to represent a disjoint sets structure is to store in each entry a value which indicates which set the entry lies in. For example, the structure $D = \{\{a, b, c, d\}, \{e,f\}, \{g\}\}$ could be represented by

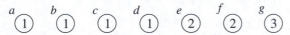

Then *same_set*$(x, y)$ would simply compare this value in the two entries. Unfortunately, a *union* operation would have to change all the values of one set to the values of the other, which in the worst case would take $O(n)$ time.

There is another, very clever data structure for representing disjoint sets, due to Galler and Fischer (1964). Each set is a tree with references from children to parents – the reverse of the usual direction. For example, if the structure is

$$\{\{a, b, c, d\}, \{e,f\}, \{g\}\}$$

the representation might be the forest

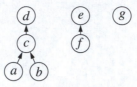

Each node is an entry, containing just the entry's value and a reference to the parent. With this representation, the operations are remarkably simple to implement. There is a private operation called *find(x)* which finds the entry at the root of *x*'s tree by following parent references until it can go no further. The *same_set(x, y)* operation compares the roots of the trees containing *x* and *y*. The *union(x, y)* operation makes the parent of *x*'s root be *y*'s root, linking the two trees into one:

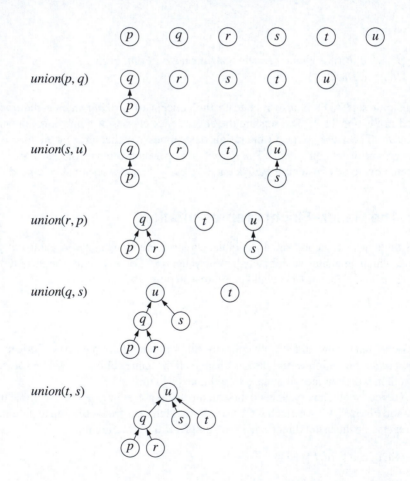

See Figure 10.2 for an implementation.

```
class DISJSETS_GF[VALUE_TYPE]

inherit

    DISJSETS_ADT[VALUE_TYPE] redefine entry_type, out end;

feature { NONE }

    find(x: like entry_type): like entry_type is
        do
            from Result := x until Result.ds_parent = Void loop
                Result := Result.ds_parent
            end
        end;

feature

    entry_type: DISJSETS_GF_ENTRY[VALUE_TYPE];

    new_entry(v: VALUE_TYPE): like entry_type is
        do
            !!Result.make(v)
        end;

    make_set(x: like entry_type) is
        do
            x.put_ds_parent(Void);
        end;

    same_set(x, y: like entry_type): BOOLEAN is
        do
            Result := (find(x) = find(y))
        end;

    union(x, y: like entry_type) is
        local
            xp, yp: like entry_type;
        do
            xp := find(x);
            yp := find(y);
            if xp /= yp then
                xp.put_ds_parent(yp)
            end
        end;

end -- DISJSETS_GF
```

**Figure 10.2** The Galler–Fischer implementation of the Disjoint Sets ADT; *make* does nothing and has been omitted.

The *make_set* operation has $O(1)$ complexity. For the *same_set* and *union* operations, a realistic characteristic operation to choose is the edge-traverse that occurs within *find*$(x)$. Clearly the cost of *find*$(x)$ is $d(x)$, the depth of $x$ in its tree. If the height of a forest is defined to be the height of the tallest tree in it, then the worst-case complexity of *find*$(x)$, when $x$ lies in forest $F$, is $h(F) - 1$. This is maximized for fixed $n$ when $F$ consists of a single skew tree:

when its value is $W(n) = n - 1$. Thus the worst-case time complexities of *same_set* and *union* are $O(n)$, but, as will be seen in the next section, this result is very easy to improve dramatically.

## 10.3 Union by size

The obvious way to improve the performance of the Galler–Fischer data structure is to ensure that the trees are balanced. There is a simple way to do this, known as *union by size*: keep a record of the size of each tree in its root, and, when taking a union, always link the smaller tree to the larger. If the trees have equal size, either may be linked to the other. For example:

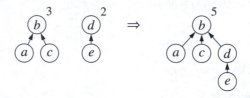

Union by size has been attributed by Knuth (1973a) to M. D. McIlroy.

The following theorem shows that this strategy is effective. Recall that the tree rooted at $v$ is denoted $T_v$, and $s(T_v)$ denotes the size (number of nodes) of $T_v$.

**Theorem 10.1:**  Consider any sequence $p_0, p_1, \ldots, p_m$ of disjoint sets operations, such that $p_0$ is *make* and the unions employ union by size. Let $x$ be any node in existence after $p_m$. Then $2^{h(T_x)-1} \le s(T_x)$.

**Proof:**  As usual with proofs of representation invariants, the proof is by induction on $m$, the length of the operation sequence.

**Basis step:** $m = 0$. Then the ADT is empty, and the theorem is vacuously true.
**Inductive step:** $m > 0$. The inductive hypothesis states that, before $p_m$ begins, $2^{h(T_x)-1} \le s(T_x)$ for all nodes $x$ in existence at that time. It must be shown to be true after $p_m$ is complete.

If $p_m$ is *make_set(x)*, it introduces a new tree $T_x$ of size $s(T_x) = 1$ and height $h(T_x) = 1$, which satisfies the condition. If $p_m$ is *same_set(x, y)*, there is no change in the structure.

Finally, suppose $p_m$ is *union(x, y)*. Let $v$ be the root of the tree containing $x$, and let $w$ be the root of the tree containing $y$. Without loss of generality, it may be assumed that $s(T_v) \le s(T_w)$. In this situation the effect of *union(x, y)* is to link $v$ to $w$, creating the new tree

$T =$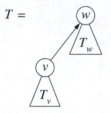

It must be shown that $2^{h(T)-1} \le s(T)$. Since $h(T) = \max(1 + h(T_v), h(T_w))$,

$$2^{h(T)-1} = 2^{\max(1+h(T_v), h(T_w))-1}$$

$$= \max(2^{h(T_v)-1+1}, 2^{h(T_w)-1})$$

$$\le \max(2s(T_v), s(T_w))$$

by the inductive hypothesis applied to $v$ and $w$. Now from $s(T) = s(T_v) + s(T_w)$ and $s(T_v) \le s(T_w)$, it follows that $2s(T_v) \le s(T)$ and $s(T_w) \le s(T)$. Consequently,

$$2^{h(T)-1} \le \max(s(T), s(T))$$

$$= s(T)$$

and the theorem is proved. $\square$

Taking logarithms, in a forest built by *make_set* and *union* operations employing union by size, every tree $T$ must satisfy $h(T) - 1 \le \log_2 s(T)$. Since $s(T) \le n$, the cost of any *find*, and hence any *same_set* or *union*, is at most $\log_2 n$.

To summarize, then, the implementation of the Disjoint Sets ADT using trees and union by size has $O(1)$ worst-case complexity for *make* and *make_set*, and $O(\log n)$ for *same_set* and *union*. Its efficiency is comparable with good implementations of other ADTs, and the code is exceptionally simple.

## 10.4 Path compression

This section presents a method called *path compression* for reducing the cost of *find* operations to virtually $O(1)$ each, by exploiting more fully the fact that a node may have arbitrarily many children.

Path compression begins by traversing the path from some node $x$ to its root $y$ in the usual way. After this is done, the path from $x$ to $y$ is traversed a second time, and every reference on it is changed to point directly to $y$:

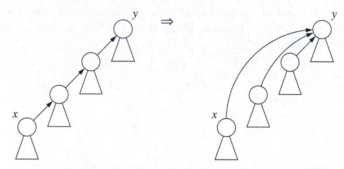

This ensures that subsequent finds along that path will run faster. This optimization is called *path compression*, and it has been attributed by Knuth (1973a) to A. Tritter. The code for path compression may be found in Figure 10.3.

### Analysis of path compression

It turns out that path compression, in conjunction with union by size, reduces the cost of *find* operations considerably, to the point where they are virtually $O(1)$ each, in the amortized sense. The proof of this is quite difficult.

It is convenient for the analysis to separate the *find* operations from the *same_set* and *union* operations that contain them. So, in the following discussion, *find* operations will appear explicitly, *same_set* operations will not be mentioned, and a *union* operation will be just the final linking of one root to another.

Path compression cannot reduce the cost of the first *find* in a sequence of operations, so no improvement can be expected in worst-case complexity. Instead, it is hoped to reduce the total cost of a sequence of operations, and this brings us into the realm of amortized complexity. As before, the measure of complexity will be the number of edges traversed during the scan from $x$ to the root. The cost of the second (compressing) scan is ignored. This is realistic, because the second scan traverses the same path.

In the following discussion, $p$ is a sequence of disjoint sets operations beginning with *make*, and containing $m_1 = n$ *make_set*, $m_2$ *find*, and $m_3$ *union* operations in any order. Let $x$ be any node in existence after operation sequence $p$ is complete, and define $r(x)$, the *rank* of $x$, as follows:

(1)  Execute $p$ with path compression turned off.

(2)  Let $r(x) = h(x) - 1$, where $h(x)$ is the height of $x$ in the forest after (1).

For example, here is an operation sequence $p$ and the forest resulting from (1). For brevity, the *make* and *make_set* operations are omitted. Each node contains its rank, and is displayed at an appropriate level in the diagram:

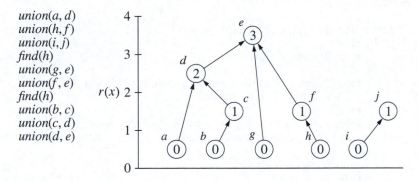

The values $r(x)$ will be used in the definition of the potential function $\Phi(F)$, which is unusual, because $\Phi(F)$ is supposed to be a function of the current state $F$, yet the $r(x)$ are determined by the final state. This is justified by observing that, once $p$ is fixed, the $r(x)$ are constants. In effect, $p$ is run with path compression off to determine the $r(x)$, then $F$ is reset to empty, and $p$ is run a second time with path compression on, using the $r(x)$ to aid the analysis of this second run.

In the diagram just given, the edges all point upwards (in other words, $r(x) < r(x.parent)$ for all non-root nodes $x$). This must always be the case, because $r(x) = h(x) - 1$, and the height of a node is always strictly greater than the height of each of its children. But what if the nodes are drawn in these positions (determined by the constants $r(x)$) at some intermediate moment in $p$, perhaps with path compression on? Would the edges point upwards then?

For example, if the sequence $p$ given above is run, employing path compression, and stopped after *union(c, d)*, the picture is

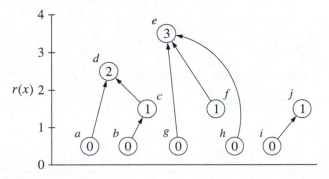

```
class DISJSETS_LINKED[VALUE_TYPE]

inherit

    DISJSETS_ADT[VALUE_TYPE] redefine entry_type, out end;


feature { NONE }

    find(x: like entry_type): like entry_type is
        local
            y, yp: like entry_type;
        do
            from Result := x until Result.ds_parent = Void loop
                Result := Result.ds_parent
            end;
            from y := x; yp := x.ds_parent until y = Result loop
                y.put_ds_parent(Result);
                y := yp;
                yp := yp.ds_parent
            end
        end;

feature

    entry_type: DISJSETS_LINKED_ENTRY[VALUE_TYPE];

    new_entry(v: VALUE_TYPE): like entry_type is
        do
            !!Result.make(v)
        end;

    make is
        do
        end;

    make_set(x: like entry_type) is
        do
            x.put_ds_parent(Void);
            x.put_size(1);
        end;

    same_set(x, y: like entry_type): BOOLEAN is
        do
            Result := (find(x) = find(y))
        end;
```

```
union(x, y: like entry_type) is
    local
        xp, yp: like entry_type;
    do
        xp := find(x);
        yp := find(y);
        if xp = yp then
            -- do nothing, already in same set
        elseif xp.size < yp.size then
            xp.put_ds_parent(yp);
            yp.put_size(xp.size + yp.size);
        else
            yp.put_ds_parent(xp);
            xp.put_size(yp.size + xp.size);
        end
    end;

end -- DISJSETS_LINKED
```

**Figure 10.3** Implementation of the Disjoint Sets ADT using the Galler–Fischer structure with both union by size and path compression.

There are fewer edges, but they all point upwards.

The proof that $r(x) < r(x.parent)$ at all times for all non-root nodes $x$, with or without path compression, is in two parts. First, turn path compression off, stop $p$ at some intermediate moment, and consider any edge $x \to y$. At this moment, $h(x) < h(y)$, and since $x$ is not a root, its height cannot change from now on. The height of $y$ cannot decrease (path compression is off, remember), so $h(x) < h(y)$ at the end of $p$, hence $r(x) < r(y)$.

Second, run $p$ again with path compression on. The union operations link together the same nodes that they did before, so the links $x \to y$ introduced by unions satisfy $r(x) < r(y)$. Path compression always links a node $x$ to one of its proper ancestors $y$:

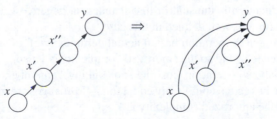

An inductive argument may assume that $r(x) < r(x')$, $r(x') < r(x'')$, and so on, and so $r(x) < r(y)$.

The picture of $F$ at some intermediate moment, with path compression on, is becoming clear: the nodes in fixed positions, the edges pointing upwards. The final element in the picture is a sequence of numbers $A_0, A_1, \ldots, A_k, A_{k+1}$. These numbers may be chosen freely, subject only to the condition

$$0 = A_0 < A_1 < \ldots < A_k \leq \lfloor \log_2 n \rfloor < A_{k+1}$$

The $A_i$ are horizontal lines cutting across the picture. If $k = 1$, for example, with $A_0 = 0, A_1 = 3$, and $A_2 = 4$, we have

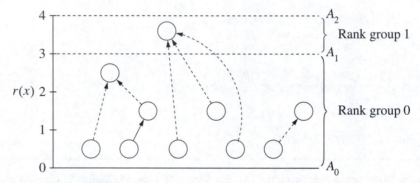

Node $x$ is said to be in *rank group i* if $A_i \leq r(x) < A_{i+1}$. By Theorem 10.1, union by size guarantees $0 \leq r(x) \leq \lfloor \log_2 n \rfloor$, and therefore every node must lie in exactly one rank group.

As shown in the diagram just given, the edges of $F$ are divided into two types: *dashed* and *solid*. Edges that connect nodes lying in different rank groups are shown dashed. Edges leading into root nodes are also dashed. The remaining edges are solid.

As an aid to analysis, a *count* field is introduced into each node, holding a non-negative integer. Actual implementations do not have this field; it is only an analytical device. Define

$$\Phi(F) = -\sum_{x \in F} x.count$$

This potential function is unusual in that it takes on negative values. Amortized analysis is nevertheless well defined in this case.

The *make_set(x)* operation has an actual complexity of 1 (say). The *x.count* field is initialized to 0, and so the amortized complexity is 1 also.

The *union(v, w)* operation (just the root linking, remember, not the two *find* operations) also has actual complexity equal to 1. No changes are made to the count fields, so again the amortized complexity is 1.

The *find(x)* operation traverses a path composed of dashed and solid edges. Its actual complexity is the number of edges on this path. However, whenever a solid edge $y \to z$ is traversed, 1 is added to *y.count*. This decreases the potential by 1, canceling the cost of traversing the solid edge, and so the amortized complexity of *find(x)* is the number of dashed edges traversed. For example, consider

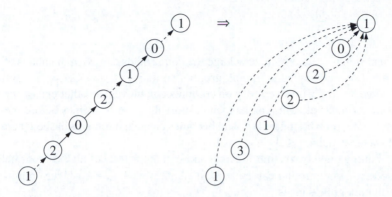

where the count values are shown inside the nodes. The actual complexity is 6, but three count fields were incremented, for an amortized complexity of 3.

Since the edges point upwards, a path can cross each of the $k$ rank group boundaries at most once, giving at most $k$ dashed edges on any path; but there is also the final dashed edge leading into the root. It follows that the amortized complexity of $find(x)$ is at most $k + 1$.

This completes the analysis of the operations. The total actual complexity of any sequence of $m_1$ *make_set*, $m_2$ *find*, and $m_3$ *union* operations satisfies

$$\sum_{i=1}^{m} t_i = \sum_{i=1}^{m} a_i - \Phi(F_m) + \Phi(F_0)$$

$$\leq m_1 + m_2(k + 1) + m_3 - \Phi(F_m),$$

since $\Phi(F_0) = 0$. It remains to determine $-\Phi(F_m)$, the total of all the count fields when the sequence ends.

The first step is to show that in any union-by-size forest $F$ containing $n$ nodes, there are at most $n/2^r$ nodes of rank $r$. Let $x_1, x_2, \ldots, x_j$ be the nodes of rank $r$ in $F$. Since these nodes all have height $r + 1$, one cannot be a proper descendant of another, so the subtrees rooted at these nodes are disjoint. By Theorem 10.1, each subtree contains at least $2^r$ nodes, making a total of $j2^r$ nodes. But this cannot exceed $n$, so $j \leq n/2^r$.

Summing this over the ranks $A_i, \ldots, A_{i+1} - 1$ shows that the total number of nodes in rank group $i$ is at most

$$\sum_{r=A_i}^{A_{i+1}-1} \frac{n}{2^r} = \frac{n}{2^{A_i}} \sum_{r=0}^{A_{i+1}-1-A_i} \frac{1}{2^r}$$

$$< \frac{n}{2^{A_i}} \sum_{r=0}^{\infty} \frac{1}{2^r}$$

$$= \frac{2n}{2^{A_i}}$$

The next step is to determine how large the count fields can be in the nodes of rank group $i$. Let $x$ be any node in rank group $i$, so that $A_i \leq r(x) < A_{i+1}$. Each time a solid edge leaving $x$ is traversed, path compression moves the other end of the edge up at least one level. This can happen at most $A_{i+1} - A_i - 1$ times before the edge crosses rank group boundary $A_{i+1}$ and becomes dashed; it remains dashed thereafter. It follows that $x.count \leq A_{i+1} - A_i - 1$.

Putting these two results together shows that the total of all the count fields of the nodes of rank group $i$ can be at most $(2n/2^{A_i}) \times (A_{i+1} - A_i - 1)$. Summing this over all rank groups gives

$$-\Phi(F_m) = \sum_{x \in F_m} x.count$$

$$\leq \sum_{i=0}^{k} \frac{2n}{2^{A_i}}(A_{i+1} - A_i - 1)$$

and the total complexity of any sequence of $m_1 = n$ *make_set* operations, $m_2$ *find* operations, and $m_3$ *union* operations satisfies

$$T \leq n + m_2(k + 1) + m_3 + \sum_{i=0}^{k} \frac{2n}{2^{A_i}}(A_{i+1} - A_i - 1)$$

The numbers $A_i$ may now be chosen freely so as to minimize this expression. If the choice is $k = 0, A_0 = 0$, and $A_1 = \lfloor \log_2 n \rfloor + 1$, then

$$T \leq n + m_2 + m_3 + 2n\lfloor \log_2 n \rfloor$$

with the total cost of traversing solid edges dominant. At the other extreme, if the choice is $k = \lfloor \log_2 n \rfloor$, and $A_i = i$ for all $i$, then $A_{i+1} - A_i - 1 = 0$, and so

$$T \leq n + m_2(\lfloor \log_2 n \rfloor + 1) + m_3$$

with the cost of the dashed edges dominant (not surprisingly, since there are no solid edges). Finally, there is an extraordinary intermediate choice. Let

$$A_0 = 0$$
$$A_{i+1} = 2^{A_i}$$

for all $i$, and let $k$ be such that $A_k \leq \lfloor \log_2 n \rfloor < A_{k+1}$. This gives

$$T \leq n + m_2(k + 1) + m_3 + \sum_{i=0}^{k} \frac{2n}{2^{A_i}}(A_{i+1} - A_i - 1)$$

$$\leq n + m_2(k + 1) + m_3 + \sum_{i=0}^{k} \frac{2n}{2^{A_i}}A_{i+1}$$

$$= n + m_2(k + 1) + m_3 + \sum_{i=0}^{k} 2n$$

$$= n + (2n + m_2)(k + 1) + m_3$$

In practice, $k$ is virtually a small constant, because the $A_i$ grow at a truly alarming rate: $A_0 = 0, A_1 = 1, A_2 = 2, A_3 = 4, A_4 = 16, A_5 = 65\,536, A_6 = 2^{65536}$. For example, if $n = 2^{65536} - 1$ (a truly enormous number), then $A_4 \leq \lfloor \log_2 n \rfloor < A_5$, so that $k = 4$. The total complexity is therefore virtually linear in the number of operations.

This analysis is due to Hopcroft and Ullman (1973); the presentation is adapted from Purdom and Brown (1985). An even tighter bound has been given by Tarjan (1975).

## 10.5 Exercises

10.1   Find a sequence of *make_set*, *same_set*, and *union* operations which proves that the time complexity bounds given in Section 10.3, for union by size without path compression, cannot be improved.

10.2   Show that the following tree will never be constructed by unions that employ union by size:

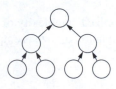

10.3   Given the tree

$$\textcircled{a} \rightarrow \textcircled{b} \rightarrow \textcircled{c} \rightarrow \textcircled{d} \rightarrow \textcircled{e} \rightarrow \textcircled{f} \rightarrow \textcircled{g}$$

suppose the operations *find(a)*, *find(b)*, ... , *find(g)* are executed in any order, employing path compression. Define the cost of the operation *find(x)* to be the number of edges traversed on the first pass (as usual). For example, in the tree above, *find(g)* costs 0, *find(a)* costs 6, and a second *find(a)* costs 1.

(a) Irrespective of the order of the operations, what will the tree look like finally?

(b) In what order should the seven *find* operations be performed so as to minimize their total cost? Prove your result.

10.4 Consider any sequence of *make_set*, *union*, and *find* operations in which all of the *union* operations precede all of the non-trivial *find* operations (as will occur when all of the unions happen to connect two roots). Show that, employing path compression with or without union by size, the total cost of the sequence is linear in its length. Hint: let $\Phi$ be the number of nodes that possess a grandparent.

10.5 Consider extending the Disjoint Sets ADT to include the operations

> *delete*(*x*: **like** *entry_type*);
> *find_all*(*x*: **like** *entry_type*): *LIST*[**like** *entry_type*];

where *delete*(*x*) deletes entry *x* from whatever set it lies in, and *find_all*(*x*) returns a list of all the entries in the set containing *x*. Implement this extended ADT in a way that preserves the good complexity bounds of the other operations.

10.6 Show that, in the analysis of Section 10.4, the sequence of numbers $A_i$ could have been defined by

$$A_0 = 0$$
$$A_{i+1} = 2^{A_i} + A_i + 1$$

without jeopardizing the analysis. What effect does this refinement have on the value of $k$?

10.7 Investigate the amortized complexity of the Disjoint Sets ADT when path compression but not union by size is employed.

# Chapter 11

# Graphs

Graphs model the real world. Problems as diverse as minimizing the cost of microwave communications networks, generating efficient assembly code for evaluating expressions, measuring the reliability of telephone networks, and many others, are naturally formulated with graphs.

For example, consider the problem of finding the shortest route between two towns on a map. The information needed to solve this problem can be clearly represented as a *graph*:

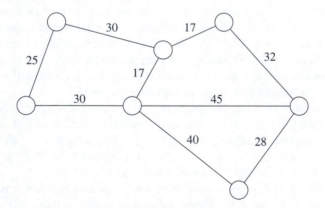

Lines represent roads, nodes represent intersections and towns, and the number attached to each line is the length of each road, or perhaps an estimate of the time it would take to travel it.

Many important problems about graphs have never been efficiently solved; for others there are elegant algorithms whose correctness requires careful study. A comprehensive account of these problems would fill volumes; only a few central ones can be treated in the two chapters devoted to the subject here.

## 11.1 Definitions

In this section some basic definitions for directed and undirected graphs are presented. These definitions are approximately standard, but the reader must be prepared for minor variations among authors.

A *directed graph* or *digraph* $G = \langle V, E \rangle$ is a set $V$ of *vertices* together with a set $E$ of *edges*. Each edge is a sequence of two vertices, and is represented diagrammatically by an arrow from the first vertex to the second. For example, here is a digraph with four vertices and four edges:

$$V = \{a, b, c, d\}$$
$$E = \{\langle a, a \rangle, \langle a, c \rangle, \langle c, d \rangle, \langle d, c \rangle\}$$

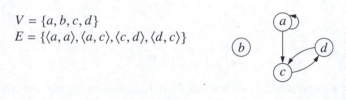

This definition permits *self-loops* (edges of the form $\langle v, v \rangle$), but prohibits *parallel edges* (two equal edges $\langle v, w \rangle$ in $E$). If $\langle v, w \rangle \in E$, $v$ is a *predecessor* of $w$, and $w$ is a *successor* of $v$. The *indegree* of $w$ is the number of its predecessors; the *outdegree* of $v$ is the number of its successors.

A sequence of vertices $\langle v_1, v_2, \ldots, v_k \rangle$, where $k \geq 1$, is a *path* if $\langle v_i, v_{i+1} \rangle \in E$ for $1 \leq i \leq k - 1$. It is a *proper path* if $k \geq 2$. If $\langle v_1, v_2, \ldots, v_k \rangle$ is a path, $v_k$ is said to be *reachable* from $v_1$. Thus, every vertex is reachable from itself. Two vertices $v$ and $w$ are *strongly connected* if $w$ is reachable from $v$, and $v$ is reachable from $w$. A path $\langle v_1, v_2, \ldots, v_k \rangle$ is a *cycle* if $v_1 = v_k$; it is *simple* if its vertices are all distinct, except that $v_1 = v_k$ is allowed, in which case the path is a *simple cycle*. For example, in the digraph above, $\langle a \rangle, \langle a, a \rangle$ and $\langle c, d, c \rangle$ are simple cycles; $\langle a, a \rangle$ and $\langle c, d, c \rangle$ are proper cycles. The *length* of a path is the number of edges on it.

A *rooted tree* is a directed graph in which, for every vertex $v$, there is exactly one path of the form $\langle a, \ldots, v \rangle$, where $a$ is a distinguished vertex called the *root* of the tree. A *subgraph* of a directed graph $G = \langle V, E \rangle$ is a digraph $G' = \langle V', E' \rangle$ such that $V' \subseteq V$ and $E' \subseteq E$. A *spanning tree* of a digraph $G = \langle V, E \rangle$ is a subgraph $T = \langle V', E' \rangle$ of $G$ such that $T$ is a rooted tree, and $V' = V$.

The complexity of graph algorithms will be measured as a function of $n$, the number of vertices, and $m$, the number of edges. Typically, there will be one characteristic operation related to vertices, and another related to edges; the number of each will be determined and their sum reported. Only finite graphs will be considered here.

### Graphs

An *undirected graph* or just *graph* $G = \langle V, E \rangle$ is a set $V$ of vertices and a set $E$ of edges. Each edge is a two-element set of distinct vertices. For example, here is a graph with four vertices and three edges:

$$V = \{a, b, c, d\}$$
$$E = \{\{a, c\}, \{c, d\}, \{a, d\}\}$$

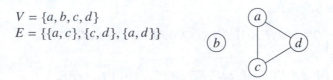

This definition prohibits self-loops and parallel edges. If $\{v, w\} \in E$, $v$ and $w$ are said to be *adjacent*. The *degree* of vertex $v$ is the number of vertices adjacent to $v$.

A sequence of $k \geq 1$ vertices $\langle v_1, v_2, \dots, v_k \rangle$ is a *path* if $\{v_i, v_{i+1}\} \in E$ for $1 \leq i \leq k - 1$. It is a *proper path* if $k \geq 2$; it is a *cycle* if $k \geq 3$ and $v_1 = v_k$; and it is *simple* if its vertices are all distinct, except that $v_1 = v_k$ is allowed. The *length* of a path is the number of edges on it.

A *tree* (or *free tree*) is a graph in which, for every pair of vertices $v, w$, there is exactly one simple path of the form $\langle v, \dots, w \rangle$. A *subgraph* of a graph $G = \langle V, E \rangle$ is a graph $G' = \langle V', E' \rangle$ such that $V' \subseteq V$ and $E' \subseteq E$. A *spanning tree* of a graph $G = \langle V, E \rangle$ is a subgraph $T = \langle V', E' \rangle$ of $G$ such that $T$ is a tree, and $V' = V$.

If $\langle v_1, v_2, \dots, v_k \rangle$ is a path, $v_1$ and $v_k$ are said to be *connected*. A graph is connected if every pair of vertices in it is connected. Otherwise, the graph is made up of a number of *connected components*: maximal subgraphs which are connected. The graph $G$ above has two connected components.

## 11.2 Specification and representation

Although one can think of a number of operations to apply to graphs – modifying them, enquiring whether a certain edge is present, and so on – we will mainly be interested in traversing a fixed graph in various ways. Accordingly, the ADT specification in Figure 11.1 concentrates on operations which implement the traversals that will be needed.

Unlike previous container ADTs, each of which had a single associated entry type, *DIGRAPH* has two such types, one for vertices and one for edges. The ADT allows for the insertion of vertices, and of edges between two existing vertices. Vertices and edges may have associated values, such as edge costs for example. Any digraph may be built by a sequence of these operations.

The *first_vertex* and *next_vertex(v)* operations allow for visiting all the vertices of digraph $g$ in an unspecified order, using the code

```
from v := g.first_vertex until g.nil_vertex(v) loop
    visit(v);
    v := g.next_vertex(v)
end
```

Both operations return the special nil vertex when there is no suitable vertex.

**class interface** *DIGRAPH_ADT[VERTEX_VALUE_TYPE,*
    *EDGE_VALUE_TYPE]*

  *vertex_type*: *DIGRAPH_ADT_VERTEX[VERTEX_VALUE_TYPE,*
    *EDGE_VALUE_TYPE]*;

  *edge_type*: *DIGRAPH_ADT_EDGE[VERTEX_VALUE_TYPE,*
    *EDGE_VALUE_TYPE]*;


  *new_vertex(value*: *VERTEX_VALUE_TYPE*): **like** *vertex_type*
      -- A new vertex with this value

  *new_nil_vertex*: **like** *vertex_type*
      -- A new nil vertex

  *new_edge(value*: *EDGE_VALUE_TYPE*): **like** *edge_type*
      -- A new edge with this value

  *nil_vertex(v*: **like** *vertex_type*): *BOOLEAN*
      -- **true** if *v* is the special nil vertex, else **false**

  *nil_edge(e*: **like** *edge_type*): *BOOLEAN*
      -- **true** if *e* is the special nil edge, else **false**

  *insert_vertex(v*: **like** *vertex_type*)
      -- Insert vertex *v* into this digraph

  *insert_edge(e*: **like** *edge_type*; *v*, *w*: **like** *vertex_type*)
      -- Insert edge *e* into this digraph, from *v* to *w*

  *first_vertex*: **like** *vertex_type*
      -- The first vertex of the digraph in some arbitrary but fixed order

  *next_vertex(v*: **like** *vertex_type*): **like** *vertex_type*
      -- The next vertex after *v* in the arbitrary but fixed order

  *first_edge(v*: **like** *vertex_type*): **like** *edge_type*
      -- The first edge leading out of *v* in some arbitrary but fixed order

  *next_edge(v*: **like** *vertex_type*; *e*: **like** *edge_type*): **like** *edge_type*
      -- The next edge out of *v* after *e* in the arbitrary but fixed order

  *end_point(e*: **like** *edge_type*): **like** *vertex_type*
      -- The endpoint of edge *e*

**end** -- *DIGRAPH_ADT*

**Figure 11.1** Specification of the Digraph ADT.

The *first_edge(v)* and *next_edge(v, e)* operations allow for visiting all the edges leading out of vertex *v*, again in an unspecified order. The *end_point(e)* operation returns the endpoint of an edge (that is, the vertex it points to). Thus, to visit each successor *w* of a given vertex *v*, the code

> **from** *e* := *g.first_edge(v)* **until** *g.nil_edge(e)* **loop**
>    *w* := *g.end_point(e)*;
>    *visit(w)*;
>    *e* := *g.next_edge(v, e)*
> **end**

may be used. Both *first_edge(v)* and *next_edge(v, e)* return the special nil edge when there is no suitable edge.

Unlike symbol tables and priority queues, this ADT is quite easy to implement so that all operations are $O(1)$ in the worst case. The representation is called *adjacency lists*. A linked list of records denoting edges is grown out of each vertex. Each contains a reference to the endpoint of the edge. For example, here is a digraph and its adjacency lists representation:

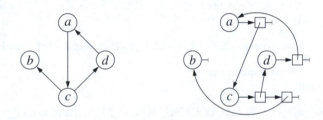

An ADT implementation using adjacency lists is given in Figure 11.2. The edges leading out of a vertex *v* are linked together through their *next_edge* fields, beginning with *v.first_edge*, and ending with a void reference. The vertices are linked together through their *next_vertex* fields. Type *DIGRAPH* is a header containing just a reference to the first vertex on this list, and a void reference terminates the list. (Alternatively, the vertices could be stored sequentially in an array.)

A variant of the Digraph ADT may be used for undirected graphs as well. Simply ensure that *insert_edge(v, w)* adds two new edges: one from *v* to *w*, and one from *w* back to *v*. The name *Graph* may be given to this variant of the ADT.

## 11.3 Relations and digraphs

Since this chapter contains algorithms on directed graphs, undirected graphs, and directed graphs without cycles, it is worth asking why these variants of the basic idea arise. The best way to answer this question is to review the mathematical theory of *relations*, which underlies all kinds of graphs.

```
class DIGRAPH_LISTS[VERTEX_VALUE_TYPE, EDGE_VALUE_TYPE]

inherit

    DIGRAPH_ADT[VERTEX_VALUE_TYPE, EDGE_VALUE_TYPE]
        redefine vertex_type, edge_type, out end;

feature { NONE }

    vertex_type: DIGRAPH_LISTS_VERTEX[VERTEX_VALUE_TYPE,
        EDGE_VALUE_TYPE];

    edge_type: DIGRAPH_LISTS_EDGE[VERTEX_VALUE_TYPE,
        EDGE_VALUE_TYPE];

feature

    make is
        do
            first_vertex := Void;
        end;

    new_vertex(value: VERTEX_VALUE_TYPE): like vertex_type is
        do
            !!Result.make(value)
        end;

    new_nil_vertex(value: VERTEX_VALUE_TYPE): like vertex_type is
        do
            Result := Void
        end;

    new_edge(value: EDGE_VALUE_TYPE): like edge_type is
        do
            !!Result.make(value)
        end;

    nil_vertex(v: like vertex_type): BOOLEAN is
        do
            Result := (v = Void);
        end;

    nil_edge(e: like edge_type): BOOLEAN is
        do
            Result := (e = Void);
        end;
```

```
insert_vertex(v: like vertex_type) is
    do
        v.put_next_vertex(first_vertex);
        v.put_first_edge(Void);
        first_vertex := v;
    end;

insert_edge(e: like edge_type; v, w: like vertex_type) is
    do
        e.put_next_edge(v.first_edge);
        v.put_first_edge(e);
        e.put_end_point(w);
    end;

first_vertex: like vertex_type;

next_vertex(v: like vertex_type): like vertex_type is
    do
        Result := v.next_vertex;
    end;

first_edge(v: like vertex_type): like edge_type is
    do
        Result := v.first_edge;
    end;

next_edge(v: like vertex_type; e: like edge_type): like edge_type is
    do
        Result := e.next_edge;
    end;

end_point(e: like edge_type): like vertex_type is
    do
        Result := e.end_point;
    end;

end -- DIGRAPH_LISTS
```

**Figure 11.2**  Adjacency lists implementation of the Digraph ADT.

Beginning with a set $S$, let the *Cartesian product* of $S$ with itself, $S \times S$, be the set of all two-element sequences of elements of $S$. For example, if $S = \{a, b, c, d\}$,

$$S \times S = \begin{Bmatrix} \langle a, a \rangle, & \langle a, b \rangle, & \langle a, c \rangle, & \langle a, d \rangle, \\ \langle b, a \rangle, & \langle b, b \rangle, & \langle b, c \rangle, & \langle b, d \rangle, \\ \langle c, a \rangle, & \langle c, b \rangle, & \langle c, c \rangle, & \langle c, d \rangle, \\ \langle d, a \rangle, & \langle d, b \rangle, & \langle d, c \rangle, & \langle d, d \rangle \end{Bmatrix}$$

A *binary relation* (or just *relation*) $R$ on $S$ is a subset of $S \times S$. For example,

$$R = \{\langle a, a \rangle, \langle b, b \rangle, \langle b, c \rangle, \langle c, b \rangle\}$$

is a binary relation on the set $S$ given above. Thus, from a formal point of view, a digraph $G = \langle V, E \rangle$ is just a relation, taking $V = S$ and $E = R$.

Relations are commonly met with as boolean conditions between numbers. For example, the '$\leq$' condition between whole numbers is a binary relation:

$$'\leq' = \begin{cases} \langle 0,0 \rangle, & \langle 0,1 \rangle, & \langle 0,2 \rangle, & \dots \\ & \langle 1,1 \rangle, & \langle 1,2 \rangle, & \dots \\ & & \langle 2,2 \rangle, & \dots \end{cases}$$

Instead of writing $\langle a, b \rangle \in$ '$\leq$' to denote membership in this relation, it is conventional to use the simpler notation $a \leq b$. In the same way, the notation $a \mathrel{R} b$ will be used instead of the formal $\langle a, b \rangle \in R$ for other relations as well.

No restriction is made as to which pairs may appear in a relation, and in general the corresponding digraph may be a random collection of vertices and edges. In practice, however, certain patterns or properties appear frequently in applications, especially the following five.

*Reflexivity.* A binary relation $R$ is reflexive if $x \mathrel{R} x$ for all $x$ in $S$. In digraph terms, every vertex has a self-loop:

For example, the relation '$\leq$' over the integers is reflexive: $x \leq x$ for all integers $x$. In the same way, '$=$' is also reflexive. But the relation $R$ given above is not reflexive, because $\langle c, c \rangle$ and $\langle d, d \rangle$ are missing.

*Irreflexivity.* A relation $R$ is irreflexive if $x \mathrel{R} x$ is false for all $x$. There are no self-loops in the corresponding digraph. For example, the relation '$<$' over the integers is irreflexive: $x < x$ is false for all integers $x$.

*Symmetry.* A relation $R$ is symmetric if $x \mathrel{R} y$ implies $y \mathrel{R} x$, for all $x$ and $y$. In digraph terms, all edges except self-loops occur in pairs:

For example, the equality relation is symmetric: $x = y$ implies $y = x$, for all $x$ and $y$. The relation $R$ given above is also symmetric.

*Antisymmetry.* A relation $R$ is antisymmetric if $x \mathrel{R} y$ and $y \mathrel{R} x$ together imply $x = y$, for all $x$ and $y$. The relation '$\leq$' is antisymmetric: $x \leq y$ and $y \leq x$ together imply $x = y$, for all $x$ and $y$. It is sometimes preferable to think of antisymmetry in its contrapositive form: $x \neq y$ implies $x \mathrel{R} y$ is false or $y \mathrel{R} x$ is false. The corresponding digraph can have no edge pairs like the one above.

*Transitivity.* A relation $R$ is transitive if $x\ R\ y$ and $y\ R\ z$ together imply $x\ R\ z$, for all $x$, $y$, and $z$. In digraph terms, the endpoints of all proper paths are connected:

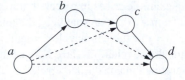

The meaning of this diagram is that the presence of the solid edges implies the presence of the dashed ones. The edge $\langle a, d \rangle$ must be present, since $\langle a, b \rangle$ and $\langle b, d \rangle$ are present. Most interesting relations are transitive. For example, '$\le$' is transitive: $x \le y$ and $y \le z$ together imply $x \le z$.

Two particular combinations of these properties are met with so frequently that they deserve special attention: equivalence relations and partial orders.

## Equivalence relations

An *equivalence relation* is a reflexive, symmetric, and transitive relation. Informally, equivalence relations arise when things are essentially the same, but not necessarily strictly equal. The archetypal equivalence relation is =, the equality relation, but there are others. The fundamental fact about any equivalence relation $R$ is that it partitions its domain $S$ into pairwise disjoint subsets $E_x$ of the form

$$E_x = \{y \mid y\ R\ x\}$$

called the *equivalence classes* of $R$. For example, the equivalence relation

$$R = \{\langle a, a \rangle, \langle b, b \rangle, \langle b, c \rangle, \langle c, b \rangle, \langle c, c \rangle\}$$

partitions its domain into the equivalence classes $\{a\}$ and $\{b, c\}$. This result will not be proved here (see, for example, Stanat and McAllister (1977) for a full discussion of relations). Instead, here are several examples.

Consider the relation 'is connected to' between vertices of a graph:

It is easy to check that this is an equivalence relation: vertex $x$ is connected to $x$ for all $x$; $x$ is connected to $y$ implies that $y$ is connected to $x$; $x$ is connected to $y$ and $y$ is connected to $z$ together imply that $x$ is connected to $z$ (via the path $\langle x, \dots, y, \dots, z \rangle$). The equivalence classes are of the form

$$E_x = \{y \in V \mid y \text{ is connected to } x\}$$

and, for the graph above, they are $E_a = \{a, b, c\}$, $E_d = \{d\}$, and $E_f = \{e, f, g, h\}$. These are just the vertices of the connected components of $G$.

A more interesting example arises in directed graphs. Define $x \leftrightarrow y$ if there is a path from $x$ to $y$ and from $y$ to $x$. Alternatively, the relation could be defined by saying that it holds when $x = y$ or there is a cycle containing $x$ and $y$. It is not hard to verify that '$\leftrightarrow$' is an equivalence relation. Here is an example of a digraph $G$, with the equivalence classes grouped inside dashed circles:

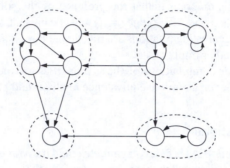

The graph can be factored into the parts within the equivalence classes, and the part outside. For the outside part a new digraph can be drawn whose vertices are equivalence classes:

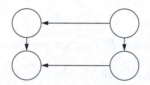

It is not hard to see that this *reduced digraph* must have no cycles. The subgraphs whose vertices are the equivalence classes of this relation are strongly connected, and they are known as the *strongly connected components of* $G$. An algorithm for finding them will be presented in Section 11.7.

## Partial orders

A partial order is a reflexive, antisymmetric, and transitive relation. The archetypal partial order is '$\leq$', but there are others.

An important fact about partial orders (in fact, all antisymmetric and transitive relations) is that their digraphs have no proper cycles. This is proved as follows. Suppose, on the contrary, that there is a proper cycle $\langle x, y, \ldots, x \rangle$ in the digraph corresponding to an antisymmetric and transitive relation $R$. It follows immediately that $x\ R\ y$; and from transitivity applied to the path $\langle y, \ldots, x \rangle$ it follows that $y\ R\ x$. But then antisymmetry implies $x = y$, a contradiction.

Knowledge of antisymmetry and transitivity is valuable information for algorithms which traverse digraphs, since they need not guard against the danger of looping endlessly around a cycle. Such algorithms are studied in Section 11.4.

## Representing relations

Suppose now that a relation $R$ has to be represented as a digraph $G$, and $R$ has one or more of the five properties defined above. Can this knowledge be used to simplify the representation? It turns out that it can.

Consider a relation $R$ which is known to be reflexive. The self-loops may be omitted from $G$, and simply assumed to be there. Similarly, if $R$ is transitive, the edges implied by transitivity may be omitted. For example, consider this heap-ordered tree:

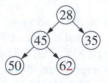

The only pairs represented explicitly are the four shown: $28 \le 45, 45 \le 50, 45 \le 62$, and $28 \le 35$. Yet, since '$\le$' is reflexive and transitive, in fact a larger relation is being represented whose digraph is

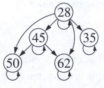

A different kind of simplification is possible if $R$ is known to be symmetric. The following replacement may be made:

The digraph has become a graph.

To summarize this section: digraphs may be used to represent arbitrary relations; directed acyclic graphs arise when the relation is antisymmetric and transitive; and undirected graphs are the natural representation for symmetric relations.

## 11.4 Directed acyclic graphs

It is the possibility of cycles that makes graphs more difficult to deal with than trees. A cycle creates the risk of infinite loops; and, more subtly, there is no natural place to begin on a cycle. For these reasons, it is natural to consider first the *directed acyclic graph*, or *dag*, which is a directed graph with no cycles.

Dags arise whenever certain activities must be carried out in some order, but not just any order. For example, the dag

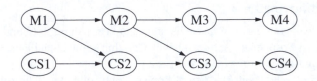

represents the prerequisite structure of the mathematics and computer science courses at a hypothetical university. It shows, for example, that both M2 and CS2 must be completed before CS3 is undertaken. Clearly, a sensible prerequisite structure will always be acyclic.

A *topological ordering* of the vertices of a digraph is a way to visit the vertices, one by one, in a sequence that satisfies all the prerequisite constraints. For example, M1, CS1, CS2, M2, M3, M4, CS3, CS4 is one of 47 possible topological orderings for the vertices of the graph given above. Formally, a topological ordering of the vertices of a directed graph $G = \langle V, E \rangle$ is a sequence $\langle v_1, v_2, \ldots, v_n \rangle$, such that $V = \{v_1, v_2, \ldots, v_n\}$ and, for all $\langle v_i, v_j \rangle$ in $E$, $v_i$ precedes $v_j$ in the sequence.

The idea of modeling constrained activities with a dag, then using a topological ordering to solve the problem of performing the activities correctly, arises frequently. Consider evaluating the arithmetic expression

$$(a - b * c) + (d - e)$$

The addition must be performed after the subtractions, but either subtraction may be performed first. These constraints are expressed by the following dag:

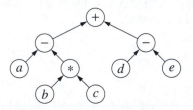

For example, $b \rightarrow *$ means that $*$ cannot be performed until $b$ is known. Notice that this dag does not say which argument of $-$ is subtracted from the other; for that, it would be necessary to specify an ordering on incoming edges.

In cases where the dag is a tree with its edges pointing towards the root, a postorder traversal will yield a topological ordering. In this example the ordering is $a\ b\ c\ * \ - \ d\ e\ - \ +$. However, more complex expressions do arise. Consider the efficient evaluation of the two roots of a quadratic equation:

$$\frac{-b + \sqrt{b^2 - 4ac}}{2a} \quad \text{and} \quad \frac{-b - \sqrt{b^2 - 4ac}}{2a}$$

The corresponding dag is no longer a tree:

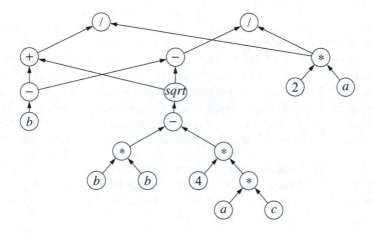

To evaluate this correctly, the dag must be traversed in topological order.

It should be clear that if a digraph has a cycle, there can be no topological ordering of its vertices; but the converse statement, that the vertices of every dag can be topologically ordered, is less obvious. The following theorem, first published by Szpilrajn (1930), is the first step in the proof of this fact:

**Theorem 11.1:** In any directed acyclic graph $G$ with $n \geq 1$ vertices, there exists a vertex of indegree 0.

**Proof:** Here is a constructive proof of the contrapositive, which states that, if all the vertices of a digraph $G$ have indegree at least 1, then $G$ contains a cycle.

Assume that all vertices have indegree at least 1. Starting at any vertex $v_1$, trace back along any one of its incoming edges to a vertex $v_2$. From $v_2$ trace back to $v_3$, and so on. Since all vertices have indegree at least 1, this process need never stop; but since $G$ is finite, eventually a vertex must be reached that was passed through before. So $G$ contains a cycle. □

The vertex of indegree 0 that this theorem provides is a suitable first element of a topological ordering, since it is not constrained to follow any other vertex. This leads to an efficient algorithm, known as *topological sort*, for finding a topological ordering of the vertices of a directed acyclic graph $G$: repeatedly find and delete a vertex of indegree 0 in $G$, until the graph is empty. The order in which the vertices are deleted is $S$, the desired topological order. The following example shows the first few stages of the algorithm:

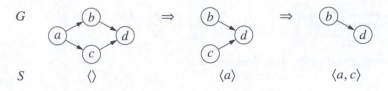

$G$

$S$      $\langle\rangle$                 $\langle a\rangle$               $\langle a, c\rangle$

Eventually $G$ becomes empty and $S = \langle a, c, b, d\rangle$. After $a$ is deleted, both $b$ and $c$ have indegree 0, and the algorithm is free to choose either.

Topological sort resembles selection sort, in that a smallest element is repeatedly deleted in both; so it is an incremental algorithm of the second kind, in the classification of Section 4.2. This suggests the loop invariant '$S$ may be extended to a topological ordering of the vertices of $G$.' Unfortunately, a topological ordering of $G$ is not known to exist, so even if $S = \langle\rangle$ it will not be possible to prove that this condition holds. The following loop invariant cleverly avoids this problem:

**Theorem 11.2 (Loop invariant of topological sort):** Let $G = \langle V, E\rangle$ be a directed acyclic graph. Then, at the beginning of the $k$th iteration of the topological sort algorithm, $S = \langle v_1, v_2, \ldots, v_{k-1}\rangle$ has the following property: for all edges $\langle v_i, v_j\rangle$ in $E$, if $v_j$ is in $S$, then $v_i$ precedes $v_j$ in $S$.

**Proof:** by induction on $k$. Let $S_k = \langle v_1, v_2, \ldots, v_{k-1}\rangle$ be the value of $S$ at the beginning of the $k$th iteration, and let $G_k$ be the value of $G$.

**Basis step:** $k = 1$. Then $S_1 = \langle\rangle$, so the theorem is vacuously true.

**Inductive step:** The inductive hypothesis concerning $S_k$ is as above; it must be shown that it is true of $S_{k+1} = \langle v_1, v_2, \ldots, v_k\rangle$, where $v_k$ is the vertex of indegree 0 in $G_k$ selected by the algorithm during the $k$th iteration. Now $v_k$ exists, by Theorem 11.1 applied to the directed acyclic graph $G_k$. Since $v_k$ has indegree 0 in $G_k$, in the original digraph $G$ it must be the case that all of $v_k$'s predecessors lie in $\{v_1, v_2, \ldots, v_{k-1}\}$, which means that, for all $\langle v_i, v_k\rangle$ in $E$, $v_i$ precedes $v_k$ in $S_{k+1}$. So the theorem holds for $S_{k+1} = \langle v_1, v_2, \ldots, v_k\rangle$.        $\Box$

At termination, the loop invariant implies that $S_{n+1}$ is a topological ordering of the vertices of $G$. The conclusion is, not just that topological sort is correct, but also that the vertices of any dag may be topologically ordered.

## Implementation and analysis of topological sort

The following implementation of topological sort is due to Knuth (1973a). Each vertex contains an *indegree* field, which holds the current indegree of the vertex, and simulates the deletion of edges from $G$ by gradually decreasing. When the indegree reaches 0, the vertex is ready for inclusion in the result sequence.

The Simple Set ADT of Section 3.1 is used to hold those vertices of indegree 0 that have not yet been included in the result; this cleverly avoids searching for them, except to begin with. The List ADT of Section 5.1 holds the result list.

```
topological_sort(g: like digraph_type): like list_type is
    local
        s: like simpleset_type;
        v, w: like vertex_type;
        e: like edge_type;
    do

        -- initialize the indegrees of all vertices
        from v := g.first_vertex until g.nil_vertex(v) loop
            v.put_indegree(0);
            v := g.next_vertex(v)
        end;
        from v := g.first_vertex until g.nil_vertex(v) loop
            from e := g.first_edge(v) until g.nil_edge(e) loop
                w := g.end_point(e);
                w.put_indegree(w.indegree + 1);
                e := g.next_edge(v, e);
            end;
            v := g.next_vertex(v)
        end;

        -- initialize s to contain all vertices of indegree zero
        !!s.make;
        from v := g.first_vertex until g.nil_vertex(v) loop
            if v.indegree = 0 then s.insert(v) end;
            v := g.next_vertex(v)
        end;

        -- perform the topological sort
        !!Result.make;
        from until s.empty loop
            v := s.delete_any;
            Result.insert_last(v);
            from e := g.first_edge(v) until g.nil_edge(e) loop
                w := g.end_point(e);
                w.put_indegree(w.indegree - 1);
                if w.indegree = 0 then s.insert(w) end;
                e := g.next_edge(v, e)
            end
        end
    end
```

The initialization visits each vertex three times and each edge once, so is $O(n + m)$. The main loop is also $O(n + m)$, since it visits each vertex and edge once.

## Critical paths

A number of problems concerned with directed acyclic graphs may be solved efficiently by visiting the vertices in topological order. The *critical path problem* is one such problem.

Consider a large project, such as the construction of a building. The project divides into a number of subprojects: laying the foundation, building the walls, installing the electrical wiring, and so on. Each subproject takes some amount of time to complete; each cannot begin until certain other subprojects are complete. This can all be represented by a dag with a cost on each edge. For example,

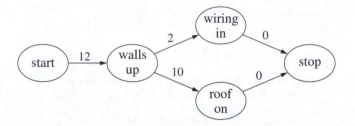

represents a simple building project, in which it takes 12 units of time to get the walls up, at which point the roof construction and wiring may proceed independently, taking 10 and 2 units of time respectively. An edge $\langle v, w \rangle$ represents a subproject, and its label, $c(v, w)$, represents the cost in units of time of the subproject. Vertices represent states, or moments in time between subprojects. Projects have a natural *start state*, when nothing has been done, and a natural *stop state*, when all is complete, so it will be assumed that there is a unique *start vertex* which is an ancestor of every vertex, and a unique *stop vertex* which is a descendant of every vertex.

The natural question to ask is, 'what is the earliest possible time this project can be finished?' In the example, this is clearly 22 units of time after commencement. Let $a$ be the start vertex, and for every vertex $v$ of $G$, let $d(a, v)$ be the earliest possible time to reach $v$. If $b$ is the stop vertex, the problem is to find $d(a, b)$.

A vertex $w$ will be reached at the earliest possible time if all its predecessor vertices are reached at their earliest possible times, and the subprojects leading from them to $w$ are commenced immediately. These subprojects must all complete before $w$ can be said to have been reached, and this gives the recurrence equation

$$d(a, a) = 0$$
$$d(a, w) = \max_{v \in P(w)} [d(a, v) + c(v, w)]$$

where $P(w)$ is the set of predecessors of $w$. Note that every vertex except $a$ must have at least one predecessor, since it has $a$ for a proper ancestor, so the max operation is performed over a non-empty set.

The recurrence leads to an obvious recursive algorithm for calculating $d(a, v)$ for all $v$. It is more efficient, however, to employ dynamic programming, and compute the $d(a, v)$ by visiting the vertices in topological order. By recording in each vertex $w$ a predecessor $v$ for which $d(a, w) = d(a, v) + c(v, w)$, at termination it will be possible to reconstruct a path from $b$ back to $a$ of total cost $d(a, b)$. Such a path is called a *critical path*; it represents a bottleneck in the project.

In the following algorithm, which is $O(n + m)$ like topological sort, each vertex $v$ contains a *distance* field which holds a value which increases to a final value of $d(a, v)$. The field is undefined until $v$'s *visited* field is set to **true**. The predecessor $v$ of $w$ for which $d(a, w) = d(a, v) + c(v, w)$ is stored in $w$'s *parent* field. The *cost* field of each edge holds the cost of the edge.

```
critical_path(g: like digraph_type;  a: like vertex_type) is
    local
        s: like simpleset_type;
        v, w: like vertex_type;
        e: like edge_type;
    do

        -- initialize the visited and indegree fields
        from v := g.first_vertex until g.nil_vertex(v) loop
            v.put_indegree(0);
            v.put_visited(false);
            v := g.next_vertex(v)
        end;
        from v := g.first_vertex until g.nil_vertex(v) loop
            from e := g.first_edge(v) until g.nil_edge(e) loop
                w := g.end_point(e);
                w.put_indegree(w.indegree + 1);
                e := g.next_edge(v, e);
            end;
            v := g.next_vertex(v)
        end;

        -- run the critical path algorithm from a
        a.put_visited(true);
        a.put_parent(new_nil_vertex);
        a.put_distance(0);
        from !!s; s.insert(a) until s.empty loop
            v := s.delete_any;
            from e := g.first_edge(v) until g.nil_edge(e) loop
                w := g.end_point(e);
                if not w.visited then
                    w.put_visited(true);
                    w.put_distance(v.distance + e.cost);
                    w.put_parent(v)
                elseif w.distance < v.distance + e.cost then
                    w.put_distance(v.distance + e.cost);
                    w.put_parent(v)
                end;
                w.put_indegree(w.indegree − 1);
                if w.indegree = 0 then s.insert(w) end;
                e := g.next_edge(v, e)
            end
        end
    end
```

The same method may be used to compute a variety of other recurrence equations efficiently, such as this one for calculating shortest paths:

$$d(a, a) = 0$$
$$d(a, w) = \min_{v \in P(w)} [d(a, v) + c(v, w)]$$

Exercise 11.11 discusses another useful recurrence.

## 11.5 Breadth-first search

The two most widely used algorithms for traversing graphs are called *breadth-first search* and *depth-first search*. Both face the same problem: how to visit every vertex without looping endlessly around any cycle.

Breadth-first search visits the vertices in order of increasing distance from some *start vertex*, which may be chosen arbitrarily. The *distance* of a vertex $v$ from start vertex $a$ is defined to be the length of (number of edges on) a shortest path from $a$ to $v$. For example, starting at $a$ in the graph

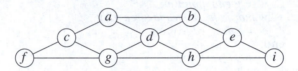

the graph may be redrawn to show distances from $a$ clearly like this:

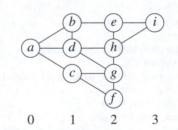

Breadth-first search will visit the vertices from left to right; vertices of equal distance from $a$ may be visited in any order.

This redrawn graph suggests an algorithm. Let $S_k$ be the set of vertices of distance $k$ from the start vertex $a$. Then $S_0 = \{a\}$, and for all $k > 0$, $S_k$ may be constructed by taking each vertex $v$ of $S_{k-1}$, following each edge $\langle v, w \rangle$ out of $v$, and adding $w$ to $S_k$ unless $w$ is already in some set. A boolean flag in each vertex $v$ called $v.visited$ may be used to remember whether $v$ has been added to any set yet.

Here is the algorithm applied to $G$ above. Vertices whose *visited* flag is **true** are shown with an asterisk. Initially, $S_0 = \{a\}$ and only $a$ has been visited:

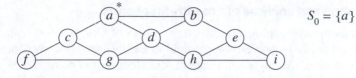

$S_0 = \{a\}$

Following every edge out of $a$ leads to $b$, $c$, and $d$, and since none have been visited yet, they all go into $S_1$:

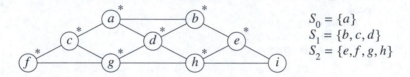

$S_0 = \{a\}$
$S_1 = \{b, c, d\}$

Following every edge out of $b$, $c$, and $d$ leads to $a$, $d$, $e$, $a$, $g$, $h$, $b$, $a$, $f$, and $g$, but the only unvisited vertices in this set are $f$, $g$, $h$, and $e$, so these go into the next set, $S_2$:

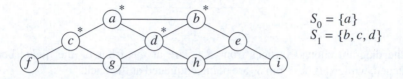

$S_0 = \{a\}$
$S_1 = \{b, c, d\}$
$S_2 = \{e, f, g, h\}$

The next set will be $S_3 = \{i\}$, and then $S_4$ is empty, which is the signal to stop.

It is easy to prove by induction on $k$ that for every vertex $v$ in $S_k$ there is a path of length $k$ from the start vertex to $v$. And there can be no shorter path to $v$, for then $v$ would have appeared in an earlier set. So the algorithm just given does indeed visit the vertices in increasing order of distance from the start vertex.

Each vertex $w$ in $S_k$ is there because there was some vertex $v$ in $S_{k-1}$ and an edge $\langle v, w \rangle$. The collection of these edges $\langle v, w \rangle$ forms a spanning tree of the graph rooted at the start vertex, called a *breadth-first search spanning tree*. For the example above, this tree is

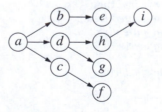

It is a concise summary of the shortest paths.

## Implementation and analysis of breadth-first search

It is easy to implement breadth-first search using an array of Simple Sets to represent $S_0$, $S_1$, $S_2$, and so on, and a boolean *visited* field in each vertex. However, there is a clever optimization. At any given moment, the algorithm is doing *delete_any* operations on some $S_{k-1}$, and *insert* operations on $S_k$, and these may be replaced by *dequeue* and *enqueue* operations respectively on a single queue:

$$q = \langle \underbrace{a, b, c, d}_{S_{k-1}}, \underbrace{e, f, g, h}_{S_k} \rangle$$

As the diagram shows, vertices from $S_{k-1}$ are at the front of the queue being dequeued, while vertices from $S_k$ are being enqueued at the back.

The code for this follows. In addition to the *visited* field, each vertex contains a *parent* field which is set to its parent in the breadth-first spanning tree:

```
breadth_first_search(g: like digraph_type;  a: like vertex_type) is
    local
        q: like queue_type;
        v, w: like vertex_type;
        e: like edge_type;
    do

        from v := g.first_vertex until g.nil_vertex(v) loop
            v.put_visited(false);
            v := g.next_vertex(v)
        end;

        a.put_visited(true);
        a.put_parent(new_nil_vertex);
        !!q.make;
        from q.enqueue(a) until q.empty loop
            v := q.dequeue;
            from e := g.first_edge(v) until g.nil_edge(e) loop
                w := g.end_point(e);
                if not w.visited then
                    w.put_visited(true);
                    w.put_parent(v);
                    q.enqueue(w)
                end;
                e := g.next_edge(v, e)
            end
        end
    end
```

Since the Queue operations are all $O(1)$, and the algorithm visits every vertex and every edge once, its worst-case time complexity on a graph or digraph containing $n$ vertices and $m$ edges is $O(n + m)$.

## 11.6 Depth-first search

A generalization of the preorder traversal of a tree, known as *depth-first search*, provides perhaps the simplest way to traverse a graph or digraph: beginning at a given vertex *v*, visit *v* and then traverse the graph, beginning at each successor of *v* in turn. Avoid visiting any vertex twice (thereby also avoiding infinite loops) by marking each vertex after it has been visited, and refusing to revisit marked vertices. A boolean *visited* field in each vertex holds this mark:

```
dfs(g: like digraph_type; v: like vertex_type) is
    local
        w: like vertex_type;
        e: like edge_type;
    do
        visit(v);
        v.put_visited(true);
        from e := g.first_edge(v) until g.nil_edge(e) loop
            w := g.end_point(e);
            if not w.visited then
                dfs(g, w);
                w.put_parent(v)
            end
            e := g.next_edge(v, e)
        end
    end
```

The precondition includes '*v* is unvisited'; the postcondition includes 'all descendants of *v* are visited.' If the graph is not connected, *dfs* may be called repeatedly:

```
depth_first_search(g: like digraph_type) is
    local
        v: like vertex_type;
    do

        from v := g.first_vertex until g.nil_vertex(v) loop
            v.put_visited(false);
            v := g.next_vertex(v)
        end;

        from v := g.first_vertex until g.nil_vertex(v) loop
            if not v.visited then
                dfs(g, v)
            end;
            v := g.next_vertex(v)
        end
    end
```

Depth-first search may be used to construct a *depth-first spanning forest F* for the graph, by adding the edge ⟨*v, w*⟩ to *F* after the recursive call to *dfs(g, w)* in procedure *dfs*, as done by *put_parent* above. For example, given the undirected graph

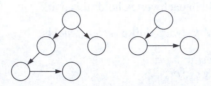

one depth-first spanning forest is

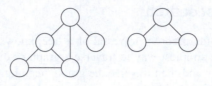

Whether or not the graph is directed, it is conventional to direct the edges of $F$ the way the search went, making these trees rooted trees. There are of course many different depth-first spanning forests, since their shape is determined by which node is chosen to begin the search, and the order in which the edges leading out of each node are explored.

The edges of $F$ are called *tree edges*, and if the graph is undirected, the non-tree edges are called *back edges*. This term is justified by the following theorem, which shows that these edges always point up the tree, never across it:

**Theorem 11.3:** Let $G$ be an undirected graph, let $F$ be a depth-first spanning forest of $G$, and let $\{v, w\}$ be any back edge. Then either $v$ is an ancestor of $w$, or $w$ is an ancestor of $v$.

**Proof:** by contradiction. Suppose neither vertex is an ancestor of the other. Without loss of generality, assume that $v$ was visited before $w$:

When $v$ was first entered by the search, $w$ was unvisited. Since $w$ is not a descendant of $v$, when the search left $v$ for the last time, $w$ was still unvisited. But this contradicts the fact that depth-first search visits every unvisited vertex adjacent to $v$ before leaving $v$ for the last time. □

Depth-first search thus imposes a useful structure on a graph – the tree edges forming a forest, the back edges pointing strictly to ancestors:

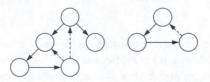

This regularity has proved to be very useful in a number of applications, such as the test for biconnectivity given in Section 11.8. A similar, but more complicated result holds in directed graphs (Exercise 11.19). Tarjan (1972) contains several applications of depth-first search.

## 11.7 Strongly connected components

Recall that two vertices of a directed graph are said to be strongly connected if each is reachable from the other, and that a strongly connected component of a digraph $G$ is a maximal subgraph of $G$ whose vertices are all strongly connected with each other. For example, the following digraph is shown with each of its strongly connected components enclosed in a dashed outline:

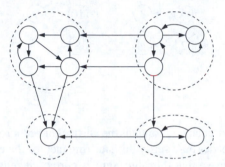

The problem of finding the strongly connected components of a digraph is a good example of the power of depth-first search. The algorithm to be described is given by Aho et al. (1983), who attribute its ideas to R. Kosaraju (unpublished), and also to Sharir (1981).

The first step is to perform a depth-first traversal of the given digraph $G$, numbering its vertices in postorder. For the digraph shown above, the result of this step might be

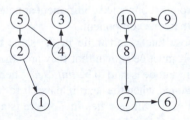

depending on the order that edges are chosen. The next step is to reverse all the edges, creating an *inverse graph* $G_r$:

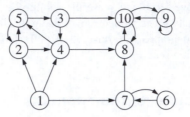

Finally, perform a depth-first traversal of $G_r$, beginning at the highest-numbered vertex. If this search does not visit all the vertices of $G_r$, choose the highest-numbered unvisited vertex and resume the search there, carrying on in this way until all the vertices have been visited:

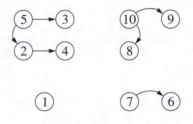

In the resulting forest, each tree contains the vertices of one strongly connected component of $G$. The reader may verify this startling fact for the example just given.

In order to prove that this algorithm is correct, it must be shown that two vertices $v$ and $w$ lie in the same strongly connected component of $G$ if and only if they lie in the same tree of the depth-first spanning forest of $G_r$ constructed by the algorithm.

Suppose first that $v$ and $w$ lie in the same strongly connected component of $G$. Then there is a path in $G_r$ from $v$ to $w$ and from $w$ to $v$, which implies immediately that $v$ and $w$ must lie in the same tree of any depth-first spanning forest of $G_r$, since otherwise the depth-first search of $G_r$ would have failed to explore all the paths open to it. This part of the proof is nicely illustrated by the first depth-first traversal shown above, in which each strongly connected component appears within one tree, but the tree may contain more than one component.

Conversely, suppose that $v$ and $w$ lie in the same tree $T$ of the depth-first spanning forest of $G_r$. It must be shown that they are strongly connected in $G$. In the following discussion, a node is said to be *initiated* when the search reaches it for the first time, and *terminated* when the search leaves it for the last time.

Let $x$ be the root of $T$. Since $v$ lies in $T$, there is a path in $G_r$ from $x$ to $v$. Therefore there is a path in $G$ from $v$ to $x$.

During the first depth-first traversal, $x$ was terminated later than $v$. This is so because $v$ was not visited when the second depth-first traversal initiated $x$, implying that $x$'s number must have been larger than $v$'s number.

Furthermore, during the first depth-first traversal, $x$ was initiated before $v$. For suppose, on the contrary, that $x$ was initiated after $v$. From the existence of the path in $G$ from $v$ to $x$ established above, it follows that $x$ must be a descendant of $v$ and hence that $x$ was terminated before $v$, which contradicts the previous paragraph.

So $x$ was initiated before $v$ and terminated after $v$. It follows that $x$ is an ancestor of $v$ in the first depth-first spanning forest, and hence that there is a path from $x$ to $v$ in $G$. So $v$ and $x$ are strongly connected in $G$.

This same argument may be used to show that $w$ and $x$ are strongly connected in $G$, and so to conclude that $v$ and $w$ are strongly connected in $G$ (via paths through $x$). So the algorithm is correct.

## 11.8 Biconnectivity

The problem of *reliability* in communication networks is of great practical importance. If a bridge is washed away in a flood, does the road network provide an alternative route? If one computer in a network fails, can the others still communicate with each other?

A graph may be used to model a communication network in the usual way: vertices represent towns or computers, edges represent the roads or cables that connect them. Undirected graphs may as well be used, since most communication networks are two-way. Our questions are equivalent to asking whether a graph remains connected whenever a single edge or vertex is deleted (when a vertex is deleted, its associated edges are deleted also). This section concentrates on vertex failures; Exercise 11.20 looks at edge failures.

For example, if the graph is a tree:

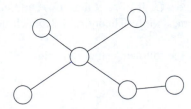

then deletion of any vertex of degree greater than one will disconnect the tree; so this network is not very reliable. If the graph is a *ring*:

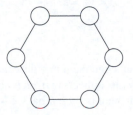

it will tolerate any single failure, assuming that the network is able to re-route its messages along the alternative path.

A graph is said to be *k-connected* if the removal of any $k - 1$ vertices leaves the remaining subgraph connected. So to be 1-connected is to be connected; to be 2-connected (or *biconnected*) means that one vertex failure can be tolerated, as in the ring above.

If a graph is not biconnected, it has *articulation points*: vertices whose removal would disconnect the graph. For example, the articulation points of

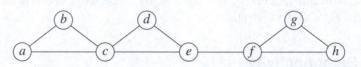

are $c$, $e$, and $f$. The obvious way to find the articulation points of a graph is to take each vertex in turn, delete it, and check whether the remaining subgraph is connected. Since the check for connectedness takes $O(n + m)$ time, finding all the articulation points of a graph is $O(n(n + m))$ using this method.

A much faster algorithm was developed by J. E. Hopcroft and presented in Aho et al. (1974). It finds all the articulation points during the course of a single depth-first traversal of the graph. The method is based on the following theorem:

**Theorem 11.4:** Let $G$ be a connected graph with depth-first spanning tree $T$. Then $v$ is an articulation point of $G$ if and only if $v$ is the root of $T$, and $v$ has at least two children; or $v$ is not the root of $T$, and for some child $w$ of $v$ in $T$ there is no back edge from any descendant of $w$ to any proper ancestor of $v$.

**Proof:** Suppose first that $v$ is the root of $T$. If $v$ has no children or one child, deleting $v$ will clearly not disconnect $G$. If $v$ has at least two children, $w$ and $x$, then deletion of $v$ must disconnect them, since by Theorem 11.3 there is no cross edge connecting $T_w$ with $T_x$.

If $v$ is not the root, the following situation holds:

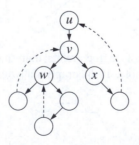

If, as is shown, there is no back edge from any descendant of $w$ to a proper ancestor of $v$, then deletion of $v$ clearly disconnects $w$ from $u$, since by Theorem 11.3 there are no other edges leaving $T_w$. If there is such a back edge, as there is within $T_x$ above, that edge provides an alternative path from $u$ to $x$, so that $v$ can be deleted without disconnecting $u$ from $x$.                                                                        □

The first step in applying this theorem to a graph $G$ is to perform a depth-first search, numbering the vertices from 1 to $n$ in the order they were first visited by the search (that is, in preorder). The number assigned to vertex $v$ will be stored in $v.num$. If $\langle v, w \rangle$ is any tree edge, then clearly $v$ was first visited before $w$, so $v.num < w.num$; while for any back edge $\langle v, w \rangle$, Theorem 11.3 says that $w$ is an ancestor of $v$, so $v.num \geq w.num$, with equality only if self-loops are allowed.

Let $\langle v, w \rangle$ be a tree edge like the one shown above in the proof of the theorem. We want to know whether or not there is a back edge from some descendant of $w$ to some proper ancestor of $v$. So define $v.low$ to be the number of the smallest-numbered vertex reachable from $v$ by following down zero or more tree edges, then up at most one back edge. For example, here is the graph of the diagram above; for each vertex $v$ the value of $v.num$ is shown inside the vertex, and the value of $v.low$ is shown adjacent to it:

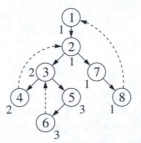

If $w.low \geq v.num$, then by following zero or more tree edges down from $w$, then at most one back edge, we cannot arrive at an ancestor of $v$; therefore, by Theorem 11.4, $v$ must be an articulation point. Conversely, if $w.low < v.num$ for all children $w$ of $v$, then $v$ is not an articulation point. Thus, if $v.low$ can be found for all $v$, the problem is solved.

Let $\langle v, t_1 \rangle, \langle v, t_2 \rangle, \ldots, \langle v, t_i \rangle$ be the tree edges leading down from $v$, and let $\langle v, b_1 \rangle, \langle v, b_2 \rangle, \ldots, \langle v, b_j \rangle$ be the back edges leading up from $v$. By considering the definition of $v.low$, it is not hard to see that it satisfies the recurrence equation

$$v.low = \min(v.num, t_1.low, \ldots, t_i.low, b_1.num, \ldots, b_j.num)$$

and so $v.low$ may be calculated for all $v$ as the depth-first search proceeds: all the quantities on the right-hand side are known by the time the search finally leaves $v$.

The following algorithm performs a depth-first search of $G$, beginning at vertex $v$. The third parameter $u$ equals the parent of $v$, or else it is a nil vertex if $v$ has no parent. The algorithm calculates $v.low$ according to the recurrence equation just given, and uses it to set $v.articulationpt$ to **true** if and only if $v$ is a non-root articulation point of $G$.

```
fap(g: like digraph_type; v, u: like vertex_type) is
    local
        w: like vertex_type; e: like edge_type;
    do
        count := count + 1;
        v.put_num(count);
        v.put_low(count);
        v.put_child_count(0);
        v.put_articulation_point(false);
        v.put_visited(true);
        from e := g.first_edge(v) until g.nil_edge(e) loop
            w := g.end_point(e);
            if not w.visited then
                fap(g, w, v);
                v.put_low(min(v.low, w.low));
                if w.low >= v.num and not g.nil_vertex(u) then
                    v.put_articulation_point(true)
                end;
                v.put_child_count(v.child_count + 1);
            elseif w /= u then
                v.put_low(min(v.low, w.num))
            end;
            e := g.next_edge(v, e)
        end
    end
```

The test $w /= u$ ensures that no tree edge is traversed backwards. The algorithm also calculates the number of children of $v$ in $T$, for use in determining whether the root of $T$ is an articulation point. The following procedure makes this determination, and also provides the appropriate initialization:

```
find_articulation_points(g: like graph_type) is
    local
        v, w: like vertex_type;
    do
        if not g.nil_vertex(g.first_vertex) then
            from v := g.first_vertex until g.nil_vertex(v) loop
                v.put_visited(false);
                v := g.next_vertex(v)
            end;
            count := 0;
            v := g.first_vertex;
            fap(g, v, new_nil_vertex);
            if v.child_count >= 2 then
                v.put_articulation_point(true)
            end
        end
    end
```

There is no need to look for unvisited vertices after executing *fap*, since $g$ is assumed connected. Like depth-first search, this algorithm has $O(n + m)$ complexity.

## 11.9 Exercises

11.1    Trace the following sequence of Digraph ADT operations, first abstractly, and then concretely using the adjacency lists implementation.

> *g.make*;
> *a := g.new_vertex('a')*;
> *b := g.new_vertex('b')*;
> *c := g.new_vertex('c')*;
> *d := g.new_vertex('d')*;
> *u := g.new_edge('u')*;
> *v := g.new_edge('v')*;
> *w := g.new_edge('w')*;
> *x := g.new_edge('x')*;
> *y := g.new_edge('y')*;
> *z := g.new_edge('z')*;
> *g.insert_vertex(a)*;
> *g.insert_vertex(b)*;
> *g.insert_vertex(c)*;
> *g.insert_edge(u, a, b)*;
> *g.insert_edge(v, a, c)*;
> *g.insert_edge(w, b, c)*;
> *g.insert_edge(x, c, a)*;
> *g.insert_vertex(d)*;
> *g.insert_edge(y, a, d)*;
> *g.insert_edge(z, d, a)*;

11.2    The *adjacency matrix* is an alternative data structure for implementing the Digraph ADT. Each vertex is represented by a number between 1 and $n$, and the adjacency matrix $a$ is defined by

$$a.item(i, j) = 1 \quad \text{if there is an edge from vertex } i \text{ to vertex } j$$
$$= 0 \quad \text{otherwise}$$

This representation efficiently implements the operation 'determine whether there is an edge from vertex $i$ to vertex $j$,' but in practice this operation is little used; and the matrix is often filled with zeros, a waste of space. What is the worst-case time complexity of this implementation of the Digraph ADT, and how does it compare with adjacency lists?

11.3    What changes would you make to the adjacency lists implementation of the Digraph ADT if the operations

> *delete_edge(e*: **like** *edge_type)*;
> *delete_vertex(v*: **like** *vertex_type)*;

were required? Try not to lose the desirable $O(1)$ time complexity per operation. It is simplest to specify that *delete_vertex* may only be applied to a vertex with no incoming or outgoing edges, but you may wish to also consider the case where the deleted vertex may have such edges.

11.4    Let $d(v, w)$ be the length of (number of edges on) a shortest path between $v$ and $w$ in a connected undirected graph $G$. Define a relation '$v$ is close to $w$' to hold when $d(v, w) \leq 10$. Which of the five properties (reflexivity, irreflexivity, symmetry, antisymmetry, and transitivity) does this relation have?

11.5    Let $G$ be a graph, and let $a$ be a fixed vertex of $G$. Define a relation $R(v, w)$ between vertices of $G$ to hold when there exists a shortest path from $a$ to $w$ which contains $v$. Which of the five properties holds in all graphs $G$? Be careful with antisymmetry.

11.6    Trace the topological sort algorithm on the dag

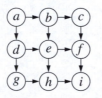

There are 42 different correct answers.

11.7    It was observed in Section 11.4 that a directed acyclic graph may have many distinct topological orderings. Which dag with $n$ nodes has the minimum possible number of topological orderings? Which has the maximum?

11.8    Verify the statement made in Section 11.4 that the directed acyclic graph

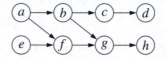

has 47 topological orderings.

11.9    Design an algorithm to list all the topological orderings of a given directed acyclic graph.

11.10   (This question requires expertise with binomial coefficients.) Let $T$ be an arbitrary non-empty binary tree:

$T =$

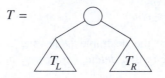

Show that $f(T)$, the number of topological orderings of $T$, satisfies the recurrence equation

$$f(T) = \binom{s(T)-1}{s(T_L)} f(T_L) f(T_R)$$

where $s(T)$ is the number of internal nodes of $T$. Solve this recurrence equation by repeated substitution to obtain the formula

$$f(T) = \frac{s(T)!}{\displaystyle\prod_{x\in I(T)} s(T_x)}$$

for the number of topological orderings of $T$, where $s(T_x)$ is the size of the subtree rooted at $x$. A good way to approach this problem is to notice that the number of topological orderings of an $n$-node tree $T$ is equal to the number of ways to place the numbers $1, 2, \dots, n$ in its nodes such that the tree is heap-ordered. For example, the tree

has three topological orderings, corresponding to

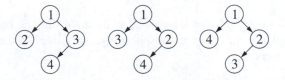

11.11  Find a recurrence equation which computes the number of paths between two vertices of a directed acyclic graph. For example, in the dag

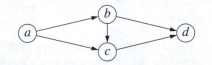

there are three paths from $a$ to $d$: $abd$, $abcd$, and $acd$.

11.12  The critical path algorithm of Section 11.4 finds the earliest possible time that a project could finish. Now suppose that we need to know the latest time at which each subproject could begin, without jeopardizing the earliest possible finish time that has been determined. For example, in the project

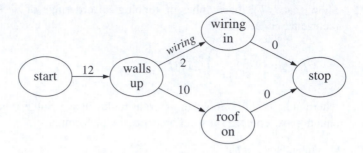

the subproject *wiring* could be started as late as time 20. Adapt the critical path algorithm to find these times.

11.13  Trace the breadth-first search algorithm, starting from $a$, on the digraph

Show the resulting spanning tree. There are many correct answers.

11.14  Consider the edges of an undirected graph $G$ which are not included in a breadth-first spanning forest $F$. Show that these edges never connect a vertex to one of its proper ancestors in $F$.

11.15  Trace the depth-first search algorithm on the digraph from Question 11.13, starting at $a$. Show the resulting spanning tree. There are many correct answers.

11.16  Let $G = \langle V, E \rangle$ be an arbitrary connected graph, and let $T$ be any depth-first spanning tree of $G$. Show that $|E| \le i(T)$, where $|E|$ is the number of edges in $E$, and $i(T)$ is the internal path length of $T$ (Section 6.3). Hence show that any depth-first spanning tree for a complete graph (that is, a graph containing all possible edges) must be skew.

11.17  Find an $O(n + m)$ algorithm which, given a graph or digraph, either prints a cycle of the graph or else prints a message stating that no cycle exists.

11.18  Give a non-recursive implementation of *dfs*, using a stack to hold the pending vertices. Compare your algorithm with *breadth_first_search*.

11.19  Use depth-first search to classify the edges of a directed graph, in a manner similar to Theorem 11.3 for undirected graphs.

11.20  Find an $O(n + m)$ algorithm for determining which edges of a connected graph, when deleted, cause the graph to become disconnected.

11.21  Show that the relation '$v$ and $w$ lie in the same biconnected component of $G$' is not an equivalence relation.

11.22  Prove that any triconnected graph with $n$ vertices has at least $3n/2$ edges, assuming $n \geq 4$. Find a family of triconnected graphs with exactly this many edges, for all even $n$.

11.23  Show that the strongly connected components algorithm given in Section 11.7 can be implemented in $O(n + m)$ time.

11.24  Consider the problem of finding the unique path between two specified vertices of a free tree $T$. For example, if

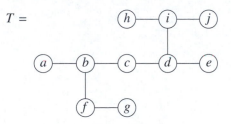

$T =$

then the path from $a$ to $g$ is $\langle a, b, f, g \rangle$.

One way to solve this problem is to perform a search (depth-first or breadth-first) beginning at one of the two given vertices. When the other one is reached, the search may be halted; parent references give the path. Unfortunately, this method may visit every vertex in the tree, even if the path itself contains only a few nodes.

If many such paths through a single tree must be found, it may be worthwhile to do some preprocessing. For example, each vertex could be assigned a number in the range 1 to $n$, and a two-dimensional array *next* constructed, where *next.item*$(v, w)$ is the first vertex on the path from $v$ to $w$. This would guarantee that any path could be found in time proportional to its length, but it requires $O(n^2)$ storage, which may be prohibitive both in size and in the time it takes to initialize.

Find a method which solves this problem efficiently, yet employs only a modest amount (say, $O(n)$) of precomputed information.

11.25  Let $T$ be a rooted tree, and let $nca(x, y)$ be the *nearest common ancestor* of $x$ and $y$. For example, in

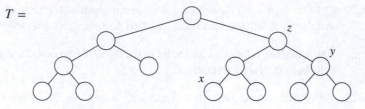

$nca(x, y) = z$. Find an algorithm which, without any preprocessing of $T$ except for the construction of parent references, calculates $nca(x, y)$ in time proportional to the length of the path $\langle x, \dots, nca(x, y), \dots, y \rangle$. Can $O(n)$ preprocessing reduce this?

# Chapter 12

# Five Classic Graph Problems

The five graph problems studied in this chapter are all classics. Important in themselves and difficult to solve, they test our techniques of design, correctness, and analysis to their limits.

## 12.1 Shortest paths

The graph most frequently encountered in the real world is probably the road network, and its most characteristic problem is that of finding the shortest route from one place to another. Graphs represent road networks in the obvious way; vertices represent towns and road intersections, and edges represent roads:

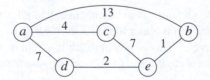

Directed edges may also be used, to allow for one-way streets; two-way links like those in the example just given stand for two one-way links in the usual way. Each edge $\langle v, w \rangle$ has an associated numeric *cost* $c(v, w)$, which usually represents the length of the road, but could represent travel time, fuel cost, and so on.

Given a directed graph $G$ whose edges have costs, and two vertices $a$ and $b$ of $G$, the problem is to find a shortest path (that is, a path of minimum total cost) from $a$ to $b$ if one exists. The total cost of a shortest path is called the *distance* from $a$ to $b$, and will be denoted $d(a, b)$. For example, it is easy to see that a shortest path from $a$ to $b$ in the graph above is

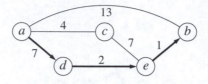

and its distance is $d(a, b) = 7 + 2 + 1 = 10$.

In virtually every real-world instance, the distances have non-negative cost. Nevertheless, we will permit negative edges, for generality and because the algorithm for weighted bipartite matching presented in Section 12.4 requires them.

Some care is needed here, because along with negative edges comes the possibility of *negative cycles* (cycles whose total cost is negative):

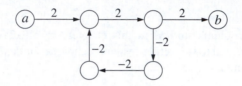

By detouring repeatedly around such a cycle, a path from $a$ to $b$ of arbitrarily small cost is obtained, so no shortest path exists.

A natural response to this is to require that the shortest paths be *simple* (free of cycles). There can only be a finite number of simple paths between any two vertices, so there must be a shortest simple path whenever $b$ is reachable from $a$. Unfortunately, the problem thus created turns out to be a close relative of the traveling salesperson problem (Section 12.5), and so is NP-complete and unlikely to be solvable in any reasonable time.

A more feasible response is to permit negative edges but prohibit negative cycles. That is, the problem is either to find a shortest path or else to report that the graph has a negative cycle. This is the approach that will be taken here.

The following theorem is basic to all work on shortest paths.

**Theorem 12.1 (Triangle inequality):** Let $G$ be a directed graph with edge costs and no negative cycles, and let $u$, $v$, and $w$ be any three vertices of $G$ such that $v$ is reachable from $u$, and $w$ is reachable from $v$. Then $w$ is reachable from $u$ and $d(u, w) \leq d(u, v) + d(v, w)$, with equality if and only if $v$ lies on a shortest path from $u$ to $w$.

**Proof:** Since $G$ has no negative cycles and $v$ is reachable from $u$, a shortest path $P_1$ from $u$ to $v$ exists with distance $d(u, v)$. Similarly, a shortest path $P_2$ from $v$ to $w$ exists with distance $d(v, w)$. Joining these paths end to end yields a path from $u$ to $w$ of total cost $d(u, v) + d(v, w)$. Since this path from $u$ to $w$ exists, a shortest path from $u$ to $w$ exists, and its total cost cannot exceed $d(u, v) + d(v, w)$, for then it would not be a shortest path. If $d(u, w) = d(u, v) + d(v, w)$, then $P_1$ joined to $P_2$ is a shortest path from $u$ to $w$ on which $v$ lies, and conversely. □

An important corollary arises in the case when $v$ and $w$ are connected by an edge: $d(u, w) \leq d(u, v) + c(v, w)$. This is immediate since $d(v, w) \leq c(v, w)$.

Road network problems have the advantage that one can use the direction of the destination as a guide: if the destination is to the north, the shortest path will rarely begin by going south. It is possible to incorporate this kind of guidance by increasing the cost of edges pointing in unpromising directions. The $A^*$ search algorithm, which may be found in any artificial intelligence text such as Winston (1992), transforms the edge weights in this way, and is otherwise identical to Dijkstra's algorithm presented below.

Although such techniques may help, ultimately a shortest path algorithm may need to search the entire graph. For this reason, research has concentrated on the *single-source shortest path problem*, which is to find a shortest path from a given start vertex $a$ to each vertex in the graph. The following theorem shows that if such shortest paths exist, they can be assembled into a spanning tree.

**Theorem 12.2:** Let $G$ be a digraph with edge costs, and suppose that every vertex is reachable from some start vertex $a$. Then either $G$ contains a negative cycle, or else it contains a spanning tree $T$, rooted at $a$, such that for every vertex $v$ in $G$, the total cost of the path through $T$ from $a$ to $v$ is equal to $d(a, v)$.

**Proof:** If $G$ contains a negative cycle, there is nothing more to prove. Otherwise, consider any vertex $v$. By assumption, $v$ is reachable from $a$, so there is a shortest path $P$ from $a$ to $v$. Any cycle on $P$ cannot have negative total cost, by assumption, nor can it have positive total cost, for then deleting it from $P$ would leave behind a shorter path from $a$ to $v$ than $P$. Such cycles must therefore have zero total cost, and they may be deleted from $P$ without changing its cost; the conclusion is that for any vertex $v$ there is a simple (cycle-free) path from $a$ to $v$ of total cost $d(a, v)$.

These simple paths may be assembled into a spanning tree by the following algorithm. Initialize $T$ to $\langle \{a\}, \{\} \rangle$. Choose any vertex $v$ not yet in $T$, and let $\langle a, \ldots, x, \ldots, v \rangle$ be a simple path from $a$ to $v$ of total cost $d(a, v)$, where $x$ is the last vertex on the path which is already in $T$. Since $T$ already contains a shortest path to $x$, $\langle a, \ldots, x \rangle$ is not needed and $T$ may be extended to include $v$ by adding $\langle x, \ldots, v \rangle$ to it. Repeat until $T$ extends to every vertex.  □

Such a tree is called a *shortest path spanning tree*. For example, the graph above has shortest path spanning tree

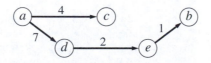

rooted at $a$. The single-source shortest path problem is either to find a shortest path spanning tree for the part of the graph that is reachable from the start vertex, or else to report the existence of a negative cycle.

Three main algorithms exist for this problem. Depending on the application, any one of them might be the method of choice.

First, there is an algorithm based on topological sorting which has already been presented, at the end of Section 11.4. It applies only to acyclic digraphs, and it has $O(n + m)$ time complexity.

Next, there is the algorithm due to Dijkstra presented later in this section. It applies to arbitrary digraphs, but all the edge costs must be non-negative. It has $O(n\log n + m)$ time complexity.

Finally, there is the Bellman–Moore algorithm presented just below. It applies to arbitrary digraphs, and the edges may have negative costs, but it is $O(nm)$.

## The Bellman–Moore algorithm

Suppose that $G$ has no negative cycles and that every vertex is reachable from $a$. Then $d(a, v)$ is well defined for all $v$, and the following equations hold:

$$d(a, a) = 0$$
$$d(a, v) = \min_{u \in P(v)} [d(a, u) + c(u, v)]$$

where $P(v)$ is the set of predecessors of $v$. This is easy to prove: if $v = a$, the absence of negative cycles means that the empty path of cost 0 is a shortest path from $a$ to itself; while if $v \neq a$, any shortest path from $a$ to $v$ must have the form $\langle a, \dots, u, v \rangle$ where $u$ is a predecessor of $v$ and $\langle a, \dots, u \rangle$ is itself a shortest path.

Unfortunately, the above does not qualify as a recurrence equation, or at least not a useful one, because when evaluating $d(a, v)$ it eventually evaluates $d(a, x)$ for every proper ancestor $x$ of $v$, and if $G$ has a cycle containing $v$, $v$ is one of its own proper ancestors so the recursion will not terminate. So this recurrence is only useful in acyclic digraphs, where it works well and is the basis of the $O(n + m)$ algorithm based on topological sorting that was mentioned above.

The algorithm due independently to Bellman (1958) and Moore (1959) relies on an alternative recurrence which avoids this cycle problem. Let $d_k(a, v)$ be the cost of a shortest path from $a$ to $v$ among all paths of length (number of edges) at most $k$. For example, in

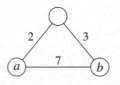

$d_1(a, b) = 7$ and $d_2(a, b) = 5$. The path need not be simple.

If there is no path from $a$ to $v$ of length at most $k$, it will be convenient to define $d_k(a, v)$ to be $\infty$. Implementations may use for $\infty$ any number guaranteed to be larger than the total cost of any path of length up to $n - 1$; for example, $n$ times the largest positive edge cost or 0 if all edge costs are negative.

Now $d_k(a, v)$ can be calculated using the following recurrence:

$$d_0(a, a) = 0$$
$$d_0(a, v) = \infty$$
$$d_k(a, v) = \min\{d_{k-1}(a, v), \min_{u \in P(v)} [d_{k-1}(a, u) + c(u, v)]\}$$

It states that a shortest (in fact the only) path of length at most 0 from $a$ to itself has cost 0; there is no path of length at most 0 from $a$ to any other vertex $v$; and a shortest path of length at most $k > 0$ from $a$ to any vertex $v$, including $a$ itself, is either a path of length at most $k - 1$ from $a$ to $v$, or else it is a path of length at most $k - 1$ from $a$ to some predecessor $u$ of $v$, followed by $\langle u, v \rangle$.

If any one of these alternatives cannot offer any suitable path, it will contribute $\infty$, which has no effect on the result of the minimizing operations, unless all terms are $\infty$ in which case the result, quite correctly, is $\infty$.

This recurrence cannot cycle because $k$ strictly decreases with every call. It is not troubled by unreachable vertices (they have infinite distance throughout) or negative cycles (paths around these cycles are permitted, but infinite ones are avoided by the limit on length). When converted into a dynamic programming algorithm as in Section 4.4, a two-dimensional table indexed by $v$ and $k$ is required:

|           | $k = 0$ | $k = 1$ | $\cdots$ | $k = n - 1$ |
|-----------|---------|---------|----------|-------------|
| $a = v_1$ | 0       |         |          |             |
| $v_1$     | $\infty$ |        |          |             |
| $\vdots$  | $\infty$ |        |          |             |
| $v_n$     | $\infty$ |        |          |             |

If $G$ has no negative cycles, at least one shortest path to every reachable vertex is a simple path (Theorem 12.2), and so has length at most $n - 1$, because no simple path can be longer. Hence $d_{n-1}(a, v) = d(a, v)$ if $v$ is reachable from $a$, and $d_{n-1}(a, v) = \infty$ otherwise; so the last column needed is $k = n - 1$. If $G$ has a negative cycle, this can be ascertained by calculating one more column and seeing whether $d_n(a, v) < d_{n-1}(a, v)$ for any $v$; if so, the path to $v$ must contain a negative cycle.

A suitable topological ordering is easily found: fill in the columns from left to right, and use any ordering within each column. By remembering which predecessor contributed the smallest $d_{k-1}(a, u) + c(u, v)$, or alternatively that $d_{k-1}(a, v)$ was minimum, actual paths can be found in addition to their costs.

The time complexity of calculating one entry in the table is clearly of the order of $1 + |P(v)|$, the number of predecessors of $v$ plus a constant. The cost of calculating one column is therefore of the order of $n + \sum_v |P(v)| = n + m$. So the total time complexity, summing over $n$ or $n + 1$ columns, is $O(n(n + m))$.

### Dijkstra's algorithm

For large graphs, the Bellman–Moore algorithm may be too slow. A much faster method, due to Dijkstra (1959), may be used if the edges have non-negative cost.

Each vertex $v$ contains three attributes: $v.visited$, which is boolean, $v.distance$, which is a number, and $v.parent$, which is a reference to a vertex. A shortest path spanning tree can be represented using these attributes: in each vertex $v$ reachable from the start vertex $a$, set $v.visited$ to *true*, $v.distance$ to $d(a, v)$, and $v.parent$ to the parent of $v$ in the spanning tree (or to *Void* in the case of $a$, the root of the tree).

Dijkstra's algorithm finds a shortest path spanning tree represented in this way. Initially, $a.visited$ is set to true, $a.distance$ to 0, and $a.parent$ to *Void*. In all other vertices $v$, $v.visited$ is set to false and $v.distance$ and $v.parent$ are not defined. As the algorithm progresses, the *distance* attributes gradually decrease to their correct values, and the *parent* attributes gradually settle on the correct parents.

The algorithm also maintains a set $Q$ of some of the visited vertices (that is, vertices whose *visited* field is true), which is initialized to $\{a\}$. During each iteration of the main loop, a vertex $v$ of minimum $v.distance$ is deleted from $Q$. For each edge $\langle v, w \rangle$ leading out of $v$ such that $w$ is unvisited, $w.visited$ is set to true, $w.distance$ is set to $v.distance + c(v, w)$, $w.parent$ is set to $v$, and $w$ is added to $Q$. For each edge $\langle v, w \rangle$ such that $w$ is visited and $v.distance + c(v, w) < w.distance$, the same assignments are made to $w$'s attributes but, since $w$ must have been added to $Q$ previously, this is not done again. The algorithm terminates when $Q$ becomes empty.

This algorithm will now be traced on the graph

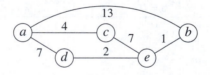

Visited vertices will have their distances shown adjacent, and their incoming edges emboldened; vertices currently in $Q$ will be shaded. The initial state is

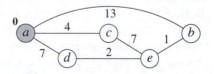

with $a$ being the only vertex in $Q$. During the first iteration, $a$ is deleted from $Q$ and its successors are modified as described above and inserted into $Q$, giving

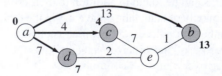

During the second iteration, since $c$ has minimum distance among the vertices in $Q$, it is deleted from $Q$ and all its outgoing edges (except the one back to $a$, which does not satisfy the conditions) are followed and their endpoints modified:

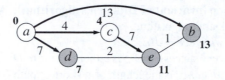

During the third iteration, $d$ has minimum distance, so afterwards the state is

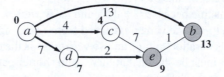

Notice at this point how the old path $\langle a, c, e \rangle$ was abandoned in favor of the new, shorter path $\langle a, d, e \rangle$. Continuing,

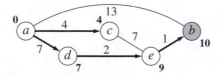

and then after deleting $b$ the algorithm terminates, since $Q$ is empty. The algorithm has found the right tree and distances in this example, but of course its correctness is far from clear.

## Correctness of Dijkstra's algorithm

While Dijkstra's algorithm is running, it partitions the vertices of $G$ into three sets: $L$, the set of vertices that have been extracted from $Q$; $Q$ itself; and $R$, the vertices not yet visited. A path $P$ from $a$ to $v$ is said to go *via $L$* if all the vertices in $P$, except $v$, are in $L$. For example, in this diagram $P_1$ goes via $L$, but $P_2$ does not:

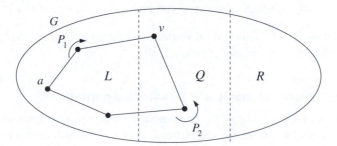

It should be clear that as soon as one path from $a$ to $w$ is found, $w.parent$ always points to the predecessor of $w$ on some path from $a$ to $w$, and $w.distance$ is always the cost of this path. It must be shown that eventually this path is a shortest path.

**Theorem 12.3 (Loop invariant of Dijkstra's algorithm):** At the beginning of the $k$th iteration of Dijkstra's algorithm,
(1) For all $z \in L$, $z.distance = d(a, z)$;
(2) For all $z \in L$, every successor of $z$ is either in $L$ or in $Q$;
(3) For all $z \in Q$, $z.distance$ is the length of a shortest path from $a$ to $z$ via $L$.
**Proof:** by induction on $k$.
**Basis step:** At the beginning of the first iteration, $L$ is empty so (1) and (2) are vacuously true; (3) is true because $Q = \{a\}$, and $a.distance = 0$ which is correct.
**Inductive step:** Let $v$ be the vertex extracted from $Q$ during the $k$th iteration. At the beginning of this iteration, $v \in Q$, and so $v.distance$ is the cost of a shortest path from $a$ to $v$ via $L$. It must be shown that there is no shorter path to $v$ via vertices not in $L$, so as to justify the inclusion of $v$ into $L$.

Consider any path $P$ from $a$ to $v$ that does not go via $L$. $P$ contains at least one vertex which is not in $L$, and not equal to $v$. Let $x$ be the first such vertex on $P$:

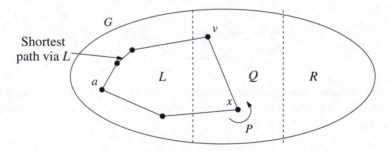

Since $x$ is adjacent to $L$, $x \in Q$ by (2). So $x.distance$ is the cost of a shortest path to $x$ via $L$, by the inductive hypothesis. But $P$ contains a path from $a$ to $x$ via $L$, so the cost of $P$ is at least as great as $x.distance$. Now $x.distance \geq v.distance$, since the algorithm chose $v$, not $x$. It follows that the cost of $P$ is at least as great as $v.distance$. Therefore $v$ may be included into $L$, with (1) holding at the beginning of the next iteration. Clearly (2) and (3) are preserved also, because the algorithm updates $w.distance$ and $Q$ to reflect the discovery of path $\langle a, \dots, v, w \rangle$ for all $w$. $\square$

At termination, $L = V$ (assuming all vertices are reachable from $a$), and (1) says that for all $z \in V$, $z.distance = d(a, z)$ as required.

## Implementation and analysis of Dijkstra's algorithm

It is clear that the set $Q$ should be implemented using a priority queue whose keys are distances and whose entries are vertices. When a new path to $w$ is found which is shorter than a previous one, $w$'s distance decreases while it is in $Q$, and so the *decrease_key* operation is required.

In the following implementation of Dijkstra's algorithm, each vertex has a *visited* field which is true if the vertex has been visited, in which case the *distance* field contains the distance of the shortest path to the vertex found so far, and the *parent* field contains the predecessor of the vertex on this path. Multiple inheritance is used to express the idea that a vertex is simultaneously a vertex in a graph and an entry in a priority queue whose key is its *distance* field.

```
dijkstra(g: like digraph_type; a: like vertex_type) is
    local
        q: like priqueue_extended_type;
        v, w: like vertex_type;
        e: like edge_type;
    do

        from v := g.first_vertex until g.nil_vertex(v) loop
            v.put_visited(false);
            v := g.next_vertex(v)
        end;

        a.put_visited(true);
        a.put_distance(0);
        a.put_parent(new_nil_vertex);
        from !!q.make; q.insert(a) until q.empty loop
            v := q.delete_min;
            from e := g.first_edge(v) until g.nil_edge(e) loop
                w := g.end_point(e);
                if not w.visited then
                    w.put_visited(true);
                    w.put_distance(v.distance + e.cost);
                    w.put_parent(v);
                    q.insert(w)
                elseif v.distance + e.cost < w.distance then
                    w.put_parent(v);
                    q.decrease_key(w, v.distance + e.cost)
                end;
                e := g.next_edge(v, e)
            end
        end
    end
```

The complexity of this algorithm is just $O(n + m)$ plus the total complexity of the operations on $q$, assuming that every vertex of the graph is reachable from $a$. Since every vertex is inserted once and deleted once, there must be $n$ *insert* and $n$ *delete_min* calls. Each iteration of the inner loop corresponds to one edge of the graph, so the body of the inner loop is executed exactly $m$ times. Inside the inner loop, either one *insert*, one *decrease_key*, or nothing is performed. There are $n - 1$ insertions performed in the inner loop, so there are at most $m - (n - 1)$ *decrease_key* operations. The worst-case complexity of Dijkstra's algorithm is therefore

$$W(n, m) = O(n \times \text{cost of } \textit{insert} + n \times \text{cost of } \textit{delete\_min} +$$
$$m \times \text{cost of } \textit{decrease\_key})$$

where the maximum size of the priority queue is $n$.

It is an interesting exercise to look through the summary of priority queue implementations given in Section 8.7, to find the one best suited to Dijkstra's algorithm. The unsorted linked list gives

$$W(n, m) = O(n \times 1 + n \times n + m \times 1)$$

$$= O(n^2)$$

since $m \leq n^2$. The 2-3 tree and the heap give

$$W(n, m) = O(n \times \log n + n \times \log n + m \times \log n)$$

$$= O(m \log n)$$

since $m \geq n - 1$ in a connected digraph. The winner is the Fibonacci heap, with

$$W(n, m) = O(n \times 1 + n \times \log n + m \times 1)$$

$$= O(n \log n + m)$$

Chapter 13 will show that this is the best possible asymptotic complexity that could be hoped for: there is no more efficient way to implement Dijkstra's algorithm.

### Breadth-first search revisited

If each edge is assigned a cost of 1, the cost of any path will equal its length, and Dijkstra's algorithm may be used to solve the breadth-first search problem of Section 11.5. The algorithm may be simplified significantly in this special case, however, as will now be shown.

Let $P_1 = \langle a, \dots, v_1, w \rangle$ be the first path from $a$ to $w$ found by Dijkstra's algorithm in the case when all edges have cost 1. It will be shown that this is a shortest path from $a$ to $w$. Let $P_2 = \langle a, \dots, v_2, w \rangle$ be another path from $a$ to $w$ found by Dijkstra's algorithm. At the time $P_1$ was found, $v_1$ had just been extracted from $Q$, so $v_1.distance = d(a, v_1)$, and the cost of $P_1$ is $d(a, v_1) + 1$. Similarly, the cost of $P_2$ is $d(a, v_2) + 1$. But $P_1$ was found before $P_2$, so $v_1$ was extracted from $Q$ before $v_2$, $d(a, v_1) \leq d(a, v_2)$, and the length of $P_1$ is no greater than the length of $P_2$.

It follows that the *decrease_key* part of Dijkstra's algorithm will never be executed in this special case. During each iteration of the main loop, then, some vertex of distance $x$, say, is extracted from $Q$, and some other vertices of distance

$x + 1$ are inserted. From this, it can easily be shown by induction that at any moment, all of the entries of $Q$ have distance $x$ or $x + 1$, for some $x$, and that the distance of every vertex inserted is the larger of these two numbers. The priority queue may therefore be replaced with a fifo queue, and it is easy to verify that the result is exactly the routine given in Section 11.5.

## 12.2 Minimum spanning trees

Consider the following problem. There are a number of cities, and it is desired to connect them by an electric power network, in such a way as to minimize the cost of the network. As described by Graham and Hell (1985), this problem was first studied by O. Borůvka, who learnt of it from friends employed in the electrification of Southern Moravia (now part of the Czech Republic).

Borůvka's solution involved an assumption that will also be made here: that junctions in the network may occur only within cities. This allows the problem to be represented as a graph. Each city is a vertex, and whenever a direct link between two cities is feasible, the corresponding vertices are connected by an edge $e$, labeled with a non-negative number $c(e)$, equal to the cost of the link. For example,

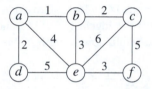

represents six cities; the cost of a direct link between $a$ and $d$ is 2, and so on.

The desired electric power network is a subgraph of $G$ that connects all of the vertices of $G$ together, using edges whose total cost is minimum. No cycles are needed, since one edge of a cycle can always be deleted without increasing the total cost of the network, or disconnecting any vertices. So the network is a spanning tree of minimum total cost: a *minimum spanning tree*. For example,

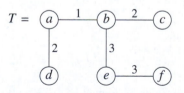

is a minimum spanning tree of the graph $G$ above, and its total cost is 11. The total cost of $T$ is denoted $c(T)$. If $G$ is not connected, a minimum spanning tree can be found for each connected component. Taken together, these trees form a *minimum spanning forest*.

There are several algorithms for finding minimum spanning forests, but in general terms they all work in the same way. Two sets of edges, which will be called $X$ and $Y$, are used. The sets are initially empty, and are gradually enlarged while maintaining the loop invariant

'There exists a minimum spanning forest of $G$ which contains all of the edges of $X$, and none of the edges of $Y$'

This invariant is easily established by initializing $X$ and $Y$ to empty. If $X \cup Y = E$ at termination, the invariant implies that $F = \langle V, X \rangle$ is a minimum spanning forest of $G$. The following theorem shows how to add one edge to $X$ while maintaining this invariant:

**Theorem 12.4:** Let $G = \langle V, E \rangle$ be a graph, and suppose there are two subsets of $E$, called $X$ and $Y$, that obey the following condition: there exists a minimum spanning forest $F$ of $G$ which contains all of the edges of $X$, and none of the edges of $Y$. Let $C$ be any connected component of the subgraph $\langle V, X \rangle$, and let

$$J(C) = \{\{u, v\} \in E - Y \mid u \in C \text{ and } v \notin C\}$$

be the edges of $G$ that join $C$ to the rest of $G$, excluding any edges of $Y$. Suppose $e$ is an edge of minimum cost in $J(C)$. Then there exists a minimum spanning forest $F'$ of $G$ which contains all of the edges of $X \cup \{e\}$, and none of the edges of $Y$.
**Proof:** An example will be helpful to start with. Consider

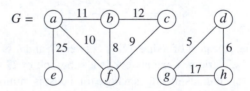

and suppose that $X = \{\{b, f\}, \{d, g\}, \{d, h\}\}$ and $Y = \{\}$. Then

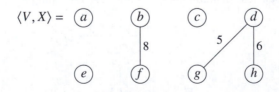

Choose $C$ to be the connected component of $\langle V, X \rangle$ whose vertices are $b$ and $f$, so that $J(C) = \{\{b, a\}, \{b, c\}, \{f, a\}, \{f, c\}\}$. Since the edge $\{f, c\}$ has minimum cost among the edges of $J(C)$, the theorem says that $\{f, c\}$ may be added to $X$.

Now for the proof. For convenience of notation, treat $F$ and $F'$ as sets of edges. If $e \in F$, take $F' = F$ and the theorem is proved. So suppose that $e \notin F$. Let

$e = \{u, v\}$. Since $u$ and $v$ are connected by $e$, there must be some path in $F$ connecting $u$ with $v$. This path begins at $u$ in $C$ and ends at $v$ outside $C$, and it contains no edges from $Y$; so it must contain at least one edge $e'$ from $J(C)$:

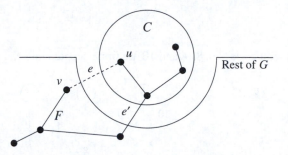

Since $e$ is of minimum cost in $J(C)$, $c(e) \le c(e')$. Now let

$$F' = F \cup \{e\} - \{e'\}$$

Then $F'$ is a spanning forest of $G$, and $c(F') = c(F) + c(e) - c(e') \le c(F)$. But $F$ was a minimum spanning forest, so $c(F) \le c(F')$. It follows that $c(F) = c(F')$, $c(e) = c(e')$, and $F'$ is also a minimum spanning forest. Clearly $F'$ contains all of the edges of $X \cup \{e\}$ and none of the edges of $Y$. $\qquad\square$

It is not hard to use this theorem to build minimum spanning trees by hand: choose any component $C$, which will initially be a single vertex, add a smallest incident edge, and repeat until the forest is complete. A simple implementation of this method will be studied next.

## Kruskal's algorithm

The algorithm due to Kruskal (1956) for finding a minimum spanning forest of a graph $G = \langle V, E \rangle$ examines the edges of the graph one by one in order of increasing cost. If an edge can be added to the growing forest without creating a cycle, this is done; otherwise the edge is discarded:

```
X := { }; Y := { };
from Q := E until Q = { } loop
    Take out of Q an edge {v, w} of minimum cost;
    if v, w lie in different components of <V, X> then
        Insert {v, w} into X
    else
        Insert {v, w} into Y
    end
end;
Result := <V, X>
```

For example, if

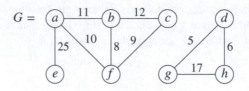

then the edges with costs 5, 6, 8, 9, and 10 are first accepted into $X$, giving

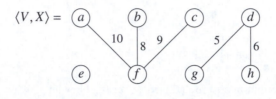

After that, the algorithm considers and rejects the edges with costs 11, 12, and 17, finally accepting the last edge with cost 25, and returning

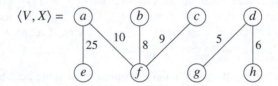

With the help of Theorem 12.4 above, it is quite easy to prove that Kruskal's algorithm is correct:

**Theorem 12.5 (Loop invariant of Kruskal's algorithm):** At the beginning of the $k$th iteration of the loop in Kruskal's algorithm applied to $G = \langle V, E \rangle$,
(1) There exists a minimum spanning forest of $G$ which contains all of the edges of $X$, and none of the edges of $Y$; and
(2) $Q = E - X - Y$.
**Proof:** The invariance of $Q = E - X - Y$ is obvious, since it is true initially and, during each iteration, one edge is deleted from $Q$ and inserted into $X$ or $Y$. It remains to prove (1) by induction on $k$.
**Basis step:** Initially, $X$ and $Y$ are empty, so any minimum spanning forest satisfies the condition.
**Inductive step:** The inductive hypothesis is as given above; it must be shown to be true for $k + 1$. Let $e = \{v, w\}$ be the edge extracted from $Q$ at the beginning of the $k$th iteration.

First, suppose that $v$ and $w$ lie in different components of $\langle V, X \rangle$. Then it must be the case that $e \in J(C)$ for some $C$. Since $e$ is of minimum cost among the edges of $Q = E - X - Y$, and $J(C) \subseteq E - X - Y$, $e$ is of minimum cost in $J(C)$. By Theorem 12.4, $e$ may be added to $X$.

Second, suppose that $v$ and $w$ lie in the same component of $\langle V, X \rangle$. This means there is a path $\langle v, \dots, w \rangle$ in $\langle V, X \rangle$, and the minimum spanning forest $F$ which exists by the inductive hypothesis also contains this path, since $F$ contains all the edges of $X$. Therefore $e$ cannot be in $F$, since if it was, $F$ would contain the cycle $\langle v, \dots, w, v \rangle$. Thus $e$ may be added to $Y$. □

When the algorithm terminates, every edge is either in $X$ or in $Y$, and so (1) assures us that $\langle V, X \rangle$ is a minimum spanning forest of $G$.

## Implementation and analysis of Kruskal's algorithm

Clearly, the edges of $G$ should be stored in a priority queue ordered by cost. The most interesting issue is how to decide whether adding a given edge $\{v, w\}$ will cause a cycle. It will do so if $v$ and $w$ lie in the same connected component of $\langle V, X \rangle$, so some means of storing the connected components is required. It turns out that the Disjoint Sets ADT from Chapter 10 is the right way to do this. For example, if

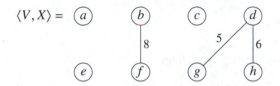

then the disjoint sets structure is $\{\{a\}, \{b,f\}, \{c\}, \{d, g, h\}, \{e\}\}$. To determine whether $v$ and $w$ lie in the same component of $\langle V, X \rangle$, the test *same_set*$(v, w)$ may be used; and when two components of $\langle V, X \rangle$ are merged into one by the insertion of an edge into $X$, a *union* operation merges the corresponding sets of vertices. There is no need to maintain $Y$, since its value is never used.

When $G$ is connected and dense (that is, contains many more edges than vertices), it is often worthwhile to optimize Kruskal's algorithm in the following way. Keep a record of how many edges have been added to $F$, and if this ever reaches $n - 1$, $F$ must be a spanning tree and the algorithm can stop immediately. Although this gives no improvement in worst-case complexity, in practice it is likely to speed up the algorithm significantly. At best, the first $n - 1$ edges considered by the algorithm will be included, and the time complexity will be reduced to $O(n \log m)$.

In the following implementation, each edge contains a *cost* field containing its cost, a boolean flag *in_forest* which will be set to **true** in each edge which is included in the minimum spanning forest, and two fields, *end_point_1* and *end_point_2*, containing the two endpoints of the edge. Multiple inheritance is used to express the idea that each vertex is simultaneously a vertex in a graph and an entry in a disjoint sets structure, and that each edge is simultaneously an edge in a graph and an entry in a priority queue whose key is its *cost* field.

```
kruskal(g: like graph_type) is
    local
        s: like disjsets_type;
        q: like priqueue_type;
        v, w: like vertex_type;
        e: like edge_type;
    do

        -- initialize vertices and priority queue of edges
        !!s.make; !!q.make;
        from v := g.first_vertex until g.nil_vertex(v) loop
            s.make_set(v);
            from e := g.first_edge(v) until g.nil_edge(e) loop
                w := g.end_point(e);
                e.put_end_point_1(v);
                e.put_end_point_2(w);
                e.put_in_forest(false);
                q.insert(e);
                e := g.next_edge(v, e)
            end;
            v := g.next_vertex(v)
        end;

        -- build the forest
        from until q.empty loop
            e := q.delete_min;
            if not s.same_set(e.end_point_1, e.end_point_2) then
                e.put_in_forest(true);
                s.union(e.end_point_1, e.end_point_2)
            end
        end
    end
```

The disjoint sets operations may be implemented so as to be virtually $O(1)$ each, according to Section 10.4, and the initialization, excluding $q.insert$, is $O(n + m)$, so the time complexity is dominated by the $m$ insert and $delete\_min$ operations. Their total complexity is $O(m \log m)$ using any one of a variety of priority queue implementations from Chapter 8.

## Prim's algorithm

The second algorithm for finding a minimum spanning forest is due to V. Jarník, as Graham and Hell (1985) explain; it was rediscovered and implemented by Prim (1957), and independently by Dijkstra (1959), and has come to bear Prim's name.

Theorem 12.4 permits any component $C$ of the growing forest $\langle V, X \rangle$ to be chosen when deciding which edge to include next. Kruskal's algorithm jumps from component to component; the idea of Prim's algorithm is to stay with one component throughout. For example, applying this approach to the graph

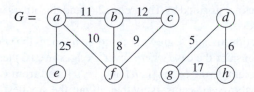

$$G =$$

and letting $C$ initially be the component of $\langle V, X \rangle$ that contains the single vertex $a$, the following trace is obtained. The edges of $C$ will be shown as solid, and of $J(C)$ as dashed. A dashed edge of minimum cost is made solid at each stage:

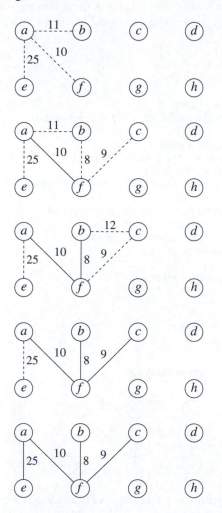

Now $J(C)$ is empty and the algorithm must be restarted on another component of $G$. The correctness of this algorithm follows in the same way as Kruskal's algorithm:

the included edges are justified by Theorem 12.4, and the others would cause a cycle so must be excluded.

This restriction to a single growing component opens the way for an interesting optimization. Consider the case where several edges in $J(C)$ lead from $C$ to some vertex $w$, as for example the edges $\{a, b\}$ and $\{f, b\}$ lead from $C$ to $b$ in the second step of the trace above. It seems likely that all but the smallest of these edges can be ruled out, and in fact this is so (see Theorem 12.6 below).

Prim's algorithm, then, combines the growing of a single component $C$ from a start vertex $a$, with the optimization of remembering only a smallest edge leading from $C$ to any vertex $w$. For convenience in the following code, these remembered edges are directed: $\langle v, w \rangle \in Q$ implies that $v \in C$ and $w \notin C$.

```
X := {}; Y := {}; Q := {};
for each vertex w adjacent to a
    Insert <a, w> into Q;

from until Q = {} loop
    Take out of Q an edge <u, v> of minimum cost;
    Insert {u, v} into X;
    for each vertex w adjacent to v
        if w has never been visited then
            Insert <v, w> into Q;
        elseif a path connects w to a in <V, X> then
            -- do nothing
        else -- there must be an edge <x, w> in Q
            if c(v, w) < c(x, w) then
                Replace <x, w> in Q by <v, w>;
                Insert {x, w} into Y
            else
                Insert {v, w} into Y
            end
        end
    end
end;
Result := <V, X>
```

For example, consider again the graph

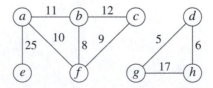

Executing Prim's algorithm on this graph, and taking $a$ as the start vertex, yields the following trace. As usual, the edges of $X$ are shown as solid, and of $Q$ as dashed:

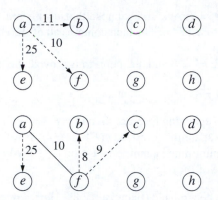

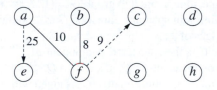

Here $\langle a, b \rangle$ has been discarded in favor of the shorter edge $\langle f, b \rangle$. Next comes

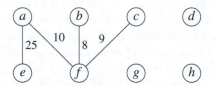

At this point, the edge $\langle b, c \rangle$ might be expected to enter $Q$; but since $\langle f, c \rangle$ has smaller cost, $\langle b, c \rangle$ is discarded. Also $\langle b, a \rangle$ is not inserted into $Q$. Two more stages give

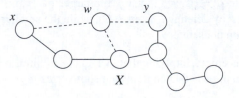

and now the algorithm must be restarted at some vertex in the other component.

The first step in proving Prim's algorithm correct is to show the validity of its optimization, that of remembering only a shortest edge from $C$ to any vertex.

**Theorem 12.6:** Let $G = \langle V, E \rangle$ be a graph, and suppose there are two subsets of $E$, called $X$ and $Y$, such that there exists a minimum spanning forest $F$ of $G$ which contains all of the edges of $X$, and none of the edges of $Y$. Let $\langle w, x, \dots, y, w \rangle$ be a simple cycle with no edges from $Y$, such that the edges of $\langle x, \dots, y \rangle$ are in $X$:

Let $e = \langle x, w \rangle$ and $e' = \langle y, w \rangle$, and suppose that $c(e) \geq c(e')$. Then there exists a minimum spanning forest $F'$ of $G$ which contains all of the edges of $X$, and none of the edges of $Y \cup \{e\}$.

**Proof:** If $e \notin F$, take $F' = F$ and the theorem is proved. So assume $e \in F$. Let

$$F' = F \cup \{e'\} - \{e\}$$

It is clear that $F'$ is a spanning forest of $G$, and $c(F') = c(F) + c(e') - c(e) \leq c(F)$. But $F$ is a minimum spanning forest, so $c(F) \leq c(F')$. It follows that $c(F') = c(F)$, and so $F'$ is also a minimum spanning forest of $G$. Clearly $F'$ contains all of the edges of $X$, and none of the edges of $Y \cup \{e\}$. $\qquad \square$

This theorem can be generalized (Exercise 12.8). Here now is the main theorem:

**Theorem 12.7 (Loop invariant of Prim's algorithm):** At the start of the $k$th iteration of Prim's algorithm applied to graph $G = \langle V, E \rangle$ with start vertex $a$,
(1) There exists a minimum spanning forest of $G$ that contains all of the edges of $X$, and none of the edges of $Y$;
(2) $Q = J(C)$, where $C$ is the connected component of $\langle V, X \rangle$ that contains $a$. (A direction is imposed on the edges of $Q$: if $\langle x, y \rangle \in Q$, then $x \in C$ and $y \notin C$.)
**Proof:** by induction on $k$. A definition of $J(C)$ is given within Theorem 12.4. Note that $J(C)$ excludes the edges of $Y$.
**Basis step:** When the main loop is entered for the first time, $X$ and $Y$ are empty, so (1) is true. The connected component $C$ of $\langle V, X \rangle$ that contains $a$ is $\langle \{a\}, \{\} \rangle$, and $J(C)$ is just the set of edges adjacent to $a$. These have been inserted into $Q$.
**Inductive step:** The two conditions are assumed to hold at the beginning of the $k$th iteration, and must be proved to hold at the beginning of the $(k + 1)$st iteration.

Since $Q = J(C)$, the edge $\{u, v\}$ of minimum cost in $Q$ may be added to $X$, by Theorem 12.4, and this the algorithm does. But now $C$ has changed and $Q$ must be updated to equal the new value of $J(C)$. All edges $\{v, w\}$ leading out of $v$ are now potential members of $J(C)$, but they cannot simply be inserted into $Q$, because there are a number of special cases.

First of all, if $w$ has never been visited, then $\{v, w\}$ is now in $J(C)$, and must be added to $Q$. This the algorithm does.

Next, if $w$ already lies in $C$, then $\{v, w\}$ is not in $J(C)$ and must not be added to $Q$. It is not hard to verify that $\{v, w\} \in X$ or $\{v, w\} \in Y$ already in this case, so that nothing should be done with this edge.

Finally, $w$ must be the endpoint of an edge $\langle x, w \rangle$ in $J(C)$. By Theorem 12.6 applied to the cycle $C = \langle w, x, \ldots, v, w \rangle$, the larger of $\{v, w\}$ and $\{x, w\}$ may be inserted into $Y$, thereby deleting it from $J(C)$, while the smaller one goes into $J(C)$. Again, the algorithm does this. $\qquad \square$

At termination, $Q$ is empty, implying that $\langle V, X \rangle$ is a minimum spanning tree of the connected component of $G$ that contains the start vertex $a$.

## Implementation and analysis of Prim's algorithm

The executable implementation of Prim's algorithm given below follows the high-level code quite closely. The major difference is that instead of inserting the edge $\langle v, w \rangle$ into $Q$, its endpoint $w$ is inserted, and $v$ is stored in $w$'s *parent* field as a record of which edge leading into $w$ is intended. At termination, the set $X$ consists of all edges $\{w.parent, w\}$ except for $w = a$; the set $Y$ is not explicitly represented.

The *visited* and *in_tree* flags of each vertex indicate respectively that the vertex has been visited previously, and that it is in $C$; the *visited* flags must be initialized to false at the start of this algorithm. Multiple inheritance is used to express the idea that each vertex is simultaneously also an entry in a priority queue, whose key is the vertex's *distance* field.

```
prim(g: like digraph_type; a: like vertex_type) is
   local
        q: like priqueue_extended_type;
        v, w: like vertex_type;
        e: like edge_type;
   do

        from v := g.first_vertex until g.nil_vertex(v) loop
           v.put_visited(false);
           v := g.next_vertex(v)
        end;

        a.put_visited(true);
        a.put_in_tree(false);
        a.put_distance(0);
        a.put_parent(new_nil_vertex);
        from !!q.make; q.insert(a) until q.empty loop
           v := q.delete_min;
           v.put_in_tree(true);
           from e := g.first_edge(v) until g.nil_edge(e) loop
              w := g.end_point(e);
              if not w.visited then
                 w.put_visited(true);
                 w.put_in_tree(false);
                 w.put_distance(e.cost);
                 w.put_parent(v);
                 q.insert(w)
              elseif w.in_tree then
                 -- do nothing
              elseif e.cost < w.distance then
                 w.put_parent(v);
                 q.decrease_key(w, e.cost)
              end;
              e := g.next_edge(v, e)
           end
        end
   end
```

As explained above, if this algorithm fails to visit all the vertices of $G$, an unvisited vertex must be selected and the algorithm restarted there, in the manner of *depth_first_search* at the end of Section 11.6.

The reader has probably noticed a strong resemblance between this code for Prim's algorithm and the code given in Section 12.1 for Dijkstra's shortest path algorithm. The only difference between them is that Dijkstra's algorithm chooses a vertex as close as possible to the start vertex at each stage, while Prim's algorithm chooses a vertex as close as possible to the growing tree. Their correctness proofs seem very different, so too much should not be made of this connection; but it makes the task of analysis very easy.

As for Dijkstra's algorithm, Prim's algorithm makes $n$ *insert* and $n$ *delete_min* calls, and at most $m - (n - 1)$ *decrease_key* calls, for a worst-case complexity of

$$W(n, m) = O(n \times \text{cost of } insert + n \times \text{cost of } delete\_min + $$
$$m \times \text{cost of } decrease\_key)$$

assuming that the graph traversal operations are $O(1)$ each. This leads to an $O(n^2)$ implementation using an unsorted linked list for the priority queue, or $O(n\log n + m)$ using Fibonacci heaps.

Unlike the implementation of Dijkstra's algorithm, however, this implementation can be bettered. By growing many small components $C$, and keeping each $J(C)$ in a Fibonacci heap, it is possible to build minimum spanning trees in almost linear time. See Fredman and Tarjan (1987) and Gabow et al. (1984).

## 12.3 Network flows

Consider the following problem. Every day, a coal mine produces 12 000 tonnes of coal which must be transported by train from the mine to a port, where it is loaded onto ships. Each segment of the railway network has its own individual capacity (measured in thousands of tonnes per day):

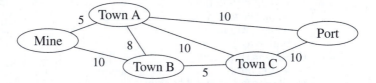

Can the 12 000 tonnes be transported each day? What is the maximum amount that can be transported? This is the *network flow* problem.

Owing to the two bottlenecks of capacity 5, the two apparently direct routes, via $A$, and via $B$ and $C$, can carry only 5 000 tonnes per day each. But by diverting some of the flow away from the bottleneck between $B$ and $C$, the total flow can be increased to 13 000 tonnes per day:

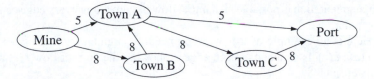

In fact, it is easy now to see how to increase the flow even further, to 15 000 tonnes per day, which is clearly the maximum possible because the railways leaving the mine can take no more.

Although coal flows continually through the network, there is really no element of time in the network flow problem. The problem is concerned with the *rate of flow*, measured in thousands of tonnes per day or whatever, which does not change over time.

Formally, define a *flow graph G* to be a directed graph with two distinguished vertices. One, the *source*, has only outgoing edges, while the other, the *sink*, has only incoming edges. (In the example above, the mine was the source and the port was the sink.) Each edge *e* has a non-negative integer *capacity* $c(e)$, representing the maximum possible rate of flow along that edge.

A *flow* in *G* is an assignment to each edge of a non-negative integer $f(e)$, called the *current rate of flow along e*, or more briefly and inaccurately the *flow along e*. The total flow along edges entering any vertex must equal the total flow along edges leaving that vertex, the source and sink excepted. This requirement amounts to saying that material may not accumulate anywhere in the network; it must flow continually.

The *network flow problem* asks for a flow in *G* such that the total flow along edges leaving the source (called the *size* of the flow) is as large as possible. Because material may not accumulate in the network, this flow out of the source must always equal the flow into the sink.

Setting up the problem in a directed graph gives the option of one-way links, such as unpumped water pipes running downhill. Bi-directional links may be modeled in the usual way with a pair of directed edges:

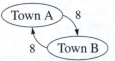

It is even possible to have a different capacity in each direction.

Network flow problems arise in the transport of other commodities, such as water and electricity. But there are also applications that have nothing to do with transportation, such as the application to bipartite matching that will be presented in Section 12.4.

Following the incremental design strategy of Section 4.2, it is natural to try to design an incremental algorithm that constructs successively larger flows, until no further augmentation is possible. An initial flow of zero along every edge can be the starting point.

Here is an example of a flow graph needing augmentation. A label of the form '$f(e) : c(e)$' is attached to each edge $e$, showing the current flow $f(e)$ and the capacity $c(e)$:

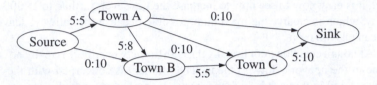

This is not exactly the earlier example, because the edges are directed now. There is a current flow of 5 from source to sink via $A$, $B$ and $C$.

Clearly, the edge from the source to $A$ is of no use in augmenting this flow, because it is already flowing to capacity. On the other hand, the edge from the source to $B$ does have spare capacity. It would seem to be a good idea to construct a graph having just the edges with spare capacity, showing how much:

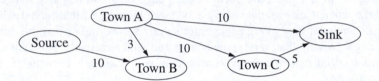

Prospects for augmenting the flow do not look good, because extra flow can only go through $B$, from which there is apparently no outlet.

However, this analysis overlooks a peculiar but important possibility. Consider this path in the original flow graph:

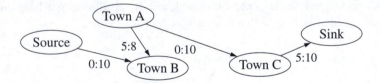

Even though the edge from $A$ to $B$ is pointing the wrong way, it is still possible for five extra units to flow along this path:

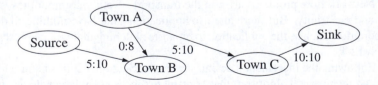

What has happened is this. Five new units of flow from the source to B have displaced the five units that previously flowed from A to B. These five units have been diverted along the edge from A to C and on to the sink. The total flow has increased by five.

Formally, then, given a flow graph G with some current flow, the *residual graph* R is constructed as follows. The vertices of R are the vertices of G. For each edge e of G such that $f(e) < c(e)$, there is an edge of R labeled with $c(e) - f(e)$. And for each edge of G such that $f(e) > 0$, there is an edge of R going the opposite way to e and labeled with $f(e)$.

For example, the flow graph

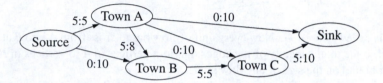

has residual graph

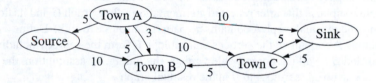

The two links connecting A and B show that up to three more units than at present may flow from A to B, or alternatively up to five more units than at present may flow from B to A (by canceling the existing flow from A to B).

The residual graph is easily constructed by following its definition. Any path in it from source to sink is a path along which flow may be increased, by an amount equal to the minimum of the labels on its edges. For example, the path

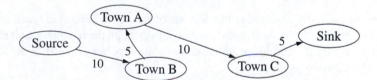

in the residual graph above permits five extra units to flow from source to sink.

This is a good point to pause and summarize the work done so far. By starting with a flow of size zero, building the residual graph, increasing the flow as much as possible along one path from source to sink, then building a new residual graph and so on, a flow can be found whose residual graph has no path from source to sink.

Two questions remain. Is this final flow a maximum flow? And how many iterations are required to reach it? The following theorem answers the first of these questions.

**Theorem 12.8:** Let $G$ be a flow graph with some flow. Suppose that the residual graph $R$ contains no path from source to sink. Then the flow is a maximum flow.
**Proof:** Suppose the set of vertices of a flow graph $G$ is divided into two sets, $A$ and $B$, such that $A$ contains the source and $B$ contains the sink:

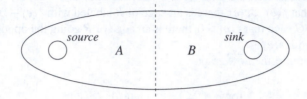

This is called a *cut* of $G$. Now every unit of flow has to cross from $A$ into $B$ at some point, so the total capacity of the edges that join vertices in $A$ to vertices in $B$ is an upper bound on the size of any flow in $G$.

For example, if $A$ contains only the source and $B$ contains the rest of the vertices, the edges in question are just the edges leaving the source, and this says that their total capacity is an upper bound on the size of any flow.

Now suppose that after repeated augmentation a flow graph $G$ and its flow are such that the residual graph $R$ contains no path from source to sink. Define a cut of $G$ by letting $A$ contain all the vertices reachable in $R$ from the source (including the source), and $B$ be all the unreachable vertices (including, by assumption, the sink). There can be no edge from $A$ to $B$ in the residual graph.

Every edge from $A$ to $B$ in the flow graph $G$ is flowing at capacity, for otherwise it would have given rise to an edge in the residual graph. Every edge from $B$ to $A$ has zero flow, for otherwise it would have given rise to an opposite edge from $A$ to $B$ in the residual graph.

In other words, a flow equal to the total capacity of all the edges from $A$ to $B$ is currently flowing from $A$ to $B$; this must be the size of the flow. But no flow can exceed the capacity of these edges. Therefore the flow is a maximum flow. □

The second question, concerning the number of iterations needed to reach a maximum flow, is more difficult. If the particular path through the residual graph may be chosen arbitrarily, the number of iterations could be very large indeed, as the following example shows:

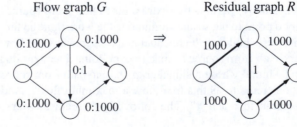

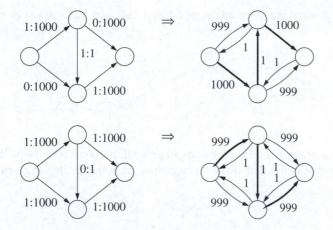

The chosen path is shown in bold at each stage. This disaster can go on for 2000 steps. If the maximum flow has size $C$, then $C$ iterations could be required, because the total flow might increase by as little as one each iteration. The situation is even worse if the capacities may be irrational numbers: Ford and Fulkerson (1962), who originated all of the ideas so far, show that the successive flow values, although always increasing, may converge to a value strictly less than the maximum flow.

Perhaps the most natural response to this problem is to choose an augmenting path in the residual graph that causes the largest possible increase in flow; in other words, the path from source to sink whose edge of minimum capacity is as large as possible. It is not difficult to see how to find this path using a modification of Dijkstra's algorithm for shortest paths. The meaning of 'distance' must be changed from 'sum of edge costs' to 'minimum of edge capacities,' and the vertex of maximum 'distance' must be chosen at each iteration. Edmonds and Karp (1972), who suggested this approach, were able to show that after at most $2m$ augmentations, where $m$ is the number of edges in the graph, the difference in size between the maximum flow and the current flow is at least halved. Hence this method requires about $2m\log_2 C$ augmentations at most, where $C$ is the size of the maximum flow. Since each augmentation requires one run of the modified Dijkstra's algorithm, the worst-case complexity is $O((n\log n + m)m\log C)$ altogether using Fibonacci heaps.

Another idea from Edmonds and Karp (1972) is to augment along a path of minimum length (number of edges) in the residual graph, using breadth-first search to find the path. An advanced version of this idea is the basis of Dinic's algorithm.

## Dinic's algorithm

The fastest algorithms for the network flow problem are all based on an algorithm due to Dinic (1970), which is the subject of this section. In this work it will be convenient to forget about flow graphs and deal exclusively with residual graphs. Let us first see how this may be done.

In a residual graph the edges are labeled only with capacities, not flows:

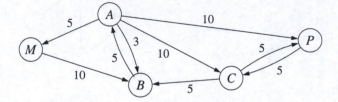

The original graph is a residual graph. In general, two vertices may be linked by a pair of opposite edges with different capacities, as in the graph just given:

Now suppose that some flow is found for the residual graph whose effect is to send $x$ units of flow from $A$ to $B$ (a symmetrical argument holds if the new flow goes the other way). The new flow graph contains

and so the new residual graph contains

because $x$ less flow is possible now from $A$ to $B$, and $x$ more flow is possible now from $B$ to $C$. If $c_1 - x = 0$, the edge from $A$ to $B$ is said to be *saturated*, and it must be deleted.

In this way it is possible to proceed directly from one residual graph to the next, and the course of the solution may be plotted as a sequence of residual graphs $R_1, R_2, R_3, \ldots$ where $R_1$ is the original graph of the problem. Of course, the flow $f_i$ that transforms $R_i$ into $R_{i+1}$ at each stage must be remembered so that the total flow can be reported, but that is an implementation detail.

Here is the example above worked through using only residual graphs. Each augmenting flow in this example happens to lie on just one path from source to sink, but that is not a requirement; any flow is acceptable. Here is the original graph:

$R_1 =$

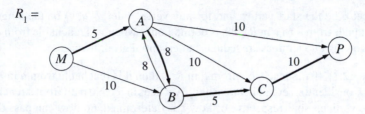

The path to be used first in augmenting the flow is shown in bold. After pushing five units of flow along this path, the residual graph is

$R_2 =$

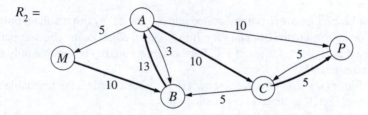

showing the next path to be used. This also allows five units of flow, giving

$R_2 =$

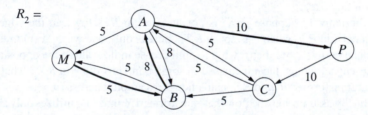

and finally another five units along this path produces

$R_2 =$

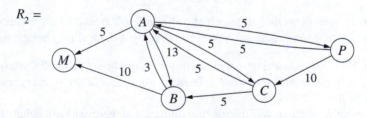

in which the sink is unreachable.

Earlier work has established that choosing any non-zero flow $f_i$ at each stage guarantees that the algorithm will eventually find a maximum flow and terminate. The remaining problem is to choose $f_i$ at each stage in a way that leads to few iterations. Dinic achieved this by restricting $f_i$ to utilizing only edges on shortest paths in $R_i$; that is, paths with the minimum possible number of edges. This restriction does not jeopardize the correctness of the algorithm, because if the sink is reachable at all, then it is reachable along a shortest path.

Let $a$ be the start vertex, and for any vertex $v$ let $d_i(a, v)$ be the length of a shortest path from $a$ to $v$ in $R_i$; this is defined only when $v$ is reachable from $a$ in $R_i$. The following two lemmas are tedious but essential groundwork.

**Lemma 12.1:** If $v$ is reachable from $a$ in $R_{i+1}$ then it is reachable from $a$ in $R_i$.
**Proof:** Consider the set of all unreachable vertices in $R_i$. No path from $a$ reaches any of these vertices, so, irrespective of how $f_i$ is determined, no flow can pass through them and no edges can be created (or destroyed) adjacent to them. Hence they remain unreachable from $a$ in $R_{i+1}$. The statement of the lemma is just the contrapositive of this. □

**Lemma 12.2:** Suppose $R_i$ is transformed into $R_{i+1}$ by a flow $f_i$ that utilizes only edges that lie on shortest paths from $a$ in $R_i$. If $\langle x, y \rangle$ is an edge on any shortest path from $a$ in $R_{i+1}$, then $d_i(a, y) \leq d_i(a, x) + 1$. Furthermore, equality is possible only if $\langle x, y \rangle$ is also an edge in $R_i$.
**Proof:** Since $\langle x, y \rangle$ lies on a shortest path in $R_{i+1}$, both vertices are reachable in $R_{i+1}$. By Lemma 12.1, they are also reachable in $R_i$.

Now $\langle x, y \rangle$ is an edge in $R_{i+1}$, but it may or may not be an edge in $R_i$. Suppose first that $\langle x, y \rangle$ is an edge in $R_i$. Then immediately $d_i(a, y) \leq d_i(a, x) + 1$, since this is true for any edge.

Alternatively, suppose $\langle x, y \rangle$ is not an edge in $R_i$. How can the edge $\langle x, y \rangle$ come to exist in $R_{i+1}$ when it is not in $R_i$? There is only one way: $\langle x, y \rangle$ must have had capacity 0 in $R_i$, and then, owing to an increase in flow along the opposite edge $\langle y, x \rangle$, its capacity must have increased to some non-zero value in $R_{i+1}$. That is, the flow that transformed $R_i$ into $R_{i+1}$ had a non-zero amount across $\langle y, x \rangle$.

But, by assumption, the flow that transformed $R_i$ into $R_{i+1}$ utilizes only shortest path edges in $R_i$. Hence $\langle y, x \rangle$ lies on a shortest path in $R_i$, so $d_i(a, x) = d_i(a, y) + 1$, and $d_i(a, y) = d_i(a, x) - 1 < d_i(a, x) + 1$. □

The next lemma shows that the length of a shortest path from $a$ to any vertex cannot decrease as the algorithm progresses, if augmenting is done along shortest paths.

**Lemma 12.3:** Suppose $R_i$ is transformed into $R_{i+1}$ by a flow $f_i$ that utilizes only edges that lie on shortest paths from $a$ in $R_i$. Then $d_{i+1}(a, v) \geq d_i(a, v)$ for every reachable vertex $v$ in $R_{i+1}$.
**Proof:** by contradiction. Assume, on the contrary, that there exists a reachable vertex $v$ in $R_{i+1}$ such that $d_{i+1}(a, v) < d_i(a, v)$. Note that $d_{i+1}(a, v)$ is well defined because $v$ is reachable in $R_{i+1}$, and then $d_i(a, v)$ is well defined by Lemma 12.1.

Arrange the reachable vertices $v$ of $R_{i+1}$ in order of increasing $d_{i+1}(a, v)$, with ties broken arbitrarily, and let $y$ be the first vertex in the sequence such that

$$d_{i+1}(a, y) < d_i(a, y) \tag{12.3.1}$$

Such a $y$ must exist by assumption.

Now $y$ cannot be $a$, because $d_{i+1}(a, a) = d_i(a, a) = 0$. Therefore a shortest path from $a$ to $y$ in $R_{i+1}$ has the form $\langle a, \ldots, x, y \rangle$ for some $x$. Both $x$ and $y$ are reachable in $R_{i+1}$, and so in $R_i$ by Lemma 12.1. Since this is a shortest path in $R_{i+1}$,

$$d_{i+1}(a, y) = d_{i+1}(a, x) + 1 \qquad (12.3.2)$$

Therefore $x$ precedes $y$ in the arrangement of vertices constructed earlier. Since $y$ was the first vertex in that sequence such that $d_{i+1}(a, y) < d_i(a, y)$,

$$d_{i+1}(a, x) \geq d_i(a, x) \qquad (12.3.3)$$

Putting these three relations together gives

$$
\begin{aligned}
d_i(a, y) &> d_{i+1}(a, y) && \text{by (12.3.1)} \\
&= d_{i+1}(a, x) + 1 && \text{by (12.3.2)} \\
&\geq d_i(a, x) + 1 && \text{by (12.3.3)}
\end{aligned}
$$

So $d_i(a, y) > d_i(a, x) + 1$. Since $\langle x, y \rangle$ lies on a shortest path in $R_{i+1}$, this contradicts Lemma 12.2. □

Of course, a *strictly* increasing distance would have been a more striking result, but that is too much to hope for. Suppose there are two shortest paths to $v$, and $f_i$ only augments one; then the other remains, and the distance to $v$ is unchanged.

Intuitively, a *blocking flow* is needed: one which saturates at least one edge on every shortest path from source to sink in $R_i$. Then these saturated edges will not appear in $R_{i+1}$, every shortest path to the sink will be destroyed, and the distance to the sink should increase. It can increase at most $n - 1$ times before reaching $n$, an impossibly large value since no simple path in a graph containing only $n$ vertices can be this long. This will indicate that the sink must have become unreachable.

Unfortunately, although a blocking flow will certainly destroy every shortest path from source to sink, new short paths could appear in $R_{i+1}$ owing to new edges being introduced. Such paths cannot in fact appear, but their possibility considerably complicates the proof given in the next two lemmas: intuition might suggest this approach, but hard work is needed to verify it.

**Lemma 12.4:** Suppose $R_i$ is transformed into $R_{i+1}$ by a flow that utilizes only edges that lie on shortest paths from $a$ in $R_i$. Suppose that $d_{i+1}(a, v) = d_i(a, v)$ for some reachable vertex $v$ in $R_{i+1}$, and let $P$ be a shortest path from $a$ to $v$ in $R_{i+1}$. Then, for every vertex $w$ on $P$, $d_{i+1}(a, w) = d_i(a, w)$.
**Proof:** by contradiction. Assume, on the contrary, that path $P$ contains a vertex $w$ such that $d_{i+1}(a, w) \neq d_i(a, w)$. Let $x$ be the last such vertex on path $P$. Since $d_{i+1}(a, x) \neq d_i(a, x)$, and Lemma 12.3 says that $d_{i+1}(a, x) \geq d_i(a, x)$,

$$d_{i+1}(a, x) > d_i(a, x) \qquad (12.3.4)$$

Now $x$ cannot be $v$, because $d_{i+1}(a, v) = d_i(a, v)$ by assumption. Therefore the path $P$ contains an edge $\langle x, y \rangle$ for some $y$. Both $x$ and $y$ are reachable in $R_{i+1}$ since they lie on $P$, hence they are reachable in $R_i$ by Lemma 12.1. Since $x$ is the last vertex on $P$ such that $d_{i+1}(a, x) \neq d_i(a, x)$,

$$d_{i+1}(a, y) = d_i(a, y) \tag{12.3.5}$$

Since $\langle x, y \rangle$ lies on $P$, a shortest path in $R_{i+1}$,

$$d_{i+1}(a, y) = d_{i+1}(a, x) + 1 \tag{12.3.6}$$

Putting these relations together gives

$$
\begin{aligned}
d_i(a, y) &= d_{i+1}(a, y) && \text{by (12.3.5)}\\
&= d_{i+1}(a, x) + 1 && \text{by (12.3.6)}\\
&> d_i(a, x) + 1 && \text{by (12.3.4)}
\end{aligned}
$$

So $d_i(a, y) > d_i(a, x) + 1$. Since $\langle x, y \rangle$ lies on a shortest path in $R_{i+1}$, once again this contradicts Lemma 12.2. □

**Lemma 12.5:** Suppose $R_i$ is transformed into $R_{i+1}$ by a flow that utilizes only edges that lie on shortest paths from $a$ in $R_i$. Suppose that this flow is a *blocking flow* for some vertex $v$ reachable in $R_{i+1}$; that is, that every shortest path from $a$ to $v$ in $R_i$ contains at least one edge that is saturated by this flow. Then $d_{i+1}(a, v) > d_i(a, v)$.
**Proof:** by contradiction. Assume, on the contrary, that $d_{i+1}(a, v) \leq d_i(a, v)$. Since $d_{i+1}(a, v) \geq d_i(a, v)$ by Lemma 12.3, it follows that $d_{i+1}(a, v) = d_i(a, v)$.

Let $P$ be any shortest path in $R_{i+1}$ from $a$ to $v$; $P$ has length $d_{i+1}(a, v)$. Now $P$ cannot also be a path in $R_i$, because, since $d_{i+1}(a, v) = d_i(a, v)$, $P$ would have to be a shortest path to $v$ in $R_i$, and by assumption all such shortest paths contain a saturated edge which is deleted when $R_i$ is transformed into $R_{i+1}$.

Since $P$ is a path in $R_{i+1}$ but not in $R_i$, it must contain at least one edge $\langle x, y \rangle$ which is not in $R_i$. Since $P$ is a shortest path in $R_{i+1}$,

$$d_{i+1}(a, y) = d_{i+1}(a, x) + 1 \tag{12.3.7}$$

Since $P$ is a shortest path from $a$ to $v$ in $R_{i+1}$ and $d_{i+1}(a, v) = d_i(a, v)$, Lemma 12.4 says that

$$d_{i+1}(a, x) = d_i(a, x) \tag{12.3.8}$$

and

$$d_{i+1}(a, y) = d_i(a, y) \tag{12.3.9}$$

Putting these relations together gives

$$d_i(a, y) = d_{i+1}(a, y) \qquad \text{by (12.3.9)}$$
$$= d_{i+1}(a, x) + 1 \qquad \text{by (12.3.7)}$$
$$= d_i(a, x) + 1 \qquad \text{by (12.3.8)}$$

But, since $\langle x, y \rangle$ is not an edge in $R_i$, Lemma 12.2 says that $d_i(a, y) < d_i(a, x) + 1$, a contradiction. □

Applying Lemma 12.5 to the sink, it is clear that by augmenting using a blocking flow, the distance from source to sink must increase by at least one on each iteration. As observed earlier, this means that there can be at most $n - 1$ iterations of Dinic's algorithm before the distance to the sink becomes impossibly large, indicating that the sink is unreachable and the algorithm has terminated.

### Finding a blocking flow

The above work shows that a maximum flow can be found by finding a blocking flow in each of at most $n - 1$ residual graphs. There have been many suggestions by researchers as to how best to do this.

A blocking flow is a flow along shortest path edges that saturates at least one edge on every shortest path from source to sink. This suggests the following simple algorithm.

Given a residual graph $R_i$, delete from it all edges except those $\langle x, y \rangle$ such that $d_i(a, y) = d_i(a, x) + 1$. The remaining edges are exactly the shortest-path edges, and every path from source to sink is a shortest path.

Use any traversal algorithm to find any path from source to sink, find the minimum of the capacities of the edges on the path, subtract this quantity from all the capacities on the path, and delete any saturated edges. Then start another traversal, repeating until there is no path from source to sink.

For example, given the residual graph

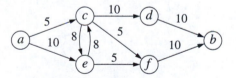

after deleting all non-shortest-path edges the graph becomes

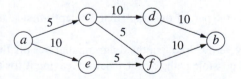

Augmenting along the path $\langle a, e, f, b \rangle$, subtracting the minimum capacity, and deleting the saturated edge produces

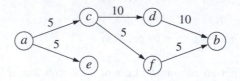

A second augment along the path $\langle a, c, f, b \rangle$ produces

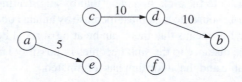

in which there is now no path from source to sink, so a blocking flow (but not a maximum flow) has been found.

Each successful traversal deletes at least one (saturated) edge, so there can be at most $m + 1$ traversals including the last, unsuccessful one. Each traversal costs $O(n + m)$ using depth-first or breadth-first search, which is $O(m)$ since only vertices reachable from $a$ are visited, hence the graph traversed is connected and $m \geq n - 1$. This gives a total cost of $O(m^2)$ for finding one blocking flow, and $O(nm^2)$ for finding a maximum flow.

It is fairly easy to improve on this. Use depth-first search for the traversal (it will still find shortest paths, since only shortest-path edges are used). If the traversal fails to find a path, a blocking flow has been found. Otherwise, the depth-first search is aborted at the moment a path from source to sink has been found:

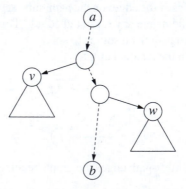

This diagram shows the part of the graph that the depth-first search has explored up to that moment.

Consider any vertex, like $v$ in the diagram, that lies off the path. Depth-first search explores all possible paths out of $v$ before leaving it for the last time; hence there can be no path from $v$ to the sink, for then depth-first search would have found that path before this path. When this path is augmented, the graph changes, but only by the deletion of saturated edges, and this cannot create a path from $v$ to the sink. Thus $v$ may be marked as useless and never visited again by any traversal during the entire course of this construction of a blocking flow.

In order to obtain a better time bound, it is necessary not just to mark $v$ as useless, but to actually delete all edges leading to it so that time will not be wasted following them during future traversals. A vertex may be declared useless at the moment the depth-first search backs out of it, having explored all paths leading from it without success; at that moment, all edges leading into it may be deleted.

The cost of one depth-first search, up to the moment when a path from source to sink is found and the search is aborted, may be divided into two parts: the on-path cost and the off-path cost. Clearly the on-path cost is $O(n)$, since the path has length $n - 1$ at most. The off-path cost could be as much as $O(n + m)$, but every vertex and edge encountered off-path will never be encountered again during the course of construction of this blocking flow; hence the total off-path cost over all traversals is $O(n + m)$.

As noted previously, there can be at most $m + 1$ traversals, since each deletes at least one edge, so the total on-path cost is $O(nm)$, the total cost of finding one blocking flow is $O(nm + n + m) = O(nm)$, and the cost of finding a maximum flow is $O(n^2 m)$.

It is probably clear to the reader that this is not likely to be the fastest possible algorithm for finding a blocking flow. Researchers have developed a series of faster and faster ways to do this. A description of the $O(nm\log n)$ method due to Sleator and Tarjan (1980), which is the current best, may be found in Tarjan (1983).

## 12.4 Matchings

Consider the following little problem. Four people, $A, B, C$, and $D$, want to go for a drive. Their car has four seats, two in the front and two in the back. Only $A$ and $B$ can drive; $B$ and $C$ refuse to sit in the back. Can everyone find a suitable seat?

This problem can be expressed very clearly using a graph:

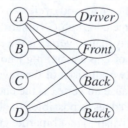

Down one side are the people, and down the other are the four seats. An edge joins a person to a seat if that person can sit in that seat. For example, $B$ can sit in either front seat, so $B$ is joined to them.

Clearly $C$ must sit in the non-driving front seat, which leaves only the driver's seat for $B$. $A$ and $D$ must therefore take the two back seats, so there are exactly two solutions:

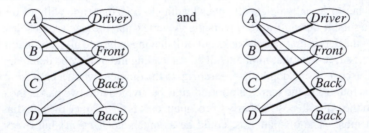

The bold edges connect the people with their seats.

Large versions of this problem are quite common in real life. For example, suppose a school has 50 teachers who each teach up to 30 classes (one group of students occupied for one hour) each week. The school offers 1490 classes to its students, which is feasible since $1490 < 50 \times 30$. However, each teacher is qualified to teach only some of the classes; some teach Mathematics and Computing only, others teach Science and Computing only, and so on. Can it be done? This is just a large version of the travelers-and-seats problem, with 1490 vertices down one side and 1500 vertices down the other.

A graph is *bipartite* if its vertices can be divided into two sets $V_1$ and $V_2$, called its *parts*, such that every edge joins a vertex in $V_1$ to a vertex in $V_2$, never $V_1$ to $V_1$ or $V_2$ to $V_2$. In the graph above, taking $V_1$ to be the people and $V_2$ to be the seats shows that the graph is bipartite.

In a bipartite graph, every cycle has even length, because every path crosses the gulf between $V_1$ and $V_2$ on each step, and so can only end where it began after an even number of steps. The converse is also true: if every cycle in a graph has even length, then the graph is bipartite. The proof of this divides the graph into two parts by letting $V_1$ be the vertices whose distance from some arbitrarily chosen vertex is even, and $V_2$ be the vertices whose distance is odd. Then it shows that any edge from $V_1$ to $V_1$ or from $V_2$ to $V_2$ must lie on an odd cycle.

A *matching* of an undirected graph $G$ (bipartite or otherwise) is a subset of the edges of $G$ with the property that no vertex is the endpoint of two or more of the edges. A *maximum matching* of $G$ is a matching whose number of edges is as large as possible. For example, the two solutions of the travelers-and-seats problem above are maximum matchings, because no vertex is the endpoint of two bold edges, and clearly there are as many bold edges as possible. In general, the size of a maximum matching can be at most $\min(|V_1|, |V_2|)$ in a bipartite graph, and at most $\lfloor |V|/2 \rfloor$ in a general graph.

For an example of a matching problem in a general graph, suppose a class of 12 students has to undertake a project, working in pairs. Not all students are compatible: some are too different to be able to work together, others simply hate each other. The data can be represented by a graph with one vertex for each student, and an edge joining two vertices whenever the corresponding students are compatible:

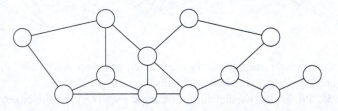

A maximum matching in this graph will be a way to pair the students together so that as many students as possible have a compatible partner:

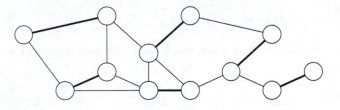

## The augmenting path method

Matching is a frustrating problem for algorithm designers. Divide-and-conquer is unable to find any useful way to divide the graph into two parts; dynamic programming seems to lead to an exponential number of subproblems; and an incremental algorithm of the second kind must begin by finding an edge which is in some maximum matching, something that noone knows how to do in any reasonable time.

The only possibility seems to be an incremental algorithm of the first kind, one which finds a sequence of larger and larger matchings, each a modification of the previous one:

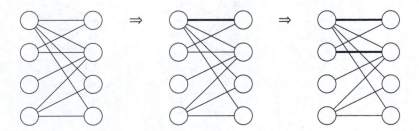

So far the modifications have been easy, but now comes

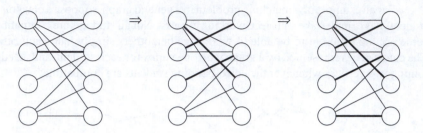

showing that radical modifications are sometimes necessary, and that careful attention needs to be given to how to do this.

Let $M_1$ and $M_2$ be two matchings for some graph $G$, bipartite or otherwise. In order to change $M_1$ into $M_2$, the edges of the set $M_1 - M_2$ must be deleted from $M_1$, and then the edges of $M_2 - M_1$ must be added. Together, these two sets form the *symmetric difference* of $M_1$ and $M_2$, denoted $\oplus$:

$$M_1 \oplus M_2 = (M_1 - M_2) \cup (M_2 - M_1)$$

Put another way, $M_1 \oplus M_2$ contains everything that lies in one set but not the other. For example,

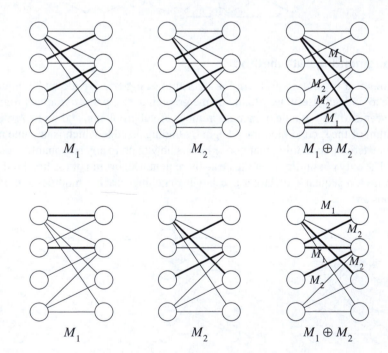

and

The edges of $M_1 \oplus M_2$ seem to form themselves into simple paths and cycles, with the edges coming alternately from $M_1$ and $M_2$. On reflection this is obviously always the case, because any vertex can be adjacent to at most one edge from $M_1$ and at most one edge from $M_2$ (because $M_1$ and $M_2$ are matchings), so every vertex has degree at most 2; and in any graph whose vertices all have degree at most 2, simple paths and cycles are the only possible structures.

The symmetric difference operator has a very useful property, easily proved: if $M_1 \oplus M_2 = S$, then $M_1 \oplus S = M_2$. This shows how to transform one matching $M_1$ into another one $M_2$, by finding an $S$ and calculating $M_1 \oplus S$:

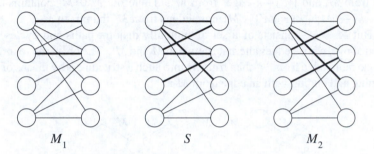

$$M_1 \qquad\qquad S \qquad\qquad M_2$$

This particular $S$ produces a larger matching $M_2$ from a smaller one $M_1$. This is because, viewed from the point of view of $M_1$, $S$ is a path beginning at an unmatched vertex, passing along an alternating sequence of edges not in $M_1$ and edges in $M_1$, ending at another unmatched vertex:

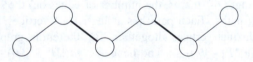

When $M_1$ is replaced by $M_1 \oplus S$, this path becomes

increasing the size of the matching by one.

A simple path of length at least one that alternates between matching edges and non-matching edges is called an *alternating path*. If the two endpoints are unmatched it is an *augmenting path*. By repeatedly finding and applying augmenting paths, larger and larger matchings can be constructed. But what if there is no augmenting path? The following key theorem, first proved in this form by Hopcroft and Karp (1973), shows that in that case, the matching has maximum size. In fact it shows much more, but its full power will not be used just yet.

**Theorem 12.9:** Let $G$ be any graph (bipartite or otherwise), and let $M$ be any matching in $G$. Suppose that some other matching $M'$ of larger size than $M$ also exists for $G$. Then $G$ contains a set of at least $|M'| - |M|$ disjoint augmenting paths for $M$, and the length of the shortest augmenting path for $M$ is at most $n/(|M'| - |M|) - 1$.

**Proof:** Consider $M \oplus M'$. From the formula

$$M \oplus M' = (M - (M \cap M')) \cup (M' - (M \cap M'))$$

which is easily proved, it is clear that, if $k = |M \cap M'|$, then $M \oplus M'$ contains $|M| - k$ edges from $M$, and $|M'| - k$ edges from $M'$. Therefore $M \oplus M'$ contains exactly $(|M'| - k) - (|M| - k) = |M'| - |M|$ more edges from $M'$ than from $M$.

But $M \oplus M'$ consists of a set of mutually disjoint paths and cycles, as explained above, whose edges alternate between $M$ and $M'$. The only way to introduce even one more edge from $M'$ than from $M$ into such a structure is by means of a path beginning and ending with an edge from $M'$:

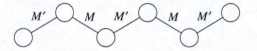

The path may have any odd length. There must be at least $|M'| - |M|$ such paths to account for the $|M'| - |M|$ more edges from $M'$ than from $M$ in $M \oplus M'$, and each such path is an augmenting path for $M$. Here then are the $|M'| - |M|$ augmenting paths for $M$ promised by the theorem.

Let $j$ be the length of (that is, the number of edges on) the shortest of these disjoint augmenting paths. Each path has at least $j + 1$ vertices, making at least $(j + 1)(|M'| - |M|)$ distinct vertices altogether. But the entire graph contains only $n$ vertices, so $(j + 1)(|M'| - |M|) \le n$ and hence $j \le n/(|M'| - |M|) - 1$. But $j$ is the length of some augmenting path for $M$, so the length of the shortest augmenting path for $M$ is at most $n/(|M'| - |M|) - 1$. $\qquad\square$

The work so far can be summarized as follows. A matching of maximum size in a graph $G$ (bipartite or otherwise) may be found by beginning with the empty matching and repeatedly finding and applying an augmenting path. Eventually, a matching will be reached for which there is no augmenting path, and at that point the theorem just proved shows that this matching has maximum size. This is the *augmenting path method* for constructing matchings, and it is due to Kuhn (1955), who actually solved the more general weighted problem; we will be considering that later in this section.

### Unweighted bipartite matching

The augmenting path method assumes that augmenting paths can be found, and it is at this point that bipartite graphs become much easier to deal with than general graphs. Here is an algorithm for finding an augmenting path in a bipartite graph $G$ with matching $M$. As will shortly be shown, this algorithm is guaranteed to find an augmenting path if one exists.

First, convert $G$ into a directed graph $G'$ by directing non-matching edges from left to right, and matching edges from right to left:

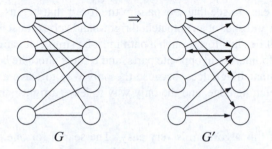

$$G \qquad\qquad G'$$

(It is at this point that we part company with general graphs: there is nothing to tell us which way to draw the arrows in a general graph.) Next, construct any spanning forest $F$ of $G'$ whose roots are the unmatched left-hand vertices of $G'$:

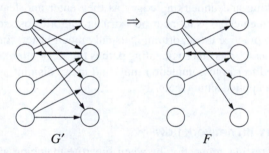

$$G' \qquad\qquad F$$

Strictly speaking, the forest can of course only go to vertices reachable from the set of unmatched left-hand vertices; but we require that it go to all such vertices. This step is easily accomplished using a traversal algorithm such as depth-first search or breadth-first search. Finally, if there is a path in $F$ from any unmatched left-hand vertex to any unmatched right-hand vertex, declare that path to be an augmenting path; otherwise declare that no augmenting path exists.

**Theorem 12.10:** The algorithm just given will find an augmenting path if and only if such a path exists.

**Proof:** If no augmenting path exists, then clearly this algorithm will not find one. We need prove only the converse, that if an augmenting path exists, one will be found.

So assume that an augmenting path $P$ exists in $G$. Think of $P$ as directed, from an unmatched left-hand vertex $v$ to an unmatched right-hand vertex $w$. $P$ must also be a path in $G'$, because the arrows of $G'$ go the same way that $P$ must: left to right on non-matching edges, right to left on matching edges.

Since $w$ is reachable from $v$ in $G'$ (via $P$), the spanning forest constructed in the second step of the algorithm must go to $w$. Since the forest is rooted at the unmatched left-hand vertices, this means that there is a path (through the forest) from some unmatched left-hand vertex $x$ to $w$. But this is a path from an unmatched left-hand vertex to an unmatched right-hand vertex, so the algorithm must declare that this path (or some other such path) is an augmenting path.

It is very easy to see that *any* path in the forest that begins at an unmatched left-hand vertex and ends at an unmatched right-hand vertex must be an augmenting path. Because it lies in a forest, such a path must be simple; it cannot have length 0 because the endpoints are in opposite parts; and it must alternate between matching edges and non-matching edges, because the only way to leave a left-hand vertex is via a non-matching edge, and the only way to leave a right-hand vertex is via a matching edge. □

The analysis of this algorithm is very easy. The search for one augmenting path requires at most one complete traversal of $G'$, costing $O(n + m)$ using any standard traversal algorithm. This will occur at most $n/2 + 1$ times, since the size of the current matching increases by 1 after each traversal, and can be at most $n/2$ in a bipartite graph (the extra 1 counts the final, unsuccessful traversal). Other operations (finding directions, marking and unmarking edges as they enter and leave the matching) are easily implemented so as to incur no extra asymptotic cost, so the total cost is $O(n(n + m))$. In practice the algorithm is usually much faster, since each traversal may be aborted as soon as one augmenting path is found, or alternatively, a traversal which is allowed to run to completion may find many disjoint augmenting paths, which can all be applied simultaneously.

### A connection with network flow

There is an interesting connection between bipartite matching and network flow. Take any instance of the unweighted bipartite matching problem:

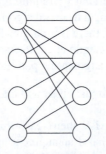

Add a source vertex at the left, and a sink vertex at the right. Connect them to the adjacent vertices, and make every edge in the resulting graph directed from left to right with capacity 1:

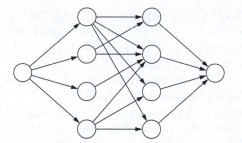

(All capacities are 1; they have been omitted for clarity.) It is quite easy now to see that every integral flow corresponds to a matching in the original graph, with the same size:

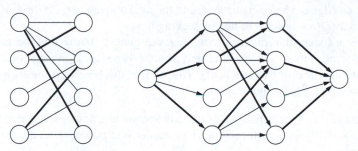

The bold edges denote matching edges as usual in the matching graph, and edges of flow 1 in the flow graph. So the unweighted bipartite matching problem can be converted (or *transformed*, in the terminology of Chapter 13) into a network flow problem, and solved in that way. In fact, the graph $G'$ constructed during the search for an augmenting path by the algorithm given earlier in this section is essentially the same as the residual graph that would be searched by a network flow algorithm at the same stage.

At first sight it might seem possible to solve weighted bipartite matching problems (presented below) with the same transformation, using the edge weights in the matching graph to define edge capacities in the flow graph. But this fails, since there is nothing to prevent an integral maximum flow from partly filling some edges, whereas in matchings an edge is used completely or not at all. (A related problem, *minimum-cost flow*, does permit such a transformation; it lies beyond our scope.) And there seems to be no transformation to network flow for general graphs, not even unweighted ones.

Now consider the algorithm for unweighted bipartite matching which applies the transformation given above, then runs Dinic's algorithm from Section 12.3, using the simple depth-first search method of finding a blocking flow given there. According to Section 12.3, the time complexity of this algorithm is $O(n^2(n + m))$, where $m$ has been replaced by $n + m$ to account for the extra $n$ edges added by the transformation. But it will now be shown that in this very special case, Dinic's algorithm in fact has $O(\sqrt{n}(n + m))$ time complexity. This is the fastest algorithm known for this problem. It was first presented, in a form unrelated to network flow, by Hopcroft and Karp (1973); the connection with Dinic's algorithm was pointed out later, by Even and Tarjan (1975).

It takes $O(n + m)$ time to convert the matching graph into a flow graph. The resulting graph has $n + 2$ vertices and $n + m$ edges.

Dinic's algorithm proceeds in stages; each stage except the last finds one blocking flow. The time complexity of each stage is $O(n + m)$ for the initial breadth-first search, plus the time taken to find a blocking flow by depth-first search. In Section 12.3, this latter was divided into two parts, the off-path cost, totalling $O(n + m)$, and the on-path cost, totalling $O(nm)$. However, in this special case, every on-path edge has capacity 1, is saturated by the flow sent along the path, and is deleted. Consequently, no edge can be on-path twice, and the total on-path cost is $O(n + m)$. Thus, it takes only $O(n + m)$ time to find a blocking flow.

Dinic's algorithm requires $O(n)$ stages in general, but in this special case it terminates much more quickly, after only about $1.4\sqrt{n}$ stages, giving a total cost for the whole algorithm of $O(\sqrt{n}(n + m))$. The proof of this is very ingenious, but, given results we already have, quite simple.

**Theorem 12.11:** When Dinic's algorithm is applied to a flow graph derived from a bipartite graph by the transformation given earlier, it terminates after approximately $\sqrt{2n}$ stages.

**Proof:** Run the algorithm for $k$ stages, where $k$ is an integer that will be chosen later. Pause, let $R$ be the residual graph at this point, and let $M$ be the matching corresponding to the current flow. It is assumed that $k$ is small enough to ensure that $M$ does not have maximum size.

The length of a shortest path from source to sink in the residual graph is initially 3, is always odd owing to the flow graph's bipartite antecedent, and increases by at least 1 during each stage, according to Lemma 12.5 from Section 12.3. So the length of a shortest path from source to sink in $R$ is at least $2k + 3$.

But now, every augmenting path for $M$ in $G$ corresponds to a path from source to sink in $R$. The corresponding paths have the same edges except that there are two extra edges in $R$, one coming from the source and the other going to the sink. So the length $l$ of a shortest augmenting path for $M$ in $G$ is at least $2k + 1$.

Let $M'$ be any maximum matching. By the assumption about $k$, $|M'| > |M|$, and so by Theorem 12.9,

$$l \leq n/(|M'| - |M|) - 1$$

from which comes $2k + 1 \leq n/(|M'| - |M|) - 1$, and

$$|M'| - |M| \leq n/(2k + 2)$$

Every stage of Dinic's algorithm increases the size of the current matching by at least

1, so the algorithm must halt after at most $|M'| - |M| + 1$ more stages, where the extra
1 counts the final, unsuccessful stage. Adding this to $k$, the number of stages so far,
gives at most

$$k + n/(2k + 2) + 1$$

stages altogether. Now $k$ may be chosen freely so as to minimize this expression, and
it is a simple matter to use calculus to show that the best choice for $k$ is approximately
$\sqrt{n/2} - 1$, giving approximately $\sqrt{2n}$ stages altogether. □

## Weighted bipartite matching

Sometimes the edges of a matching graph have weights, and the aim is to find a
matching of maximum total weight. For example, in the problem of grouping
children into compatible pairs mentioned at the beginning of this section, weights
might be used to express preferences for certain pairs. This problem is usually called
*weighted matching*, although the bipartite version has frequently been called the
*assignment problem*, taking the view that a bipartite matching is an assignment of
left-hand vertices to right-hand ones.

A little care is needed with the definition of the weighted matching problem.
Consider this graph:

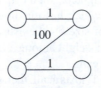

The overall maximum weight matching has size 1 and weight 100. If a size 2
matching is required, the best one has weight only 2. So we can ask for a matching of
maximum weight overall, or we can ask for a matching of maximum weight among
all matchings of a given size; but we cannot ask for a matching which has maximum
weight and size simultaneously.

Fortunately, the algorithm to be presented finesses these distinctions by
successively finding a matching of maximum weight among all matchings of size 0,
then of size 1, then of size 2, and so on:

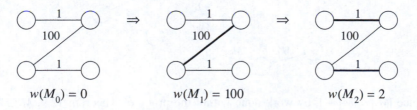

Those who need a matching of maximum weight overall can select the largest in weight of all these matchings; those who need a matching of maximum weight among all matchings of maximum size can select the last matching generated before the algorithm halts. The algorithm is due to Kuhn (1955), who named it the *Hungarian method* in recognition of the earlier work of the mathematicians König and Egerváry.

The algorithm is simple to state. For any set of edges $S$, let $w(S)$ be their total weight. To find, for all $k \geq 0$, a matching $M_k$ of maximum weight among all matchings of size $k$, proceed as follows. There is always exactly one matching of size zero, namely the empty matching, so let $M_0 = \{\}$. Given $M_k$, find an augmenting path $P$ such that $w(M_k \oplus P)$ is as large as possible, and let $M_{k+1} = M_k \oplus P$. Repeat until there is no augmenting path.

Previous work shows that $M_0$, $M_1$, $M_2$, and so on is indeed a sequence of matchings of size 0, 1, 2, and so on, and that the algorithm terminates only when no matching of larger size exists. It is also clear that $M_{k+1}$ has maximum weight among all matchings of size $k + 1$ that have the form $M_k \oplus P$ for some augmenting path $P$, because that is merely a restatement of the definition of $M_{k+1}$. But there could conceivably be matchings of larger weight than $w(M_{k+1})$, not obtainable by augmenting $M_k$ with a single path in this way. The following theorem rules out this possibility, thereby proving the correctness of the Hungarian method.

**Theorem 12.12:** Let $G$ be a weighted graph (bipartite or otherwise), and let $M$ be a matching in $G$ of size $k \geq 0$ which has maximum weight among all matchings of size $k$. Then, if a matching of size $k + 1$ exists at all, a matching $M \oplus P$ of size $k + 1$ exists which has maximum weight among all matchings of size $k + 1$, where $P$ consists of a single augmenting path.

**Proof:** If a matching of size $k + 1$ exists at all, then a matching $M'$ of size $k + 1$ exists which has maximum weight among all matchings of size $k + 1$.

Consider $M \oplus M'$. As usual, this symmetric difference of two matchings consists of a set of disjoint simple paths and cycles whose edges alternate between $M$ and $M'$:

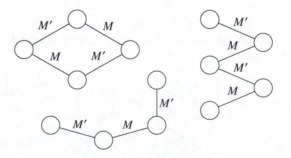

Since $|M'| = |M| + 1$, by work done within the proof of Theorem 12.9, $M \oplus M'$

contains exactly one more edge from $M'$ than from $M$, and it contains at least one path $P$ of odd length which has one more edge from $M'$ than from $M$.

Let $C = M \oplus M' - P$. Since $M \oplus M'$ has one more edge from $M'$ than from $M$, and so does $P$, $C$ has an equal number of edges from $M$ and from $M'$. For future reference, note that since $P \subseteq M \oplus M'$, $C = M \oplus M' - P = M \oplus M' \oplus P$, and by the properties of $\oplus$ we can conclude $C \oplus M' = M \oplus P$.

Let $C_1$ be the edges of $C$ that come from $M$, and let $C_2$ be the edges of $C$ that come from $M'$. Then $w(M' \oplus C) = w(M') - w(C_2) + w(C_1)$. But $M' \oplus C$ is a matching of the same size as $M'$, and since $M'$ has maximum weight among all matchings of its size, $w(M' \oplus C) \leq w(M')$. It follows that $w(C_1) \leq w(C_2)$.

But now an identical argument, applied to $M$ instead of $M'$, shows that $w(C_2) \leq w(C_1)$. Therefore $w(C_2) = w(C_1)$ and $w(M' \oplus C) = w(M')$. So $M' \oplus C$ also has maximum weight, and since $M' \oplus C = M \oplus P$, the theorem is proved. $\square$

Now that the Hungarian method has been proved correct, the remaining problem is to find an augmenting path $P$ for a maximum-weight matching $M$ such that $w(M \oplus P)$ is as large as possible. Once again, this is beyond our scope for the case of general graphs, but in bipartite graphs it is quite easy to do, as follows.

To the graph $G$ containing $M$, add a start vertex $a$ at the left and a destination vertex $b$ at the right, connected by edges of weight zero to neighboring unmatched vertices. Make non-matching edges directed from left to right with their weights negated, and matching edges directed from right to left with their weights unmodified. For example, if $G$ is

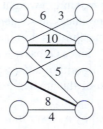

then the transformed version $G'$ is

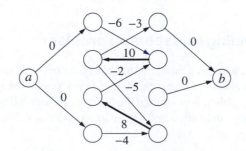

By arguments familiar from the treatment of unweighted bipartite matching early in this section, every augmenting path $P$ in $G$ corresponds to a path $P'$ from $a$ to $b$ in $G'$, and vice versa. Furthermore, $w(M \oplus P) - w(M) = -w(P')$. For example,

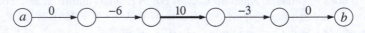

in $G'$ has $w(P') = -6 + 10 - 3 = 1$, and applying the corresponding $P$ to $M$ causes a change in weight of $w(M \oplus P) - w(M) = 6 - 10 + 3 = -1$. Thus, the path $P'$ of minimum total weight corresponds to the desired augmenting path $P$, the one for which $w(M \oplus P)$ is as large as possible.

$P'$ can be found by applying a shortest path algorithm to $G'$, with start vertex $a$. Section 12.1 offers a choice of three algorithms. In this application, $G'$ is not acyclic, and it contains negative edges, so the Bellman–Moore algorithm is indicated.

The Bellman–Moore algorithm will fail if $G'$ contains a negative cycle, but luckily this cannot be. For suppose that $G'$ contains a negative cycle $C$, such as

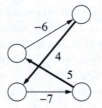

Then $M \oplus C$ is a matching of size $|M|$ and weight strictly greater than $w(M)$, contradicting the fact that $M$ has maximum weight among all matchings of its size.

The Hungarian method produces a sequence of up to $\lfloor n/2 \rfloor$ matchings before stopping. The cost per matching is dominated by the cost of applying the Bellman–Moore algorithm to $G'$. Since $G'$ has $n + 2$ vertices and up to $m + n$ edges, the cost of the Bellman–Moore algorithm is $O(n(n + m))$ by the analysis given in Section 12.1. Thus the total cost of this implementation of the Hungarian method is $O(n^2(n + m))$.

This result can be improved by a clever transformation of the edge costs into non-negative equivalents, thus permitting Dijkstra's algorithm to be used instead of the Bellman–Moore algorithm. The details may be found in Tarjan (1983).

## 12.5 The traveling salesperson problem

This chapter concludes with a problem that has never been satisfactorily solved, despite the ingenious efforts of researchers over many years: the *traveling salesperson problem*. The problem is to arrange the itinerary of a traveling salesperson, who wants to visit some widely scattered towns in an order which minimizes the total amount of traveling.

Despite this somewhat whimsical description, the traveling salesperson problem has important applications. Consider, for example, a computer-controlled spot welding machine. Its task is to make a number of spot welds on a metal plate. The welder begins in a rest position away from the plate and ends in the same position, so that the plate can be removed and the next one loaded. Here is a typical plate and a path which seems to visit all the welding sites economically:

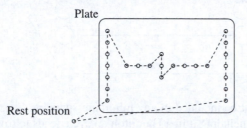

By minimizing the total distance the welder has to travel, the time taken to complete the job is minimized. Similar situations arise frequently in manufacturing.

An instance of the traveling salesperson problem may be represented in the usual way: each town is a vertex of an undirected graph; edge $e$ of cost $c(e)$ joins two vertices when there is a road of length $c(e)$ between the corresponding towns. In the spot welding case, every pair of weld points (including the rest position) would be connected with an edge whose cost is the distance between the two points.

A *Hamiltonian cycle* of a graph $G$ is a cycle which visits every vertex of $G$ exactly once. (The name honors the mathematician W. R. Hamilton.) The problem is to find a Hamiltonian cycle whose total cost is minimum. For example, given

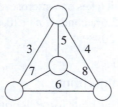

there are three different Hamiltonian cycles:

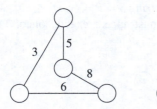 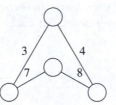 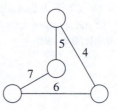

Curiously, they all happen to have cost 22, so they are all minimum.

The traveling salesperson problem is hard, as this example tries to show:

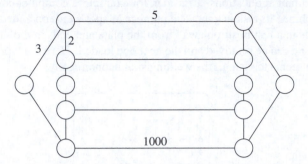

The edge of cost 2 must be included in any minimum spanning tree, by Theorem 12.4. However, rashly including it in a Hamiltonian cycle leads to trouble later: it is not hard to verify that the edge of cost 1000 must then be included as well. There seems to be no clever theorem which tells how to choose the right edges.

The traveling salesperson problem is one of a large number of problems, from all fields of computer science, which are known to be equally hard, and for which no efficient algorithms are known. They are the *NP-complete problems* (although technically the traveling salesperson problem is called *NP-hard*). Their theory is regrettably beyond the scope of this book; see Garey and Johnson (1979).

The traveling salesperson problem can be solved by 'brute force search,' which means generating all the permutations of the $n$ vertices, checking each permutation to see if it defines a Hamiltonian cycle, and if so what its cost is, and remembering the smallest. Unfortunately, there are $n!$ permutations, so this algorithm is ruled out for all but small $n$. For example, if it takes one microsecond to process one permutation, then the algorithm takes about 3.6 seconds if $n = 10$, about six months if $n = 15$, and about one million years if $n = 20$.

## A dynamic programming algorithm

An interesting improvement to the brute force algorithm has been made by Held and Karp (1962), who noticed some duplication in the method and were able to eliminate it using dynamic programming. Let $S = \{x_1, x_2, \ldots, x_k\}$ be a subset of the vertices of $G = \langle V, E \rangle$. Say that a path $P$ goes from $v$ to $w$ *covering* $S$ if $P = \langle v, x_1, \ldots, x_k, w \rangle$, where the $x_i$ may appear in any order, but each must appear exactly once. For example, the path

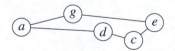

goes from $a$ to $a$, covering $\{c, d, e, g\}$.

The next step is to define $d(v, w, S)$ to be the total cost of a shortest path from $v$ to $w$, covering $S$. If there is no such path, let $d(v, w, S) = \infty$. A minimum Hamiltonian cycle $C_{min}$ of $G$ must have total cost

$$c(C_{min}) = d(v, v, V - \{v\})$$

where $v$ is any vertex of $G$, and this provides a way to calculate $C_{min}$. If $|V| = 1$, clearly $c(C_{min}) = 0$. Otherwise the following recurrence holds for $d(v, w, S)$:

$$d(v, w, \{\}) = c(v, w)$$
$$d(v, w, S) = \min_{x \in S}[c(v, x) + d(x, w, S - \{x\})]$$

where $c(v, w)$ is the cost of edge $\{v, w\}$ if it exists, or $\infty$ otherwise. The second line is for non-empty $S$; it says that a shortest path from $v$ to $w$ covering $S$ first goes to some vertex $x$ in $S$, then follows a shortest path from $x$ to $w$, covering $S - \{x\}$.

The recursive evaluation of this recurrence equation is straightforward, and by keeping track of the value of $x$ which minimized $d(v, w, S)$ at each stage, a minimum Hamiltonian cycle can be found along with its cost. Unfortunately, it can be shown that $d(v, w, \{\})$ is evaluated $(n - 1)!$ times, where $n$ is the number of vertices in $G$, during the evaluation of $d(v, v, V - \{v\})$ (Exercise 12.16). The recurrence equation searches through all Hamiltonian cycles, and no improvement has been made.

But now, observe that $d(x, y, \{\})$ can only take on $n(n - 1)$ values – one for each pair of vertices $x$ and $y$. There must be a great deal of repeated evaluation of subproblems going on, so the situation calls for dynamic programming – solving all the subproblems where $|S| = 0$ first, then $|S| = 1$, and so on.

How many subproblems $d(x, y, S)$ are there? $S$ could be any one of the $2^{n-1}$ distinct subsets of $V - \{v\}$, while $x$ could be any one of the $n$ vertices of $G$. A close look at the recurrence equation above will show that $y$ must always equal $v$; so this gives $n2^{n-1}$ subproblems, and in fact there are somewhat fewer than this, owing to the restriction $x \notin S$.

To determine the value of $d(v, w, S)$ using the recurrence equation, once all the $d(x, w, S - \{x\})$ are known, takes $O(n)$ time. With a careful implementation, this leads to an $O(n^2 2^{n-1})$ algorithm for the traveling salesperson problem.

Although this algorithm is still hopelessly infeasible for large $n$, and there is the added problem of a huge memory requirement for the table, it is very much faster than brute force search. For example, if it takes one microsecond for each of the $n^2 2^{n-1}$ steps, then $n = 20$ can be solved in about three minutes.

## An approximate solution to the traveling salesperson problem

Since all known algorithms for the traveling salesperson problem are infeasible, it becomes worthwhile to ask whether the problem can be solved efficiently on the average, or whether a good but non-minimum Hamiltonian cycle can be found quickly, and so on. The remainder of this section is devoted to a method which is guaranteed to produce a Hamiltonian cycle of reasonably low cost.

An assumption about $G$ is needed that fortunately is justifiable in nearly all applications. It is that $G$ is a complete graph whose edges satisfy the *triangle inequality*: for every three vertices $u$, $v$ and $w$, the relation $c(u, w) \leq c(u, v) + c(v, w)$ must hold. For example, the assumption holds if vertices are points in space, and costs are distances between points:

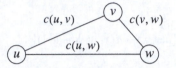

since there is a way to get from any point to any other, and the shortest path between two points is the direct one.

Here is the method. First, find a minimum spanning tree $T$ of $G$:

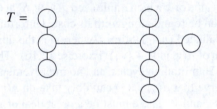

Next, construct a cycle $P$ by a clockwise traversal of $T$:

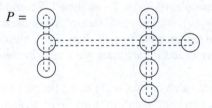

Finally, transform $P$ into a Hamiltonian cycle $C$ by cutting corners to avoid revisiting any vertices:

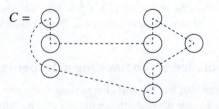

The shortcut edges must exist because the graph is assumed to be complete, and the triangle inequality guarantees that cutting corners cannot increase the cost, so $c(C) \le c(P) = 2c(T)$.

Take any minimum Hamiltonian cycle $C_{min}$. Deleting any edge $e$ of $C_{min}$ gives a (skew) spanning tree of $G$. Since $T$ is a minimum spanning tree,

$$c(T) \le c(C_{min} - \{e\})$$

$$\le c(C_{min})$$

and so $c(C) \le 2c(C_{min})$. In other words, the Hamiltonian cycle $C$ has no more than twice the minimum possible cost. The reader is urged to try out this algorithm on the spot welding example at the beginning of this section.

Christofides (1976) has shown how to tighten up this method to produce a Hamiltonian cycle $C$ satisfying $c(C) \le 1.5c(C_{min})$. His method requires a matching of minimum total cost in a general graph, which is a trivial variation of the weighted matching problem discussed in Section 12.4.

The first step is to find a minimum spanning tree $T$ as before:

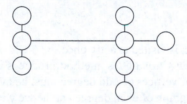

Next, identify the vertices of odd degree in $T$ (shown in gray):

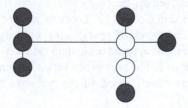

Find a matching $M$ of maximum size and minimum total cost for these 'odd' vertices, and add its edges to those of $T$:

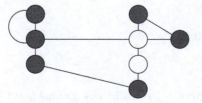

Parallel edges are acceptable at this stage. Next find an *Euler cycle* for this graph, that is, a cycle that traverses every edge exactly once:

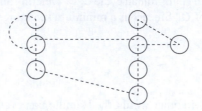

Select a vertex that the Euler cycle visits more than once, and construct a shortcut that eliminates one of the visits:

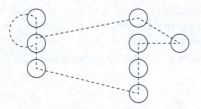

Repeat until every vertex is visited exactly once.

Here is a proof that Christofides' method produces a Hamiltonian cycle. In any graph, the number of vertices of odd degree must be even, so the matching step is applied to a complete graph of even degree and hence will produce a set of edges $M$ that touches each odd vertex exactly once. When these edges are added to those of $T$, they increase the degree of every odd vertex by one, creating a connected graph in which every vertex has even degree. By a well-known theorem from graph theory, due to Euler and proved in Cohen (1978) or any graph theory text, such a graph contains an Euler cycle, and the proof provides a simple algorithm for constructing one. Shortcutting a vertex that appears more than once on the cycle cannot disconnect the cycle or cause it to fail to visit every vertex. Eventually, after sufficiently many shortcuts, every vertex must appear on the cycle exactly once, so the cycle is a Hamiltonian cycle.

The cost of the Christofides cycle $C$ is clearly at most $c(T) + c(M)$, since it is obtained from $T$ plus $M$ by shortcuts. If it can be shown that $c(M) \le 0.5c(C_{min})$, the result will follow since then

$$c(C) \le c(T) + c(M)$$

$$\le c(C_{min}) + 0.5c(C_{min})$$

$$= 1.5c(C_{min})$$

To prove that $c(M) \le 0.5c(C_{min})$, consider any optimal tour $C_{min}$:

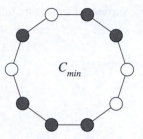

The vertices of odd degree in $T$ are shown in gray. Apply shortcuts to $C_{min}$ to produce another cycle $C'$ that bypasses all the even vertices:

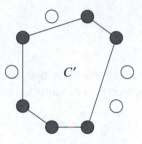

Clearly $c(C') \leq c(C_{min})$ since $C'$ is produced from $C_{min}$ by shortcuts. Taking every second edge of $C'$ produces a matching $M_1$ of the odd vertices:

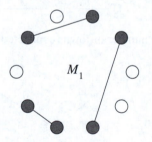

The unused edges of $C'$ form a second matching $M_2$ of the same vertices:

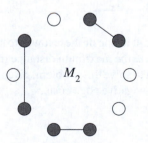

Now $M$ is a matching of these vertices of minimum total cost, so $c(M) \leq c(M_1)$ and $c(M) \leq c(M_2)$. Hence

$$2c(M) \leq c(M_1) + c(M_2)$$

$$= c(C')$$

$$\leq c(C_{min})$$

and so $c(M) \leq 0.5c(C_{min})$, and the cost of the Christofides cycle $C$ is at most $1.5c(C_{min})$. This is perhaps the deepest result known about the traveling salesperson problem. Twenty years have passed since it was obtained, but no improvement on it has been found.

## 12.6 Exercises

12.1    Trace Dijkstra's shortest path algorithm on the following graph. Each undirected edge corresponds to two directed edges.

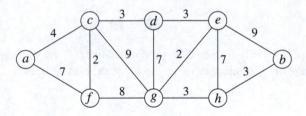

12.2    A region contains a number of towns connected by roads:

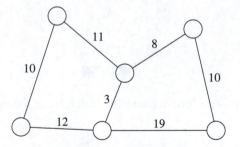

A hospital is to be built in one of these towns to service them all. Its site must be chosen to minimize the maximum distance from any town to the hospital. Devise an algorithm to solve this problem, given an arbitrary road map which is a graph with non-negative edge costs.

12.3    Trace Kruskal's algorithm for minimum spanning trees on the graph

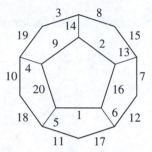

12.4    Repeat the previous question, using Prim's algorithm starting anywhere.

12.5    Consider finding a minimum spanning forest under the restriction that a specified subset of the edges must be included or excluded. Can Kruskal's or Prim's algorithm be adapted to handle these restrictions?

12.6    Does the loop invariant of Prim's algorithm, plus termination, guarantee that every edge in the connected component of $G$ containing $a$ has been inserted into $X$ or $Y$? Or could the algorithm overlook some edges?

12.7    The analysis of Prim's algorithm says that there are at most $m - (n - 1)$ *decrease_key* operations. Since $G$ is undirected, each edge is represented by two edge records. So shouldn't this be $2m - (n - 1)$?

12.8    Prove the following generalization of Theorem 12.6:

**Theorem 12.13:** Let $G = \langle V, E \rangle$ be a graph, and suppose there are two subsets of $E$, called $X$ and $Y$, that obey the following condition: there exists a minimum spanning forest $F$ of $G$ which contains all of the edges of $X$, and none of the edges of $Y$. Let $C$ be any simple cycle of $G$ not containing any edges from $Y$, and let $e$ be an edge of maximum cost among the edges of $C$ not in $X$. Then there exists a minimum spanning forest $F'$ of $G$ which contains all of the edges of $X$, and none of the edges of $Y \cup \{e\}$.

12.9    Investigate algorithms for the minimum spanning tree problem based primarily on the theorem from the preceding question.

12.10   Trace the augmenting path method for network flow on the following graph. Give the current flow graph and its residual graph at each stage.

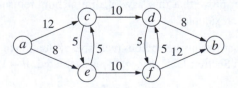

12.11   Repeat the previous question, but follow Dinic's algorithm.

12.12   Trace the augmenting path method for unweighted bipartite matching on

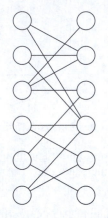

12.13   In applications it often happens that one wants to maintain a maximum size matching under such operations as the addition or deletion of a vertex or an edge. Can you find ways to implement these operations more quickly than by rebuilding the entire matching from the beginning again?

12.14   Trace the Hungarian method for weighted matching on this graph:

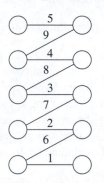

12.15   It is noticeable while tracing the Hungarian method that, as the size of the matching increases, its weight also increases up to some point and thereafter decreases. In fact, the sequence of values $w(M_i) - w(M_{i-1})$ seems to be monotone decreasing, which if true would imply the previous observation. Can you prove that this 'law of diminishing returns' always holds, or find a counterexample?

12.16   Show that, during the obvious recursive evaluation of the recurrence equation given in Section 12.5, $d(v, w, \{\})$ is evaluated $(n - 1)!$ times.

12.17  Call a path which visits every vertex exactly once a *salesperson path*:

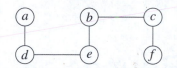

One idea for an algorithm for finding a salesperson path of minimum cost, modelled on Kruskal's algorithm for minimum spanning trees, is to examine the edges in order from smallest cost to largest. If the inclusion of an edge would create a three-way junction or a loop in the growing path, it is discarded; otherwise it is added to the path.

(a)  Trace the algorithm on the following graph. It turns out that the algorithm does find a minimum salesperson path in this graph.

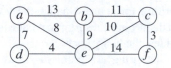

(b)  There are graphs, even connected graphs, for which no salesperson path exists. For example,

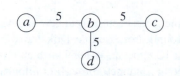

is such a graph. Find a graph which shows that the algorithm may fail to find *any* salesperson path, even when such a path exists.

(c)  Find a graph which shows that the algorithm may fail to find a minimum salesperson path, even if it does find a salesperson path.

12.18  Let $T$ be a free tree with edge costs, and define the *diameter* of $T$ to be the cost of the longest simple path in $T$. For example, the diameter of

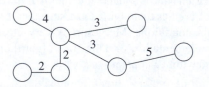

is 12. Devise a linear algorithm for finding the diameter of a tree.

# Chapter 13

# Lower Bounds

Enjoyable as it is to study elegant and efficient algorithms, such as Quicksort or Dijkstra's algorithm for shortest paths, the very ingenuity we admire in these algorithms raises a disturbing question: to what extent is algorithm design dependent upon the brilliant idea, the lucky guess?

Even more disturbing are problems for which no efficient algorithm has ever been found, despite the efforts of researchers over many years. The traveling salesperson problem (Section 12.5) is perhaps the best known such problem – and it is of great practical importance. Has a brilliant idea been missed, or is no efficient algorithm possible?

After a problem has been solved, new and better algorithms and implementations may still be found. For example, Dijkstra's algorithm for finding shortest paths in graphs (Section 12.1) began in 1959 with an $O(n^2)$ implementation based on an unsorted array, then progressed through $O(m\log n)$ and $O(m\log_{2+m/n} n)$ implementations to the current best, $O(n\log n + m)$ using Fibonacci heaps, in 1983. Will the algorithms of today be superseded by more efficient ones in the future? For which problems is it worth trying to find better algorithms?

Ultimately, such questions can only be answered by a theorem of the form 'All algorithms for problem $P$ have complexity $T(n) \geq f(n)$.' A function $f(n)$ appearing in such a theorem is called a *lower bound on the complexity of P*. If we are so fortunate as to have an algorithm of complexity $f(n)$ for $P$, that algorithm is *optimal*: it cannot be bettered.

This chapter introduces some techniques that have been developed for finding lower bounds, and applies them with some success. It will be shown, for example, that under certain conditions, Mergesort is very close to optimal, and that the $O(n\log n + m)$ implementation of Dijkstra's algorithm is asymptotically optimal (that is, optimal to within a constant factor).

## 13.1 Models of computation

When some algorithm's characteristic operation is declared to be realistic, an assumption is being made about the class of physical machines on which the algorithm will be run. For example, in the analysis of binary search, one comparison between keys was considered realistic. This ruled out physical machines whose memory consists of a magnetic tape, because on those machines the cost of binary search is dominated by winding the tape backwards and forwards.

Whenever $f(n)$ is asserted to be a lower bound on the complexity of a problem $P$, it is necessary to specify these assumptions about the physical machines. Presumably a machine which implements the operation 'solve $P$' for arbitrary instances of $P$ in $O(1)$ time would be excluded, for example, unless $P$ was very trivial. No attempt will be made to use the laws of physics to exclude such machines.

This set of assumptions is called a *model of computation*, and it can be clearly described by an ADT defining the permitted assembly level operations:

**class interface** *TYPICAL_MACHINE*

*add_integer(x, y: DATA_ADDRESS)*
*jump_if_zero(x: DATA_ADDRESS; a: INSTRUCTION_NUMBER)*
*...*

**end** -- *TYPICAL_MACHINE*

*By definition*, each operation has a certain cost, which at this low level is usually $O(1)$. The only algorithms allowed are those which can be expressed as a numbered sequence of these operations; the complexity of such an algorithm is the total cost of the operations it executes.

This places the study of lower bounds on firm ground, because it precisely specifies what algorithms are permitted and how their cost is to be measured. The theorems may now take the form, 'With respect to model of computation $M, f(n)$ is a lower bound on the complexity of problem $P$.'

A model of computation may be a real, physically existing machine, in which case the ADT, the meaning of each operation, and the costs may all be obtained from the manufacturer's documentation. When this is done, the following problem always arises. The types *DATA_ADDRESS* and *MACHINE_INTEGER* have fixed upper limits, typically $2^{32} - 1$ or $2^{64} - 1$ at the time of writing. To remove this restriction, which prevents the solution of truly arbitrary instances of problems, it is necessary to construct a *virtual machine*, which is just a second ADT implemented using the operations of the first, whose data types do not carry this restriction. There is no difficulty in doing this – arbitrary-length arithmetic, for example, is quite easy to implement – but the price is an increase in the cost of each operation from $O(1)$ to $O(\log N)$, where $N$ is the largest number or address needed to solve the particular instance. A few operations, notably multiplication and division, become more expensive still.

The analyses of this book have all been based on a somewhat unrealistic model of computation, in which arbitrary instances may be solved, yet only $O(1)$ is charged per operation. This model is useful because in practice integers or addresses larger than $2^{32} - 1$ are never needed, and it is best not to clutter up the analyses with allowances for them. Readers who are uncomfortable with this model can easily redo the analyses, charging $O(\log N)$, or whatever is appropriate, per operation.

Throughout this book a *sequential* model of computation is used; that is, it is assumed that only one computational process exists. There are also *concurrent* models, which allow many processes to run simultaneously. Their theory is quite well developed, and will increase in importance as parallel and distributed computing become more widespread; but they are beyond the scope of this book.

## 13.2 Adversary bounds

Consider the problem of summing the array *entries.item*(1..*n*). Every element contributes something to the result, so every element must be examined. But, under any reasonable sequential model of computation, only a fixed number of elements can be examined in $O(1)$ time. Therefore any algorithm for this problem is $\Omega(n)$; in other words, its complexity is bounded below by some constant times *n*.

This argument is called an *input lower bound*. It is extremely general, and it can be used to derive an $\Omega(n)$ bound for most problems. Not every algorithm examines all of its input, however: binary search, for example, does not.

Another, quite useful way to express this argument is to use an *adversary*: someone who watches as the algorithm runs, and tries to break it. For the summing problem, this version of the argument is as follows. Suppose some algorithm does not examine every element. The adversary watches and, when the algorithm terminates, it moves in and changes the value of some unexamined element. The algorithm is run again, and it gives the same result as before, since it does not see the change. But the true result has changed, so the algorithm is incorrect. It follows that any correct algorithm examines every element, and so is $\Omega(n)$.

If something more specific than an asymptotic bound is wanted, it is necessary to be more specific about the model of computation. Consider finding the index of a minimum element of the array *entries.item*(1..*n*), assuming that

**if** *entries.item*(*i*) < *entries.item*(*j*) **then** *jump to x*

is the only operation capable of examining *entries* in any way. (Recall that assembly level operations are being used here.) This rules out, for example, hashing the values or comparing sums of values, and it is reasonable to ask what point there is in finding a lower bound under such a restrictive model. The answer is that one algorithm that obeys this model already exists, and it makes $n - 1$ comparisons (Section 2.1); we want to know whether it can be improved, but we don't want to become side-tracked into difficult questions about the usefulness of comparing sums of elements.

Clearly at least $\lceil n/2 \rceil$ of these comparisons must be made, for otherwise some element is left unexamined. But an adversary can do better than this. Represent the elements of *entries* by nodes of a directed graph $G$, and whenever the algorithm discovers that *entries.item(i)* < *entries.item(j)*, draw an edge from *entries.item(i)* to *entries.item(j)*. When the algorithm terminates, mark the element that it declares to be a minimum with an $m$:

Now the adversary examines this graph. If it is not connected, take any component $C$ not connected to $m$. The values in $C$ may all be made smaller than $m$, without contradicting what the algorithm discovered. Run the algorithm again: it declares $m$ to be a minimum element, which is incorrect. It follows that $G$ must be connected, hence that at least $n - 1$ comparisons are necessary, and that the algorithm from Section 2.1 is optimal.

Consider the problem of merging two sorted sequences, containing $n$ and $m$ elements respectively, into one sorted sequence:

$$\langle 28, 35, 50, 62 \rangle + \langle 11, 45 \rangle \Rightarrow \langle 11, 28, 35, 45, 50, 62 \rangle$$

This problem was studied in Section 9.3, where an algorithm of worst-case complexity $W(n, m) = n + m - 1$ comparisons was presented. Is this optimal?

If $n$ and $m$ are very different, the algorithm is certainly not optimal:

$$\langle 28, 35, 50, 62 \rangle + \langle 45 \rangle \Rightarrow \langle 28, 35, 45, 50, 62 \rangle$$

If $m = 1$, the algorithm degenerates to linear search, with worst-case complexity $W(n) = n$. Binary search would be much more efficient, and this suggests that it would be better to store the larger sequence in a binary search tree and insert the elements of the smaller sequence into it, but that idea will not be pursued here.

Merging is most often done on sequences of equal length, so it would seem to be a good idea to consider what can be done with the assumption $n = m$. Suppose the two sorted sequences are $\langle a_1, \dots, a_n \rangle$ and $\langle b_1, \dots, b_n \rangle$. Let the adversary choose the values to ensure that

$$a_1 < b_1 < a_2 < \dots < a_n < b_n$$

Every correct algorithm must compare $a_1$ with $b_1$, $b_1$ with $a_2$, and so on to $a_n$ with $b_n$ at some stage. For suppose on the contrary that some merging algorithm does not compare $b_i$ with $a_{i+1}$ (the case of $a_i$ and $b_i$ is similar). Since no elements lie between $b_i$ and $a_{i+1}$, the adversary is free to exchange their values without contradicting what the algorithm discovered. Thus the algorithm is incorrect.

Therefore at least $2n - 1$ comparisons between elements must be made in the worst case, and so the merging algorithm of Section 9.3 is optimal when $n = m$. Knuth (1973b) reports that this result was discovered independently by R. L. Graham and R. M. Karp about 1968.

## 13.3 Decision trees

Suppose that a problem specification says that, in certain circumstances, the result is to be 0, otherwise the result is to be 1. It seems intuitively clear that any algorithm for this problem must decide at some point whether the circumstances hold or not: the algorithm must make a test with a boolean outcome. If more than two distinct values for the result are possible, more tests must be made.

Unfortunately for this argument, an algorithm can produce a large number of distinct results without making any tests, just by echoing its input. However, by adopting a model of computation that restricts the ways in which an algorithm may access its input, some valuable lower bounds can be derived.

Let $I$ be an instance of some problem $P$. Divide $I$ into two parts, the *free part* $f$, and the *restricted part* $r$, so that $I = \langle f, r \rangle$. Adopt a model of computation which allows an algorithm to use $f$ in any way it wishes, but restricts all access to $r$ to operations of the form

**if** $b(v, f, r)$ **then** *jump to* $x$

where $b(v, f, r)$, hereafter called a *restricted test*, is an arbitrary boolean function of $v$ (the working variables of the program), $f$, and $r$. The restricted tests must be free of side-effects. The number of restricted tests executed is taken to be the measure of complexity. This is called the *decision tree* model of computation, for a reason that will become clear shortly.

For example, let $P$ be the problem of sorting the array *entries. item*$(1..n)$ into non-decreasing order. Let $n$ itself be free, but make the values within *entries* restricted. That is, these values may only be accessed in boolean tests such as

**if** *entries.item*$(i)$ < *entries.item*$(j)$ **then** ...

or

**if** *entries.item*$(i)/i$ + *entries.item*$(j)/j$ > $n$ **then** ...

Notice that this model prohibits assignments of restricted input, so the sorted sequence can never be written to output. Instead, the output will be a permutation of the numbers 1 to $n$ which indicates how to rearrange *entries* into sorted order.

It is easy to verify that all of the sorting algorithms of Chapter 9 except radix sort can be implemented using this model of computation. (They must be modified to manipulate an array of indices of *entries*, not the elements of *entries* itself.) Another

example is the problem of finding a shortest path spanning tree in a directed graph
$G$ with edge costs. Here it is appropriate to let $G$ itself be free, but make the edge
costs restricted. An algorithm may access the edge costs, in tests such as

>**if** *length of path $P_1$ < length of path $P_2$* **then** ...

which is a comparison of sums of edge costs, selected by the working variables $P_1$
and $P_2$. Dijkstra's algorithm is implementable under this model, a fact which will be
exploited in Section 13.5 to derive a lower bound on its complexity.

As a simple example of an algorithm implemented under the decision tree
model of computation, consider this algorithm for finding the index of a minimum
element of the array *entries.item*$(1..n)$:

```
min_index(n: INTEGER): INTEGER is
    local
        i, m: INTEGER
    do
        from m := 1; i := 2 until i > n loop
            if entries.item(i) < entries.item(m) then
                m := i
            end;
            i := i + 1
        end;
        Result := m
    end
```

Take $n$ to be free and the contents of *entries* to be restricted. The algorithm obeys the
model because the only access to the contents of *entries* is in the test *entries.item*$(i)$ <
*entries.item*$(m)$. Here is a trace of the algorithm on the input $\langle 35, 18, 76 \rangle$, presented
in a graphical form that emphasizes the restricted tests:

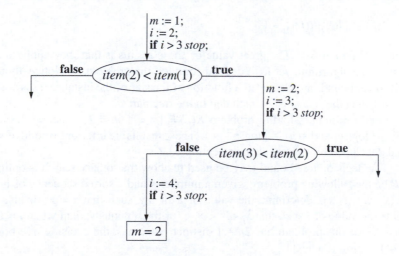

The algorithm's output is written in the square node at the end, but it may be generated at any intermediate point. Clearly, this trace is one path through a binary tree, from the root to an external node. If the free part of the input is kept fixed (in this example, fix $n = 3$), and the restricted part is varied, the whole tree appears:

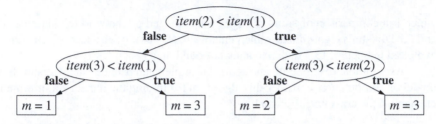

This is a *decision tree*, and it is clear that any algorithm implemented under the decision tree model of computation can be expressed as such a tree, simply by tracing it as has been done above.

Let $R(f)$ be the set of all possible results of problem $P$, for a given $f$. For example, if $P$ is the minimum-finding problem, then $R(3) = \{m = 1, m = 2, m = 3\}$. It is clear that the decision tree must have at least $|R(f)|$ external nodes, one for each distinct result. By Theorem 6.4, any binary tree with at least $|R(f)|$ external nodes has height at least $\lceil \log_2 |R(f)| \rceil$, so it follows that the worst-case complexity of any decision tree algorithm for problem $P$ is

$$W(f) \geq \lceil \log_2 |R(f)| \rceil$$

if the measure of complexity is the number of restricted tests performed. By $W(f)$ is meant the worst case over all instances $I$ whose free part is $f$. Similarly, if the $|R(f)|$ outputs have equal probability of occurring, the average complexity is

$$A(f) \geq \lceil \log_2 |R(f)| \rceil - 1$$

again by Theorem 6.4. The great value of these results is that they apply to any decision tree algorithm, yet $R(f)$ depends only on the problem $P$. Notice, though, that if lower bounds are wanted as a function of the size of the instance (as is always the case), then the size must be included in the free part.

For the minimum-finding problem, $R(f) = \{m = 1, m = 2, \ldots, m = n\}$, and so $W(n) \geq \lceil \log_2 n \rceil$ and $A(n) \geq \lceil \log_2 n \rceil - 1$. These results are inferior to the adversary bound developed for this problem in Section 13.2.

The decision tree bound may be used to show that binary search is optimal. Let $P$ be the following problem: given a number $x$ and a sorted sequence of numbers $\langle x_1, x_2, \ldots, x_n \rangle$, determine the value of $i$, if any, such that $x = x_i$; or else determine the value of $i$ such that $x_i < x < x_{i+1}$ (or the obvious variant when $i = 0$ or $i = n$). Since this problem has $2n + 1$ distinct outcomes, the decision tree bound is $W(n) \geq \lceil \log_2 (2n + 1) \rceil$.

This does not fit quite comfortably with the analysis of binary search in Section 2.2, because there the characteristic operation was one comparison with a *three-way* result. The bound could be changed to $W(n) \geq \lceil \log_3(2n + 1) \rceil$, but it is better to proceed as follows. Assume that $x \neq x_i$, for all $i$. For this restricted problem, the comparisons of binary search have two-way results. Now there are only $n + 1$ distinct outcomes, and the bound is $W(n) \geq \lceil \log_2(n + 1) \rceil$, which is achieved by binary search. In this sense, then, binary search is optimal.

If $P$ is the problem of sorting $n$ distinct numbers, then $R(f)$ is the set of all permutations of the numbers $1, \dots, n$. Therefore the worst-case complexity of any decision tree sorting algorithm is at least $\lceil \log_2 n! \rceil$, and the average complexity is at least $\lceil \log_2 n! \rceil - 1$. Since $n! \simeq (n/e)^n$ by Stirling's approximation, $\log_2 n! \simeq n\log_2 n - 1.44n$, and the lower bounds are a very satisfactory $\Omega(n\log n)$. Mergesort, whose worst-case complexity is $n\log_2 n - (n - 1)$ comparisons between keys in the worst case, for $n$ a power of 2, is very close to optimal.

## 13.4 Entropy

In the previous section, a lower bound on the average complexity of decision tree algorithms was found under the assumption that each outcome was equally likely. A fascinating theory, due to Shannon (1949), arises when this restriction on the probabilities is dropped.

Let $p_1, p_2, \dots, p_k$ be a probability distribution; that is, $p_i \geq 0$ for all $i$, and $\sum_{i=1}^{k} p_i = 1$. Define the *entropy* of the distribution by

$$H(p_1, p_2, \dots, p_k) = -\sum_{i=1}^{k} p_i \log_2 p_i$$

Since $p_i \leq 1$ for all $i$, it follows that $\log_2 p_i \leq 0$, and so $H(p_1, p_2, \dots, p_k) \geq 0$. If $p_i = 0$, $\log_2 p_i$ is undefined; however, since $\lim_{x \to 0} x\log_2 x = 0$, it is safe to define $0\log_2 0$ to be $0$. In effect, zero probabilities are ignored.

The entropy of a probability distribution is a measure of how uniform the distribution is. Its minimum value is 0, which occurs when one of the $p_i$ is 1 and the others are 0; its maximum value, $\log_2 k$, occurs when the probabilities are all equal. The general shape of the entropy function can be seen in the following graph of $H(p, 1 - p)$:

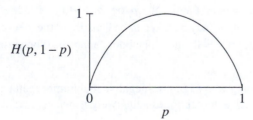

**Theorem 13.1 (Decomposition of entropy):** Let $p_1, p_2, \ldots, p_k$ be a probability distribution, and suppose $k \geq 2$. Divide the distribution into two non-empty parts, $p_1, p_2, \ldots, p_j$ and $p_{j+1}, p_{j+2}, \ldots, p_k$, and let $u = \sum_{i=1}^{j} p_i$ and $v = \sum_{i=j+1}^{k} p_i$. Then

$$H(p_1, p_2, \ldots, p_k) = uH(p_1/u, p_2/u, \ldots, p_j/u) + $$
$$vH(p_{j+1}/v, p_{j+2}/v, \ldots, p_k/v) + H(u, v)$$

**Proof:** To begin with, assume that both $u$ and $v$ are non-zero. Then

$$uH(p_1/u, p_2/u, \ldots, p_j/u) = -u\sum_{i=1}^{j}(p_i/u)\log_2(p_i/u)$$

$$= -\sum_{i=1}^{j}(p_i\log_2 p_i - p_i\log_2 u)$$

$$= -\sum_{i=1}^{j}p_i\log_2 p_i + u\log_2 u$$

Similarly,

$$vH(p_{j+1}/v, p_{j+2}/v, \ldots, p_k/v) = -\sum_{i=j+1}^{k}p_i\log_2 p_i + v\log_2 v$$

and the result follows from adding these two equations together:

$$uH(p_1/u, p_2/u, \ldots, p_j/u) + vH(p_{j+1}/v, p_{j+2}/v, \ldots, p_k/v)$$

$$= -\sum_{i=1}^{j}p_i\log_2 p_i + u\log_2 u - \sum_{i=j+1}^{k}p_i\log_2 p_i + v\log_2 v$$

$$= -\sum_{i=1}^{k}p_i\log_2 p_i + u\log_2 u + v\log_2 v$$

$$= H(p_1, p_2, \ldots, p_k) - H(u, v)$$

If $u = 0$, then $p_1 = p_2 = \ldots = p_j = 0$, and $-\sum_{i=1}^{j}p_i\log_2 p_i + u\log_2 u$ has been defined to be 0, so $uH(p_1/u, p_2/u, \ldots, p_j/u)$ may be taken to be 0 also, and the theorem is trivial. A similar argument applies if $v = 0$; and since both cannot be 0 because $u + v = 1$, the theorem is proved. $\square$

Let $T$ be a binary tree with a *weight* (a non-negative real number) attached to each external node. If there are $k$ external nodes and $k$ weights $w_1, w_2, \ldots, w_k$, define the *weighted external path length of T by*

$$wepl(T) = \sum_{i=1}^{k} w_i d_i$$

where $d_i$ is the depth of the external node to which $w_i$ is attached. For example, if

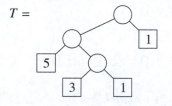

$$T =$$

then $wepl(T) = 5 \times 2 + 3 \times 3 + 1 \times 3 + 1 \times 1 = 23$. The quantity $wepl(T)$ has been defined previously, when studying Huffman trees (Section 6.4).

Let $T$ be a decision tree with $k$ external nodes, and let $w_i$ be the probability that an instance occurs which leads to the $i$th external node. Then, since $d_i$ is the time complexity of that instance, the average complexity $A(n)$ of the decision tree algorithm is $wepl(T)$.

In order to get a lower bound on the average complexity of a problem under the decision tree model, a lower bound is needed for $wepl(T)$ that holds for all $T$ yet depends only on the probabilities $w_1, w_2, \ldots, w_n$ of the instances, not on the shape of $T$. This is what entropy provides:

**Theorem 13.2 (Entropy lower bound):** Let $T$ be any binary tree with $k$ external nodes, and suppose that non-negative weights $w_1, w_2, \ldots, w_k$ are attached to these external nodes in any order. Then

$$wepl(T) \geq wH(w_1/w, w_2/w, \ldots, w_k/w)$$

where $w = \sum_{i=1}^{k} w_i$ is the total weight.
**Proof:** If $w = 0$, the right-hand side is taken to be 0 in the usual way, and the result is trivial. The remainder of the proof is by induction on $k$.
**Basis step:** $k = 1$. Then $H(w_1/w) = 0$, and the result is again trivially true.
**Inductive step:** $k \geq 2$. Define $p_i = w_i/w$ for all $i$, so that $p_1, p_2, \ldots, p_k$ is a probability distribution. Let $T'$ be $T$ with $w_1$ replaced by $p_1$, $w_2$ replaced by $p_2$, and so on. Since $T'$ has at least two external nodes,

$$T' =$$

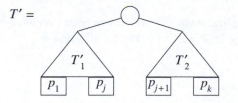

for some $j$. Although the $p_i$ are shown in order from left to right, they may appear in any order. Now, if $d_i$ is the depth of the external node containing $p_i$,

$$wepl(T') = \sum_{i=1}^{k} p_i d_i$$

$$= \sum_{i=1}^{k} p_i (d_i - 1) + 1$$

$$= \sum_{i=1}^{j} p_i (d_i - 1) + \sum_{i=j+1}^{k} p_i (d_i - 1) + 1$$

$$= wepl(T'_1) + wepl(T'_2) + 1$$

$$\geq uH(p_1/u, p_2/u, \dots, p_j/u) + vH(p_{j+1}/v, p_{j+2}/v, \dots, p_k/v) + 1$$

by the inductive hypothesis applied to $T'_1$ and $T'_2$, where we have set $u = \sum_{i=1}^{j} p_i$ and $v = \sum_{i=j+1}^{k} p_i$. Now $H(u, v) \leq \log_2 2 = 1$, so

$$wepl(T') \geq uH(p_1/u, p_2/u, \dots, p_j/u) + vH(p_{j+1}/v, p_2/v, \dots, p_k/v) + H(u, v)$$

$$= H(p_1, p_2, \dots, p_k)$$

by Theorem 13.1. Now recalling the definitions of $T'$ and the $p_i$,

$$wepl(T) = \sum_{i=1}^{k} w_i d_i$$

$$= w \sum_{i=1}^{k} p_i d_i$$

$$= w \cdot wepl(T')$$

$$\geq wH(p_1, p_2, \dots, p_k)$$

$$= wH(w_1/w, w_2/w, \dots, w_k/w)$$

and the theorem is proved. $\qquad\qquad\qquad\qquad\qquad\qquad\qquad\qquad\qquad\qquad$ □

This theorem has a number of applications. To find a lower bound on the average complexity of decision tree sorting, let $k = n!$, $w_i = 1/n!$ for all $i$, and so

$$A(n) \geq wH(w_1/w, w_2/w, \dots, w_k/w)$$

$$= H(1/n!, 1/n!, \ldots, 1/n!)$$

$$= -n! \times (1/n!)\log_2(1/n!)$$

$$= \log_2 n!$$

which is a slight improvement on the lower bound obtained in the last section.

The entropy bound is most interesting, however, in cases where the probabilities differ. It shows, for example, that the weighted external path length of a Huffman tree built from the weights $w_1, w_2, \ldots, w_n$ is at least $wH(w_1/w, w_2/w, \ldots, w_k/w)$. Since this weighted external path length is the length of the encoded message, it is clear that the possibility of the message being very short exists only when the weights differ significantly from each other.

## 13.5 Transformations

When two problems are closely related, it may be possible to transfer a lower bound from one problem to the other.

Let $P$ and $P'$ be two problems. Suppose an arbitrary instance $I$ of $P$ may be solved by converting $I$ into an instance $I'$ of $P'$, solving $I'$, and converting the solution $S'$ thus obtained back into a solution $S$ of $I$:

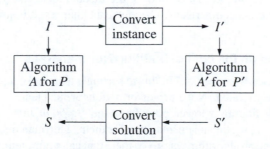

If algorithms exist for converting $I$ into $I'$ and $S'$ into $S$, a *transformation from P to P'* is said to exist; this is written $P \propto P'$. For example, the problem of finding the median of a set of $n$ numbers (that is, the $\lceil n/2 \rceil$th smallest) transforms to sorting:

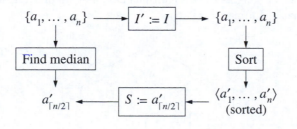

The two conversion algorithms are trivial, since $I' = I$ and $S$ is just the $\lceil n/2 \rceil$th element of the sorted sequence $S'$.

The consequences of the relationship $P \propto P'$ for the worst-case complexity of the two problems are expressed by the following theorem:

**Theorem 13.3 (Transformation lower bound):** Suppose that $P \propto P'$, and that the worst-case complexities of the algorithms that convert $I$ into $I'$ and $S'$ into $S$ are $f_1(n)$ and $f_2(n)$ respectively, where $n$ is the size of $I$. Then
(1) For every algorithm for $P'$ of worst-case complexity $W'(n)$, there is an algorithm for $P$ of worst-case complexity $f_1(n) + W'(n) + f_2(n)$;
(2) If $g(n)$ is a lower bound on the complexity of $P$, then $g(n) - f_1(n) - f_2(n)$ is a lower bound on the complexity of $P'$.
**Proof:** It is assumed that all algorithms and bounds are with respect to a single model of computation. The proof of (1) is obvious; the proof of (2) is by contradiction: if an algorithm for $P'$ of complexity less than $g(n) - f_1(n) - f_2(n)$ existed, then by (1) an algorithm for $P$ of complexity less than $g(n)$ would exist, contradicting the assumption that $g(n)$ was a lower bound on the complexity of $P$. $\qquad\square$

For example, the theorem applies to the transformation from median-finding to sorting, under the decision tree model; $f_1(n) = f_2(n) = 0$. It follows from the existence of (say) Mergesort that an $O(n\log n)$ median-finding algorithm exists, and, from the lower bound $n - 1$ on the cost of finding the median (Exercise 13.1), that sorting requires at least $n - 1$ comparisons. Of course, neither result is striking.

## A lower bound on the cost of building Huffman trees

The transformation from median-finding to sorting is a natural one; the two problems are clearly closely related. Not all transformations are so clear.

Consider finding a lower bound for the *Huffman tree problem*: given $n$ weights $w_1, w_2, \dots, w_n$, find a Huffman tree for them. Huffman trees were presented in Section 6.4, and an algorithm was given there that can be implemented in $O(n\log n)$ time (Exercise 8.7).

It would be desirable to transform sorting to the Huffman tree problem, so as to prove an $\Omega(n\log n)$ lower bound, but this requires some way to read off a sorted sequence of weights from a Huffman tree. For example, if the weights are $4, 7, 3, 2, 4$, then a Huffman tree is

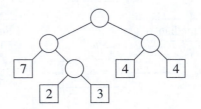

and it is not clear how to retrieve the sorted sequence $\langle 2, 3, 4, 4, 7 \rangle$ from this tree. Smaller weights appear deeper in the tree, however, so there is hope. In fact, if the Huffman tree turns out to be skew, then the weights are sorted with the largest at depth 1, the second largest at depth 2, and so on.

So define the following problem, which will be called Sort*. We are given a set of $n$ distinct positive numbers $w_1, w_2, \dots, w_n$, and we are told that there is a permutation $w'_1, w'_2, \dots, w'_n$ of these numbers such that $w'_i > \sum_{j=1}^{i-1} w'_j$ for all $i$. The problem is to sort the numbers.

It is easy to see that the $\Omega(n\log n)$ decision tree bound for sorting applies equally well to Sort*, since the new condition does not change the number of external nodes in the decision tree. Now transform Sort* to the Huffman tree problem:

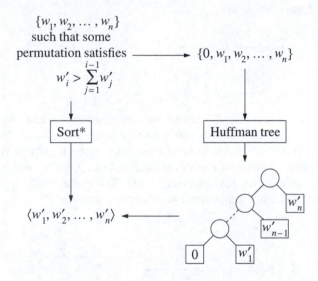

The Huffman tree must be a skew tree like the one shown, as will now be proved. Since $w'_n > \sum_{j=1}^{n-1} w'_j$, clearly $w'_n$ contains over half the total weight and must appear at depth 1. The same argument applies to the remaining weights within their subtree. But now the transformation back to the sorted sequence $\langle w'_1, w'_2, \dots, w'_n \rangle$ is easily accomplished by an $O(n)$ traversal of the tree. It follows that any decision tree algorithm for constructing Huffman trees is $\Omega(n\log n)$, and therefore that Huffman's algorithm is asymptotically optimal: there is no substantially faster algorithm.

## A lower bound on the cost of Dijkstra's algorithm

We conclude this section with a proof that the Fibonacci heaps implementation of Dijkstra's algorithm is optimal to within a constant factor, under the decision tree model. The result is interesting in that it shows that there are only two possible ways in which some new algorithm for the shortest path problem can be made asymptotically faster than Dijkstra's.

Consider the following problem, which will be called $P'$. Given an edge-weighted directed graph $G$ with distinguished vertex $v_0$, the problem is to determine a shortest path spanning tree of $G$, rooted at $v_0$, *and* a sequence of all the vertices of $G$, ordered by non-decreasing distance from $v_0$. For example, given the instance

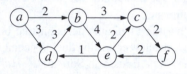

with $v_0 = a$, the solution is to be

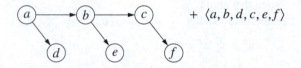

$+ \langle a, b, d, c, e, f \rangle$

This problem is quite artificial, because the *real* problem – finding shortest paths – requires only that the shortest path spanning tree be produced. Nevertheless, Dijkstra's algorithm solves this artificial problem, because it extracts vertices from its priority queue in order of non-decreasing distance from $v_0$, and it is a trivial modification to remember this ordering and include it in the result.

Sorting of distinct non-negative numbers transforms to $P'$:

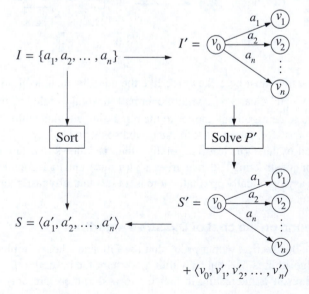

Given a set of numbers to sort, use them as costs in the directed graph $I'$ shown, thus producing an instance of $P'$. The solution to this instance is a shortest path spanning tree which is identical with $I'$, plus the sequence $\langle v_0, v'_1, \ldots, v'_n \rangle$ of vertices in non-decreasing order of distance from $v_0$; in other words, in non-decreasing order of the $a_i$. Dropping $v_0$ from the sequence and replacing each $v'_i$ with its corresponding $a'_i$ yields the original numbers in non-decreasing order.

It is easy to see that the two conversion algorithms are both $O(n)$, and in fact under the decision tree model, $f_1(n) = f_2(n) = 0$. So it follows from Theorem 13.3 and the $\Omega(n\log n)$ sorting lower bound that any decision tree algorithm for problem $P'$ must be $\Omega(n\log n)$. By the usual adversary argument, any algorithm for problem $P'$ must be $\Omega(n + m)$, where $m$ is the number of edges. It follows that, under the decision tree model, any algorithm for problem $P'$, including any implementation of Dijkstra's algorithm, must be $\Omega(n\log n + m)$.

The argument shows clearly that there are only two possible ways to improve on Dijkstra's algorithm implemented using Fibonacci heaps. The first is to go outside the decision tree model. For example, use Dijkstra's algorithm, but implement the priority queue with methods analogous to radix sorting.

The second way is to devise a shortest path spanning tree algorithm which is not capable of generating the sequence of vertices in non-decreasing order of distance from $v_0$. In fact, such an algorithm has already been studied. It was based on topological sorting, and it ran in linear time (Section 11.4); but unfortunately it works only on directed *acyclic* graphs.

These remarks show the great practical value of lower bound results in guiding the search for better algorithms. There are a large number of problems, such as matrix multiplication, minimum spanning trees, and the traveling salesperson problem, where the lower bounds that are known are not strong enough to show that any existing algorithm is asymptotically optimal. Our knowledge of algorithms and data structures, therefore, is very far from complete.

## 13.6 Exercises

13.1 Use the adversary argument for minimum-finding given in Section 13.2 to show that the problem of finding the $k$th smallest of a set of $n$ numbers requires at least $n - 1$ comparisons for any $k$, under the model of computation employed for minimum-finding.

13.2 Using an adversary argument and induction, prove that any algorithm for the Towers of Hanoi problem must make at least $2^n - 1$ disk moves, and so conclude that the algorithm given in Section 2.2 is optimal.

13.3 Use an adversary argument to prove that any algorithm which finds the $k$th smallest of a set of $n$ numbers must also find which of the remaining numbers are smaller, and which are larger.

13.4 (This question requires expertise with binomial coefficients.) Using the result of the previous question, find a decision tree lower bound on the cost of finding the median of a set of $2k + 1$ distinct numbers. How does this bound compare with the adversary bound of Exercise 13.1?

13.5 Draw a decision tree for the Mergesort of the array *entries.item*(1..3). Is Mergesort optimal for $n = 3$?

13.6 Mergesort will sort five numbers in eight comparisons in the worst case, but, since $\lceil \log_2 5! \rceil = 7$, it is possible that some other algorithm, requiring at most seven comparisons, exists. Find one.

13.7 Show how to simulate the $r$-way branch of radix sort by a decision tree of depth $O(\log r)$, and so produce a decision tree lower bound for radix sort.

13.8 (This question requires expertise with binomial coefficients). Find a decision tree bound on the complexity of merging a sorted list of $n$ numbers with a sorted list of $m$ numbers. Investigate the special cases $n = m$ and $m = 1$.

13.9 Find an $\Omega(n \log n)$ decision tree bound for the problem solved by Huffman's algorithm.

13.10 Show that the problem of finding a longest common subsequence of two sequences (as discussed in Section 4.4) has

$$\sum_{k=0}^{\infty} \binom{n}{k}\binom{m}{k} = \binom{n+m}{n}$$

distinct outcomes, where $n$ and $m$ are the lengths of the two sequences. The right-hand side is a well-known simplification of the left. Use it to find a decision tree bound for this problem.

13.11 What is the set of all outcomes of the problem solved by Dijkstra's algorithm? What can you say about the decision tree bound for this problem?

13.12 Prove that $H(p_1, p_2, \ldots, p_n)$ achieves its maximum value when $p_1 = p_2 = \ldots = p_n = 1/n$, and show that this value is $\log_2 n$.

13.13 This question characterizes the binary trees of minimal weighted external path length, and shows that the entropy bound cannot be improved.

(a) Let $T$ be a binary tree with $k$ external nodes, containing weights $w_1, w_2, \ldots, w_k$, and let $w = \sum_{i=1}^{k} w_i$. Show that

$$wepl(T) = wH(w_1/w, w_2/w, \ldots, w_k/w)$$

if and only if, for every internal node $x$ of $T$, the total weight of the left and right subtrees of $T_x$ is equal.

(b)    Use (a) to show that $wepl(T) = wH(w_1/w, w_2/w, \ldots, w_k/w)$ if and only if $w_i/w = 2^{-d(x_i)}$ for all $i$, where $x_i$ is the external node containing $w_i$, and $d(x_i)$ is its depth.

13.14   What does the $\Omega(n\log n)$ sorting bound imply about the complexity of the Priority Queue and Ordered Symbol Table ADTs?

13.15   Show that the binary relation $\propto$ is reflexive (that is, $P \propto P$ for all problems $P$) and transitive (that is, if $P \propto Q$ and $Q \propto R$, then $P \propto R$).

# Appendix A

# Reading Eiffel

This brief appendix is intended as an aid to reading Eiffel for those familiar with Pascal, Modula-2, Ada, or C. It is not an introduction to object-oriented programming, nor to Eiffel. Meyer (1997) is recommended for those subjects.

Within procedures (or *routines* in Eiffel terminology), Eiffel looks very much like other languages:

```
add_root(i, n: INTEGER) is
    local j: INTEGER;
    do
        j := 2 * i;
        if j <= n then
            if j < n and then entries.item(j).key < entries.item(j+1).key then
                j := j + 1
            end;
            if entries.item(i).key < entries.item(j).key then
                swap(entries, i, j);
                add_root(j, n)
            end
        end
    end

build_heap(n: INTEGER) is
    local i: INTEGER;
    do
        from i := n // 2 until i < 1 loop
            add_root(i, n);
            i := i - 1
        end
    end
```

There are no **begin** keywords, and semicolons are optional. The **if** statement has the general form

> **if** *condition* **then**
> > *statements*
>
> **elseif** *condition* **then**
> > *statements*
>
> **else**
> > *statements*
>
> **end**

where there may be any number of **elseif** parts and the **else** part is optional. There is only one loop statement in Eiffel, with the general form

> **from** *statements* **until** *condition* **loop**
> > *statements*
>
> **end**

The statements after **from** are executed, then *condition* is evaluated. If it is **true** the loop exits, otherwise the statements after **loop** are executed, *condition* tested again, and so on. This is the **while** loop of other languages with *condition* negated.

The // operator is integer division; \\ is integer remainder. The **and then** operator is logical **and** except that the second argument is not evaluated if the result of the first is **false**. There is a similar **or else** operator.

When a routine is a function, it automatically has a local variable called *Result* whose value becomes the value of the function upon exit. An assignment to *Result* sets the result value but does not cause an exit from the function.

The notation *x.y* is equivalent to *x↑.y* in Pascal and Modula-2, and to *x->y* in C. In Eiffel, as in C, *y* may be a routine. In most languages, values are assigned to and retrieved from arrays by the statements *a[i] := x* and *x := a[i]* respectively. The Eiffel equivalents are *a.put(x, i)* and *x := a.item(i)*.

Data abstraction (Section 3.1), expressed by the **class** construct, is of central importance in Eiffel. A class is similar to a record in Pascal or a *struct* in C:

> **class** *POINT[T]*
>
> **feature** { *NONE* }
>
> > *x, y: T;*
>
> **feature**
>
> > *set_point(new_x, new_y: T)* **is**
> > **do**
> > > *x := new_x;*
> > > *y := new_y;*
> >
> > **end**
>
> **end**

*NONE* indicates that the following features are to be private; that is, not accessible except to other features of this class, such as *set_point*. *T* is a generic type parameter which must be supplied when points are declared. For example,

> *p*: *POINT*[*INTEGER*];

declares a variable which is a reference to a point whose coordinates are integers. The reference is initially *Void* (that is, nil); a point may be created using the !! symbol (equivalent to *new* in Pascal or *malloc* in C), as in the statement

> !!*p.set_point*(5, 7)

which allocates a new record, assigns *p* to point to it, and calls *set_point* to initialize its two attributes, which are integers in this case. It is not necessary to free memory when it is no longer needed, because Eiffel implementations are supposed to do this automatically.

The declaration

> *v*: **like** *vertex_type*;

states that variable *v* is to have the same type as some previously declared variable *vertex_type*. The reader may safely assume that this means what it seems to mean: that *v* has the type of a graph vertex.

# Appendix B

# Recommended Reading

Aho A. V., Hopcroft J. E. and Ullman J. D. (1974). *The Design and Analysis of Computer Algorithms*. Reading, MA: Addison-Wesley. A seminal book of extraordinary breadth and depth, which collects together areas as diverse as data structures, arithmetic, pattern-matching, and complexity theory.

Cohen D. I. A. (1978). *Basic Techniques of Combinatorial Theory*. New York: Wiley. A clear account of binomial coefficients, generating functions, permutations, graphs, and other topics, with many captivating examples and exercises.

Dijkstra E. W. (1976). *A Discipline of Programming*. Prentice-Hall. An influential and much-discussed book presenting formal correctness as a design method.

Garey M. R. and Johnson D. S. (1979). *Computers and Intractability: a Guide to the Theory of NP-completeness*. San Francisco: Freeman. Still the standard reference for the profound theory of the NP-complete problems.

Knuth D. E. (1973a). *The Art of Computer Programming, Vol. 1: Fundamental Algorithms* 2nd edn. Reading, MA: Addison-Wesley. This pioneering volume, first published in 1968, is still the best introduction to the advanced techniques of combinatorial algorithm analysis.

Knuth D. E. (1973b). *The Art of Computer Programming, Vol. 3: Sorting and Searching*. Reading, MA: Addison-Wesley. A thorough and inspirational treatment of symbol table data structures and sorting. Essential reading.

Manber U. (1989). *Introduction to Algorithms – A Creative Approach*. Reading, MA: Addison-Wesley. A unified algorithm design method, with many interesting case studies.

Meyer B. (1997). *Object-Oriented Software Construction* 2nd edn. Prentice-Hall. An introduction to object-oriented analysis, design, and programming, and the Eiffel programming language.

Sedgewick R. (1988). *Algorithms* 2nd edn. Reading, MA: Addison-Wesley. A good reference for a broad range of algorithms, including sorting, searching, string matching, parsing, cryptography, computational geometry, graph algorithms, and mathematical algorithms.

Tarjan R. E. (1983). *Data Structures and Network Algorithms*. Philadelphia, PA: Society for Industrial and Applied Mathematics. A study of four classic graph problems (minimum spanning trees, shortest paths, network flows, and matchings) and associated data structures.

# References

Adel'son-Vel'skii G. M. and Landis E. M. (1962). An algorithm for the organization of information. *Dokl. Akad. Nauk SSSR*, **146**, 263–6. In Russian; English translation in *Soviet Math.* **3** (1962), 1259–63

Aho A. V., Hopcroft J. E. and Ullman J. D. (1974). *The Design and Analysis of Computer Algorithms*. Reading, MA: Addison-Wesley

Aho A. V., Hopcroft J. E. and Ullman J. D. (1983). *Data Structures and Algorithms*. Reading, MA: Addison-Wesley

Allen B. and Munro I. (1978). Self-organizing binary search trees. *Journal of the ACM*, **25**, 526–35

Bayer R. and McCreight E. (1972). Organization and maintenance of large ordered indexes. *Acta Informatica*, **1**, 173–89

Bellman R. E. (1958). On a routing problem. *Quart. Appl. Math.*, **16**, 87–90

Bitner J. R. (1979). Heuristics that dynamically organize data structures. *SIAM Journal on Computing*, **8**, 82–110

Blum M., Floyd R. W., Pratt V., Rivest R. L. and Tarjan R. E. (1973). Time bounds for selection. *Journal of Computer and System Sciences*, **7**, 448–61

Brown R. (1988). Calendar queues: a fast $O(1)$ priority queue implementation for the simulation event set problem. *Communications of the ACM*, **31**, 1220–7

**368** References

Christofides N. (1976). Worst-case Analysis of a New Heuristic for the Travelling Salesman Problem. *Tech. Rep.*, Graduate School of Industrial Administration, Carnegie-Mellon University, Pittsburgh, Pennsylvania, USA

Cohen D. I. A. (1978). *Basic Techniques of Combinatorial Theory*. New York: Wiley

Dijkstra E. W. (1959). A note on two problems in connexion with graphs. *Numerische Mathematik*, **1**, 269–71

Dijkstra E. W. (1976). *A Discipline of Programming*. Prentice-Hall

Dinic E. A. (1970). Algorithm for solution of a problem of maximum flow in a network with power estimation. *Soviet Math. Dokl.*, **11**, 1277–80

Driscoll J. R., Gabow H. N., Shrairman R. and Tarjan R. E. (1988). Relaxed heaps: an alternative to Fibonacci heaps with applications to parallel computation. *Communications of the ACM*, **31**, 1343–54

Edmonds J. and Karp R. M. (1972). Theoretical improvements in algorithmic efficiency for network flow problems. *Journal of the ACM*, **19**, 248–64

Even S. and Tarjan R. E. (1975). Network flow and testing graph connectivity. *SIAM Journal on Computing*, **4**, 507–18

Floyd R. W. (1964). Algorithm 245 – Treesort 3. *Communications of the ACM*, **7**, 701

Floyd R. W. (1967). Assigning meanings to programs. In *Proceedings of the 19th Symposium in Applied Mathematics*, pages 19–32

Ford L. R. and Fulkerson D. R. (1962). *Flows in Networks*. Princeton, NJ: Princeton University Press

Fredman M. L., Sedgewick R., Sleator D. D. and Tarjan R. E. (1986). The pairing heap: a new form of self-adjusting heap. *Algorithmica*, **1**, 111–29

Fredman M. L. and Tarjan R. E. (1987). Fibonacci heaps and their uses in improved network optimization algorithms. *Journal of the ACM*, **34**, 596–615

Gabow H. N., Galil Z. and Spencer T. H. (1984). Efficient implementation of graph algorithms using contraction. In *Proc. 25th Annual IEEE Symposium on Foundations of Computer Science*, pages 347–57

Galler B. A. and Fischer M. J. (1964). An improved equivalence algorithm. *Communications of the ACM*, **7**, 301–3

Garey M. R. and Johnson D. S. (1979). *Computers and Intractability: a Guide to the Theory of NP-completeness*. San Francisco: Freeman

Graham R. L. and Hell P. (1985). On the history of the minimum spanning tree problem. *Annals of the History of Computing*, **7**, 43–57

Gries D. (1981). *The Science of Programming*. Springer-Verlag

Held M. and Karp R. M. (1962). A dynamic programming approach to sequencing problems. *Journal of the Society for Industrial and Applied Mathematics*, **10**, 196–210. Since renamed *SIAM Journal on Applied Mathematics*

Hoare C. A. R. (1962). Quicksort. *Computer Journal*, **5**, 10–15

Hoare C. A. R. (1969). An axiomatic basis for computer programming. *Communications of the ACM*, **12**, 576–83

Hopcroft J. E. and Karp R. M. (1973). An $O(n^{5/2})$ algorithm for maximum matching in bipartite graphs. *SIAM Journal on Computing*, **2**, 225–31

Hopcroft J. E. and Ullman J. D. (1973). Set merging algorithms. *SIAM Journal on Computing*, **2**, 294–303

Huffman D. A. (1952). A method for the construction of minimum-redundancy codes. *Proceedings of the IRE*, **40**, 1098–101

Hunt J. W. and Szymanski T. G. (1977). A fast algorithm for computing longest common subsequences. *Communications of the ACM*, **20**, 350–3

Jones D. W. (1986). An empirical comparison of priority-queue and event-set implementations. *Communications of the ACM*, **29**, 300–11

Karatsuba A. and Ofman Y. (1962). Multiplication of multidigit numbers on automata. *Dokl. Akad. Nauk SSSR*, **145**, 293–4. In Russian

Knuth D. E. (1973a). *The Art of Computer Programming, Vol. 1: Fundamental Algorithms* 2nd edn. Reading, MA: Addison-Wesley

Knuth D. E. (1973b). *The Art of Computer Programming, Vol. 3: Sorting and*

*Searching.* Reading, MA: Addison-Wesley

Kruskal J. B. Jr (1956). On the shortest spanning subtree of a graph and the traveling salesman problem. *Proceedings of the American Mathematical Society,* **7,** 48–50

Kuhn H. W. (1955). The Hungarian method for the assignment problem. *Naval Research Logistics Quarterly,* **2,** 83–98

Liskov B. and Guttag J. (1986). *Abstraction and Specification in Program Development.* Cambridge, MA: MIT Press

Meyer B. (1997). *Object-Oriented Software Construction* 2nd edn. Prentice-Hall

Moore E. F. (1959). The shortest path through a maze. In *Proceedings of the International Symposium on the Theory of Switching, Part II*

Paterson M. S. and Wegman M. N. (1978). Linear unification. *Journal of Computer and System Sciences,* **16,** 158–67

Perlis A. J. and Thornton C. (1960). Symbol manipulation by threaded lists. *Communications of the ACM,* **3,** 195–204

Peterson G. L. (1987). A Balanced Tree Scheme for Meldable Heaps with Updates. *Tech. Rep. GIT-ICS-87-23,* School of Information and Computer Science, Georgia Institute of Technology, Atlanta, GA

Prim R. C. (1957). Shortest connection networks and some generalizations. *Bell System Technical Journal,* **36,** 1389–401. This journal has since been renamed *AT&T Technical Journal*

Purdom P. W. Jr. and Brown C. A. (1985). *The Analysis of Algorithms.* Holt, Rinehart and Winston

Sedgewick R. (1988). *Algorithms* 2nd edn. Reading, MA: Addison-Wesley

Shannon C. E. (1949). Communication in presence of noise. *Proceedings of the IRE,* **37,** 10–21

Sharir M. (1981). A strong-connectivity algorithm and its applications in data flow analysis. *Computers and Mathematics with Applications,* **7,** 67–72

Singleton R. C. (1969). Algorithm 347: an efficient algorithm for sorting with minimal storage. *Communications of the ACM*, **12**, 185–87

Sleator D. D. and Tarjan R. E. (1980). An $O(nm\log n)$ Algorithm for Maximum Network Flow. *Tech. Rep. STAN-CS-80-831*, Computer Science Department, Stanford University, Stanford, CA

Sleator D. D. and Tarjan R. E. (1985a). Amortized efficiency of list update and paging rules. *Communications of the ACM*, **28**, 202–8

Sleator D. D. and Tarjan R. E. (1985b). Self-adjusting binary search trees. *Journal of the ACM*, **32**, 652–86

Stanat D. F. and McAllister D. F. (1977). *Discrete Mathematics in Computer Science*. Prentice-Hall

Strassen V. (1969). Gaussian elimination is not optimal. *Numerische Mathematik*, **13**, 354–6

Szpilrajn E. (1930). Sur l'extension de l'ordre partiel. *Fundamenta Mathematicae*, **16**, 386–9

Tarjan R. E. (1972). Depth-first search and linear graph algorithms. *SIAM Journal on Computing*, **1**, 146–60

Tarjan R. E. (1975). Efficiency of a good but not linear set union algorithm. *Journal of the ACM*, **22**, 215–25

Tarjan R. E. (1983). *Data Structures and Network Algorithms*. Philadelphia, PA: Society for Industrial and Applied Mathematics

Tarjan R. E. (1985). Amortized computational complexity. *SIAM Journal on Algebraic and Discrete Methods*, **6**, 306–18

Vuillemin J. (1978). A data structure for manipulating priority queues. *Communications of the ACM*, **21**, 309–15

Williams J. W. J. (1964). Algorithm 232: heapsort. *Communications of the ACM*, **7**, 347–8

Winston P. H. (1992). *Artificial Intelligence* 3rd edn. Reading, MA: Addison-Wesley

# Index

## DATE DUE

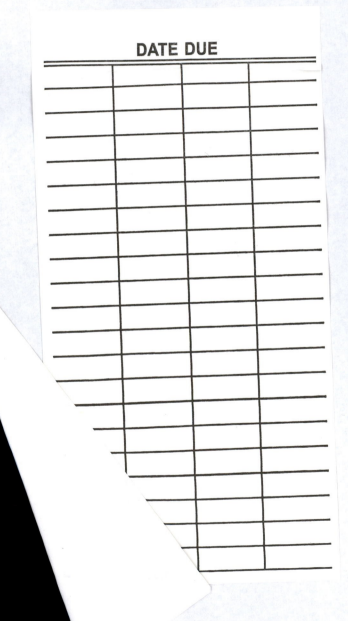